Changing the World,
Changing Oneself

Protest, Culture and Society

General editors:

Kathrin Fahlenbrach, University of Halle Wittenberg, Germany.

Martin Klimke, German Historical Institute, Washington, DC / Heidelberg Center for American Studies (HCA), University of Heidelberg.

Joachim Scharloth, Department of German, University of Zurich, Switzerland.

Protest movements have been recognized as significant contributors to processes of political participation and transformations of culture and value systems, as well as to the development of both a national and transnational civil society.

This series brings together the various innovative approaches to phenomena of social change, protest and dissent which have emerged in recent years, from an interdisciplinary perspective. It contextualizes social protest and cultures of dissent in larger political processes and socio-cultural transformations by examining the influence of historical trajectories and the response of various segments of society, political and legal institutions on a national and international level. In doing so, the series offers a more comprehensive and multi-dimensional view of historical and cultural change in the twentieth and twenty-first century.

Volume 1
Voices of the Valley, Voices of the Straits:
How Protest Creates Communities
Donatella della Porta and Gianni Piazza

Volume 2
*Transformations and Crises: The Left and the Nation
in Denmark and Sweden, 1956–1980*
Thomas Ekman Jørgensen

Volume 3
*Changing the World, Changing Oneself:
Political Protest and Collective Identities in
West Germany and the U.S. in the 1960s and 1970s*
Edited by Belinda Davis, Wilfried Mausbach,
Martin Klimke, and Carla MacDougall

Changing the World, Changing Oneself

Political Protest and Collective Identities in West Germany and the U.S. in the 1960s and 1970s

Edited by

Belinda Davis, Wilfried Mausbach,
Martin Klimke, and Carla MacDougall

Berghahn Books
New York • Oxford

First published in 2010 by
Berghahn Books
www.berghahnbooks.com

Library of Congress Cataloging-in-Publication Data

Changing the world, changing oneself : political protest and collective identities
in West Germany and the U.S. in the 1960s and 1970s / edited by Belinda
Davis … [et al.]. — 1st ed.
    p. cm. — (Protest, culture and society ; 3)
    Includes bibliographical references and index.
    ISBN 978-1-84545-651-1 (hardback : alk. paper)
    1. United States—Relations—Germany (West) 2. Germany (West)—
Relations—United States. 3. Youth protest movements—United
States—History—20th century. 4. Youth protest movements—Germany
(West)—History—20th entury. 5. Youth—United States—Political
activity—History—20th century. 6. Youth—Germany (West)—Political
activity—History—20th century. 7. Youth—United States—Attitudes—
History—20th century. 8. Youth—Germany (West)—Attitudes—
History—20th century. 9. Group identity—United States—History—20th
century. 10. Group identity—Germany (West)—History—20th century.
I. Davis, Belinda.
    E183.8.G3C347 2010
    327.73043—dc22
                                                              2009025367

British Library Cataloguing in Publication Data
A catalogue record for this book is available from the British Library
Printed in the United States on acid-free paper

ISBN 978-1-84545-651-1 hardback

Contents

Acknowledgments

This volume represents the fruits of the conference "The 'Other' Alliance: Political Protest, Intercultural Relations, and Collective Identities in West Germany and the United States, 1958–77," held in Heidelberg. We would like to thank all the institutions and individuals involved in making the conference a success beyond the wildest hopes of the four organizers. The Volkswagen Foundation generously sponsored the conference as well as the larger three-year research project, "Das Fremde im Eigenen: Interkultureller Austausch und kollektive Identitäten in der Revolte der 1960er Jahre," from which it originated. We are especially thankful to Antje Gunsenheimer for efficiently backstopping the project at the Volkswagen Foundation. We also owe a special debt of gratitude to Detlef Junker, Founding Director of the Heidelberg Center for American Studies (HCA) at the University of Heidelberg, who raised the seed money that allowed us to prepare the initial grant application to the Volkswagen Foundation, and who accompanied and encouraged the project throughout. Significant contributions for the conference came from the University of Heidelberg, the Hamburg Institute for Social Research (HIS), the German-American Institute in Heidelberg (DAI), and Rutgers University. The *Internationales Wissenschaftsforum Heidelberg* (IWH) kindly agreed to include the conference in its program of prestigious international symposiums, thus admitting us to its splendid Art Deco villa and facilitating a magnanimous grant from the *Stiftung Universität Heidelberg*. Theresa Reiter and her team at the IWH created an atmosphere that proved congenial for presentations and discussions alike. Generous support of the HIS was crucial in bringing contemporary activists from both sides of the Atlantic to the conference, some of whom had not seen each other for more than 40 years. We would like to acknowledge a particular debt to Bernd Greiner who not only mustered this support from Hamburg but also masterfully moderated a most entertaining roundtable discussion at the conference. The DAI and its director, Jakob J. Köllhofer, provided the venue for a wonderful film series with comments and open discussion by contemporary activists, which added a rich accompaniment to the conference. We would also like to thank all those who chaired sessions or contributed papers, comments, and observations at the conference but are not represented in this volume, among them Manfred Berg, Ingo Cornils, Philipp Gassert, Uta Gerhardt, Thomas Gijswijt, Sara Hakemi, Karrin M. Hanshew, Madeleine Herren-Oesch, Roman Luckscheiter, Stan Nadel, Jacco Pekelder, Joachim Scharloth, Heiner Stahl, Alexander Vazansky, Tim Warneke, and Thomas P. Wheatland. The thinking behind this conference was also informed by two previous and most stimulating workshops: "Protest 1960s–1980s:

Trans- and Intercultural Perspectives" which was both generously sponsored by and held at Rutgers University on October 13, 2003; "Atlantic Crossings? Transcultural Relations and Political Protest in Germany and the U.S., 1958–1977" enjoyed munificent funding from, again, the Volkswagen Foundation as well as the German Historical Institute in Washington, D.C., where it was held. Our heartfelt thanks go out not only to these three institutions but also to everyone who participated in these meetings.

International scholarly conferences always entail considerable organizational challenges. In our case, these were more than met by Danijela Albrecht who conjoined cheerfulness and assiduous administrative efforts far beyond the call of duty in order to make the conference the thrilling success it turned out to be. We offer our most grateful thanks to her, also for making the larger research project run so smoothly. For the administration of finances we were fortunate to be able to rely on the good offices of Noemi Huber. We would also like to express our appreciation to Katja Nagel and Christiane Rösch for their substantial assistance at various stages of the larger project. Thanks are also due to Ana Maric for skillfully compiling the index for this book.

Finally, we are deeply indebted to those at Berghahn Books who so ably shepherded this volume to its completion, including Marion Berghahn, Ann Przyzycki, Melissa Spinelli, and Jaime Taber.

Heidelberg and New Brunswick
December 2009

Introduction

Belinda Davis, Wilfried Mausbach,
Martin Klimke, and Carla MacDougall

The keyword "1968"—and the longer period it signifies—automatically evokes thoughts of global action and transnational relations. These relations took place at the "highest" and "lowest" levels, including at the level of the self-image of contemporary activists. The observation of Daniel Cohn-Bendit, a leading activist in Paris and then in Frankfurt, is a typical product of this cosmopolitan panopticon: "Paris, Berlin, Frankfurt, New York, Berkeley, Rome, Prague, Rio, Mexico City, Warsaw—those were the sites of a revolt that traveled around the globe and that conquered the hearts and dreams of an entire generation. The year 1968 was, in the truest sense of the word, international."[1] Heidelberg activist Joscha Schmierer added in retrospect: "In our eyes, the shrinking world … once again coalesced into a unified world in 1968, in which not only was everything bound up with everything else, but everyone could also act globally in an effective way."[2]

Such remarks evince the "global" dimension of the era in four ways, foremost in the idea of a world that had shrunk to manageable size—what today we might in various contexts call globalization, a new kind of globalization. Secondly, the remarks call to mind the ideological construction of a revolutionary context of the first, second, and third worlds. Thirdly, they reveal a strong sense of the transnational as well as the international, suggesting not only that similar events and transformations happened to be taking place within numerous countries, but also that these transformations were highly interactive and porous across national boundaries, even if national and local cultures remained significant. Stemming from these two characteristics, finally, the global dimension becomes clear in the potential for significant action at once locally and globally.

This volume attempts to address these issues through a particular (if not exclusive) focus on West Germans, Americans, and their "relations." It offers new perspectives on Cold War and broader global relations in the 1960s and 1970s, from the angle of the youth movements that shook the United States, Western Europe, and beyond, resulting in the transformation of diplomatic relations and domestic political cultures, ideas about democracy and notions of who best understood and promoted it. (Thus, except where it refers to a specific date, "1968" is used here as an imperfect shorthand for a longer period, a periodization many of these essays directly address and problematize, though we avoid the distracting quotation marks. This applies too to the notion of "'68er.") Bringing together scholars from four countries, three disciplines, and numerous methodologies, this collection also features the reflections of former activists on these issues.

In the first instance, the present book is another sprout in the growing field of transnational history.[3] In the United States, this field has emerged from a longstanding effort to internationalize American history.[4] Here, as elsewhere, it has been strongly influenced by postcolonial studies and the notion of hybridization as well as by works on migrations and diasporas.[5] Not surprisingly, then, transnational history's major interest is in the movements, flows, and circulation of people, practices, and ideas, and in their interaction, interpenetration, and entanglement. In contrast with international history, it moves well beyond state actors to include a far wider range of groups and individuals. Overall, it has evolved into an approach that aims to extricate history from the iron cage of the nation-state, thereby decentering hitherto presumed stable markers of space, belonging, and identity.

The 1960s have lately emerged as a major field of inquiry for scholars interested in both intercultural transfers and cross-national comparisons. Beginning particularly in the late 1980s, with the twenty-year anniversary of '68, social scientists have repeatedly addressed the world-historical effect of the movements of the 1960s and 1970s.[6] Immanuel Wallerstein, for instance, viewed the '68ers as those who helped bring to prominence the articulation of minority concerns against the domination of national and social total worldviews, and in this way brought about a revolution in the world system.[7] Likewise suggestive is Beate Fietz's discussion of a globalized generational context, which allowed the insubordinate students of the 1960s to act as the bearers of a process of transformation that swept the entire world.[8] Such projects identify and investigate macro-level processes, and as such, they inform and inspire a number of the contributions to this volume. At the same time, many of these contributions—including some of the same ones—seek to bring better into view "micro-level" relations, including specifically the intercultural exchanges among the various social sites of action and even among particular individuals, with surprising consequences.

Closely linked to this idea of macro- and micro-processes, and of the movement's international nature, some of the recent historical work on the era draws on and advances the now longstanding social scientific research on new social movements. Thus, historian Ingrid Gilcher-Holtey and others have looked at the way in which ideas structure process, how they guide people to particular behaviors, and how these behaviors in turn inform a common cognitive orientation, once again transcending national boundaries.[9] Those brought together by these practices thus contributed to the foundation of a thickly woven network of alternative presses, newspapers, and publishers that produced in turn a kind of transnational alternative public sphere.[10] This was among the most significant and lasting effects of these processes, with implications for both Europe and the United States.

This volume taps into such conceptualizations of the transfer of ideas across borders, and of the way in which collective identities stimulated particular courses of action grounded in these transfers. At the same time, the following chapters attempt to overcome the limitation to constitutive ideas and their diffusion within particular networks that has so far characterized much of the relevant literature. For one, the present contributions attempt to ground the influential sallies of intellectual luminaries in more social-historical, textual, and otherwise more concrete and specific fashion. In this way, too, the lived-in world and everyday life of both the transmitters and the recipients of such ideas (insofar as they can be thus divided) warrant closer attention. This work attempts thus to reclaim the voices and the vitality of individuals as well as groups, instead of drowning them out in monolithic mass movements and enqueuing them in faceless networks. Finally, this book aims to reach beyond ideas to institutions, lifestyles, and cultural practices that presumably were much more crucial to processes of diffusion both within and across different societies than were sometimes arcane edifices of thought. As Jakob Tanner has observed: "On the one hand, protest arose out of eccentric, dark, cynical, surreal-dadaist traditions and subcultures, scarcely compatible with the socialist humanism of the student movement and the rational, even economical utopias of the New Left. ... On the other hand, these subcultural impulses were astonishingly easy to integrate into that universal spiral of commercialization, which consumer society deepened, and which promoted globalization in the sign of an American dream."[11] Contemporary activists have concurred, ascribing pervasive consequences to countercultural commune experiments, reaching "from the cultivation of myths—between 'Maoist love nests,' the 'nexus of terrorism,' and 'self-realization'—to tangible social ramifications," such as the spread of group houses, the breaking of taboos, and a novel conflation of matters private and public.[12] Understanding such consequences as a piece of transnational cultural transfer in the broad sense is a central aim of this collection.

Even more important to the present volume is its resolve to finally give due credit to the fact that cultural transfer is never a one-way street but always a story of constant circulation. Too often, and particularly in the case of the relationship between West Germany and the United States, processes of interdependence and adaptation have been depicted as monodirectional. To be sure, timeworn notions of cultural imperialism have long since given way to more refined understandings of "Americanization."[13] These have in turn been amplified and amended by theories of "Westernization" that seek to replace the semblance of a unidirectional transmission from the United States with the concept of a more intercultural transfer. Yet although this approach has yielded important and highly illuminating results, it has remained focused for the most part on concepts of sociopolitical order, slighting the purview of lifestyles and cultural practices. More important, none of the studies employing the Westernization paradigm has actually investigated the transfer of German ideas, dispositions, or practices to the United States.[14] Thus, the circular moment of intercultural transfer continues to be remarkably understudied—a problem to which we hope to offer some redress.

This volume is centrally informed by a notion of interculturality that avoids reproducing existing paradigms by focusing, first, on the nexus between, rather than always on the separation of, the "self" and the "other." Secondly, it focuses on the modes of enmeshment and overlap rather than on patterns of example and emulation within processes of cultural transfer. From the vantage point of such a broadened perspective, a uniquely historical dimension of interculturality comes into view in a dual sense. First, historical facts and contemporary events can be read as texts that impinge upon different social and cultural experiences. Secondly, these experiences are, of course, themselves historically marked, which in turn has notable effects on the reception of foreign cultural products as well as their refraction and eventual realization in the construction of one's own identity. With a particular attentiveness to these interactions, the following chapters trace various instances of circulation throughout West German and American protest movements of the 1960s and 1970s, in an effort to attempt a genuinely transnational social and cultural history of that period. They do so in five specific domains, reflecting the openness of transnational history to different methodological approaches: (1) intellectual history, (2) the realm of memory, (3) diplomatic history in the broader sense of transnational relations, (4) questions concerning violence, and (5) the field of social practices, cultural norms, and everyday life.

The first section, "Atlantic Crossings: From Germany to America and Back," offers an initial sense of the "back-and-forth" of ideas, but even this title belies the complexity of exchanges highlighted in the pieces by sociologist (and contemporary) Detlev Claussen and intellectual historian John Abromeit. Looking here particularly at intellectual genealogies, a basis for the "praxis," or theoretically informed activism, that many hoped to achieve, we find movement across numerous axes, characteristic as well of the other chapters in the book. There is the axis of time as well as that of space: the movement of ideas in space, embodied naturally in and also across a number of real persons, takes place over time. At the same time, the spatial argument itself must be complicated: ideas are never simply in one place or (then) another. As these authors demonstrate, in this context ideas are palimpsests: they are overdetermined by new situations, but the old versions don't disappear. New settings work to both transform and fix ideas—via the specific individuals who think them. Ideas may travel through a variety of conduits, but they come from one person, or sometimes many simultaneously, and are interpreted by another, or others: interpreted, adopted, reacted against, and transformed, sometimes in a classroom, but into a larger world.

Building the human element very directly back into the discussion is a critical theme of this book on intercultural transfer and exchange. The Nazi exile of

Frankfurt School thinker Theodor W. Adorno to the United States paradoxically later breathed new life into the ideas associated with that school, influenced already before the war by German-American exchanges. The roles of the long-standing influence of, for example, Adorno's fellow exiles Max Horkheimer and Erich Fromm, and of the experience of fascism, naturally remained critical. At the same time, both Adorno's and Herbert Marcuse's influence, coming from the United States to the new/old country of (West) Germany, was perhaps far greater than it might have been without these transatlantic wanderings. Yet, as Claussen notes, Adorno never felt so much a European as he did while in the US: the difference of the latter country seemed to crystallize for him who he was—and who he wasn't. Still, it was his experience in the United States, indeed his peregrinations back and forth, that brought Adorno to challenge the notion of "German peculiarity" on the question of fascism. Celebration of his perceived difference from others around him was part of the achievement for Adorno himself, as Claussen demonstrates: the ability to be able to celebrate difference and diversity, of both thought and person.

For his part, Abromeit challenges myths concerning Adorno's and Marcuse's involvement with the protest movements of the 1960s. Noting the significance of the Frankfurt School's transatlantic character from early on, Abromeit argues that the persistent memory of Adorno's notorious confrontation with students in Frankfurt in 1969 has obscured the significance of his work for contemporary activists as well as Adorno's frequent support of their acts. In turn, Marcuse's support of student activism was hardly uncritical; his criticisms were informed by the concepts developed over time and space within the Frankfurt School.

The emphasis on place and space in these entries marks the next section as well, which also focuses on these elements' role in forging identity—and identities—with and against others, here among larger populations. In these contributions, by historians Wilfried Mausbach and Carla MacDougall, and by literary critic Susanne Rinner, space intersects with and "borrows" from time, as two populations reconcile with or butt up against particular pasts and presents, as history and as memory, in the "afterlives" of the era. Wilfried Mausbach observes the astonishing degree to which young West Germans and Americans—among other populations—appropriated one another's histories, fitting themselves both within and against the different trajectories. Thus, many West Germans adopted the Vietnam War as a means to understanding—or otherwise contending with—their own national history and their place in it. At the same time, swaths of Americans found the Holocaust a particularly usable frame of reference for fitting themselves into their own national story. Remarkably, the upshot was, as Mausbach argues, that activists on both sides of the Atlantic not only came to inhabit a "shared moral universe" but also developed a new "transnational memory."

Carla MacDougall's piece moves us forward to the early 1980s, and to the consequences of this most recent past, addressing the question of place and space in far more "local" fashion that is concrete if also metaphorical. Taking President Ronald Reagan's 1982 visit to West Berlin as her point of departure, MacDougall examines the efforts of a newly vibrant leftist scene to relocate the former German capital's symbolic place in Cold War discourse, by challenging the political mainstream's vision of the city as closely tied to America. Throughout this discursive struggle, the different sides invoked Berlin as a site of meaningful memories, albeit very different ones. Although squatters, punks, and other contrarians were clearly informed by the '68ers' exposure of American innocence, they nevertheless, as MacDougall argues, precipitated a profound transformation in German anti-Americanism through a redefinition of their city's relationship with the United States.

Finally in this section, Susanne Rinner moves us forward still a few years more, examining novels written in the decade after German reunification and bringing us along the axis of time into the future of the movement, as well as into its past. Like Mausbach, Rinner documents the transatlantic arrogation of "others'" histories to oneself; she too observes an extraordinary commonality of reference to "America" and its role as place, as a "lieu de mémoire," in the process of "remembering, forgetting, story-telling, and silence." Rinner examines the longstanding and contradictory views of America in Germany in this recent incarnation, and, in this instance, how they provide a backdrop against which authors like Ulrike Kolb, Bernhard Schlink, and Peter Schneider develop their characters' identities. These novelists demonstrate a self-reflectiveness, ironic or otherwise, in identifying the US as "fascist"—and, frequently, as a lopsided counterpart, their own characters as "victims." Rinner reminds us not only of the long history of US-German relations and its uses before the 1960s, but also of a continued process, well beyond although influenced by that period. In turn, she raises the question of generation in more complex fashion than it is sometimes deployed, including in terms of concepts of "post-memory," the appropriation of others' memories as one's own.

The next section extends these cross-cultural encounters, real and imagined, onto a new terrain. We might have called it "protest *versus* power"—except that "new diplomatic" historians Martin Klimke and Jeremi Suri unveil the vulnerabilities of those in power as they themselves perceived them. United States officials fit protesting West Germans into a particular vision, most pronouncedly informed by the Cold War, and spent less time thinking about their own place in that scenario than acting to transform it. As international power brokers, they shared a sense of the voluntarism that Ingrid Gilcher-Holtey and others discuss among the protestors: a belief in the ability—and responsibility—to shape the world according to their own vision. But, as these authors demonstrate, officials quickly came up against the limitations of their abilities to mold the present and future. These pieces raise cases of "other alliances" and unparallel relations—relations that clearly refute any notion of simple, one-way influences from the United States. As Klimke shows us, US State Department officials had already installed an institutional infrastructure designed to draft and coordinate the effort to win over the hearts and minds of the young generations overseas at the beginning of the decade. In the mid 1960s, they increasingly utilized these existing youth programs to come to terms with the mounting hostility toward US foreign policies and the global dimension of student unrest. American officials worried terribly about the prospect of American domestic protest being transported to and picked up by West German students through a variety of various transnational channels. This concern reflected an apparent great transformation in this unparallel relation, at least in the eyes of US officials, who had previously envisioned themselves to be "allied" with West German youth: the future of that country, untainted by Nazism—and raised under a Cold War *Weltbild*. But, ironically, by the late 1960s, US officials seemed to share West German protestors' own vision of "borrowed history," imagining these protestors as a "new Viet Cong" to be reckoned with. In consequence, they attempted to counter the potentially detrimental impact of student protestors on US foreign policy interests with regard to West Germany by closely monitoring and reaching out to what they saw as the country's future political elite through a variety of cultural diplomatic efforts.

The parallels in the ways these different populations imagined one another is revealing. But this "uneven relation" was hardly the only one of its type. Looking beyond formal foreign relations and their informal counterparts among protestors, one finds all kinds of such connections, both actual and confined to the heads of various actors. These relations did not remain only between these two countries, of course, but spread rather well beyond, yet another theme that several pieces in this volume take up. Jeremi Suri continues with this story of transcontinental "uneven relations"—and of its unintended consequences. He builds on the notion of the "Frankenstein effect" American officials feared they had unleashed, as US-inspired educational reform seemed to create new enemies of West German youth, a situation these authorities feared they could not afford in the strained Cold War context. Significantly, the results of the varied responses led to redefined international alignments and relations—as well as to new splits and side-taking within West Germany itself, as the new right began to grow and the conservative Christian Democratic Union (CDU), newly out of power, coalesced transnationally with Richard Nixon, the new American president.

In the fourth section, the sociologically informed historian Ingrid Gilcher-Holtey and literary critic Karin Bauer address the question of violence. As both pieces make clear in their different ways, looking across the dimensions of space as well as time is critical in properly characterizing and contextualizing this violence. Gilcher-Holtey makes evident indeed that a transnational approach is essential to an understanding of violence and its meaning among contemporary activists, including through notions of "symbolic" and "playful" violence. Taking seriously the combined significance of ideas, traditions, and practices as widespread as those of Karl Marx, situationist Guy Debord, dadaists, and surrealists, as well as of contemporaries such as Che Guevara, Régis Debray, and members of the American SNCC, Gilcher-Holtey makes manifest another extremely important dimension of the movements' transnationalism—meanwhile demonstrating how problematic it would be to assert any linear connection between activists of the '68 movement and those who took up "armed struggle" in West Germany.

The latter subject forms the basis for Bauer's piece, which also looks at an individual person in order to trace the transfer of ideas and emphasizes, again, the complexity of identity formation. As she places Ulrike Meinhof for the reader, we don't see the "activist," whose move from masterfully plying words to deploying violent action seems in some characterizations incomprehensible. Rather, the very brutal official response to activism of words and of political theater in both the United States and West Germany inspired Meinhof's adoption of American SDS leader Carl Davidson's notion of a move "from protest to resistance." Once more, the idea traveled via an indirect route, through a number of individuals. Once more too we see how an idea got transformed in its transfer, both across and within national boundaries. It is the context of the escalation of the Vietnam War that formed the ostensible basis for this shift, in West Germany as in the US—but, of course, not exactly equivalently. Likewise, the particularities of Meinhof's own cultural, experiential, and ideational influences inform her own reception of this notion.

These differences within as well as between and among different national cultures form a critical plank of the next section, "(En)counter-Culture," with contributions by historians Detlef Siegfried, Maria Höhn, and Belinda Davis, and by sociologist Georgy Katsiaficas. Siegfried's contribution on "White Negroes" exhibits how fractures within a national culture created new "bedfellows," often across national boundaries—and well before the explosive late 1960s, but still very much a part of them. As others in the volume also observe, for some Germans the perceived link to African-Americans reflected their adoption, conscious and otherwise, of a number of identity characteristics: from "outsider" and "minority" to representative of "authentic" culture to "victim"—the last, naturally, a far more comfortable shroud to take on than that of "perpetrator." And, once more, the flow of influence was hardly monodirectional. West German and European appreciation for African-American performers gave the latter new stature and a new self-understanding to some degree back in the United States. This chapter speaks too to cross-generational links and the transfer of traditions within West Germany, as well as to rupture: the older West Germans who brought African-American musicians to West Germany found their most eager audience in young people, who embraced thereby an incipient "alternative culture" within West Germany.

Höhn treats this same relation—in this instance in an intensely direct and interactive sense, between American GIs stationed in West Germany and young West Germans—as another example of the "other alliance," or "second front," as she puts it. Here too this interaction drew the attention and concern of US officials, who feared young West Germans' role in influencing soldiers' views of the war and of the US, as well as in influencing American protestors. Within West Germany, Höhn offers the sense of intermediality that Siegfried also demonstrates: the transfer of "knowledge" between more local and/or more alternative media, including between the West German/African-American *Voice of the Lumpen* and the mainstream press. Some African-Americans began to see their own country through the eyes of German characterizations of "Amerika" (and "Amerikkka," sending the historical borrowings back and forth again!). Likewise, some began to proclaim a "natural" link to struggles in the Third World—in turn creating the possibility for both the direct and the indirect "experiential solidarity" that many young West Germans yearned for. All this formed the background to a transnational murder trial, during which all these relations were raised in haut-relief.

The piece by Belinda Davis also takes on this interculturality, claiming that young West Germans' widespread and frequent exposure to different cultures from their earliest years—including, significantly, to American culture, but well beyond Coca-Cola and Elvis Presley—was a central piece of bringing them to activism. This early and regular experience of "difference," with its broad range of sources, led hundreds of thousands to embrace and even seek out such difference, whether through school exchanges in the US or through regular informal, independent travel, which significantly contributed to the kinds of widespread transnational communications networks that help explain '68's global simultaneity. Such exposure led later activists to see their own culture(s) with fresh eyes and to imagine how that culture could be changed—and how they could change it.

Georgy Katsiaficas's essay picks up the question of counterculture and transnational simultaneity raised in a number of these pieces. Like Davis, he draws our attention to a far greater number and range of activists than sometimes wins focus. His contribution argues for the critical spontaneity of "autonomous" movements beginning in the late 1960s and marking the 1970s. This reflected the significant globalization of the circumstances that provoked this move across national boundaries and into countercultural groupings, from anti-nuclear to women's to peace movements and beyond. Katsiaficas thus sees Cold War structures as the primary spurs to this "people power," an Eros or "politics of the first person," in turn expressed far more broadly as direct action, rather than in words and the exchange of words and theories that so many others have emphasized. Indeed, the essay argues, this is the means to understanding the participation of great numbers of activists that went well beyond the intense discussion of ideas among a relative few who were, as he sees it, of relatively little importance.

In our effort to take advantage of our good fortune in having living "sources" to talk back to us, we include here as a last section excerpts from discussions with a number of contemporary activists from the United States and West Germany (and indeed reflecting, precisely in the nature of the era, a set of far more international and transnational experiences). The participation of Bernardine Dohrn, Helen Garvy, Tom Hayden, Rainer Langhans, Robert Pardun, Michael Vester, and KD Wolff, as well as Detlev Claussen and Georgy Katsiaficas (who served also as a scholarly contributor), was a central and always enlightening and thoughtful aspect of the conference the contributions of which form this volume, and we are deeply grateful for their willingness to join us. A particularly electrifying aspect of this participation was the reunion, across national cultures and boundaries, of activists who had not seen one another since those turbulent and yeasty years but who were very much living testimony to the critical role of the interactions and entanglements explored in this book.

Notes

1. Daniel Cohn-Bendit, *Wir haben sie so geliebt, die Revolution* (Frankfurt am Main, 1987), 15. Lutz Schulenburg has captured this "great world awakening" in a compilation of contemporary documents from all over the world. See Lutz Schulenburg, ed., *Das Leben ändern, die Welt verändern! 1968 – Dokumente und Berichte* (Hamburg, 1998), here 5. The activists' antagonists, in fact, shared this appraisal. Thus, US National Security Adviser Henry A. Kissinger informed President Richard M. Nixon that "[s]tudent unrest is a worldwide phenomenon, and has been for some time. ... There is a worldwide revolt against some of the basic conditions of modern society—the impersonality of institutions, the boredom of living in secure and prosperous societies, the decline of religious belief, and a pervasive relativism about moral belief and skepticism about moral authority." Memorandum for the President, Subject: Dr. Heard's Memorandum on Campus Unrest, 6 August 1970, box 333, Records of the Policy Planning Council – Director's Files (Winston Lord) 1969–1977, Record Group 59, National Archives, College Park, MD.
2. Joscha Schmierer, "Der Zauber des großen Augenblicks: Der internationale Traum von '68," in *Die Früchte der Revolte: Über die Veränderung der politischen Kultur durch die Studentenbewegung,* ed. Lothar Baier et al. (Berlin, 1988), 107–26, here 124–25.
3. There has recently been an explosion of literature, theoretical and historically specific, on transnationalism. Compare as a sampling: Akira Iriye, "On the Transnational Turn," *Diplomatic History* 31, no. 3 (2007): 373–76; idem, "AHR Conversation: On Transnational History," *American Historical Review* 111, no. 5 (2006): 1440–64; Claire F. Fox, "Commentary: The Transnational Turn and the Hemispheric Turn," *American Literary History* 18, no. 3 (2006): 638–47; Gunilla Budde, Sebastian Conrad, and Oliver Janz, eds., *Transnationale Geschichte: Themen, Tendenzen und Theorien* (Göttingen, 2006), and the ensuing review symposium on that volume on the *H-Soz-u-Kult* listserv with contributions by Matthias Middell, Michael Geyer, Barbara Lüthi, Dominic Sachsenmaier, and Andreas Eckert (http://hsozkult.geschichte. hu-berlin.de/rezensionen/type=revsymp); Shelley Fisher Fishkin, "Crossroads of Cultures: The Transnational Turn in American Studies: Presidential Address to the American Studies Association, November 12, 2004," *American Quarterly* 57, no. 1 (2005): 17–57; Kiran Klaus Patel, "Überlegungen zu einer transnationalen Geschichte," *Zeitschrift für Geschichtswissenschaft* 52, no. 7 (2004): 626–45. See also

Akira Iriye and Pierre Saunier, eds., *The Palgrave Dictionary of Transnational History* (London, forthcoming 2009).

4. See in particular Ernest R. May, "Writing Contemporary International History," *Diplomatic History* 8, no. 2 (1984): 103–14; Akira Iriye, "The Internationalization of History," *American Historical Review* 94, no. 1 (1989): 1–10; Ian Tyrrell, "American Exceptionalism in an Age of International History," *American Historical Review* 96, no. 4 (1991): 1031–55; David Thelen, "Of Audiences, Borderlands, and Comparisons: Toward the Internationalization of American History," *Journal of American History* 79, no. 2 (1992): 432–62; idem, "The Nation and Beyond: Transnational Perspectives on United States History," *Journal of American History* 86, no. 3 (1999): 965–75; Thomas Bender, ed., *Rethinking American History in a Global Age* (Berkeley, CA, 2002); Marcus Gräser, "Weltgeschichte im Nationalstaat: Die transnationale Disposition der amerikanischen Geschichtswissenschaft," *Historische Zeitschrift* 283, no. 2 (2006): 355–82.

5. See Kwame Anthony Appiah, "Is the Post- in Postmodernism the Post- in Postcolonial?" *Critical Inquiry* 17, no. 2 (1991): 336–57; Sebastian Conrad and Shalina Randeria, eds., *Jenseits des Eurozentrismus: Postkoloniale Perspektiven in den Geschichts- und Kulturwissenschaften* (Frankfurt am Main and New York, 2002); Sebastian Conrad, "Doppelte Marginalisierung: Plädoyer für eine transnationale Perspektive auf die deutsche Geschichte," *Geschichte und Gesellschaft* 28, no. 2 (2002): 145–69; Nina Glick Schiller, Linda Basch, and Cristina Blanc-Szanton, eds., *Towards a Transnational Perspective on Migration: Race, Class, Ethnicity, and Nationalism Reconsidered* (New York, 1992); Adesh Pal and Tapas Chakrabarti, eds., *Critiquing Nationalism, Transnationalism, and Indian Diaspora* (New Delhi, 2006); Alejandro Portes and Josh DeWind, eds., *Rethinking Migration: New Theoretical and Empirical Perspectives* (New York, 2007). See also the special issue on "Transnationalismus und Migration" of the Swiss journal *Traverse* 34, no. 1 (2005).

6. Compare e.g. David Caute, *The Year of the Barricades: A Journey through 1968* (New York, 1988); Ronald Fraser, et al, *1968: A Student Generation in Revolt* (New York, 1988); Peppino Ortoleva, *Saggio sui movimenti del 1968 in Europa e in America* (Rome, 1988); Aldo Agosti, Luisa Passerini, and Nicola Tranfaglia, eds., *La cultura et i luoghi del '68* (Milan, 1991); Ingo Juchler, *Die Studentenbewegungen in den Vereinigten Staaten und der Bundesrepublik Deutschland der sechziger Jahre: Eine Untersuchung hinsichtlich ihrer Beeinflußung durch Befreiungsbewegungen und –theorien aus der dritten Welt* (Berlin, 1996); Carole Fink, Philipp Gassert, and Detlef Junker, eds., *1968: The World Transformed* (New York, 1998); Wolfgang Kraushaar, "Die erste globale Rebellion," in idem, *1968 als Mythos, Chiffre und Zäsur* (Hamburg, 2000), 19–52; Geneviève Dreyfus-Armand, et al., eds., *Les années 68: Le temps de la contestation* (Brussels, 2001); Jeremi Suri, *Power and Protest: Global Revolution and the Rise of Détente* (Cambridge, MA, 2003); Michael Schmidtke, *Der Aufbruch der jungen Intelligenz: Die 68er Jahre in der Bundesrepublik und den USA* (Frankfurt am Main and New York, 2003); Édouard Husson, "1968: événement transnational ou international? Le cas de la France et de la République Fédérale d'Allemagne, *Revue d'Allemagne et des pays de langue allemande* 35, no. 2 (2003): 179–88; Jeremy Varon, *Bringing the War Home: The Weather Underground, the Red Army Faction, and Revolutionary Violence in the Sixties and Seventies* (Berkeley, CA, 2004); Jeremi Suri, ed., *The*

Global Revolutions of 1968 (New York, 2007); Martin Klimke and Joachim Scharloth, eds., *1968 in Europe: A History of Protest and Activism, 1956–77* (New York and London, 2008); also Belinda Davis, "What's Left? Popular and Democratic Political Participation in Postwar Europe," *American Historical Review* 113, no. 2 (2008): 363–90; Norbert Frei, *1968: Jugendrevolte und globaler Protest* (Munich, 2008); Jens Kastner and David Mayer, eds., *Weltwende 1968? Ein Jahr aus globalgeschichtlicher Perspektive* (Vienna, 2008); Martin Klimke, *The Other Alliance: Student Protest in West Germany and the United States in the Global Sixties* (Princeton, 2010); Karen Dubinsky, et al., eds., *New World Coming: The Sixties and the Shaping of Global Consciousness* (Toronto, 2009); Philipp Gassert and Martin Klimke, eds., *1968: Memories and Legacies of a Global Revolt* (Washington, D.C., 2009). See also the forum in *American Historical Review*: "The International 1968, Part I & Part II," in: idem, 114, no. 1 (February 2009), 42–135; idem, 114, no. 2, (April 2009), 329–404.

7. Immanuel Wallerstein, "1968: Eine Revolution im Weltsystem," in *1968 – ein europäisches Jahr?*, ed. Etienne François (Leipzig, 1997), 19–33.

8. Beate Fietz, "'A Spirit of Unrest': Die Achtundsechziger-Generation als globales Schwellenphänomen," in *Der Geist der Unruhe: 1968 im Vergleich. Wissenschaft – Literatur – Medien,* ed. Rainer Rosenberg, Inge Münz-Koenen, and Petra Boden (Berlin, 2000), 3–25. See also Eric Hobsbawm, "The Year the Prophets Failed," in *1968. The Magnum Photographs: A Year in the World,* ed. Eugene Atget and Laure Beaumont-Maillet (Paris, 1998), 8–10.

9. Ingrid Gilcher Holtey, ed., *1968 – Vom Ereignis zum Gegenstand der Geschichtswissenschaft* (Göttingen, 1998); idem, *Die 68er Bewegung: Deutschland – Westeuropa – USA* (Munich, 2001). For a broader social science perspective see Donatella della Porta, Hanspeter Kriesi, and Dieter Rucht, eds., *Social Movements in a Globalizing World* (New York, 1999); Joe Bandy and Jackie Smith, eds., *Coalitions Across Borders: Transnational Protest and the Neoliberal Order* (Lanham, MD, 2005).

10. Ingrid Gilcher-Holtey, "Der Transfer zwischen den Studentenbewegungen von 1968 und die Entstehung einer transnationalen Gegenöffentlichkeit," *Berliner Journal für Soziologie* 10, no. 4 (2000): 485–500. See also Martin Klimke and Joachim Scharloth, eds., *1968 – Handbuch zur Kultur- und Mediengeschichte der Studentenbewegung* (Stuttgart, 2007).

11. Jakob Tanner, "'The Times They Are A-Changin' – Zur subkulturellen Dynamik der 68er Bewegungen", in Gilcher-Holtey, *1968,* 207–23, here 207–8. For West Germany, the seminal study on the entanglement of political protest, counterculture, and consumerism is Detlef Siegfried, *Time Is on My Side: Konsum und Politik in der westdeutschen Jugendkultur der 60er Jahre* (Göttingen, 2006).

12. Reinhard Mohr and Dany Cohn-Bendit, *1968 – Die letzte Revolution, die noch nichts vom Ozonloch wusste* (Berlin, 1988), 79.

13. See Jessica C. E. Gienow-Hecht, "Shame on the US? Academics, Cultural Transfer, and the Cold War: A Critical Review," *Diplomatic History* 24, no. 3 (2000): 465–94, and the commentaries by Richard Pells, Bruce Kuklick, Richard Kuisel, and John Dower, ibid., 495–528. For a lucid survey of the historiographical trends, see also Philipp Gassert, "Amerikanismus, Antiamerikanismus, Amerikanisierung: Neue Literatur zur Sozial-, Wirtschafts- und Kulturgeschichte des amerikanischen Einflusses in Deutschland und Europa," *Archiv für Sozialgeschichte* 39 (1999): 531–61.

14. See Anselm Doering-Manteuffel, *Wie westlich sind die Deutschen? Amerikanisierung und Westernisierung im 20. Jahrhundert* (Göttingen, 1999); idem, "Westernisierung: Politisch-ideeller und gesellschaftlicher Wandel in der Bundesrepublik bis zum Ende der 60er Jahre," in Axel Schildt, Detlef Siegfried, and Karl Christian Lammers, eds., *Dynamische Zeiten: Die 60er Jahre in den beiden deutschen Gesellschaften* (Hamburg, 2000), 311–41; Holger Nehring, "'Westernization': A New Paradigm for Interpreting West European History in a Cold War Context," *Cold War History* 4, no. 2 (2004): 175–91. For empirical studies see Michael Hochgeschwender, *Freiheit in der Offensive? Der Kongreß für kulturelle Freiheit und die Deutschen* (Munich, 1998); Thomas Sauer, *Westorientierung im deutschen Protestantismus? Vorstellungen und Tätigkeit des Kronberger Kreises* (Munich, 1998); Gudrun Kruip, *Das 'Welt'-'Bild' des Axel Springer Verlags: Journalismus zwischen westlichen Werten und deutschen Denktraditionen* (Munich, 1998); Julia Angster, *Konsenskapitalismus und Sozialdemokratie: Die Westernisierung von SPD und DGB* (Munich, 2003); idem, "'Safe By Democracy': American Hegemony and the 'Westernization' of West German Labor," *Amerikastudien/American Studies* 46, no. 4 (2001): 557–72; Arnd Bauerkämper, Konrad H. Jarausch, and Marcus M. Payk, eds., *Demokratiewunder: Transatlantische Mittler und die kulturelle Öffnung Westdeutschlands 1945–1970* (Göttingen, 2005).

Part I

Atlantic Crossings

From Germany to America and Back

Chapter 1

Intellectual Transfer

Theodor W. Adorno's American Experience

Detlev Claussen

By the late 1960s Theodor W. Adorno had already become a kind of institution in Germany. Adorno himself, appalled, was among the first to realize this. But at that point no one gave much thought to the fact that Adorno had also become a transatlantic institution. In 1967, when I was attending my first advanced seminar in philosophy, Angela Davis presented a paper and Irving Wohlfarth and Sam Weber were among the participants. All three played important roles in translating, introducing, and "mediating" Adorno and Walter Benjamin's relation to a larger world. In 1969 Martin Jay came to Frankfurt. His work in the 1970s kept alive a consciousness of the relation between the European critical theorists Adorno and Max Horkheimer—both of whom had passed away by the mid 1970s—and Herbert Marcuse and Leo Löwenthal, who lived longer lives in California.

In Frankfurt, students of Adorno observed these milestones, reached in the face of critical theory's often quite isolated and unhappy history, with a mixture of pleasure and distrust. For those who thought of themselves as inheriting a living tradition, it was disconcerting to be told that critical theory was already a closed book—an object of "intellectual history" rather than a framework of contemporary social analysis. In 1983 Jay became the first person to address the idea of "Adorno in America." Unfortunately, despite Jay's warnings to be on guard against anecdotes and clichés about either Adorno or the German émigré experience, those clichés have come to dominate the very idea of Adorno and America. In the centenary of Adorno's birth, 2003, the German arts and culture media did their part to perpetuate the old legends. The ostensible literature of remembrance thus tells us yet again how the intellectual elites of Weimar escaped the Nazis by fleeing into the cultural wasteland called America, and how, after finding a place for themselves in the paradise of California during its golden age, they seemed to want nothing more than to return to their Germany, the land of *Dichter und Denker.* Alas, no documentary evidence, and certainly nothing from Adorno's pen, has retired these hoary narratives.

As stories like this are told and retold, the image of Adorno and that of the transatlantic relation harden into stereotypes. In Europe, anti-Americanism has long distorted accounts of Adorno's view of America. On the American side, the clichéd image of Adorno as an intellectual whose myopias supposedly made him less than normal dovetail with a highly distorting anti-intellectualism. Thus Adorno, we are told, had no clue about sports, blindly hated jazz, and never enjoyed himself at the movies, in front of the television, or anywhere else. This litany says less about Adorno than it does about intercontinental interaction in the bad sense. If we set aside the notion that America and Europe are self-contained entities, however, and if we begin to view their relation as a changing, historical one, Adorno's life and work can point to what was in fact a highly significant transfer of experience. Simply put: without America, Adorno would never have become the person we now recognize by that name. The man who fled from Hitler was a brilliant philosopher and artist with left-radical sympathies, a polymath barely thirty years old bearing the name of Dr. Wiesengrund-Adorno. In 1949 a far more circumspect American citizen named Theodor W. Adorno returned to Europe. For many years thereafter, however, the suitcase always remained packed; only gradually, after attaining a professorship in Frankfurt in 1953, could Adorno see a future for himself as a convinced democrat and critical enlightener in West German society. Without Horkheimer's success in organizing the reestablishment of the old Institute for Social Research in Frankfurt in 1949, Adorno most likely would not have returned to Germany. In 1953, when he made the decision to stay in Germany, his closest German acquaintances and friends in California, Thomas Mann and Fritz Lang, reacted with skepticism and displeasure.

The fact that Adorno changed his name in California in 1942 was neither incidental nor trivial. But it was not to suppress his Jewish heritage—as certain of his detractors have insinuated—that Adorno abbreviated his father's name to a *W*. At the time, it was far more relevant to downplay the German overtones of Wiesengrund. According to his own account, Adorno's collaboration with Mann on *Doktor Faustus* brought Adorno closer to the German tradition than he had been. But the California period was also the moment of Adorno's departure from that tradition. He came to America a German philosopher and a *Privatdozent* from Frankfurt University;[1] he left America a social theorist and researcher, capable not only of writing *Philosophy of Modern Music* as an excursus to *Dialectic of Enlightenment* but also of making a decisive contribution to the pioneering study *The Authoritarian Personality*. Adorno did not mature into a philosophical sociologist in the good old German tradition; instead, he became a theorist who used empiricism to free traditional philosophy from dogma. It was precisely his theoretical sensibility that allowed him to break out of the narrow frameworks of social-scientific routine, making new forms of inquiry open to experience and opening up new aspects of experience to empirical research and theoretical conceptualization. But of course this is not how it is usually perceived. Take, for instance, the infamous episode involving Paul F. Lazarsfeld in 1938. We all know the clichéd version of this story, which reads almost like a sports headline:

"American academic system pummels German philosopher! Another victory for American pragmatism, and a humiliating defeat for idealism!" Yet the headlines do not square with either the broad history of social research or even the specific events and people involved.

Lazarsfeld, for one, did not become an empiricist in America. He came out of the labor movement inspired by Austro-Marxism, with its unique mixture of enlightenment goals, scientific positivism, and progressive politics. Lazarsfeld's "radio barometer" was something he invented while in Vienna; his collaboration with Horkheimer went back to the final days of the Weimar Republic. It is true that the Princeton Radio Research Project, for which Lazarsfeld hired Adorno in 1938 as the musical director, was still making use of rather primitive "likes and dislikes" studies to investigate the musical preferences of its listeners. "Like or dislike" is a question of taste, yet this simple-sounding question can be approached seriously only with great difficulty. As Adorno pointed out, an intellectually and sociologically meaningful investigation of taste can take place only through an inquiry into the way objective constellations of social forces come to be manifest in subjects. Empiricists fear such questions the way the devil fears holy water, because these questions call empiricism itself into question, and they do so on good empirical grounds, by requiring it to define what it thinks it is measuring. Adorno, who dared to ask this question in his first work as an empirical sociologist, initially met with the rejection that comes of violating a profession's strongest taboo.

In 1968 Lazarsfeld and Adorno both wrote memoirs of their experiences at the Princeton Radio Research Project and of their first encounters with one another. Both accounts have the charm of autobiographical reflections, and for that reason both must be approached with caution. Writerly intentions are altered in the process of writing, and these intentions are transformed again when read under different social circumstances. Lazarsfeld's "Episode in the History of Empirical Social Research" foregrounds an "Atlantic transfer" that, for him, meant the path from Vienna to the Ivy Leagues; Adorno's text reflects on the "scientific experiences of a European scholar" in New York and California between 1938 and 1953. Yet the difference between their accounts of transatlantic displacement, travel, and arrival is immediately apparent. Lazarsfeld wanted to and in fact did become an American scientist; he was celebrated worldwide as one of the leading American social scientists of his generation.

This Adorno did not want, yet even in his self-understanding he did not remain a German philosopher. Rather—paradoxical as it may sound—it was in the United States that he became a European, one who, like his old friend Horkheimer, came back to Frankfurt via Paris. If one reads *Minima Moralia* for traces of a European self-awareness that was emerging in California, the conclusion is inescapable: *Minima Moralia* reads like an inverted tourist guide, in which the European begins to understand himself through exile. In choosing to research Paris as the last bastion of an old Europe, Walter Benjamin had sought a similar self-understanding, and his refusal to break off his work led to his undoing. When Adorno, in New York, received Benjamin's surviving files, he did not merely obtain a set of notes toward an "incomplete research project." Contained therein were also Benjamin's insights—a kind of knowledge that a Lazarsfeld would have found wholly unsympathetic (not to mention unprofessional) had Benjamin, by a different set of circumstances, managed to make the Atlantic transfer in person. Adorno needed to return to Germany to complete the circuit, for only there could he bring Benjamin's work to press. Benjamin, who knew how to draw on the tensions between differentiated social formations as a source of intellectual insight and knowledge, had already shown the way: the relationship between France and Germany served as a thought model (*Denkmodell*) for both men.

Throughout the long nineteenth century France had embodied, from the German point of view, the utopian potential of a successful revolution that, however, had not yet come to its emancipatory conclusion. In many respects, Marx's pre-1848 critique of Germany had already drawn its power from the social differential between east and west, a line then marked by the Rhine. But the twentieth century would become, from the European point of view, the American century. In retrospect, it seems strange that America's utopian potential as the land of unlimited possibilities was often identified by those friends of Adorno who least knew America: Alban Berg, for example. Or we might note here Benjamin's choice of a title for a collection of aphorisms that he wrote partly in anticipation of an American exile: *Zentralpark* (*Central Park*). The more self-evident it became that the October Revolution had failed, the more it became clear—by the mid 1930s, inescapably clear—that hope and opportunities for change must be discovered in the most advanced society of the contemporary world.

Yet American society was experienced as one whose revolution was already over: the emancipatory mind slipped from identification with the short-lived Napoleonic empire to an almost ontological view of America as a pure bourgeois society. "La Révolution est fini" was the implicit motto of a radically bourgeois American society largely antagonistic to European traditions. Social-revolutionary critique is unthinkable in a society in which the forces of enlightenment unfold their dialectic in the absence of a hostile ancien régime. Horkheimer and Adorno returned from America not as disappointed revolutionary critics but as dialecticians of enlightenment. The essence of the American experience—of what was new to the enlightened Europeans—consisted in what Adorno called the "experience of substantive democratic forms." Those Germans who read *Minima Moralia* when it appeared in 1951 could hardly understand this, for democracy was for most of them still largely an imported good brought by the occupying power. The anti-American slant inherent to many of the German interpretations of *Minima Moralia* over the years should be viewed in terms of this social-historical context. In a new age, in which the lack of any alternative to democratic forms of social organization is a global experience, an opportunity beckons to discover again the utopian power of Adorno's social criticism.

The critical theorists' social criticism had great difficulty gaining traction in the American academic system. The politically astute émigré Horkheimer—who along with Friedrich Pollock developed the strategy for the Atlantic transfer of the Institute for Social Research—shied away from staging an open confrontation between a critical theory oriented toward social change and the academic system that served as its host. Yet it would be paradoxical to read into this reluctance the idea that the institute's research stood no chance of integrating into American society. Aside from the fact that the institute's advance representative, Franz Neumann, had already garnered considerable popularity and acclaim by the 1930s and probably would have, if not for his untimely death, been a star in the American academy, one should also remember that Marcuse and Löwenthal clearly had an easier time surviving in academic America than they would have had in postfascist Germany. Thomas Wheatland has, moreover, demonstrated that these judgments can be made in terms of broader intellectual currents.[2] His study shows that the transfer of the institute to Columbia University disproves the cliché; the overall effect of the transfer was to give what had been the purely theoretical New York school of sociology a strongly empirical turn that allowed its ideas to displace the paradigms of the better-established Chicago sociological tradition. One suspects that Horkheimer, sensing the historical shape of the American academy, sought out Lazarsfeld for precisely these reasons. Lazarsfeld had ties to the institute dating back to the Weimar years, but, having emigrated several years before Horkheimer, he also had a wealth of empirical research experience to share. Out of gratitude for Horkheimer's help, Lazarsfeld made it possible for Horkheimer to bring Adorno to America in 1938.

The true differences between the two radio researchers, though, derived from their divergent conceptions of what they were doing in America: Adorno was the émigré, Lazarsfeld the immigrant. The different structures of expectation implied by these terms run through both men's recollections from 1968. My interest is to make these latent structures explicit—as well as to show, more generally, that the Atlantic transfer succeeds only if it entails a reciprocal process, whereby not just ideas but also experiences are brought across the divide. This experiential transfer must also involve an exchange that transcends the boundaries of the "academic" habitus, at least as it is narrowly defined.

On 27 May 1945, after the defeat of Hitler's army, Adorno presented a lecture at the Jewish Club of Los Angeles titled "Questions for the Intellectual Emigration." At the time, returning to Germany was not an immediate prospect for anyone, and relatively few anticipated the starkly bipolar world political order to come. For these reasons, the natural question presenting itself was how emigration would contribute to the new American century. Adorno addressed these issues from the start by distinguishing between immigration and emigration. Lazarsfeld's model of a research career in the United States—a career that might easily enough serve the war effort—stood comfortably within the tradition of secular immigration that had allowed millions of Germans to become Americans since the nineteenth century. It fit into Adorno's concept of immigration, born of direct life experience, as well. Most of the theorists in Horkheimer's circle had also become American citizens in the early 1940s, and several of them, such as Marcuse, had worked for the Office of War Information, producing social-scientific assessments of nations in the world war. Adorno—though he had had the privilege of being employed to work with Horkheimer on *Dialectic of Enlightenment* and thus of drawing funds that the institute had managed to transfer to America—was by no means opposed to the others' efforts. Indeed, in the coming years his analyses of fascist agitators and the "authoritarian personality" were natural correlates to the intention to integrate into the American social science system. Yet Adorno also held fast to the experiential content inherent in the "émigré," a category that connotes an ongoing awareness of violence, an awareness that inhibits the ability to identify wholly with the land of refuge. The inner compulsion to integrate into a new society—a compulsion that mirrors the rules of bourgeois society more generally—also echoes the central experience in European Jewish society, the pressure to assimilate. An immigrant society imposes on the immigrant a choice: either deny or reinvent one's life history and, with it, history itself. Under this pressure, Adorno developed, beginning in 1945, a third possibility: an intellectual program, as he put it, of "transferring that which is not transferable."

Memory of tradition cannot be conclusively reconciled with the promise of liberation: even when the two principles can be alloyed, their bond is unstable and constantly risks falling into demonization or idealization. Yet this was the task that Adorno set himself in 1945. In anti-Americanism, a distorted social perception produces and internalizes the image of a wholly uncultured America; in anti-intellectualism, it produces a hypertrophic notion of culture that precludes social analysis. Today these seemingly mutually exclusive oppositions have become inseparable. The inflated culture concept has already, under the title of "cultural studies," won scientific dignity for itself, either as glorified high culture or as ethnoreligious specificity. It is from this perspective that Adorno's program of transferring the nontransferable becomes contemporary for us once again. Adorno's critique of Lazarsfeld's naive empiricist idea of measuring culture—a critique that appeared, in thinly veiled form, in the 1945 lecture—directs itself not against an empirical American style of science but against an uncritical acceptance of the developing culture industry.

Here, too, a clarifying word must be added: the culture industry is no American peculiarity; rather, the United States has, in the last hundred years, merely been ahead of the curve in the global trend toward commercializing intellectual production. Within this trend, Lazarsfeld's quantification of culture is of course wholly appropriate: it merely reflects the culture industry's drive to quantify itself in order to ease its own acceptance on the market. The US is now, as in

1945—as Adorno stated—in "the most advanced position for observing" the development of society. It was out of the tension between advanced social developments and the cultural developments of a continental Europe lagging behind that Adorno's capacity for nonconservative cultural criticism began to emerge. Anti-intellectualism has, however, repeatedly tried to categorize Adorno as a conservative cultural critic—a role that he never sought. Adorno's recognition of how Weimar culture had undermined itself—a recognition that went hand in hand with that of the Soviets' barbarous cultural politics in the 1930s—was too deeply ingrained in him, both as direct memory and as part of his constitution as a European intellectual, to allow for such self-misunderstanding. With the Hitler-Stalin pact, European culture had lost its sense of a homeland; those who ultimately were fortunate enough to escape the destruction were, of course, disproportionately those who made it to America. In this sense, it is important to remember that the intellectual emigration was not made up just of Jews, even if Adorno's audience at the Jewish Club was almost certainly composed largely of Jews from German-speaking lands.

The text that Adorno used to reintroduce himself to the West German public was called "Cultural Criticism and Society"; this—not *Prisms*—was supposed to be the title of the book introduced by this 1949 essay. It is in this, Adorno's opening foray into postwar German culture, that we find what is perhaps his most misinterpreted dictum: "To write poetry after Auschwitz is barbaric." But how often do we hear the whole sentence? "The critique of culture finds itself confronting the last stage of the dialectic of culture and barbarism: to write poetry after Auschwitz is barbaric—and that fact, that situation devours even the insight and intelligence that speak out about why poetry has become impossible."[3] This sentence encapsulates Adorno's attempt not to sacrifice the European experience to a globalized amnesia. The memory of the appearance of barbarism in the midst of culture makes his work contemporary: whereas cultural memory gains its right to exist only insofar as it is critical, the glorification of culture itself brings barbaric tendencies in its train. For this reason, it is not at all accurate to characterize Adorno as a neo-Marxist; if that were so, he not only would be boring but would also have been rightly forgotten. Lazarsfeld in his memoirs tried to portray Adorno as a neo-Marxist, but Lazarsfeld's interest lay in transcending the problem formulated by Adorno: to understand how human subjects consciously mediate objective social processes. The studies that Adorno himself undertook—of the effects of fascist agitators in America, of the techniques of horoscopes in the *Los Angeles Times*,[4] of "how to look at television" (in 1953, at which point television viewing had been universal in California, the land of cutting-edge communication technologies, for about five years)[5]—all bear a kind of witness to a still-unresolved problem in the social sciences.

If one partakes in the belief, widespread even today in the scientific community, that culture and the subject can be unproblematically identified with one another, then Adorno's American experience may become irrelevant. But if one views this identification of culture with the individual as a residual marker of the experience of a modern immigrant society—the kind of society that the societies of "old Europe" have since become—one also recognizes the problem posed by Adorno's life and thought as an aspect of experience that an uncritical science has lost the ability to articulate and analyze. In 1968 Adorno bequeathed to his German students and American readers "a kind of restitution of experience against its empirical treatment" in the form of a theoretical program. Even in remembering Adorno we must be conscious of how easy it is to diminish experience by stringing together adjectives and mistaking them for actual analysis. German, bourgeois, Jewish, half-Jewish: each classification falls short of the concrete individual—and American citizen—who, out of a mixture of external pressures and free will, renamed himself Theodor W. Adorno in California in 1942. He wished to keep alive the remembrance of the conditions that had given him his intellectual physiognomy, yet he could not, nor did he want to, be identical with what he had once been.

In closing, I wish to refer to a remark, made by Adorno in the 1968 "Scientific Experiences of a European Scholar," that to my knowledge has gone unnoticed but that speaks both to the formative and to the historical dimensions of Adorno's American experience, as well as to his attempt to raise that experience to the level of critical theory.[6] As such, it is a remark that pointed (and still points) to the future of critical theory. Observing that it is characteristic of modern society to demand that the individual increasingly conform to society's norms and thus identify with its demands, Adorno comments that this social fact would seem to require a dramatic revision of the foundational concept of identity. Without such a revision, he reasons, the embrace of identity amounts to the uncritical celebration of a backward-looking ideology that has the potential to displace humane praxis. Precisely insofar as modern society, which Adorno certainly interpreted through the all-purpose ideology of the "melting pot," hoped to do away with the Old World, so it also kept alive a central concept of all utopias—the hope, as Adorno put it in *Minima Moralia*, "of being able to be different without fear."[7] Adorno's American experience made it possible, for someone who had become conscious of himself in America, to return to Germany as a European intellectual—and indeed, to a Europe that did not yet even exist. Only through the mediation of America could Adorno become the kind of institution—and the body of thought—that brings intellectuals together from both sides of the Atlantic to think about the displacements and tensions of modern society.

Notes

This essay appeared first in *New German Critique* 33, 1 97 (2006), and is reprinted here with permission of Duke University Press.

1. The *Privatdozent* is a typical old German institution that means an adjunct professor who receives no pay.

2. Thomas Wheatland, *The Frankfurt School in Exile* (Minneapolis, MN, 2009).
3. Theodor W. Adorno, "Cultural Criticism and Society," in *Prisms,* trans. Samuel Weber and Shierry Weber (Cambridge, MA, 1981), 34. Translation modified. For the German see "Kulturkritik und Gesellschaft," in *Prismen,* vol. 10.1 of *Gesammelte Schriften,* ed. Rolf Tiedemann (Frankfurt am Main, 1977), 11–30.
4. Theodor W. Adorno, *The Stars Down to Earth, and Other Essays on the Irrational in Culture,* ed. Stephen Crook (New York, 1994).
5. Theodor W. Adorno, "How to Look at Television," *Quarterly of Film, Radio, and Television* 8, no. 3 (1954): 214–35. The essay first appeared in German in *Rundfunk und Fernsehen* 4 (1953), reprinted as "Fernsehen als Ideologie" in *Eingriffe,* vol. 10.2 of *Gesammelte Schriften,* ed. Rolf Tiedemann (Frankfurt am Main, 1977), 518–32; the English version was reprinted as "Television as Ideology" in *Critical Models: Interventions and Catchwords,* trans. Henry W. Pickford (New York, 1998), 59–70.
6. Theodor W. Adorno, "Wissenschaftliche Erfahrungen in Amerika," in *Stichworte,* appendix to *Eingriffe,* 701–38. For the English version see "Scientific Experiments of a European Scholar in America," in Pickford, *Critical Models,* 215–42.
7. Theodor W. Adorno, "Mélange," in *Minima Moralia: Reflections from Damaged Life,* trans. E. F. N. Jephcott (London, 1974), 114.

Chapter 2

The Limits of Praxis
The Social-Psychological Foundations of Theodor Adorno's and Herbert Marcuse's Interpretations of the 1960s Protest Movements

John Abromeit

There has been much research, documentation, and discussion of Theodor Adorno's and Herbert Marcuse's relationships to the protest movements of the 1960s, but the general understanding of their attitudes and involvement is still largely dominated by myth. In its most common form, the myth can be described as follows. Adorno was an aloof mandarin who refused to translate his radical theoretical positions into concrete political practice. The repressive consequences of Adorno's political quietism were demonstrated most clearly by his response to the occupation of the Institute for Social Research in January 1969 by a group of students from the Socialist German Student Union (SDS): Adorno called the cops. Marcuse, on the other hand, fully identified with the protesting students, as amply demonstrated by his appearance at numerous political events in the late 1960s and his energetic denunciation of the liberal establishment, American imperialism and capitalism more generally. Marcuse was the "guru" or "grandfather" of the student movement, who provided a theoretical justification for students' political activism.[1]

While it is true that Adorno eventually distanced himself from radical students and that Marcuse supported them more actively, the dominant understanding has prevented a more historically nuanced assessment of their respective roles in the protest movements in Germany and the US. The dominant view has not only obscured the important ways in which Adorno supported these movements and Marcuse was critical of them, it has also overlooked the common theoretical assumptions that profoundly shaped both of their interpretations of these events. In what follows, I would like emphasize, in particular, their common theoretical debt to a critical social-psychological tradition, which began in the 1930s with Max Horkheimer's and Erich Fromm's pathbreaking integration of Freudian psychoanalysis into Marx's critical theory of modern capitalism and which was appropriated and further developed by Adorno and Marcuse in the 1940s and

1950s. Revisiting the shared social- psychological categories underlying Marcuse and Adorno's critical theory will not only illuminate their interpretation of the protest movements of the 1960s; it will also demonstrate that they did not differ as much as is commonly assumed. Second, a more detailed reconstruction of Adorno's involvement with the protest movements should make clear that he not only influenced the students theoretically but was also an outspoken supporter of most of their professed goals. Although Adorno had expressed concerns from the beginning about certain tendencies in the movement to privilege praxis over theory, it was not until the occupation of the Institute for Social Research in January 1969 that he believed these tendencies had become dominant and he deemed it necessary to distance himself publicly from the movement. Finally, a reexamination of Marcuse's *theoretical* understanding of the protest movements makes it clear that he was not as sanguine about the prospects of revolutionary praxis as is commonly assumed. Although the May events in France temporarily pushed Marcuse beyond his relatively bleak political prognosis in *One-Dimensional Man,* the ferocious backlash against the protest movements in the US in the early 1970s led him to recognize ex post facto the truth content of Adorno's arguments about the potential for authoritarianism in contemporary capitalist societies. In fact, the strength of the backlash convinced Marcuse of the theoretical urgency of reexamining the social-psychological tradition inaugurated by Horkheimer and Fromm.

It lies beyond the scope of this essay to reconstruct the early development of the social-psychological tradition of Critical Theory in the work of Horkheimer and Fromm.[2] But it is worth noting, in a volume dedicated to examining the transatlantic presuppositions and relations of the protest movements of the 1960s, that this tradition was "transatlantic" from the very beginning. The first serious attempt by Horkheimer and Fromm to apply their innovative synthesis of Marxian and Freudian categories occurred in an empirical study of the attitudes of German workers and salaried employees in 1929.[3] In contrast to many of his future Institute colleagues, Horkheimer already recognized at this time the importance of empirical social research for a critical theory of society. Realizing also that American sociologists had developed more advanced empirical research methods than their German counterparts, Horkheimer looked to studies such as Robert and Helen Lynd's *Middletown* as models for the empirical work to be carried out at the Institute. But the study of German workers and salaried employees directed by Fromm also went beyond any empirical studies carried out in the US—or anywhere else—in its application of psychoanalytic techniques in both the formulation and evaluation of the questionnaires. Horkheimer and Fromm wanted to grasp not just the respondents' conscious attitudes, but also their unconscious character structures. Despite the fact that the methods used in this first study were highly experimental and unrefined, the study clearly conveyed strong authoritarian tendencies among the German lower and lower-middle classes—even among groups that professed leftist political allegiances. Based on the findings of the study, Horkheimer and Fromm presciently concluded that if the National Socialists attempted to seize power, resistance from the German working class would be minimal. So already in 1931 Horkheimer transferred the Institute's endowment to the Netherlands and sent Fromm to the United States to prepare for a forced exile—a possibility that soon became a reality.

In its next major social-psychological research project, the Institute addressed the problem of authoritarianism once again, this time with refined methods and a broader geographical scope. Already before the relocation of Institute headquarters from Frankfurt to Columbia University, questionnaires for the *Studies of Authority and Family* were distributed in France, Switzerland, Belgium, Holland, and Austria. The final version of the study also included material gathered in studies of unemployment and its effects on families in the United States. One of these studies—of families in Newark, New Jersey, in 1935–36—became the basis for a more extensive project carried out by Mirra Komarowsky and Paul Lazarsfeld and published under the Institute's auspices in 1940. The *Studies on Authority and Family* demonstrated more clearly than the 1929 study on German workers that Horkheimer and Fromm's categories were intended to address social-psychological tendencies that transcended any particular national context. This basic presupposition was made explicit in their theoretical work in the mid 1930s, which the empirical material included in the *Studies* was intended to test and refine. In his introduction to the *Studies,* which represented the culmination of a series of essays on critical social psychology from the early 1930s, Fromm developed the category of the sado-masochistic character.[4] In his essay "Egoism and Freedom Movements: On the Anthropology of the Bourgeois Epoch," which was written immediately after the publication of the *Studies on Authority and Family,* Horkheimer demonstrated how the constellation of "sado-masochistic" character structures, described in social-psychological terms by Fromm, had developed historically.[5] Through an examination of political mass mobilization at certain key historical junctures—such as the Reformation and French Revolution—Horkheimer tried to demonstrate how relations between the ascendant bourgeoisie and the lower classes had shaped the dominant character structures of both groups. Horkheimer referred to the constellation of characters structures that emerged in this historical process as the "anthropology of the bourgeois epoch." Fromm and Horkheimer's theoretical and historical reflections became the foundation for the empirical social-psychological research carried out by Institute members in the 1940s.

In light of the catastrophic events unfolding in Europe in the 1940s, the Institute's research on authoritarianism acquired new urgency. The American Jewish Committee (AJC) and the Jewish Labor Committee (JLC) agreed to finance large-scale research projects by the Institute to determine whether a similar threat existed in the United States and, if so, how best to combat it. The project financed by the JLC focused on anti-Semitism among American workers. The Institute submitted a 1,300-page report to the JLC as early as 1944, documenting that, as Martin Jay put it, "more than half the workers surveyed has shown anti-Semitic bias of one sort or another."[6] But due to Horkheimer's concerns about how the American public would react to the study, and also due to the fact that many of its findings had been duplicated in the larger *Studies in Prejudice,* financed by the AJC, the JLC study was never published. It would take us too far afield to discuss the *Studies in Prejudice* as a whole, but of the five volumes published, Leo Lowenthal's and Norbert Guterman's *Prophets of Deceit* and Theodor Adorno's contributions to *The Authoritarian Personality* certainly represented the most important attempts to test and develop the Institute's social-psychological theory and empirical research methods. Lowenthal stated explicitly in the preface to *Prophets of Deceit* that Horkheimer's essay on "Egoism and Freedom Movements" provided the theoretical foundations for his study. In order to determine the ways in which "the anthropology of the bourgeois epoch" was manifesting itself in the United States in the 1930s and 1940s, Lowenthal used content analysis to analyze newspapers, pamphlets, and speeches of American proto-fascist agitators. As Horkheimer and Fromm had done before, Lowenthal combined empirical research methods with psychoanalytic categories in order to "probe beneath the manifest content of his speeches and writings to disinter their latent content."[7]

The primary goal of the *Authoritarian Personality* was to explain, as Horkheimer stated in his preface to the volume, "the rise of an 'anthropological' species we call the authoritarian type of man."[8] As was the case with Lowenthal's *Prophets of Deceit,* Adorno benefited methodologically from the experience of the study of anti-Semitism among the American working class and its conclusion that the interrelated problems of authoritarianism and prejudice had to be approached indirectly.[9] So in the questionnaires distributed and the interviews conducted for the project, minority groups were not mentioned and the participants were not informed of the direct purpose of the research. The primary methodological goal of the study was to develop a reliable means of measuring unconscious psychological dispositions, which would betray sympathy or susceptibility to authoritarian and/or prejudiced beliefs and behavior. The most important result of the research, in this regard, was the so-called "F Scale," which gauged potential authoritarianism in terms of nine basic variables, such as conventionalism, aggression, superstition, projectivity, and attitudes toward sex.[10]

In terms of substantive results, the most important for our purposes here is the concept of the *pseudo-conservative* character structure. The category of the pseudo-conservative is most closely related to Fromm's category of the sadomasochistic character and most clearly demonstrates the continuity of what Horkheimer had called bourgeois anthropology.[11] Echoing Horkheimer, Adorno notes that the pseudo-conservative type "was probably established during the last four centuries," but that "the objective social conditions have made it easier for the character structure in question to express itself" and that "the social acceptance of pseudo-conservatism has gone a long way … it has secured an indubitable mass basis."[12] Adorno describes the pseudo-conservative as a "man who, in the name of upholding traditional American values and institutions and defending them against more or less fictitious dangers, consciously or unconsciously aims at their abolition."[13] He notes that the pseudo-conservative favors "the curtailment of individual liberties in the name of some ill-defined collectivity" and that a pseudo-conservative worldview "blends very well with the desire for authoritarian control as expressed by those who style themselves as conservatives."[14] As we shall see, this character type would figure prominently in the backlash against students in both Germany and the US.[15]

To sum up, the social psychological tradition of the Frankfurt School began as a "transatlantic" project and became increasingly so with the transfer of the Institute to the United States and its engagement in the 1930s and the 1940s with the empirical social-psychological studies mentioned above. Although research techniques were refined, Horkheimer's notion of the "anthropology of the bourgeois epoch" and Fromm's notion of the "sado-masochistic personality" remained crucial theoretical points of reference. The tacit assumption was that the constellation of character structures created by modern capitalism did not differ radically in the United States and in Europe; in fact, there had been no need to overcome feudalism and absolutism in the "New World," which led Adorno to call the United States a "radical bourgeois society."[16] While Horkheimer and Adorno were impressed with the "substantial democratic forms" they encountered in the US,[17] they by no means assumed that it was thus rendered immune to the authoritarian tendencies that were deeply rooted in modern capitalist society. The fact that the Institute for Social Research continued to conduct empirical research projects on authoritarianism after it was reestablished in Frankfurt in 1951 demonstrates once again the "transatlantic" presuppositions of their social-psychological theory. This theory would play a crucial role in both Herbert Marcuse's and Theodor Adorno's interpretations of the protest movements in Germany and the US in the 1960s.

Unlike Adorno, Herbert Marcuse was not directly involved in the Institute's empirical research projects in the 1940s. But Marcuse kept abreast of its research while working at the Office of Strategic Studies during the war.[18] He also engaged in a serious study of Freud for the first time during the war, which eventually resulted in the publication in 1955 of *Eros and Civilization: A Philosophical Inquiry into Freud.* His central argument about a baleful "dialectic of civilization" at work in Western capitalist societies echoed Horkheimer's argument about the anthropology of the bourgeois epoch in several key ways.[19] Like Horkheimer, Marcuse argued that modern capitalism created and constantly reproduced historically unprecedented levels of socially mediated repression. Marcuse also followed Horkheimer in his belief that this "surplus repression" created surplus aggression that was mobilized by political leaders to further their political aims. Marcuse departed from Horkheimer in his greater willingness to accept the late Freud's speculative concept of Thanatos. Rather than positing it as a biological constant, however, Marcuse argued that the death drive was a response to the weakening of Eros due to surplus repression, which resulted from historically specific social conditions. Marcuse was also more willing than Horkheimer to trace the subtle and often highly sublimated ways in which Thanatos manifested itself in advanced capitalist societies. Echoing Horkheimer and Adorno's arguments in *Dialectic of Enlightenment*, Marcuse demonstrated how the original impulse of civilization—to subordinate internal and external nature to rational control—had overshot its goal and turned into its opposite: the recrudescence of barbarism at the height of "civilization." Although technology had advanced far enough to make possible a "non-repressive civilization," it was used instead to develop ever more efficient and deadly weapons. Marcuse viewed the war in Vietnam, with its massive implementation of napalm and cluster bombs against Vietnamese civilians, as an unadulterated expression of this dialectic of civilization: sublimated and unsublimated Thanatos given free rein against an officially approved "enemy of the people."[20]

If Marcuse's notion of the dialectic of civilization anticipated and influenced student protests against the war in Vietnam, his arguments about the integration of the working class in *One-Dimensional Man* did the same for the New Left, with regard to its critiques of the Old Left and attempts to find "new agents of change" among students, intellectuals, women, and minorities, as well as in anti-colonial struggles. The idea that the working class had failed to perform the role assigned to it in the Marxist theoretical tradition was, of course, nothing new by this time. The empirical research project on the attitudes of the working class in Weimar Germany, mentioned above, had already alerted the Institute to the strong unconscious tendencies toward integration among large sections of the lower and lower-middle classes. Marcuse's thesis of the integration of the working class was, in other words, not just a political argument reflecting the rise of corporatism and a new labor aristocracy; it also rested upon Horkheimer and Fromm's social-psychological findings. In *One-Dimensional Man* Marcuse makes this argument in terms of both "false needs" and "false consciousness." In a consumer society, workers had much more to lose than their chains. In such a situation, marginalized groups became the placeholders of critical consciousness. Those with privileged access to critical knowledge, such as students and intellectuals, or those who were oppressed by or excluded from the benefits of the affluent society, such as minorities, women, and colonial or post-colonial subjects, could more easily understand that the affluent society still rested upon a fundamentally exploitative dynamic. But Marcuse never claimed that these groups were a new revolutionary subject. He said they could help prepare the way for a situation in which transformative possibilities would be possible. For Marcuse, the working class remained the primary agent of social transformation: in-itself, if not yet for-itself.

An Essay on Liberation marked the high point of Marcuse's optimism about the protest movements. Written at the height of global student and worker protests in 1968, Marcuse dedicated this work to the student revolutionaries in Paris. Inspired greatly by the strong aesthetic moment in the May events in Paris as well as the increasing influence of the counterculture in the United States, Marcuse argued that the protesters were developing a "new sensibility" that pointed beyond a purely political revolution, for a political revolution alone was not enough to transcend the social-psychological dynamic at work in modern capitalist societies. An objective transformation of political institutions must be preceded and accompanied by a transformation of subjective character structures in order to prevent the reoccurrence of what Marx had trenchantly described in *The Eighteenth Brumaire*, namely the fearful conjuring of ghosts from the past during the crisis situation and the reconstitution of repressive relations thereafter. Marcuse believed that the reemergence of key aspects of the historical avant-garde in the European protest movements, along with the flowering of the counterculture in the US, might signal the emergence of precisely this subjective, genuinely "radical" dimension of change, which had been lacking in the other modern revolutions. To support this argument Marcuse took recourse to an ancient concept of the aesthetic that was grounded in the structure of the senses and emotions as a whole.[21] Far from relegating it to hermetic works of art (Adorno) or its own discrete value sphere (Habermas), Marcuse pointed to the role of the aesthetic in the formation and possible transformation of character structures in modern capitalist societies. Marcuse's highly speculative concept of the "new sensibility" can best be understood in relation to Horkheimer's concept of bourgeois anthropology.[22] Marcuse believed for a brief time that the aesthetic moment in the protest movements pointed beyond bourgeois anthropology to qualitatively new forms of subjectivity, but as we shall see, he was soon disappointed.[23]

In 1957 the Institute for Social Research carried out an empirical study on West German students' attitudes toward politics. In a short piece based on these findings, which Adorno wrote two years later, his primary concern was the *lack* of student interest in politics.[24] As late as 1965, Adorno was still convinced that the dominant attitude among German students was "apolitical" and that this attitude was at least partially determined by the conservative structure of German universities.[25] Thus, it should come as no surprise that when German students became increasingly politicized in the late 1960s and began to demand democratic reforms in the structure and curriculum of the universities, Adorno supported most of their demands. For example, in a discussion about recent student protests in October 1967, Adorno agreed, in particular, with the students' criticisms of overspecialization within the university, and he supported the students' democratic rights to protest in order to bring university reforms about.[26] Adorno also supported more student input and control over the conditions of study and curriculum as well as the possibility of students forming "autonomous" study groups for which they could receive formal academic credit.[27]

Just as Adorno had anticipated and supported many of the students' criticisms of the university, so his calls for a more open and rigorous public debate about the recent Nazi past and its continued conscious and unconscious influence on contemporary society and politics in the Federal Republic articulated what would become a central concern of radicalized students. In the fall of 1959 Adorno presented his most extensive and direct engagement with the question of "The Meaning of Working through the Past" in postwar Germany.[28] It was in this essay that Adorno made the following controversial claim: "I consider the survival of National Socialism *within* democracy to be potentially more menacing than the survival of fascist tendencies *against* democracy."[29] This claim clearly demonstrated his conviction that the subjective and objective conditions that had made fascism possible had not yet been eliminated. Thus, concerning this issue as well, Adorno must have been encouraged by the efforts of the SDS during this time to "talk about the noose in the house of the executioner."[30] In 1959 the SDS organized an exhibition titled "Unexpiated Nazi Justice" that documented the continued activity in the West German judiciary system of over fifty judges and attorneys who had been active under the Nazi regime.[31] The "Spiegel affair" in 1962[32] and the Frankfurt Auschwitz trials,[33] which ran from December 1963 to August 1965, reinforced the impression among many members of the SDS that deep and unexamined continuities existed between National Socialism and the Federal Republic.[34] The increased awareness of these continuities in the mid 1960s contributed to a radicalization of students, who began to see the West German state itself as potentially or already pre-fascist. This concern with the recent Nazi past was one of the most important *differentia specifica* of the West German student movement.

Along with the growing awareness of the past came an increasing need among students, particularly those in leading positions in the SDS, to reexamine the most important theoretical debates about fascism before and during the war. With the exception of a few relatively isolated figures such as Adorno, Wolfgang Abendroth, and Ernst Bloch, who provided German students with a living link to critical analyses of fascism before 1945, such debates had completely disappeared from German public life. Even Max Horkheimer—who had returned to Frankfurt after the war to reintroduce the Critical Theoretical tradition to the next generation of German students—long resisted students', colleagues', and publishers' requests to reprint his early writings.[35] But the radical students refused to wait, and pirated editions of Horkheimer's early writings began circulating in the mid 1960s. The pseudonymously published collection of aphorisms *Dämmerung*[36] and his essay "The Authoritarian State" were particularly influential among students.[37] Adorno—himself a participant in these prewar discussions—clearly supported the students' efforts to recover these lost critical theoretical traditions in order to understand Germany's recent fascist past. He influenced students directly not just with his numerous public speeches and radio addresses, but also in his seminars. In fact, one could say that the students had fulfilled one of Adorno's deepest desires, namely to insure that these critical theoretical traditions were recovered and reestablished in Germany.

One of the main reasons politically conscious students began to view the government of the Federal Republic as proto-fascist was its long-standing efforts to amend the constitution with emergency laws that would give the state the power to restrict civil liberties in a time of crisis. Due to lingering memories of the catastrophic effects of Article 48 in the Weimar constitution, which had abetted the National Socialists' legal appropriation of power, the attempts to reenact emergency laws in the Federal Republic met with substantial opposition. In May 1965, the SDS helped organize a large conference in Bonn called "Democracy Faced with a State of Emergency." In 1966 a grand coalition was formed between the Social Democratic and the Christian Democratic parties, which could provide for the first time the two-thirds majority necessary to pass the emergency laws. Opposition to the laws continued and became a central concern of the extra-parliamentary opposition, which was transformed into a mass movement after a police officer shot and killed the student protester Benno Ohnesorg in Berlin on 2 June 1967.

Opposition to the emergency laws became the issue that united students, trade union members, and critical intellectuals like Adorno. On 11 May 1968, during the final deliberations in the Bundestag about the emergency laws, the SDS helped organize a protest march against the emergency laws in Bonn, which attracted over 60,000 people from across West Germany. Although Adorno did not participate in this march, shortly thereafter he met with Otto Brenner, the president of the powerful German Metal Workers' Union (I.G. Metall), and suggested that it initiate a general strike in order to prevent the passage of the emergency laws.[38] On 17 May Adorno signed a petition against the emergency laws, and on 28 May, the day before the final debate about them in the Bundestag, he sharply criticized the emergency laws in a public discussion on Hessian public television.[39]

Widespread support of the emergency laws made it clear to Adorno that anti-democratic tendencies were still widespread *within* West German society. So when politicized students set out to understand and oppose such tendencies by contributing to a radically democratic extra-parliamentary opposition,[40] it should come as no surprise that Adorno supported their efforts. When the students, who were attempting to bring about positive or prevent negative reforms, themselves became victims of an anti-democratic backlash, Adorno sprang to their defense. Following the murder of Benno Ohnesorg, Adorno prefaced his lecture on aesthetics by expressing his solidarity with the protesting students, criticizing the brutal actions of the Berlin police, and demanding a quick and impartial inquiry into the affair.[41] Five months later, when the police officer who shot and killed Ohnesorg was acquitted by a Berlin court of the charge of manslaughter, Adorno once again interrupted his lecture to publicly condemn the decision.[42] On this occasion, Adorno first made a statement that he would repeat several times publicly and privately in the following year—a statement that seems surprising and greatly exaggerated, at first glance—namely, that the protesting students had come to occupy the place of the Jews in West German society.[43] The full meaning and significance of this statement can only be understood against the larger background of the critical social-psychological categories developed by him and his colleagues at the Institute for Social Research.

On 11 April 1968 the leader of the Berlin SDS, Rudi Dutschke, was shot and critically wounded in Berlin by a troubled young man named Josef Bachmann. On 19 April Adorno expressed his dismay at this incident and his solidarity with the students by signing, along with fourteen other prominent scholars and writers, a letter published in the left-liberal weekly newspaper *Die Zeit*. The letter laid the blame for the incident squarely at the feet of the Springer publishing house and demanded a detailed investigation into their role in encouraging it. Two weeks later, Adorno used this incident in his introductory lecture on sociology as an example to illustrate the explanatory power of the social-psychological categories of Critical Theory. Adorno's statement is worth quoting at length, since it reveals so much not only about Adorno's understanding of the protest movements, but also of the condition of West German society as a whole:

> You can give many possible local and specific reasons why this pogrom occurred in Berlin. ... But consider the most compelling reason, namely the agitation against the students carried out over a long period of time by the Springer Press. This agitation would not have been effective, if it hadn't corresponded to a certain potential receptivity among its readers. One aspect of contemporary society is that—and this is true precisely for the so-called boulevard press—it transforms information into products for consumption; in other words, the information itself provides pleasure in a certain way or, more accurately, ersatz pleasure for those for whom it is intended. Thus, without this potential anti-intellectualism, especially the resentment against people who are not yet entirely imprisoned within the heteronomy of the labor process, as is the case with students, this agitation, which cannot by any means be completely separated from commercial motives, would not have been possible at all in this form.[44]

Adorno saw the primary cause of Dutschke's attempted murder in the powerful anti-intellectual ideology fomented by one of the largest media concerns in Germany. He argued that the Springer Press specifically targeted a working and lower-middle class readership with a lower than average educational level, provided them with compensatory pleasures by denigrating the nonconformist students as irresponsible and parasitic *Schmarotzer*[45] or dangerous agents of Moscow, and tacitly encouraged its readers to give their repressed instincts free rein in sadistic attacks upon the students.

As we have seen, Adorno believed that thoroughgoing changes were necessary within the German university, and his active public support of most of the students' demands for reforms against the persistently conservative attitudes of the majority of his colleagues placed him in an increasingly isolated position among the university faculty and administration.[46] But Adorno's defense of reforms was always on the condition that they make the university *more,* not less, rigorous. When Adorno was faced with tendencies among the students that he believed contributed to dominant anti-intellectual attitudes, he did not hesitate to oppose them. Perhaps the most important of these tendencies within the university was the SDS's increasing willingness to disrupt lectures and occupy university buildings. Adorno received his first taste of this tactic on 7 July 1967 when politicized students—including several members of the Berlin SDS—attempted to disrupt a lecture he was giving at the Free University on Goethe's neoclassical play *Iphigenia in Tauris.* Despite some commotion at the beginning, Adorno was able to deliver his talk. He was angered by the event, but he also responded positively to the SDS's request to meet with him on their home turf—at the Republican Club in West Berlin—just a few days later to discuss the contemporary political situation.[47] The event did not, in other words, lead Adorno to distance himself from the student movement or the SDS as a whole.

A few months later, the Frankfurt SDS decided to disrupt a lecture by Carlo Schmid, a professor of political science who was serving as a minister for the SPD in the grand coalition government and was also a supporter of the emergency laws. The rector of the university, Walter Rüegg, had warned the SDS not to follow through with its "Go-in" against Schmid, which he described as an "exercise in fascist terror methods." When they went ahead with the "Go-in" anyway, Rüegg attempted to have the SDS banned from the university as a whole. A few days later at the end of his lecture on aesthetics, Adorno discussed the incident with Hans-Jürgen Krahl and other members of the SDS.[48] Adorno agreed with the students that Rüegg's claim that they were using "fascist terror methods" was irresponsible and that their action could be justified if the goal was indeed an open discussion that was not simply a means of creating publicity for the SDS.[49]

The first half of 1968 witnessed a rapid escalation of the protest movement in West Germany. In February, the SDS organized a major conference and demonstration against the war in Vietnam. The attempted assassination of Rudi Dutschke in April led to massive protests in Berlin against the Axel Springer publishing house and street fighting in Berlin and Frankfurt. The protest against the emergency laws came to a head in May, with the aforementioned demonstration in Bonn. In Frankfurt, students occupied the university from 14 to 16 May and once again from 27 to 31 May in an attempt to establish a "political university" as a site for historical and theoretical reflection for the protest movement.[50] But the passage of the emergency laws in the Bundestag on 30 May—with an overwhelming majority of 384 to 100 votes—represented a major defeat for the movement. The threat of the emergency laws had given the student movement relevance beyond the university and encouraged intellectuals, union leaders, and

workers to join their cause.[51] Now that the emergency laws were a *fait accompli,*
the coalition between students, workers, and radical intellectuals began to disin-
tegrate. The end of the massive strikes and the "retour à la normale" in France in
early June also clearly indicated that support for the students among the general
population was—even in France[52]—by no means unlimited. But the SDS was
reluctant to accept the fact that it was becoming increasingly isolated in its demands. During the second half of 1968 it pursued a strategy of escalation that
would eventually lead to its dissolution.

Adorno seemed to possess a fine sensibility for this changing constellation.
By the end of July 1968 he was no longer willing to condone the disruption of
lectures in order to promote open discussion and enlightenment among students.
After a group of students attempted to transform the lectures of the professor
of German literature Martin Stern into an ongoing discussion of the ideological role of scholarship, Adorno explicitly asked his students to desist from using
such methods in struggles within or outside the university. Although Adorno
had himself been attacked by Stern and vehemently disagreed with his approach
to the study of literature, denying someone his freedom of speech was not, according to him, compatible with the democratic ideal of autonomous citizen-
ship. During this time Adorno was becoming increasingly concerned about the
prominence of voluntarist, anti-intellectual tendencies within the SDS and the
student movement as a whole. On 8 December the SDS occupied the primary
sociology building and proclaimed the beginning of an "active strike" in order to
force a complete restructuring of the curriculum, structure, and administration
of the sociology department. On 10 December Adorno co-authored a proposal
to the striking students in which he reiterated his support for many of the students' basic concerns while also rejecting the more extreme demands as a "tactic
of confrontation at all costs, which will lead necessarily to self-destruction."[53]
But the SDS refused to moderate its demands. Adorno, Habermas, and Ludwig von Friedeburg[54] issued a flyer on 17 December in which they demanded
"for the last time" that the students end their occupation. Upon learning that
evening that the police would be arriving the following morning—which they
did—the students opted to vacate the building rather than be arrested.[55]

Not surprisingly, the students were incensed by Adorno and his colleagues'
willingness to take recourse to the police in order to put an end to their strike
in the sociology department. Soon afterward another flyer appeared in which
Adorno, Habermas, and Ludwig von Friedeburg were accused of using arguments taken directly from Goebbels's propaganda arsenal and of becoming lack-
eys of the authoritarian state.[56] But the most dramatic and consequential conflict
between Adorno and the SDS was still to come: the occupation of the Institute for Social Research. The SDS had been entertaining the idea of occupying
the Institute for some time,[57] but when it finally occurred on 31 January 1969
Adorno and von Friedeburg reacted much more swiftly than they had during the
occupation of the sociology department in December. After the students refused

Friedeburg's request to leave, he and Adorno decided immediately to call the police. The seventy-five students inside were escorted out without incident and taken to the police station. With the occupation of the Institute and Adorno's swift reprisal, the already significantly strained relations between Adorno and the students collapsed.

What explains the growing distance between Adorno and the SDS? What was the foundation of their disagreement? In terms of university politics, Adorno was concerned—as we have seen—that some of the students' proposed reforms would make the university less rather than more rigorous. It is important to note that Adorno did not see any contradiction whatsoever between rigor and radical social critique; quite the contrary, he viewed the former as an absolute condition of the latter. One of the reasons why Adorno believed the reforms proposed by the SDS would undermine the rigor of the university was that they conflated authority based on one's person with authority based on the mastery of a certain body of knowledge or experience in a certain area.[58] While Adorno demanded that students should be able to participate and help determine all aspects of the educational process, he also considered it unrealistic for students to demand that they be given as much or more power than professors.[59] Adorno also criticized the students for applying a radical critique of *society* in an unmediated way to the university. Adorno stated in an interview in October 1967: "The model of society, as developed in the socialist critique, cannot be directly applied to the university for the simple reason that no one can accuse professors today of exploiting students, or exercising domination of them in the sense in which one could speak of exploitation or domination in the context of society."[60] Finally, Adorno insisted that the students distinguish more carefully between critical scholarship and direct political action. University institutions were not the place to plan the latter. In short, the fact that the students had begun to see Adorno, who supported most of their demands and shared their desire to cultivate a radical theoretical critique of late capitalist society, as just another agent of the "authoritarian state," confirmed concerns he had already begun to voice in 1967 about the students' failure to distinguish between rational and irrational authority, or between social domination and the relationship between students and professors.

But Adorno's objections to the students' university politics were secondary to deeper underlying differences he had with their interpretation of the West German state as proto-fascist and their belief that socially transformative praxis was possible at the present time. The disagreement between Adorno and the SDS about the potential for a recrudescence of fascism in the fledgling West German democracy is highly complex.[61] As we have seen, Adorno's statement in 1959 that he was more concerned about fascist tendencies within democracy than he was about those opposed to democracy, was highly influential in the theoretical development of the SDS.[62] Furthermore, Adorno's repeated affirmation that the radical students had themselves come to occupy the place of Jews clearly demonstrated his belief that the objective social conditions that had made fascism possible in the first place had not yet been eliminated. On this point, Adorno agreed with the students. However, he disagreed with their analysis of the source of the threat and their strategy for combating it. Far from viewing the Federal Republic as democratic in any meaningful sense, the students viewed its political institutions as totally corrupt, and as themselves facilitating an imminent reconstitution of fascism in West Germany.[63]

Adorno, in contrast, recognized that even the formal democracy of the Federal Republic represented a crucial step beyond, and an important bulwark against, fascism and was eminently worth defending. The students, meanwhile, believed it had become necessary to start a revolutionary movement against these political institutions in order to prevent the reemergence of fascism in West Germany and that it would be possible to expand such a movement into a broader emancipatory struggle against capitalism as such.[64] Adorno not only denied that such a movement was possible at the time, he maintained that if the students attempted to start such a movement, they could provoke a conservative backlash that could indeed lead to a serious weakening or liquidation of West Germany's formal democratic institutions and to the unshackling of the powerful authoritarian tendencies that still existed in West Germany society.

The crucial differences between Adorno and the SDS on the threat of fascism and how best to combat it were clearly articulated long before the transition "from protest to resistance" that led the SDS to pursue increasingly militant tactics in the second half of 1968 and 1969. In a discussion with Adorno after his lecture on aesthetics in November 1967, Hans-Jürgen Krahl assessed the present danger of fascism in the following way:

> A fascist mass movement in the metropoles of late capitalism is only possible under conditions that exist, for example, in the contemporary United States. An imperialist country like the US uses brutal violence in the Third World and this violence rebounds and has a brutalizing effect on the country. In the US the danger of a fascist counter-movement does in fact exist. … In countries which are no longer engaged in counter-revolutionary activities in the Third World, the danger of a fascist counter-movement does not exist. The European community today is a more or less meaningless, marginal group and the movement toward fascism here, which is not just a restoration movement, is taking place at the heart of the political and legal system itself.[65]

Adorno's response leaves no question that he saw the danger, in terms almost opposite from Krahl's, as emanating from West German *society*, not its political institutions. He stated:

> With regard to the question of the danger of right-wing radicalism and a potential for fascism, I can only say that my thoughts on the matter

are different. I view this danger as being much more serious. ... I don't fail to see the authoritarian tendencies in whole series of points within our democracy. Fascism was not a coincidence. I consider it necessary and good to draw attention to these points. But ... I believe that the difference between a fascist state and that which I think I can observe today as a potential within the rules guiding our democracy, is a qualitative difference. I would say, it would be abstract and fanatical in a problematic sense, to oversee this difference, i.e. to consider it more important to take action against a democracy, which should be improved in this or that way, than against an opponent, who is already violently rumbling.[66]

This exchange between Adorno and Krahl demonstrates the limits of the students' understanding of fascism and its relationship to their own society. As we have seen, the students were deeply concerned about fascism and the possibility of its reemergence, and they contributed greatly to beginning the process of working through the past, which had been largely repressed by their parents' generation. Nonetheless, the students' historically unmediated view of the Federal Republic as a form of "integral statism,"[67] as well as slogans such as "capitalism leads to fascism, therefore we must get rid of capitalism,"[68] betray an all-too-mechanical understanding of fascism and the conditions that could lead to its reemergence.[69] As Detlev Claussen has recently pointed out, the students' understanding of fascism reflected an overly rationalist, orthodox Marxist approach. They had not yet fully integrated the social-psychological dimension of Critical Theory, which was necessary to adequately reflect upon anti-Semitism and other forms of prejudice in general, and upon the conditions that had made Auschwitz possible in particular.[70]

For Adorno, one unfortunate incident that took place in March 1969 became symbolic of the degeneration of the student protest movement. Several members of the "leather-jacket fraction," an unapologetically voluntarist fraction within the SDS, broke into and demolished the room of a philosophy student who was friends with Krahl, in order to denounce the student's abstinence from praxis. Adorno mentioned the incident in an essay he wrote not long afterward entitled "Marginalia to Theory and Praxis":

> Today once again the antithesis between theory and praxis is being misused to denounce theory. When a student's room was smashed because he preferred to work rather than join in actions, on the wall was scrawled: "Whoever occupies himself with theory, without acting practically, is a traitor to socialism." It is not only against him that praxis serves as an ideological pretext for exercising moral constraint. The thinking denigrated by the actionists apparently demands of them too much undue effort: it requires too much work, is too practical.[71]

Adorno made such criticisms of the voluntarist tendencies in the student movement repeatedly in 1969, but it would be wrong to view his critique of praxis
simply as a reaction to the increasing militancy of the students. At the annual
meeting of German sociologists on 9 April 1968, Adorno stated his conviction
that "the entire complex of theory and practice must be thought through in a
completely new and radical manner."[72] The theoretical foundations of Adorno's
efforts during this time to rethink the relationship between theory and practice can be found in his philosophical magnum opus, *Negative Dialectics,* which
was published in 1966. Already in that work, Adorno had raised some serious
questions about the "primacy of practice."[73] Some of the same concerns voiced
at a high level of philosophical abstraction in *Negative Dialectics* reappear in
more concrete form in Adorno's criticisms of the students in 1969. For example, Adorno criticizes a common interpretation of praxis that is beholden to
the "arch-bourgeois primacy of practical reason" and that, and a result, remains
indifferent to its object. He writes:

> Despite all its eager realism, pure practical reason is devoid of object
> to the same degree that the world for manufacturing and industry be-
> comes material devoid of quality and ready for processing … Indeed,
> one could ask whether in its indifference toward its object all nature-
> dominating praxis up to the present day is not in fact praxis in name
> only… A consciousness of theory and praxis must be produced that
> neither divides the two such that theory becomes powerless and praxis
> becomes arbitrary, nor refracts theory through the arch-bourgeois pri-
> macy of practical reason proclaimed by Kant and Fichte. Thinking is
> a doing, theory a form of praxis; already the ideology of the purity
> deceives about this.[74]

Adorno saw this denigration of theory and indifference to the object in the student movement in their increasing unwillingness to reflect upon the object they
were attempting to change with their praxis: West German society. Adorno accused the student movement of refusing to accept the fact that it had become
isolated, of "refusing to reflect upon its own impotence."[75] Even though change
was still urgently needed, objective social conditions had rendered transformative
praxis impossible for the time being. It could not be brought about in the present
with force, because "desperation that, because it finds exits blocked, blindly leaps
into praxis, even with the purest intentions, joins forces with the catastrophe."[76]

But Adorno's objections to voluntarist tendencies in the student movement
still leave unanswered the crucial question of *why* praxis was impossible at that
time. To answer this crucial question we must return to the social-psychological
categories of the Critical Theorists. In response to Adorno's objection, could not
the radical students have argued that waiting for praxis to become possible again
would be like "Waiting for Godot"? As we shall see, Herbert Marcuse argued,

in view of the protesting students, that in certain situations praxis can advance theory and that remaining isolated from practice betrays the ultimate purpose of theory. Adorno might have responded to such an argument by pointing to the scene in Samuel Beckett's play in which Vladimir (Didi) attempts to improve the condition of the enslaved Lucky, who reacts to Didi's well-intentioned actions by lashing out at him and thereby asserting his desire to remain in his familiar sado-masochistic relationship with Pozzo. This scene can serve as an allegory for the social-psychological dynamics at work between the radical students and the lower and lower-middle classes in West Germany. After the disintegration of the protest movements and the rise of a powerful backlash movement against them in the early 1970s—particularly in the US—Marcuse would come to accept Adorno's more pessimistic assessment of the potential for socially transformative praxis.[77] But at the high point of the movements Marcuse did indeed believe that the students and their allies might be able to initiate what he referred to as "qualitative change." In order to examine Marcuse's differences with Adorno, let us return briefly to the three concepts, discussed earlier, that were crucial for Marcuse's interpretation of the events of the late 1960s: the integration of the working class, the new sensibility, and the dialectic of civilization.

Although the myth of Marcuse as the "guru" of the student movement makes it seem like he had been optimistic about the protest movements from the beginning, as we have seen, he was in fact better known for his pessimism, as any serious reader of *One-Dimensional Man* would have to conclude. Marcuse's analysis there of the integration of the working class, but also of key developments in the ideology of advanced industrial societies, painted a grim picture of a "society without opposition." As a result, other Marxist intellectuals criticized Marcuse for defending an updated version of Friedrich Pollock's state capitalism thesis.[78] The appropriation of surplus value and the accumulation of capital continued, while the potentially dangerous, "anarchic" aspects of capitalism, which could lead to system-threatening crisis, had been brought under control by the state, leading to a "totally administered" or "one-dimensional" society. As his 1965 essay "Repressive Tolerance" clearly demonstrated, Marcuse was encouraged by the increasing militancy of students and the civil rights movement. But contrary to what many claimed, Marcuse never viewed students or marginalized minority groups as a new revolutionary subject. He claimed they might be able to initiate a broader movement for "qualitative change," but until this movement won the support of the working classes in the advanced industrial nations, the situation would not be genuinely revolutionary. At this point, Marcuse still agreed with Adorno that the possibility for praxis in the emphatic Marxian sense was "foreclosed for an unforeseeable amount of time."[79]

But the events in France in May 1968, when nearly 10,000,000 workers went on strike, led Marcuse, who was in Paris at the time, to reconsider his argument in *One-Dimensional Man* that praxis was foreclosed for the time being. Marcuse considered renaming *An Essay on Liberation,* which he was working on at the time, "Beyond One-Dimensional Man."[80] For a moment it seemed that the integration of the working class might be weakening, and that the identification of the workers with their leaders and the cycle of bourgeois anthropology could be broken. Thus, in the second half of 1968 and the first half of 1969, at precisely the time when Adorno was becoming increasingly frustrated with the radical students' emphasis on action, Marcuse believed that a new situation had emerged. Although the situation was still "not a revolutionary one, not even a pre-revolutionary one,"[81] Marcuse nonetheless believed that radical actions could and should play an important role in the ongoing political conflicts. They could help create a situation in which "qualitative change" might become possible. This divergence in Adorno's and Marcuse's assessments of the political situation was expressed clearly in the remarkable series of letters about the protest movements that they exchanged in the first half of 1969. In a letter to Adorno on 5 April Marcuse argued:

> You know me well enough to know that I reject the unmediated translation of theory into praxis just as emphatically as you do. But I do believe that there are situations, moments, in which theory is pushed on further by praxis—situations and moments in which theory that is kept separate from praxis becomes untrue to itself.[82]

In his response to Marcuse one month later, Adorno countered:

> I know that we are quite close on the question of the relation between theory and practice ... I would also concede to you that there are moments in which theory is pushed on further by practice. But such a situation neither exists objectively today, nor does the barren and brutal actionism that confronts us here have the slightest thing to do with theory anyhow.[83]

A number of other political and theoretical factors informed Adorno and Marcuse's disagreement on the question of praxis. The former included their differing views on the war in Vietnam and the differences in the historical and political conditions in the US and West Germany.[84] The latter included a different understanding of the critical intellectual and his or her relationship to the public sphere. Unfortunately, it would take us too far afield to discuss these complex issues in detail here. We must rest content with the observation that Marcuse's understanding of the *political* situation differed from Adorno's at this juncture in time.

As we have seen, Marcuse was impressed not only by the political implications of the May events in France, but also by the strong presence of an *aesthetic* moment in the revolts. Marcuse's concept of a "new sensibility" expressed his belief that cracks were beginning to emerge in the social-psychological foundations of the bourgeois epoch. The course of modern revolutions had led Marcuse to the conclusion that a transformation of political and/or economic power must be anticipated and accompanied by a transformation in subjective character structures in order to prevent the anxious re-creation of social domination. Marcuse interpreted the aesthetic moment in the protests as a desire to abolish not only bourgeois political and property relations, but also bourgeois anthropology. As he put it in *Essay on Liberation:*

> These causes [of social domination] are economic-political, but since they have shaped the very instincts and needs of men, no economic and political changes will bring this historical continuum to a stop unless they are carried through by men who are physiologically and psychologically able to experience things, and each other, outside the context of violence and exploitation. The new sensibility has become, by this very token, *praxis:* it emerges in the struggle against violence and exploitation where this struggle is waged for essentially new ways and forms of life … does this great anti-authoritarian rebellion indicate a new dimension of radical change, the appearance of new agents of radical change, and a new vision of socialism in its qualitative difference from the established societies?[85]

Marcuse's highly speculative arguments were based on a broad concept of the aesthetic, which went beyond hermetic works of art or discrete value spheres. Marcuse's willingness at this time to expand of the concept of the aesthetic to subjective sensibility in general made him more receptive than Adorno to certain forms of popular and countercultural protest. Although he never completely abandoned the concept of artistic form, Marcuse was more willing than Adorno to reconsider the old avant-garde dream of merging art and life, of abolishing the affirmative, bourgeois institution of art.[86]

By the early 1970s Marcuse's high hopes had largely dissipated in the face of the widespread and often ferocious conservative backlash against the protest movements. With regard to both the integration of the working class and the co-optation of new forms of aesthetic protest, Marcuse had to concede that the baleful dialectic of capitalist civilization had triumphed once again. As we have seen, that this dialectic consisted in the weakening of Eros in an increasingly repressive capitalist society, which in turn reinforced authoritarian character structures and lowered restraints against the release of pent-up libidinal energy in the form of aggression against tacitly or explicitly condemned "enemies of the people." Among the many disappointing political events at the time, the reelection of Richard Nixon in 1972 in his run against the liberal anti-war candidate George McGovern seemed particularly symbolic for Marcuse of the triumph of backlash politics in the US. The fact that the heaviest bombing of the entire war in Vietnam—the so-called "Christmas Bombings"[87]—occurred soon after

Nixon's re-election, must have compounded Marcuse's dismay. Marcuse sought to explain these developments in an important essay, published just a few years ago, called "The Historical Fate of Bourgeois Democracy." There Marcuse poses the question of why the "silent majority" of Americans supported Nixon and his advocacy of hard-line policies both at home and abroad. Marcuse points to the social-psychological dynamics at work:

> Bourgeois democracy is giving itself an enlarged popular base which supports the liquidation of the remnants of the liberal period, the removal of government from popular control, and allows the pursuit of the imperialist policy. ... government of the people and by the people (self-government) now assumes the form of a large scale *identification* of the people with their rulers—caricature of popular sovereignty. ... The interplay between production and destruction, liberty and repression, power and submission ... has, with the help of technological means not previously available, created among the underlying populations a mental structure which responds to, and reflects the requirements of the system. In this mental structure are the deep individual, instinctual roots of the identification of the conformist majority with the institutionalized brutality and aggression. An instinctual, nay, libidinal affinity binds, beneath all rational justification, the subjects to their rulers. The mental structure involved here is the *sadomasochistic character*.[88]

Marcuse goes on to argue that one must return to social-psychological arguments presented by Horkheimer and Fromm in *The Studies on Authority and Family* and further developed by Adorno in *The Authoritarian Personality* in order to grasp these developments.

Although Marcuse continued to stress the importance of oppositional movements that emerged out of the protest movements in the 1970s—especially the women's liberation and the ecology movements—Marcuse's gesture to Adorno here, along with his defense of highly sublimated forms of art at the end of his life,[89] must be interpreted as an ex post facto acknowledgement of the correctness of Adorno's claim in the late 1960s that the possibility for praxis in the emphatic Marxian sense was foreclosed for the time being. The anthropology of the bourgeois epoch proved—and continues to prove—itself to be more tenacious than Marcuse had thought.

Notes

1. For a discussion of how Marcuse's involvement in the 1960s protest movements has shaped his subsequent reception in the United States, see John Abromeit and W. Mark Cobb, eds., *Herbert Marcuse: A Critical Reader* (London and New York, 2004), 1–6.

2. In what follows, Critical Theory refers specifically to the work of the theorists of the Frankfurt School.

3. Erich Fromm, *The Working Class in Weimar Germany: A Psychological and Sociological Study*, ed. Wolfgang Bonß, trans. B. Weinberger (Warwickshire, 1984).

4. Erich Fromm, "Sozialpsychologischer Teil," in *Studien über Autorität und Familie: Forschungsberichte aus dem Institut für Sozialforschung*, ed. Max Horkheimer (Paris, 1936).

5. "Egoism and Freedom Movements: On the Anthropology of the Bourgeois Era," in Max Horkheimer, *Between Philosophy and Social Science: Selected Early Writings*, trans. G. Frederick Hunter, Matthew S. Torpey and John Torpey (Cambridge, MA, 1993), 49–110. I have translated the German "Epoche" here as "epoch" rather than "era."

6. Martin Jay, *The Dialectical Imagination* (Boston, Toronto, and London, 1973), 225.

7. Leo Lowenthal, *False Prophets: Studies on Authoritarianism* (New Brunswick, NJ, and Oxford, 1987), 5. Lowenthal's name is spelled here without the umlaut as per his preference once in the US.

8. T. W. Adorno, Else Frenkel-Brunswick, Daniel Levinson, R. Nevitt Sanford, *The Authoritarian Personality* (New York, 1950), ix.

9. *The Dialectical Imagination*, 226.

10. For a more detailed discussion, see *The Dialectical Imagination*, 243ff.

11. Both in the text and in later reflections, Adorno emphasized the importance of Horkheimer's work in providing the implicit historical and sociological framework for the more explicitly psychological orientation of *The Authoritarian Personality*. Despite his earlier criticisms of Fromm, Adorno also refers positively to Fromm's analysis of the "sado-masochistic personality" as an exemplary analysis of the "authoritarian syndrome." *The Authoritarian Personality*, 752.

12. *The Authoritarian Personality*, 676.

13. Ibid.

14. Ibid., 680.

15. For another examination—which is indebted to Adorno—of the pseudo-conservative character and its impact on American politics in the 1950s and 1960s, see Richard Hofstadter, "The Pseudo-Conservative Revolt – 1954" and "Pseudo-Conservatism Revisited – 1965," *The Paranoid Style in American Politics and Other Essays* (New York, 2008), 41–92.

16. Theodor W. Adorno, "Über Tradition," *Gesammelte Schriften*, ed. Rolf Tiedemann, vol. 10.1 (Frankfurt am Main, 1977), 310.

17. As Detlev Claussen points out in his essay in this volume.

18. As Marcuse's correspondence with Horkheimer during this time makes clear. See, for example, Horkheimer's letter to Marcuse on 17 July 1943, in Max Horkheimer, *Gesammelte Schriften*, ed. Alfred Schmidt and Gunzelin Schmid Noerr, vol. 17 (Frankfurt am Main, 1996), 463–64.

19. Marcuse explicitly acknowledged his theoretical debt to Horkheimer in the preface. See *Eros and Civilization* (Boston, 1955), xviii.

20. See, for example, Herbert Marcuse, "The Inner Logic of the American Policy in Vietnam," in Marcuse, *The New Left and the 1960s: Collected Papers*, 3 vols., ed. Douglas Kellner (New York and London, 2005), 3:38–40.

21. Marcuse, *Eros and Civilization*, 157ff.

22. For a more detailed elaboration of this argument, see Alfred Schmidt, "Herbert Marcuses Idee einer 'neuen Anthropologie'," in Schmidt, *Emanzipatorische Sinnlichkeit: Ludwig Feuerbachs Anthropologischer Materialismus* (Munich, 1988), 30–71. See also Stephan Bundschuh, "The Theoretical Place of Utopia: Some Remarks on Marcuse's Dual Anthropology," in Abromeit and Cobb, *Herbert Marcuse*, 152–62.

23. As early as 1970 Marcuse began to see clearly the signs of the counterculture's descent into political apathy or worse. See his review of Charles Reich's *The Greening of America:* Herbert Marcuse, "Charles Reich: A Negative View," in *The New Left and the 1960s*, 3:46–48.

24. Theodor Adorno, "Zur Demokratisierung der deutschen Universitäten," in *Frankfurter Schule und Studentenbewegung: Von der Flaschenpost zum Molotowcocktail, 1946–1995*, 3 vols., ed. Wolfgang Kraushaar (Frankfurt am Main, 1998), 2:120–22.

25. See Adorno's foreword to Heribert Adam, *Studentenschaft und Hochschule: Möglichkeiten und Grenzen studentischer Politik* (Frankfurt am Main, 1965), in Kraushaar, *Frankfurter Schule und Studentenbewegung*, 2:194.

26. Ibid., 305.

27. On this issue, Adorno openly opposed the president of Frankfurt University, Walter Rüegg, who insisted that autonomous seminars be ignored and that under no circumstances could students receive official academic credit for them. Adorno defended the students' rights to form their own seminars and—if their work met accepted scholarly standards—receive credit for them. Kraushaar, *Frankfurter Schule und Studentenbewegung*, 2:540–41.

28. "The Meaning of Working Through the Past," trans. Henry Pickford, in Adorno, *Critical Models: Interventions and Catchwords* (New York, 1998), 89–104.

29. Ibid., 90.

30. Ibid., 89.

31. Kraushaar, *Frankfurter Schule und Studentenbewegung*, 1:156, 164, and 188.

32. In October of 1962 the Hamburg-based weekly news magazine *Der Spiegel* published an article that claimed that the military of the Federal Republic was woefully unprepared for a possible Communist attack from the East. In response, the West German government accused *Der Spiegel* of treason and proceeded to shut down the magazine, search its offices, and arrest the editors of the magazine and the author of the article. See David Schoenbaum, *The Spiegel Affair* (New York, 1968).

33. Thanks primarily to the initiative of the Hessian State Attorney General Fritz Bauer, twenty-two members of the SS who had been active in the labor, concentration, and death camps in Auschwitz were put on trial in Frankfurt between 1963 and 1965. It was the largest trial against Holocaust perpetrators in postwar Germany. On the Frankfurt Auschwitz trials, see Devin O. Pendas, *The Frankfurt Auschwitz Trial, 1963–65: Genocide, History and the Limits of the Law* (Cambridge and New York, 2006) and Rebecca Wittmann, *Beyond Justice: The Auschwitz Trial* (Cambridge, MA, 2005).

34. Detlev Claussen, "Der Kurze Sommer der Theorie," in Claussen, *Aspekte der Alltagsreligion: Ideologiekritik unter veränderten gesellschaftlichen Verhältnissen* (Frankfurt am Main, 2000), 155.

35. In 1968 Horkheimer did finally agree to republish his essays from the 1930s, although he made it clear that the ideas they contained could no longer be applied in an unmediated way to present conditions. See his "Brief an den S. Fischer Verlag"

from 1965 and his "Vorwort zur Neupublikation" from 1968 in Max Horkheimer, *Gesammelte Schriften,* 19 vols., ed. Alfred Schmidt and Gunzelin Schmid Noerr (Frankfurt am Main, 1988), 3:9–13 and 14–19 respectively. Also, Horkheimer continued to refuse to republish some of his most politically charged essays, such as "The Authoritarian State" and "The Jews and Europe."

36. Originally published as Heinrich Regius, *Dämmerung: Notizen in Deutschland* (Zurich, 1934), reprinted in Max Horkheimer, *Gesammelte Schriften,* vol. 2, ed. Gunzelin Schmid Noerr (Frankfurt am Main, 1987), 312–452. Many, but not all, of the aphorisms have appeared in English translation in Max Horkheimer, *Dawn and Decline: Notes 1926–1931 & 1950–1969,* trans. Michael Shaw (New York, 1978).

37. For example, in 1967 Hans-Jürgen Krahl and Rudi Dutschke did precisely what Horkheimer would warn against in the 1968 foreword to the republication of his writings from the 1930s: they attempted to apply Horkheimer's analysis of the authoritarian state from 1940 in an unmediated way to contemporary political conditions in the Federal Republic. See the theory of "integral statism" they present in their "Organisationsreferat" from September 1967, in Kraushaar, *Frankfurter Schule und Studentenbewegung,* 2:287–90.

38. Oskar Negt, *Achtundsechzig: Politische Intellektuelle und die Macht* (Göttingen, 1995), 172; Detlev Claussen, *Theodor Adorno: Ein Letztes Genie* (Frankfurt am Main, 2003), 398.

39. Kraushaar, *Frankfurter Schule und Studentenbewegung,* 2:384 and 392.

40. For a discussion of 1968 as a radical democratic movement, including an interesting comparison of 1968 with the democratic upsurge of 1848 in Germany, see Negt, *Achtundsechzig,* 135–76.

41. Kraushaar, *Frankfurter Schule und Studentenbewegung,* 2:241.

42. Ibid., 323–24.

43. Ibid., 324. For another discussion of this aspect of Adorno's interpretation of the protest movement, see Russell Berman, "Adorno's Politics," in *Adorno: A Critical Reader,* ed. Nigel Gibson and Andrew Rubin (Malden, MA, and Oxford, 2002), 126–31.

44. Kraushaar, *Frankfurter Schule und Studentenbewegung,* 2:376 (my translation).

45. *Schmarotzer* was a pejorative term widely used during the so-called Third Reich to brand Jews and other targets of Nazi ideology as lazy and parasitic.

46. See, for just one example, note 25 above.

47. Adorno was willing to meet with the students only on the condition that the conversations remained private. He was willing to enter into discussion with the students, but he was not, as he put it later, willing to be used as an object to further their own publicity in the media. Despite his caution, the German weekly *Der Spiegel* ran an article that made it seem like Adorno was some sort of secret adviser of the SDS. Adorno wrote a letter to the editor to protest, but *Der Spiegel* refused to print it. See Kraushaar, *Frankfurter Schule und Studentenbewegung,* 1:265.

48. Hans-Jürgen Krahl was a leading figure—and *the* leading theorist—of the Frankfurt SDS. He was also a student of Adorno's. Although they came into conflict after the SDS occupation of the Institute for Social Research in January 1969, Adorno considered Krahl "without doubt one of my most gifted students." Adorno's respect for Krahl comes through clearly in a response he wrote to Günter Grass, who accused Adorno of letting himself be intimidated by Krahl at a public discussion at the Frankfurt Book Fair in September 1968. As late as November 1968, Adorno was

still willing to defend Krahl and to refuse Grass's demand that he publicly distance himself from Krahl and the SDS. See Kraushaar, *Frankfurter Schule und Studentenbewegung,* 2:472.

49. Adorno also warned the students, however, not to make the same mistake the German Communist Party (KPD) had made in the early 1930s with their policy of "Social Fascism," which asserted that the Social Democrats were just as reprehensible politically as the fascists and should be combated with equal vigor. Kraushaar, *Frankfurter Schule und Studentenbewegung,* 2:327.

50. Kraushaar, *Frankfurter Schule und Studentenbewegung,* 1:324–26, 333–37; see also Negt, *Achtundsechzig,* 177–82.

51. For example, at the massive rally against the emergency laws held on 27 May at the Römerberg near the historic Paulskirche and Frankfurt City Hall, several leaders of the most important union organizations in Hesse spoke alongside Hans-Jürgen Krahl and other non–university-affiliated intellectuals. See Kraushaar, *Frankfurter Schule und Studentenbewegung,* 1:333–36.

52. In the so-called Easter demonstrations in Frankfurt, approximately 10,000 (mostly young) workers had participated in the actions against the Springer Verlag touched off by Rudi Dutschke's assassination. But this, the high point of worker participation in the protest movements in West Germany, paled in comparison to the May events in France, at whose high point nearly 10,000,000 workers were on strike.

53. Ibid., 502–3.

54. Friedeburg was a student of Adorno's who had worked at the Institute for Social Research since 1955. In 1966 he became a professor of sociology in Frankfurt, and he was co-director of the Institute for Social Research at this time. From 1970 to 1974 he was the minister of culture of the state of Hesse. He remained the director of the Institute for Social Research until 2001.

55. Kraushaar, *Frankfurter Schule und Studentenbewegung,* 1:381–82.

56. Ibid. 2:526–27.

57. Negt, *Achtundsechzig,* 177–78. For a brief account of the occupation of the Institute and the events leading up to it that was probably written by Adorno himself, see Kraushaar, *Frankfurter Schule und Studentenbewegung,* 2:557–58.

58. The defense of rational authority against an undifferentiated rejection of authority as such has a long history in the tradition of Critical Theory. See, for example, Horkheimer's discussion of authority in his introductory essay for *The Studies on Authority and Family:* "Authority and the Family," in Max Horkheimer, *Critical Theory,* trans. M.J. O'Connell (New York, 1992), 68–97.

59. Kraushaar, *Frankfurter Schule und Studentenbewegung,* 2:310.

60. Ibid., 308.

61. For a good overview of the debate about the continuity of fascism in the Federal Republic and the accusations of both the left and the right that their opponents were "fascist," see Belinda Davis, "New Leftists and West Germany: Fascism, Violence, and the Public Sphere, 1967–74," in *Coping with the Nazi Past: West German Debates on Nazism and Generational Conflict, 1955–1975,* ed. Philipp Gassert and Alan E. Steinweis (New York, 2006), 210–37.

62. For an overview of the influence of the Critical Theorists on the early development of the SDS, see Alexander Demirovic, *Der nonkonformistische Intellektuelle* (Frankfurt am Main, 1999), 880ff.

63. Here, once again, see the theory of "integral statism" in the "Organisationsreferat," presented by Rudi Dutschke and Hans-Jürgen Krahl at the national meeting of the SDS in September 1967. Kraushaar, *Frankfurter Schule und Studentenbewegung,* 2:287–90.

64. For example, in a press release from 19 December 1968 the SDS proclaimed openly that they "understood the struggle against the technocratic reform of the university as part of the struggle for the revolutionary transformation of this society." Kraushaar, *Frankfurter Schule und Studentenbewegung,* 2:528.

65. Ibid., 328.

66. Ibid., 328–29.

67. See notes 37 and 63.

68. This slogan appeared on a banner during the political university in May 1968. Kraushaar, *Frankfurter Schule und Studentenbewegung,* 1:330.

69. That said, the students were by no means the only ones who used the concept of fascism irresponsibly, as Jürgen Habermas's well-known denunciation of radical students as "left fascists" or Walter Rüegg's portrayal of the SDS Go-in against Carlo Schmid as a "fascist terror," clearly demonstrates. As Oskar Negt points out, the sloppy use of the concept of fascism—which, he admits, he was also guilty of at this time—was a sign that the process of working through the past had only just begun. Negt, *Achtundsechzig,* 251.

70. Claussen, "Der kurze Sommer der Theorie," 160.

71. Adorno, "Marginalia to Theory and Praxis," *Critical Models,* 263.

72. Kraushaar, *Frankfurter Schule und Studentenbewegung,* 2:354.

73. *Negative Dialektik* (Frankfurt am Main, 1966), 15.

74. Adorno, "Marginalia to Theory and Praxis," *Critical Models,* 259 and 261.

75. Ibid., 273.

76. Ibid., 265 (translation modified).

77. Despite this pessimistic turn in the early 1970s, Marcuse continued to support and praise movements in the 1970s, such as the women's and ecology movements, that emerged out of the 1960s protest movements. See "Marxism and Feminism," and "Ecology and Revolution," in Marcuse, *The New Left and the 1960s,* 165–72 and 173–76.

78. See, for example, Paul Mattick, "The Limits of Integration," in *The Critical Spirit: Essays in Honor of Herbert Marcuse,* eds. Kurt H. Wolff and Barrington Moore Jr. (Boston, 1968), 374–400.

79. Adorno, *Negative Dialektik,* 15 (translation mine).

80. See also the lecture Marcuse gave on 31 October 1968, "Beyond *One-Dimensional Man,*" in *Herbert Marcuse: Toward a Critical Theory of Society,* ed. Douglas Kellner (New York and London, 2001), 111–20.

81. "Adorno/Marcuse Correspondence on the German Student Movement," trans. Esther Leslie, *New Left Review,* no. 233 (January/February 1999): 125.

82. Ibid.

83. Ibid., 127.

84. For Marcuse's debate with Adorno on Vietnam, see "Adorno-Marcuse Correspondence on the German Student Movement," 27–9.

85. Herbert Marcuse, *An Essay on Liberation* (Harmondsworth, 1972), 32–33.

86. For a discussion of the historical avant-garde's attempts to merge art and life, see

Peter Bürger, *Theory of the Avant-Garde,* trans. Michael Shaw (Minneapolis, 1984). For Adorno's critique of the historical avant-garde and his defense of the autonomy of art see, for example, his letter to Walter Benjamin from 18 March 1936, reprinted in *Aesthetics and Politics,* ed. Fredric Jameson (London and New York), 120–6, or his essay "Looking Back on Surrealism," Theodor Adorno, *Notes to Literature,* vol. 1, trans. Shierry Weber Nicholsen (New York, 1991), 86–90.

87. Carried out between 18 and 30 December—at a time when it must have been clear to just about anyone that the war could no longer be won—Americans bombers flew nearly 4,000 sorties, dropping explosives with a cumulative power several times that of the atomic bomb dropped on Hiroshima. The urban centers of Hanoi and Haiphong were hit hardest.

88. Herbert Marcuse, "The Historical Fate of Bourgeois Democracy," in *Towards a Critical Theory of Society: Collected Papers,* vol. 2, ed. Douglas Kellner (New York and London, 2001), 167 and 170.

89. Herbert Marcuse, *The Aesthetic Dimension: Towards a Critique of Marxist Aesthetics* (Boston, 1978).

Part II

Spaces and Identities

Chapter 3

America's Vietnam in Germany— Germany in America's Vietnam

On the Relocation of Spaces and the Appropriation of History

Wilfried Mausbach

Germany—America—Vietnam. Even the well-disposed reader might be forgiven for fearing that I am pretty much doing the splits here. Yet, in starting out with this chapter, I will not flinch from adding yet another region to the roster. Recently, the German parliament debated a resolution concerning the massacres of Armenians in the Ottoman Empire between 1915 and 1917. Filed in February 2005 by Germany's conservative Christian Democrats (CDU), the resolution declares that Turkey's ongoing denial to recognize the crimes of its predecessor was inconsistent with the idea of reconciliation as a guiding principle of the European Union, to which Turkey wants to accede.[1] Elaborating on this theme in a publication of the CDU's Protestant caucus, Member of Parliament Christoph Bergner explained that this appeal to Turkey to face up to the darker chapters of its history constituted a candid attempt to introduce the country to the European culture of memory. According to Bergner, the member states of the European Union stand out in coming to terms with their respective pasts.[2] This notion is rapidly gaining currency throughout the EU. It is also being controversially discussed among scholars. Whereas some welcome the construction of a collective European identity geared to historical guilt because this would at least preclude an easy return to triumphalist notions of cultural superiority, others warn against the specter of identity politics being instigated by political and cultural elites without much regard to mainstream attitudes.[3]

At the center of Europe's assorted guilt discourses stands, of course, the Holocaust. In early 2000, the Stockholm International Forum on the Holocaust called for renewed efforts to promote education, remembrance, and research about the Holocaust. In the years since, many European countries—among them the United Kingdom, France, Italy, Poland, Belgium, and the Netherlands—have declared 27 January, the day Soviet soldiers liberated Auschwitz, a national day of remembrance, which it has been in Germany since 1996. To be sure, the Holocaust is far from being a cornerstone of collective memory in Europe alone. Indeed, the destruction of European Jewry is now remembered globally. As Konrad Jarausch and Michael Geyer have observed, when it comes to the Holocaust, "German history has become part of a web of global memory articulated worldwide."[4] Less circumspect, Daniel Levy and Natan Sznaider have suggested that "shared memories of the Holocaust … provide the foundations for a new cosmopolitan memory" that will in turn foster new forms of solidarity.[5] They envision an emerging global community of fate that refers to the central catastrophe of the twentieth century in order to articulate common concerns above and beyond the nation-state.[6]

While the big bang that set in motion the trek to a transnational memory is often identified in the NBC mini-series *Holocaust* that was broadcast in the United States in April 1978 and subsequently viewed by some 220 million people in fifty countries,[7] I will argue in this chapter that in fact the 1960s were the formative period in the transnationalization of the Holocaust. More specifically, I want to illustrate how protest against the Vietnam War in both Germany and the United States at the same time mirrored and promoted this process. Eventually, this analysis will serve to suggest that shared imaginations of the Holocaust provided "the 'other' Alliance" of student and protest movements with one essential constituent of a collective identity.

History, Geography, and the Invention of Transnational Communities

Identity, of course, is never unproblematic; even individuals have multiple identities with regard to gender, race, religion, class, or nation. To posit, then, that innumerable individuals share a collective identity seems to be highly problematic. The concept has accordingly been decried as a fiendish phrase from the dictionary of ideological mobilization.[8] However, in talking of collective identity with regard to "the 'other' Alliance," I do not mean to portray the latter as a kind of essentialist entity. Rather, I seek to single out a set of shared characteristics that endowed people with a personal sense of belonging. Jan Assmann has defined collective identity as "the image that a group establishes of itself and with which its members identify." He continues: "Collective identity is a question of *identification* on the part of the individuals involved. It does not exist 'as such' but only to the extent that certain individuals bear witness to it. It is as strong or weak as it is present in the mind and behavior of group members and as it is able to animate their thoughts and actions."[9] This essay is concerned, therefore, with the way actors saw themselves and the world and with the processes through which certain commonalties emerged and were articulated across national boundaries. I refer to collective identity, then, not as a constructed standard that is dictated to or put on a multitude of human beings, but rather as a *re*constructed set of experiences.[10]

Identity is grounded in time and space. In telling stories about our past, we explain who we are. The crucial role that collective memories and invented traditions have played in the emergence and consolidation of nation-states has consequently been a thriving field of historical analysis for the past quarter century.[11] Yet nations are far from the only "imagined communities" that use history as a constituent of identity. As this chapter will indicate, supra- and subnational groupings also erect their historical markers. Moreover, as a consequence of the process of globalization, the exposure to other cultures' experiences—past and present—has dramatically increased. Through modern telecommunications and the spread of popular culture, the preconditions for "importing" and appropriating others' (hi)stories have been greatly expanded. Two early examples of such appropriation, I would suggest, are the much discussed Americanization of the Holocaust and what we may call the Germanization of the Vietnam War.

Unlike time, space has long been viewed as a rather unproblematic constituent of identity. Only recently has it been emphasized, for instance, that maps are narratives in their own right and that as such they are as selectively constructed as is history.[12] Like history, maps can only show fractions of what Max Weber called "the meaningless infinity of global occurrences."[13] Because maps, unlike historical narratives, apparently come without author and intent, they encourage us to forget that this is a picture that someone has arranged, selected, and coded.[14] Yet spatial representations are only a particular mode to perceive historical reality, and as such they produce meaning just as historical narratives do. As Hans-Dietrich Schultz has observed: "What appears as hard 'facts' in sharp relief is merely an imagined and communicated 'truth'—shared by some and contested by others—of a mental world, whose patterns of thought are projected onto the map-sheet, only to return from there as 'natural truth.'"[15] Thus, maps were crucial in, among other things, legitimizing the nation-state and in subjugating colonial territories. As Mark Neocleous has pointed out: "A polity imagines itself, and is imagined by others, in part through its cartographic image." Anything that is apt to question the represented identity is deemed to be of no account or obsolete—that is, it is "off the map."[16]

Cartographic images also visualize and reinforce mental maps.[17] In diagrammatic representations of the Cold War world, the Soviet Union, colored in a jarring red and occupying a sixth of the globe, is leaning heavily and most intimidatingly on Western Europe and the rest of the world.[18] Sometimes the dye spills over and pours forth over neighboring and ideologically kindred regions that are then contrasted sharply with the reassuringly blue areas of the "Free World," stretching from the Americas in the West to Japan and, of course, South Vietnam in the East. At the same time, geographic distances must occasionally be made to dwindle in order to render certain propositions more meaningful to domestic audiences, to bring them "closer to home." Detlef Junker, in a different context, has referred to this technique as "zooming in the enemy."[19] Yet, as I will now go on to demonstrate, it is not only antagonists that are subject to relocation.

Relocating Vietnam

It was not "the 'other' Alliance" that started with the relocation of spaces but the alliance proper, i.e., the Atlantic Alliance. When the Cold War evolved into a global struggle and the United States took it upon itself—in the words of *Life* magazine—"to mobilize effectively … all of the more than one billion people outside the Iron Curtain,"[20] the West grew to encompass the "Free World." To be sure, "[t]he West itself is," as Peter Burke has aptly observed, "a historical construct."[21] Indeed, its boundaries had just been redrawn to incorporate the nascent West German democracy. As a homogeneous community with a continuous history unfolding through seemingly empty time, the West set out in ancient Greece and Rome, incorporating on its way Christianity, the European Renaissance and the voyages of discovery, the rise of modern science and liberal democracy, and culminating in the Atlantic community as the apex of human progress.[22] Moreover, as Americans who were confronted with European parochialism during the 1950s and 1960s were quick to point out, the United States was committed not only to preserving its heritage in Europe, but also to preserving and encouraging the part of its heritage that had spread throughout the world.[23] Throughout the 1960s, the efforts of the US to educate its allies about Vietnam relied heavily on the script and map of an imagined community called the "Free World."

Indicative of the communal character of the "Free World" is the familial rhetoric that suffuses political discourse on Vietnam. A revealing example is an important policy speech given by US Secretary of Defense Robert McNamara in March 1964. In the wake of McNamara's latest fact-finding mission to Saigon, officials within the administration of President Lyndon B. Johnson felt that the secretary should take advantage of an address before the James Forrestal Memorial Dinner at the Sheraton-Park Hotel in Washington, D.C., to "deliver a major speech covering the South Viet-Nam situation in detail and attempting to set it in deep perspective."[24] The speech aimed to target both domestic critics and wavering allies, attempting above all to nip French President Charles de Gaulle's talk of neutralization in the bud.[25] A draft sent to the president through the National Security Council (NSC) thus declared unambiguously: "First, and most important, is the simple fact that South Vietnam is a member of the family of the Free World—a member of our family of nations." At the NSC, staff member Michael Forrestal—coincidentally the son of the man whose memory was to be honored on the occasion of McNamara's speech—was uncomfortable with this rendering of the relationship. He replaced the phrase "a member of our family of nations" with "a family of which we are also members," commenting in the margins that the original "sounds as if we are head of a family." Forrestal's qualms, however, only extended to the hierarchies in the household, not to the familial rhetoric as such, which suggested a natural community of fate. A bit further down in the speech, when it was explained that "[t]he U.S. role in South Vietnam, then, is: first, to answer the call of the South Vietnamese, a member of our family of the Free World, to help them save their country for themselves," he remarked:, "o.k. here."[26] The passage was nevertheless slightly revised to read "a member nation of our Free World family" before a summary of the speech went out to countries all over the world via wireless file following McNamara's presentation on 26 March.[27]

Not every American policymaker shared Michael Forrestal's scruples with regard to American patriarchy. On a speaking tour across the United States in early 1966, the deputy chief of mission at the American embassy in Bonn asked his audiences, "Germany: Ally or Problem Child?"[28] Reflecting on the need to "develop a consensus leading to common action by the free world community of nations," the State Department's Policy Planning Staff called for an educative diplomacy, explaining that "[t]he root meaning of educate is 'to bring up a child, physically and mentally.' And that is the root of our problem … Education involves not only the impartation of knowledge but the development of mental and moral discipline. Some pupils may be very difficult. But we should not write any of them off as completely hopeless."[29]

With respect to West Germany, to be sure, American attempts to portray Vietnam as a matter of common concern proved to be far from hopeless. This endeavor was facilitated by an analogy between Berlin and Saigon that was stock-in-trade in the early 1960s. Thus, President Kennedy, in 1962, spoke of "the burden that we must bear of helping freedom defend itself all the way, from the American soldier guarding the Brandenburg Gate to the Americans now in Viet-Nam."[30] Five days after the president's assassination, his successor echoed this sentiment before a joint session of Congress, promising that the United States would "keep its commitments from South Vietnam to West Berlin."[31] Early on, West German Chancellor Ludwig Erhard assured LBJ that Germany would back the United States in its "efforts to maintain South Vietnam as a bulwark of the Free World in South East Asia."[32] His fellow countrymen, he added on the occasion of a visit to the White House, regarded Vietnam as "a kind of testing ground as to how firmly the U.S. honors its commitments. In that respect there existed a parallel between Saigon and Berlin." There was, therefore, Erhard continued, hardly a country that was more inextricably linked with South Vietnam than Germany, notwithstanding the vast geographical distance.[33] Perhaps sensing that this spatial actuality might be detrimental to emotional closeness, the chancellor soon revised his geographical expertise, telling US Ambassador at Large Averell Harriman that "Viet-Nam was at the door of Europe."[34] Not surprisingly, President Johnson's National Security Adviser McGeorge Bundy, in reviewing the Cold War line of battle, found that "the defense of Berlin, right now, is in Vietnam."[35]

Relocating Auschwitz

At the same time, however, a new generation was coming of age on both sides of the Atlantic Ocean that refused to buy into this worldview. Compared to policymakers in the United States and West Germany, students displayed a much greater sensitivity to the secular process of decolonization and the extent to which it called into question deeply ingrained Cold War certainties. Wrote James Gilbert in *Studies on the Left:* "The ... memories of the Berlin Blockade simply are not relevant to this generation of students."[36] Quite the reverse, it was the dark sides and blind spots of bipolarity that took center stage. As the American Students for a Democratic Society (SDS) observed in their manifesto *America and the New Era,* "[T]he closed, seemingly irreconcilable conflict between the two blocs created a world in which virtually every human value was distorted, all moral standards seemed weirdly irrelevant."[37] The Manichean dichotomy between "Free World" and "Captive Nations" ceased to persuade a new generation of critical students. In Germany, a yet unnoticed student named Rudi Dutschke wrote in 1964: "Today, we have truly arrived at a division of the world ... , namely, the division of the world into countries rich and poor."[38] When the chairmen of the official student government organization at West Berlin's Free University, following the start of Washington's campaign of sustained bombing in North Vietnam, signed an anti-war declaration sponsored by the East German regime, they explained that they "could not subscribe to the clichés propagated in Germany about the war in Vietnam, namely, that it is a struggle between communism and capitalism."[39]

Instead of the Berlin-Saigon analogy, another comparison was steadily gaining ground among German peace activists: the parallel between contemporary American actions in Vietnam and past German atrocities during the 1930s and 1940s.[40] Protesters pointed out that Washington was using Vietnam as a field of experimentation for new weapons in much the same way Nazi Germany had done during the Spanish Civil War.[41] In a declaration supporting the international congress on Vietnam held in Berlin in 1968, a group of well-known writers and intellectuals proclaimed: "Vietnam is our generation's Spain. We must not burden ourselves with guilt by remaining quiet or noncommittal in the face of the revolutionary struggle of the Vietnamese people."[42] But protesters did not stop at comparisons with the 1930s. When the German SDS put together an exhibition on Vietnam in 1965, captions for various pictures read: "Strategic hamlet, fascist KZ of the US and the Saigon regime" or "Innocent children in concentration camp."[43] The playwright Peter Weiss, fresh from creating a sensation with his drama *The Investigation,* a stage adaptation of the Frankfurt Auschwitz trial, proclaimed that the strategic hamlet program threatened to uproot nine million people, adding that this figure corresponded to the number of Jews overcome by Hitler. American manuals for the use of gas to smoke out the Vietcong, he claimed, "equaled the inventive genius that German manufacturers once devoted to erect gas chambers and crematories ... America," he concluded, "is left today ... as continuing the tradition of Guernica, Lidice, and Majdanek."[44] Invoking Auschwitz repeatedly in a collection of poems about Vietnam, the lyricist Erich Fried provoked a discussion in the respected journal *Der Monat* on whether, following a famous dictum about Auschwitz by Adorno, it was possible to write poems about Vietnam.[45] In February 1967 the journal *Das Argument* carried the headline "Auschwitz, Vietnam, and no end to it," and it closed out the year with a collection of aphorisms by philosopher Günther Anders, who suggested that the Vietnamese, charred by napalm, resembled the Jews cremated in Auschwitz.[46] Even journalist Klaus Harpprecht, who was usually sympathetic to the United States, concluded: "America, in agony and convulsions, wends its way to the shadowy realm of guilt—where Europe's peoples have been wandering about for a long time."[47]

The analogy between Auschwitz and Vietnam took yet another turn when a plainclothes police officer shot and killed student Benno Ohnesorg during a demonstration against the Shah of Iran in West Berlin on 2 June 1967. Now, open violence seemed to return from the periphery to the center. In the eyes of many students, Auschwitz was about to spring back from Southeast Asia to the country where it originated. The hackneyed parallel between Berlin and Saigon suddenly acquired a whole new meaning. "Isn't," asked a student newspaper, "Berlin in Vietnam or vice-versa since June 2?"[48] The relocation of spaces was coming full circle.

One peculiar result of this excursion was that students began to view *themselves* as prospective victims of extermination. As one visitor to the International Vietnam Congress in West Berlin warned, "If we want to understand the liberation struggle in Vietnam correctly, it means that we have to get rid of this government"; otherwise, he continued, "we will perish in a concentration camp one day."[49] A small minority within the movement therefore concluded that it was not enough anymore to speak up against the misdeeds of the system but that active resistance was warranted—even by force. Michael "Bommi" Baumann, reflecting on his decision to join the militant faction "Bewegung 2. Juni," which derived its name from the date of Ohnesorg's shooting, explained: "Instead of being deported to Auschwitz once again, I'd rather shoot—it's as simple as that."[50] From start to finish, the perception of Auschwitz and Vietnam as the vanishing point of their own society also haunted the members of Germany's most notorious terrorist group, the Red Army Faction (RAF). Legend has it that Gudrun Ensslin, a future leader of the group, cried out in the wake of Ohnesorg's shooting: "It's the generation of Auschwitz—you cannot argue with them."[51] Instead of arguing, Ensslin and her companion Andreas Baader committed arson in a Frankfurt department store, justifying their action in court with the complacency of their fellow citizens about the war in Vietnam. In a postscript to the defendants' closing statement, Ensslin's one-time fiancé Bernward Vesper charged that the judges, as representatives of a generation that had failed to set department stores on fire in protest against fascism in 1938, were now sending to prison those who—Vietnam being the Auschwitz of the young generation—did in fact light a fire.[52] In May 1972, having long since gone underground, the RAF bombed several US Army installations in Germany, announcing afterward that assaults were justified against a military machine that was carrying on "genocide, the murder of people, annihilation, Auschwitz" in Vietnam.[53]

After the leaders of the group were apprehended and put on trial, one of their attorneys, Otto Schily, compared the bombings to possible assaults on the Reichssicherheitshauptamt, the Third Reich's main office of persecution, and reminded the court of recent television images from Vietnam. "These are the same pictures: the Jewish child, hands up approaching SS-members in the ghetto, and the Vietnamese children who, screaming and burnt by napalm, run towards the photographer following a carpet bombing."[54] In October 1977, on the very day before he committed suicide, Andreas Baader still identified the Vietnam War as the compelling reason for the RAF's actions.[55] While the moral urgency and almost pathological rigor among members of the RAF, culminating in a suicidal errand, was certainly exceptional, the same cannot be said of the initial ideological parameters underlying their worldview. The triad of Vietnam, Auschwitz, and their own perceived oppression and persecution was part and parcel of the experiences of many activists in the late 1960s and most of the 1970s.

Coming to Terms with the Past

The fact that a few militant radicals emanating from the German student and protest movement utilized the Vietnam War as a means to arrive at a self-appointed mandate should not conceal that the moral indignation and outrage of many West Germans in the face of American actions in Vietnam was heartfelt and true. Neither, however, must this latter fact bar us from addressing some of the broader implications of those protests. It appears that a vocal minority of West Germans appropriated American experiences in Vietnam in order to work through their own nation's history. By invoking Vietnam as a present representation of Auschwitz, these Germans opened up the possibility of making up for the resistance that failed to materialize in the 1930s and 1940s, and thus of redeeming themselves of an inherited burden of guilt. If, as West Berlin's Vietnam Solidarity Committee admonished its compatriots, "[a]ll citizens who keep quiet are tacitly tolerating the US war, and they become implicated in just the same way as those who remained silent in spite of Hitler's crimes,"[56] then the protesters, by speaking up, in turn extricated themselves from these very crimes. In acting against America's purported continuation of Auschwitz in Vietnam and thereby redeeming themselves from their inherited guilt, many young Germans obtained just enough distance from their nation's past to allow them to confront it in a new way. Thus they contributed to a process whereby the Holocaust, as

Jörn Rüsen has put it, "for the first time acquired a status in historical perspective that ended up on the mental map of the German self."[57] From now on, as Clemens Albrecht has written, "To be German means to grapple with the National Socialist past."[58]

This has led many observers to accord anti-war protesters and the German student movement in general an important role in the Federal Republic's coming to terms with the past. Yet, as more and more historians have recently pointed out, the generation of 1968 in fact only accelerated and radicalized a process that was well underway by the late 1950s.[59] It was nurtured by the age cohort born around the mid to late 1920s, whose formative experience was the German collapse of 1945, and whose members now moved up to fill important positions in the realms of politics, culture, and mass media.[60] The commemorative efforts of these so-called "forty-fivers" were considerably aided and encouraged by the culture industry's discovery of the destruction of European Jewry as a product for mainstream consumption and by a number of spectacular media events, foremost among them the trial of Adolf Eichmann in Jerusalem. Only as the result of the combined effects of these developments was the fate of Europe's Jews lifted out of the general atrocities of the Second World War and perspicuously marked off as the most extraordinary crime against humanity. As Raul Hilberg once remarked, "In the beginning there was no Holocaust, when it took place in the middle of the twentieth century, its nature was not fully grasped."[61] The same could be said of Auschwitz, which for a long time held a less prominent place in Western perceptions of the Nazi concentration camp system than did Bergen-Belsen and Buchenwald, liberated by British and US troops respectively. Only after the Eichmann and Auschwitz trials established the systematic industrialized murder by gas as the defining characteristic of the Jewish catastrophe did Auschwitz become *the* symbol for the Holocaust, probably also benefiting from a visit at the scene of the crime by the court of the Frankfurt trial in December 1964, complete with several hundred journalists from the US, Europe, and Israel.[62] All those developments only created the peculiar frame of reference into which German anti-war activists were then able to project their understanding of the Vietnam War.

Transnationalizing the Holocaust

It is important to note, however, that Germany was of course not the only country affected by these trends. The trial of Adolf Eichmann, for instance, represented a huge—and perhaps the first ever—international media event. The Israeli government saw to it that much of the industrialized world was tuned in to the proceedings. Two thirds of the general seating capacity in the courtroom was reserved for members of the press. In addition, it was arranged to record the trial on videotape. The American contractor for the recording later reported that footage of the trial had been shown in thirty-eight countries. Commercial networks in the US received copies of the videotape via airmail for next-day presentation. ABC featured reports on the trial daily in its prime-time news, supplemented by a variety of special programs. The coverage of the two other national networks did not lag far behind. TV guides characterized the reporting as viewing not to be missed. Next to television, the trial was covered in theatrical newsreel and news radio broadcasts and, of course, through regular reporting in major newspapers and magazines. A bibliography published in 1969 listed more than one thousand titles about the trial.[63]

More than a quarter of the bibliography's entries accounted for reviews of Hannah Arendt's trial report *Eichmann in Jerusalem: A Report on the Banality of Evil* (1963). This catchy phrase, felicitously capturing the glaring absence of any particular wickedness, pathology, or ideological conviction on the part of the man in the glass box, together with the fierce controversy that erupted in the wake of Arendt's book, ensured that the figure of the "desk-killer" and mindless paper-pusher and the identification of the Holocaust as a harrowing tale of administrative mass murder rapidly entered public consciousness.[64] Contrary to the Israeli government's intention to use the trial for the purposes of educating the world about the Jewish fate and thereby legitimizing the Jewish state, American audiences conceptualized the trial above all as a lesson with universal significance. As Daniel Bell pointed out in his review of Arendt's book, "[t]he frightening prospect it disclosed was that, given the structural tendencies of modern societies to centralize power and to manipulate vast numbers of men through the agencies of state coercion, the totalitarian potential was an ever-recurrent one."[65] This notion was reinforced when in the mid 1960s the controversial experiments of Yale psychologist Stanley Milgram began to reach a wider audience. His easy success in urging randomly recruited citizens to inflict increasingly painful electric shocks on test persons uncovered—as one reviewer put it—the "latent Eichmann" hidden in ordinary men.[66] The critic and historian Lewis Mumford concluded: "In every country there are now countless Eichmanns in administrative offices, in business corporations, in universities, in laboratories, in the armed forces: orderly obedient people, ready to carry out any officially sanctioned fantasy, however dehumanized and debased."[67]

This rendering of the Holocaust and its prototypical perpetrator easily connected to the revulsion toward the modern bureaucratic state that was a staple of the New Left in both Europe and the United States. Unsurprisingly, protesters quickly applied the new lessons to the war in Vietnam. Thus, Carl Oglesby, president of the Students for a Democratic Society (SDS), adjured his audience at an anti-war rally in Washington, D.C., in November 1965: "Think of the men who now engineer that war—those who study the maps, give the commands, push the buttons, and tally the dead: Bundy, McNamara, Rusk, Lodge, Goldberg, the President himself. They are not moral monsters. They are all honorable men."[68] Activists daubed Eichmann's name on banners and placards and rubbed them into the faces of those who—they felt—were conducting or abetting a modern genocidal war in Southeast Asia.[69]

Needless to say, the appropriation of the Holocaust in America was not confined to the figure of Adolf Eichmann. In fact, some of the same moral imperatives that made themselves felt in Germany were also discernible among American protesters. Thus, SDS leader Carl Davidson defended the shift from protest to resistance "on the basis of the Nuremberg decisions which expected Hitler's opposition to oppose him, not debate him."[70] Similarly, the remark by Bernardine Dohrn of the militant Weather Underground that "We refuse to be 'good Germans!'" was echoed widely within the movement.[71] In addition, a sense of repression conjured up some of the same hyperbolical images of persecution that we have already noticed in West Germany. Following the conviction of the so-called Catonsville Nine, who had set fire to hundreds of draft records with a sort of home-made napalm, a supporter confided in the brother of one of the convicted men: "I am convinced that sooner or later we are all going to end in a concentration camp."[72] A German visitor reported hearing a song with the line: "We hold these truths to be self-evident: All people could be cremated equal."[73] Obviously, the interpretive repertoire in Germany and the United States overlapped to a considerable extent. This, I would argue, was mainly due to the emergence of the Holocaust as a paramount frame of reference during the 1960s.

Contrary to the impression left by authors as varied as Peter Novick and Norman Finkelstein, this process was not driven primarily by the Jewish community in the United States.[74] Instead, popular culture was the main vehicle of the Americanization of the Holocaust. As Alan Mintz, among others, has persuasively argued, the key to this process "lies in the power of cultural texts and their diffusion in the form of books, stage plays, movies and television."[75] In fact, even the documentary footage of the Eichmann trial yielded traces of popular culture, with one commentator likening the enclosed dock that held the defendant to "the glass cage used in televised quiz shows."[76] However, much more important were stage plays, Hollywood movies, or televised dramas like *The Diary of Anne Frank,* Stanley Kramer's *Judgment at Nuremberg,* or, for that matter, Peter Weiss's *The Investigation,* which suggested that the complicity of supposedly innocent bystanders made Auschwitz possible in the first place, and of which two different productions were televised in the United States in 1967.[77]

The Holocaust also made what Jeffrey Shandler has termed "guest appearances" in American serialized television programs.[78] Occasionally, the anti-war protesters' allusion to parallels between Germany's Nazi past and contemporary American actions in Vietnam even crept into this venue. Thus in a 1968 episode of the science fiction series *Star Trek,* Captain Kirk and the crew of the starship *Enterprise* encounter a replica of Nazi Germany on a planet called Ekos where they arrive looking for a prominent historian who was sent there by the interplanetary federation years earlier to act as a "cultural adviser." As it turns out, the historian found the planet fragmented and divided and, in an effort to administer a hefty dose of corporate feeling to the Ekosians, resolved to hark back to the example of an efficient and orderly state three centuries past called the Third Reich. Unfortunately, the plan goes awry when some eager-to-learn Ekosians topple their cultural adviser, initiate a campaign of racial hatred against their neighboring planet—cueingly called Zeon—and drug the historian into compliance. Captain Kirk and his science officer Mr. Spock manage to rouse the errant fellow from his befogged condition and he is able to call off the assault on the Zeons, but he has barely done so when he is fatally shot by the real bad guy. As he dies, the historian tells the spaceship's commander: "I was wrong. The noninterference direction is the only way. We must stop the slaughter. ... Even historians fail to learn from history. They repeat the same mistakes. Let the killing end."[79] In 1968, at the height of an intervention in a faraway place that had begun with the dispatch of a few token "advisers," the drama's audience could hardly have missed the insinuation.

To be sure, Vietnam was far from the only place to which the Holocaust was applied in American cultural productions of the 1960s. In Sidney Lumet's 1964 movie *The Pawnbroker,* starring Rod Steiger, a Jewish Holocaust survivor is depicted as a callous shopkeeper whose past intrudes uncontrollably into his new life in contemporary Harlem. Juxtaposing flashbacks of Holocaust memory with scenes of inner-city unrest, the film suggests, as Sara Horowitz has observed, "that American racism represents the continuation of the Holocaust into the present."[80] African-American protesters accepted the analogy with alacrity. The founding document of the Black Panther Party demanded reparations of the United States, pointing out that the Germans, having murdered six million Jews, were now aiding Israel, whereas Americans had not even started to settle their debt for the slaughter of fifty million black people.[81]

In July 1968, the Panthers sent a delegation to the United Nations' headquarters in New York calling for an investigation into Black American claims of genocide against the United States government.[82] In their eyes, this was far from a historical problem. As Stokely Carmichael, the Panthers' "honorary prime minister," remarked on the occasion of Huey P. Newton's birthday in February 1968: "Many of us feel—many of our generation feel—that they're getting ready to commit genocide against us. ... If you do not think [the honky is] capable of committing genocide, against us, check out what he's doing to our brothers in Vietnam, *check* out what he's doing in Vietnam. We have to understand that we're talking about our *survival* and nothing else, whether or not this beautiful race of people is gonna survive on the earth."[83] Likewise relating Vietnam to America, the Black Panthers' "Justice Minister" H. Rap Brown exhorted African-Americans to "refuse to participate in the war of genocide against people of color: a war that also commits genocide against us. Black men are being used on the front lines at a disproportionate rate. Forty-five percent of the casualties are Black. That's genocide!" With a swipe at more moderate groups like the National Association for the Advancement of Colored People (NAACP), Brown continued:

"Nonviolence as it is advocated by negroes is merely a preparation for genocide. Some negroes are so sold on nonviolence that if they received a letter from the White House saying to report to concentration camps, they would not hesitate. They'd be there in no time! If we examine what happened to the Jews, we find that it was not the Germans who first began to remove Jews. It was other Jews!"[84]

Brown's point of reference in this seems to have been the controversy over the role of Jewish Councils during the Third Reich triggered by Hannah Arendt's Eichmann report. David Hilliard, Chief of Staff of the Black Panther Party, decried the mainstream fixation on the Germans as Holocaust perpetrators. "The American historian," he asserted, "has a way of justifying this system by using Germany as the most vicious enemy against mankind. This is perhaps true for the people of Jewish descent. But when we really check this shit out, starting with the genocide of the Indians; the 50,000,000 Black people slaughtered by the oppressors when taken against their will at the point of guns, over 400 years ago, right here in America; then reminding ourselves of the genocidal and imperialist war against the Vietnamese people"—then, Hilliard suggested, it became easier to relate to Eldridge Cleaver's remark that the American flag and the American eagle were the true symbols of fascism.[85]

If white radicals had already replaced the c in America with one k in order to convey the country's similarity to Nazi Germany, black activists made it three ks, thus firmly inscribing their own historical experiences into this American replica of Germany.[86] At the same time, Black Nationalists were charting mental maps that sought to detach African-Americans from this frightening mongrel. "Territorial nationalists" like the Congress of Racial Equality's Roy Innis conceptualized African-American communities as black colonies representing "a series of islands" separated by land and together composing a "nation within a nation." "Revolutionary Nationalists" like the Black Panthers classified African-Americans as Third World people living in the black "internal colony of the United States." "Cultural Nationalists" like the US Organization's Ron Karenga thought of African-Americans as "a separate entity—an 'alien Nation/Race' ensnared by white sponsored ghetto colonialism."[87] The Weather Underground, temporarily strongly attracted by Black militancy, accepted this notion of American blacks actually being a part of the Third World and accordingly identified within the US a "Black Vietnam" that, by crushing the power of American imperialists, would bring the whole thing down internationally as well.[88] Vietnam was thus relocated to an America that had meanwhile—in the minds of movement participants at least—acquired conspicuous features of the German past.

Conclusion

At the beginning of the twenty-first century, political, economic, and cultural transformations have weakened the role of national histories in the making of identities.[89] There are now communities of virtual communication with a sense of belonging detached from territorial structures.[90] However, whereas our ability to actively engage in this communication has dramatically increased only in the last ten to fifteen years, we have been on the receiving end of globally transmitted information for more than half a century. The post–Second World War revolution in transportation and telecommunication, which was an integral part of a set of overlapping processes—usually called globalization—that tremendously accelerated the flows of people, ideas, and things, quickly made every part of the world responsive to every other part.[91] Especially with the advent of electronic media and satellite television, transfers of knowledge and cultural borrowing broadened to such an extent that people became able to assemble meanings and identities from almost everywhere. At the end of the Second World War, there were fewer than 200,000 television sets in American homes; ten years later that number had risen to 32 million. Germany, of course, was lagging considerably behind. Yet in 1957 the number of television subscribers in West Germany crossed the threshold of one million, and by the early 1960s a quarter of German households owned a private set, although it would take until 1974 for the market to be saturated.[92] During the 1960s, two recurrent themes on television screens, radio programs, and newspaper headlines were the contemporary American war in Vietnam and the past German atrocities in Europe that, by and by, came to be known as the Holocaust.

More specifically, and as I have argued in this chapter, the emergence of the Holocaust both provided a frame of reference for interpreting American actions in Vietnam and presented a challenge for the younger generation to come to terms with. In a sense, it created a shared moral universe for protesters on both sides of the Atlantic. However, local activists adapted and refracted the Holocaust with regard to their own needs. Thus, West German students vilified American warfare in Vietnam as a repetition of Auschwitz but at the same time used this alleged recurrence in order to distance themselves from their own nation's blemished past. This retreat yielded a new sense of self-esteem that in turn allowed them to confront the German past anew and thus contribute to a larger transformation resulting in what Bernhard Giesen has called a "Holocaust identity."[93] The Federal Republic has since subscribed to the notion that it is exactly the Holocaust—and, as far as Germans are concerned, maybe only the Holocaust—that, as an absolute opposite, is capable of setting into stark relief the normative quintessence of a democratic society under the rule of law.[94] Consequently, a permanent chafing against the National Socialist past has become a linchpin for the continued existence of German democracy, lest the country should relapse into precarious times.

American democracy has been much less endangered historically than Germany's and is therefore in no need of a similar prop. Not surprisingly, then, the adjuration of Germany in America's Vietnam did not produce equally profound consequences for American collective identity. Moreover, if America has "imported" the Holocaust into its collective memory, this had necessarily to be accompanied by a process of cultural translation. But, as Gabriel Motzkin has pointed out: "When we take over the memory of the other, we detach that memory from the other's historical experience."[95] This is also to say that we have to integrate it into our own historical experience. This integration, like all acts of collective remembrance, is always a contentious process. To be sure, appropriating German history both reflected and contributed to the fact that the meaning of America became much more complicated during the 1960s. In addition, it helped African-Americans and other minorities to claim distinction for themselves.[96] Finally, the emergence of the Holocaust and the almost simultaneous threat to the existence of Israel in the Six-Day War promoted the assertion of an American Jewish identity.[97]

Yet overall, the Vietnam War and its comparison to the Holocaust failed to effectively shatter the self-image of mainstream America. Instead, and quite the contrary, Americans eventually made the Holocaust into a major piece of the heroic jigsaw puzzle of American history. The most conspicuous manifestation of this can be found in the United States Holocaust Memorial Museum that opened next to the National Mall in Washington in 1993. By dint of placement alone, within view of the Washington and Jefferson Monuments, the museum is framed by American democratic ideals. This framing, however, also extends to the exhibition itself, which starts and finishes with examples of American self-images. Toward the end of the exhibit, emerging from the darkness into the light, the visitor will encounter a celebration of rebirth and renewal in stories of immigration that take the survivors from the ravaged "Old World" to the "New World" of Jewish statehood and American egalitarianism. Then, stepping out of the building, visitors find themselves surrounded by the great American monuments to democracy.[98] That, however, actually brings them right back to where they started—and not just topographically. As Tim Cole has observed, upon entering the museum "[w]e witness 1945 before we go back to 1933 … , experiencing 'liberation' before we experience 'destruction' and encountering American liberators before we encounter the Nazi murderers. As we start out on this telling of the 'Holocaust,' we have already been handed a mental map within which to operate. … It is a journey back to 1945 and a journey back to 'America' before we step into Germany."[99]

This is accomplished by the peculiar way in which visitors are introduced to the exhibit. Entering an elevator that takes them up to the fourth floor, they hear the words of a patrol leader, who radios in that his men have come across something that they don't quite understand, that is hard for Americans to grasp. As the elevator doors open, visitors are confronted with a large black and white photograph of General Eisenhower amid a group of US soldiers staring in disbelief and horror at a pile of half-burnt corpses at Ohrdruf concentration camp. Writes Cole: "Already a framework is established that teaches us to see the 'Holocaust' as an un-American crime."[100] Moreover, by opening the exhibit with footage from General Eisenhower's visit to Ohrdruf, the Holocaust is readily integrated into the heroic American grand narrative by suggesting that the liberation of such camps had been the rationale for the future president's Second World War campaign all along.[101] Mission accomplished.

No doubt, the commemorative paths that Germany and the United States have taken since the emergence of the Holocaust and its entanglement with the Vietnam War have diverged considerably. Yet the story of America's Vietnam in Germany and Germany in America's Vietnam demonstrates the extent to which each country's history has been implicated in the construction of the other country's collective identities.

Notes

1. Deutscher Bundestag, 15. Wahlperiode, Drucksache 15/4933, 22 February 2005.
2. Christoph Bergner, "Zum 90. Jahrestag des Beginns der Armeniervernichtung im Osmanischen Reich," *Evangelische Verantwortung,* no. 4 (2005): 1–5.
3. See respectively, Bernhard Giesen, "Europäische Identität und transnationale Öffentlichkeit. Eine historische Perspektive," in *Transnationale Öffentlichkeiten und Identitäten im 20. Jahrhundert,* ed. Hartmut Kaelble, Martin Kirsch, and Alexander Schmidt-Gernig (Frankfurt am Main and New York, 2002), 67–84; Lothar Probst, "Der Holocaust – eine neue Zivilreligion für Europa?" in *Die NS-Diktatur im deutschen Erinnerungsdiskurs,* ed. Wolfgang Bergem (Opladen, 2003), 227–38.
4. Konrad Jarausch and Michael Geyer, *Shattered Past: Reconstructing German Histories* (Princeton, 2003), 114.
5. Daniel Levy and Natan Sznaider, "Memory Unbound: The Holocaust and the Formation of Cosmopolitan Memory," *European Journal of Social Theory* 5, no. 2 (2002): 87–106, 88. For a more detailed exposition of this argument see Daniel Levy and Natan Sznaider, *Erinnerung im globalen Zeitalter: Der Holocaust* (Frankfurt am Main, 2001). For a critique see Oliver Marchart, Vrääth Öhner, and Heidemarie Uhl, "Holocaust revisited – Lesarten eines Medienereignisses zwischen globaler Erinnerungskultur und nationaler Vergangenheitsbewältigung," *Tel Aviver Jahrbuch für deutsche Geschichte* 31 (2003): 307–34, esp. 327–34.
6. Levy and Sznaider, *Erinnerung im globalen Zeitalter,* 14.
7. Jeffrey Shandler, *While America Watches: Televising the Holocaust* (New York, 1999), 176.
8. See in particular Lutz Niethammer, *Kollektive Identität: Heimliche Quellen einer unheimlichen Konjunktur* (Reinbek, 2000).
9. Jan Assmann, *Das kulturelle Gedächtnis: Schrift, Erinnerung und politische Identität in frühen Hochkulturen,* 2nd ed. (Munich, 1997), 132 (original emphasis).
10. This differentiation is indebted to Jürgen Straub, "Identität," in *Handbuch der Kulturwissenschaften,* 3 vols., ed. Friedrich Jaeger and Burkhard Liebsch (Stuttgart and Weimar, 2004), 1:277–303: "Damit geht es nicht mehr um eine *normierende Vorschrift,* sondern um eine *rekonstruierende Nachschrift* in erfahrungswissenschaftlicher Absicht." (299; original emphasis).
11. Among the classic texts are Hugh Seton-Watson, *Nations and States: An Enquiry into the Origins of Nations and the Politics of Nationalism* (London, 1977); Benedict

Anderson, *Imagined Communities: Reflections on the Origins and Spread of Nationalism* (London, 1983); Eric Hobsbawm and Terence Ranger, eds., *The Invention of Tradition* (New York, 1983); Ernest Gellner, *Nations and Nationalism* (Ithaca, NY, 1983); Eric J. Hobsbawm, *Nations and Nationalism Since 1780: Programme, Myth, Reality* (New York, 1990); John R. Gillis, ed., *Commemorations: The Politics of National Identity* (Princeton, 1994); Helmut Berding, ed., *Nationales Bewusstsein und kollektive Identität* (Frankfurt am Main, 1994). Recent case studies include John Bodnar, *Remaking America: Public Memory, Commemoration, and Patriotism in the Twentieth Century* (Princeton, 1992); Linda Colley, *Britons: Forging the Nation, 1707–1837* (New Haven, 1992); Edgar Wolfrum, *Geschichtspolitik in der Bundesrepublik Deutschland: Der Weg zur bundesrepublikanischen Erinnerung 1948–1990* (Darmstadt, 1999); Maria Bucur, *Birth of a Nation: Commemorations of December 1, 1918, and National Identity in Twentieth-Century Romania* (West Lafayette, IN, 2001); Patrice M. Dabrowski, *Commemorations and the Shaping of Modern Poland* (Bloomington, IN, 2004). See also the voluminous projects on national sites of memory in France and Germany: Pierre Nora, ed., *Les lieux de mémoire*, 7 vols. (Paris, 1984–1992); Etienne François and Hagen Schulze, eds., *Deutsche Erinnerungsorte*, 3 vols. (Munich, 2001).

12. See J. B. Harley and David Woodward, eds., *The History of Cartography*, 4 vols. (Chicago, 1987–1998); J. B. Harley, "Maps, Knowledge and Power," in *The Iconography of Landscape: Essays on the Symbolic Representation, Design and Use of Past Environments*, ed. Denis Cosgrove and Stephen Daniels (New York, 1988), 277–312; David Buisseret, ed., *Monarchs, Ministers and Maps: The Emergence of Cartography as a Tool of Government in Early Modern Europe* (Chicago, 1992); Derek Gregory, *Geographical Imaginations* (Cambridge, MA, 1994); Gearóid Ó. Tuathail, *Critical Geopolitics: The Politics of Writing Global Space* (Minneapolis, MN, 1996); Jeremy Black, *Maps and History: Constructing Images of the Past* (New Haven, and London, 1997); Matthew Edney, *Mapping an Empire: The Geographical Construction of British India, 1765–1843* (Chicago, IL, 1997); Guntram Henrik Herb, *Under the Map of Germany: Nationalism and Propaganda 1918–1945* (London and New York, 1997); Jürgen Osterhammel, "Die Wiederkehr des Raumes: Geopolitik, Geohistorie und historische Geographie," *Neue Politische Literatur* 43, no. 3 (1998): 374–97; Karl Schlögel, *Im Raume lesen wir die Zeit: Über Zivilisationsgeschichte und Geopolitik* (Munich, 2003).

13. Max Weber, "Die 'Objektivität' sozialwissenschaftlicher und sozialpolitischer Erkenntnis" (1904), in Max Weber, *Gesammelte Aufsätze zur Wissenschaftslehre*, ed. Johannes Winckelmann, 7th ed. (Tübingen, 1988), 146–214, 180.

14. See Denis Wood, *The Power of Maps* (New York, 1992).

15. Hans-Dietrich Schultz, "Raumkonstrukte in der klassischen deutschsprachigen Geographie des 19./20. Jahrhunderts im Kontext ihrer Zeit: Ein Überblick," *Geschichte und Gesellschaft* 28, no. 3 (2002): 343–77, 376.

16. Mark Neocleous, "Off the Map: On Violence and Cartography," *European Journal of Social Theory* 6, no. 4 (2003): 409–25, esp. 421, 417.

17. On mental maps see Frithjof Benjamin Schenk, "Mental Maps: Die Konstruktion von geographischen Räumen in Europa seit der Aufklärung," *Geschichte und Gesellschaft* 28, no. 3 (2002): 493–514.

18. See Schlögel, *Im Raume lesen wir die Zeit*, 95.

19. See Detlef Junker, *Power and Mission: Was Amerika antreibt* (Freiburg, 2003), 167.
20. Editorial, "Targets of Opportunity," *Life*, 14 August 1950, 30, quoted in John Fousek, *To Lead the Free World: American Nationalism and the Cultural Roots of the Cold War* (Chapel Hill, NC, and London, 2000), 176.
21. Peter Burke, "Westliches historisches Denken in globaler Perspektive – 10 Thesen," in *Westliches Geschichtsdenken: Eine interkulturelle Debatte*, ed. Jörn Rüsen (Göttingen, 1999), 31–52, 32.
22. See David Gress, *From Plato to NATO: The Idea of the West and Its Opponents* (New York, 1998), esp. 29–48.
23. See Stanford political scientist Robert A. Walker's interjection during a conference at the Institute for European History in Mainz, in Martin Göhring, ed., *Europa – Erbe und Aufgabe: Internationaler Gelehrtenkongress Mainz 1955* (Wiesbaden, 1956), 272.
24. William P. Bundy, Memorandum for Sullivan, Truehart, Jorden, and Thomson, Subject: Draft Speech for Delivery by Secretary McNamara on March 26, 17 March 1964, box 3, Records of the Special Assistant to the Under Secretary for Political Affairs, 1963–1965, Lot 67D554, Record Group (RG) 59, National Archives II, College Park, MD (hereafter: NA). For McNamara's trip and his ensuing report to the president and National Security Council see Robert D. Schulzinger, *A Time for War: The United States and Vietnam, 1941–1975* (New York, 1997), 139–41, and Fredrik Logevall, *Choosing War: The Lost Chance for Peace and the Escalation of War in Vietnam* (Berkeley, 1999), 122–29. McNamara's own recollections are in Robert S. McNamara (with Brian VanDeMark), *In Retrospect: The Tragedy and Lessons of Vietnam* (New York, 1995), 112–17.
25. See Memorandum From the Secretary of State's Special Assistant for Vietnam (Sullivan) to the Special Assistant in the Bureau of Far Eastern Affairs (Thomson), Subject: Comments on Proposed McNamara Speech, U.S. Department of State, ed., *Foreign Relations of the United States (FRUS), 1964–1968, vol. 1: Vietnam 1964* (Washington, D.C., 1992), 189–90.
26. See Michael Forrestal, Memorandum for the President, Subject: Draft Speech by Secretary McNamara on Vietnam (Forrestal Award Dinner), 21 March 1964, box 3, Country File-Vietnam, National Security File (NSF), Lyndon B. Johnson Library, Austin, TX (hereafter: LBJL). The draft copy with Forrestal's handwritten notes is ibid.; McNamara also called the president on the phone to announce that his draft was on the way. See *Taking Charge: The Johnson White House Tapes, 1963–1964*, ed. and with a commentary by Michael Beschloss (New York, 1997), 292–94.
27. News Release, Office of Assistant Secretary of Defense (Public Affairs), 26 March 1964, box 3, Country File-Vietnam, NSF, LBJL. See also Address before the James Forrestal Memorial Awards Dinner of the National Security Industrial Association at Sheraton-Park Hotel, Washington, D.C., 26 March 1964, folder: SVN - Press & Policy Statements, box 37, RG 200, Records of Robert S. McNamara, NA. The text is printed in *Department of State Bulletin*, 13 April 1964, 562–70.
28. Kiderlen to Auswärtiges Amt, Subject: Vortrag des Gesandten Martin Hillenbrand in Los Angeles, 13 January 1966, B145/3043, Bundesarchiv Koblenz.
29. Policy Planning Council, PPC 16–61: Educative Diplomacy, 6 December 1961, box 2, Records of the Special Assistant to the Under Secretary for Political Affairs, 1963–1965, RG 59, NA.

30. Address in New Orleans at the Opening of the New Dockside Terminal, 4 May 1962, in *Public Papers of the Presidents of the United States (PPP): John F. Kennedy 1962* (Washington, D.C., 1963), 357–61, 360.

31. Address before a Joint Session of the Congress, 27 November 1963, *PPP: Lyndon B. Johnson*, 1:8.

32. Letter from Chancellor Erhard to President Johnson, undated (rec'd. 9 May 1964), *FRUS 1964–1968*, 15:79–80. For the German original see Institut für Zeitgeschichte, ed., *Akten zur Auswärtigen Politik der Bundesrepublik Deutschland* 1964 (Munich, 1995), 1:514–18, esp. 516 (hereafter: *AAPD*).

33. Memorandum of Conversation, 4 June 1965, *FRUS 1964–1968*, 2:718; Gespräch des Bundeskanzlers Erhard mit Präsident Johnson in Washington, 4 June 1965, *AAPD* 1965, 2:961–67, esp. 962.

34. Memorandum of Conversation, Subject: Harriman's Moscow Conversation and Related Subjects, 24 July 1965, box 194, NSF Germany, LBJL.

35. Congressional Reception, 12 February 1965, LBJ Papers, Congressional Briefings, box 1, LBJL.

36. James Gilbert, "The Teach-in: Protest or Co-optation," reprinted in *The New Left: A Documentary History*, ed. Massimo Teodori (Indianapolis, IN, and New York, 1969), 240–46, 245.

37. SDS, "America and the New Era," ibid., 172–82, 173.

38. Rudi Dutschke, "Diskussion: Das Verhältnis von Theorie und Praxis," in *Subversive Aktion: Der Sinn der Organisation ist ihr Scheitern,* ed. Frank Böckelmann and Herbert Nagel (Frankfurt am Main, 1976), 190–95, 192.

39. Speech by Wolfgang Lefèvre before the Konvent, 26 October 1965, folder: SDS Vietnam Horlemann 1966, B1, Archivbereich 'APO und Soziale Bewegung' im Zentralinstitut für sozialwissenschaftliche Forschung der Freien Universität Berlin (hereafter: AASB). See also Wolfgang Lefèvre, "Mir schien jedes Mittel recht. Gespräch mit dem ehemaligen 1. AStA-Vorsitzenden," reprinted in *Freie Universität Berlin 1948–1973: Hochschule im Umbruch (Dokumentation)*, vol. 4: *Die Krise 1964–1967*, ed. Siegward Lönnendonker and Tilman Fichter, with Claus Rietzschel (Berlin, 1975), 245; Tilman Fichter and Siegward Lönnendonker, *Kleine Geschichte des SDS: Der Sozialistische Deutsche Studentenbund von 1946 bis zur Selbstauflösung* (Berlin, 1977), 89.

40. See Wilfried Mausbach, "Auschwitz and Vietnam: West German Protest Against America's War During the 1960s," in *America, the Vietnam War, and World: Comparative and International Perspectives,* ed. Andreas W. Daum, Lloyd C. Gardner, and Wilfried Mausbach (New York, 2003), 279–98.

41. Wilhelm Bauer, "Positionen in Vietnam," *Neue Kritik* 6, no. 29 (1965): 6–8; Georg W. Alsheimer, "Amerikaner in Vietnam," *Das Argument* 8, no. 36 (1966): 2–4.

42. Quoted in Ingo Juchler, *Die Studentenbewegungen in den Vereinigten Staaten und der Bundesrepublik Deutschland der sechziger Jahre: Eine Untersuchung hinsichtlich ihrer Beeinflussung durch Befreiungsbewegungen und –theorien aus der Dritten Welt* (Berlin, 1996), 258.

43. See the list of photographs in folder SDS, Vietnam Ausstellung 10.-20. Dez., B II 1965, AASB.

44. Peter Weiss, "Vietnam," *Dagens Nyheter*, 2 August 1966. Although first published in a Swedish newspaper, Weiss's intervention was widely disseminated in Germany. My

quotation is from a leaflet that reprints the article next to a warning that the German government might send troops to Vietnam: Hans Ewert, *Deutsche an die Front!*, box 21, Jürgen Klein collection (SDS Hamburg), Archiv des Hamburger Instituts für Sozialforschung (HIS). On Peter Weiss' *The Investigation* see Peter Reichel, *Erfundene Erinnerung: Weltkrieg und Judenmord in Film und Theater* (Munich, 2004), 228–41; Robert Cohen, "The Political Aesthetics of Holocaust Literature: Peter Weiss's *The Investigation* and Its Critics," *History and Memory* 10, no. 2 (1998): 43–67.

45. See Erich Fried, *und Vietnam und* (Berlin, 1996); Peter Härtling, "Gegen rhetorische Ohnmacht: Kann man über Vietnam Gedichte schreiben?" *Der Monat* 19, no. 224 (1967): 57–61; Harald Hartung, "Poesie und Vietnam: Eine Entgegnung," ibid., no. 226 (1967): 76–79.

46. Günther Anders, "Der amerikanische Krieg in Vietnam oder Philosophisches Wörterbuch heute," *Das Argument* 9, no. 45 (1967): 349–97, esp. 360; see also Günther Anders, *Visit Beautiful Vietnam: ABC der amerikanischen Aggressionen heute* (Cologne, 1968).

47. Klaus Harpprecht, "Im Stande der Schuld," *Der Monat* 20, no. 234 (1968): 4.

48. Monika Steffen, "Tiere an Ketten – SDS und Horkheimer," *Diskus* 17, no. 5 (1967): 11, reprinted in *Frankfurter Schule und Studentenbewegung: Von der Flaschenpost zum Molotowcocktail 1946–1995*, 3 vols., ed. Wolfgang Kraushaar (Hamburg, 1998), 2:263.

49. Der Senator für Inneres (Abteilung IV), *Bericht über die auf der 'Internationalen Vietnam–Konferenz' am 17. Februar 1968 in West–Berlin gehaltenen Reden*, Berlin 1968 (typewritten), 25.

50. Michael Baumann, *Wie alles anfing* (Munich, 1975), 40.

51. Jillian Becker, *Hitler's Children: The Story of the Baader-Meinhof Terrorist Gang* (London, 1977), 41.

52. See Andreas Baader, Gudrun Ensslin, Thorwald Proll, and Horst Söhnlein, *Vor einer solchen Justiz verteidigen wir uns nicht! Schlußwort im Frankfurter Kaufhausbrandprozeß. Mit einem Nachwort von Bernward Vesper und einer Erklärung des SDS Berlin* (Berlin, 1968), 19–25. See also Becker, *Hitler's Children*, 78–88; Gerd Koenen, *Vesper, Ensslin, Baader: Urszenen des deutschen Terrorismus* (Cologne, 2003), 171–83.

53. Quoted in Jeremy Varon, *Bringing the War Home: The Weather Underground, the Red Army Faction, and Revolutionary Violence in the Sixties and Seventies* (Berkeley, 2004), 210. See also Stefan Aust, *Der Baader Meinhof Komplex* (Hamburg, 1986), 231–37.

54. Quoted in Aust, *Der Baader Meinhof Komplex*, 388–89.

55. See ibid., 562–63. See also Martin Klimke and Wilfried Mausbach, "Auf der äußeren Linie der Befreiungskriege: Die RAF und der Vietnamkonflikt," in *Die RAF und der linke Terrorismus*, 2 vols., ed. Wolfgang Kraushaar (Hamburg, 2006), 1:620–43.

56. Richard Lindt and Peter Biesold, "Solidarität mit Vietnam," April 1965, file 117747, DY 24, Stiftung Archiv der Parteien und Massenorganisationen der DDR im Bundesarchiv, Berlin (SAPMO-DDR).

57. Jörn Rüsen, "Holocaust, Erinnerung, Identität," in *Das soziale Gedächtnis: Geschichte, Erinnerung, Tradierung*, ed. Harald Welzer (Hamburg, 2001), 243–59, 251.

58. Clemens Albrecht, Günter C. Behrmann, Michael Bock, Harald Homann, and Friedrich H. Tenbruck, *Die intellektuelle Gründung der Bundesrepublik: Eine Wirkungsgeschichte der Frankfurter Schule* (Frankfurt am Main and New York, 1999), 570.

59. See e.g. Detlef Siegfried, "Zwischen Aufarbeitung und Schlußstrich. Der Umgang mit der NS-Vergangenheit in beiden deutschen Staaten 1958–1969," in *Dynamische Zeiten: Die 60er Jahre in den beiden deutschen Gesellschaften,* ed. Axel Schildt, Detlef Siegfried, and Karl Christian Lammers (Hamburg, 2000), 77–113; Peter Reichel, *Vergangenheitsbewältigung in Deutschland: Die Auseinandersetzung mit der NS-Diktatur von 1945 bis heute* (Munich, 2001); Wilfried Mausbach, "Wende um 360 Grad? Nationalsozialismus und Judenvernichtung in der 'zweiten Gründungsphase' der Bundesrepublik," in *Wo '1968' liegt: Reform und Revolte in der Geschichte der Bundesrepublik,* ed. Christina von Hodenberg and Detlef Siegfried (Göttingen, 2006), 15–47.

60. See A. D. Moses, "The Forty-Fivers: A Generation Between Fascism and Democracy," *German Politics and Society* 17, no. 1 (1999): 94–126; Christina von Hodenberg, "Die Journalisten und der Aufbruch zur kritischen Öffentlichkeit," in *Wandlungsprozesse in Westdeutschland: Belastung, Integration, Liberalisierung 1945–1980,* ed. Ulrich Herbert (Göttingen, 2002), 278–311, esp. 298–309.

61. Raul Hilberg, "Developments in the Historiography of the Holocaust," in *Comprehending the Holocaust: Historical and Literary Research,* ed. Asher Cohen, Joav Gelber, and Charlotte Wardi (Frankfurt am Main and New York, 1988), 21.

62. See Tim Cole, *Selling the Holocaust: From Auschwitz to Schindler – How History is Bought, Packaged, and Sold* (New York, 1999), 100–101; Donald Bloxham, *Genocide on Trial: War Crimes Trials and the Formation of Holocaust History and Memory* (New York, 2001), 93–128; Sybille Steinbacher, *Auschwitz: Geschichte und Nachgeschichte* (Munich, 2004), 113–19.

63. See Shandler, *While America Watches,* 83–132; Cole, *Selling the Holocaust,* 9, 47–72.

64. For a detailed account of the controversy see Elizabeth Young-Bruehl, *Hannah Arendt: For Love of the World* (New Haven, and London, 1982), 328–78; see also Peter Novick, *The Holocaust in American Life* (Boston, and New York, 1999), 127–45.

65. Daniel Bell, "The Alphabet of Justice: Reflections on 'Eichmann in Jerusalem,'" *Partisan Review* 30, no. 3 (1963): 417–29, 427.

66. See Novick, *The Holocaust in American Life,* 136–37; Zygmunt Bauman, *Modernity and the Holocaust* (Ithaca, NY, 1992), 151–68, esp. 167.

67. Lewis Mumford, *The Myth of the Machine,* vol. 2: *The Pentagon Power* (New York, 1970), 279.

68. Carl Oglesby, "Trapped in a System," in *"Takin' It to the Streets": A Sixties Reader,* ed. Alexander Bloom and Wini Breines (New York, 1995), 220–21.

69. See Dorothy Rabinowitz, *New Lives: Survivors of the Holocaust Living in America* (New York, 1976), 193; Charles DeBenedetti, with Charles Chatfield, *An American Ordeal: The Antiwar Movement of the Vietnam Era* (Syracuse, NY, 1990), 127–28; Klaus Naumann, "Sympathy for the Devil? Die Kontroverse um Hannah Arendts Prozeßbericht 'Eichmann in Jerusalem,'" *Mittelweg 36* 2, no. 1 (1994): 65–79, 69.

70. U.S. House, *Anatomy of a Revolutionary Movement: Students for a Democratic Society.* Report by the Committee on Internal Security, 91st Congress, 2d Session, 6 October 1970 (Washington, DC, 1970), 77.

71. See Varon, *Bringing the War Home,* 6, 85–86, 120. The same is true for parts of the American Jewish community; see Judith Apter Klinghoffer, "The Transformation of the Holocaust Legacy," *SHOFAR* 14, no. 2 (1996): 53–75.

72. Dorothy Day to Daniel Berrigan, 31 May 1968, Berrigan Papers, Cornell University, quoted in DeBenedetti, *An American Ordeal,* 219.

73. Heinz Paechter, "Neuer Linksradikalismus in den USA," *Der Monat* 18, no. 211 (1966): 16–25. See also Varon, *Bringing the War Home,* 96–99.

74. Novick, *Holocaust in American Life,* passim; Norman G. Finkelstein, *The Holocaust Industry: Reflections on the Exploitation of Jewish Suffering* (New York, 2000). Tim Cole displays a similar tendency: although he realizes that the adaptation by American Jews of the Holocaust as a marker of their ethnic identity fails to explain why the same event acquired an iconographic status also for Gentiles, he ascribes the latter to the NBC miniseries of the late 1970s, thereby implicitly accepting that Jewish interests were pivotal in the 1960s. See Cole, *Selling the Holocaust,* 10–13.

75. Alan Mintz, *Popular Culture and the Shaping of Holocaust Memory in America* (Seattle and London, 2001), 16.

76. Horace Sutton, "Eichmann Goes on Trial: The Charged Air," *Saturday Review* 44, no. 14, 8 April 1961, 49, quoted in Shandler, *While America Watches,* 111.

77. See Alvin H. Rosenfeld, "Popularization and Memory: The Case of Anne Frank," in *Lessons and Legacies: The Meaning of the Holocaust in a Changing World,* ed. Peter Hayes (Evanston, IL, 1991), 243–78; Cole, *Selling the Holocaust,* 23–46; Mintz, *Popular Culture,* 17–19; 90–107; Shandler, *While America Watches,* 62–64, 69–79, 150.

78. For the following see Shandler, *While America Watches,* 133–54, esp. 147–50.

79. Quoted ibid., 148.

80. Sara R. Horowitz, "The Cinematic Triangulation of Jewish American Identity: Israel, America, and the Holocaust," in *The Americanization of the Holocaust,* ed. Hilene Flanzbaum (Baltimore and London, 1999), 142–66, 153. See also Mintz, *Popular Culture,* 107–22.

81. "Black Panther Party Platform and Program: What We Want, What We Believe," October 1966, reprinted in *The Black Panthers Speak,* 3rd ed., ed. Philip S. Foner, with a new foreword by Clayborne Carson (New York, 1995), 2–4.

82. See Jennifer B. Smith, *An International History of the Black Panther Party* (New York and London, 1999), 68.

83. Stokely Carmichael, "A Declaration of War," reprinted in Teodori, *The New Left,* 275–82, 276.

84. H. Rap Brown, *Die Nigger Die!* (1969) quoted from excerpts reprinted in *The Sixties Papers: Documents of a Rebellious Decade,* ed. Judith Clavir Albert and Stewart Edward Albert (New York, 1984), 151–58, 157. On the altercation within the African-American community over the war in Vietnam see Manfred Berg, "Guns, Butter, and Civil Rights: The National Association for the Advancement of Colored People and the Vietnam War, 1964–1968," in *Aspects of War in American History,* ed. David K. Adams and Cornelis A. van Minnen (Keele, 1997), 213–38.

85. David Hilliard, "The Ideology of the Black Panther Party," in Foner, *The Black Panthers Speak,* 123.

86. See, e.g., Michael Schmidtke, *Der Aufbruch der jungen Intelligenz: Die 68er Jahre in der Bundesrepublik und den USA* (Frankfurt am Main and New York, 2003), 150–52. The "KKK" usage was also taken up in Germany. The left-wing publishing house Verlag Roter Stern even released a primer titled *Amerikkka: Ein Lese-Bilder-Buch* (Frankfurt am Main, 1974) in its series "Learning, subversively." The spelling

was again popularized in the 1990s with the release of gangsta rapper Ice Cube's album *Amerikkka's Most Wanted.*

87. See William L. Van Deburg, *New Day in Babylon: The Black Power Movement and American Culture, 1965–1975* (Chicago and London, 1992), 129–91, esp. 138–40, 153, 170. Stokely Carmichael couched this idea in the following terms: "[M]ost importantly, we must understand that for black people the question of community is not a question of geography. It is a question of color. … For us the question of community is a question of color and our people – *not* geography, *not* land, not land, not land, not geography. That is to say that we break down the concept that black people living inside the United States are black Americans. That's nonsense." Carmichael, "A Declaration of War," 278.

88. See "You Don't Need A Weatherman To Know Which Way the Wind Blows, June 1969," in *Weatherman,* ed. Harold Jacobs (Berkeley, 1970), 51–90. Eldridge Cleaver characterized African-Americans as "a Black Trojan Horse" for Vietnam; see "The Black Man's Stake in Vietnam," *The Black Panther,* 23 March 1969, reprinted in Foner, *The Black Panthers Speak,* 100–104.

89. See Thomas Bender, "Historians, the Nation, and the Plenitude of Narratives," in *Rethinking American History in a Global Age,* ed. Thomas Bender (Berkeley, 2002), 1–21.

90. See Claus Leggewie, "Zugehörigkeit und Mitgliedschaft. Die politische Kultur der Weltgesellschaft," in Jaeger and Liebsch, *Handbuch der Kulturwissenschaften* 1:316–33.

91. See Charles Bright and Michael Geyer, "Where in the World Is America? The History of the United States in the Global Age," in Bender, *Rethinking American History,* 63–99, esp. 67.

92. See James T. Patterson, *Grand Expectations: The United States, 1945–1974* (New York, 1996), 348–55; Axel Schildt, *Moderne Zeiten: Freizeit, Massenmedien und „Zeitgeist" in der Bundesrepublik der 50er Jahre* (Hamburg, 1995), 262–83; Wulf Kansteiner, "Nazis, Viewers and Statistics: Television History, Television Audience Research and Collective Memory in West Germany," *Journal of Contemporary History* 39, no. 4 (2004): 575–98.

93. Bernhard Giesen, *Intellectuals and the German Nation: Collective Identity in an Axial Age,* trans. Nicholas Levis and Amos Weisz (New York, 1998), 145–63.

94. See Jürgen Habermas, "Zur Auseinandersetzung mit den beiden Diktaturen in Deutschland in Vergangenheit und Gegenwart," in *Materialien der Enquete-Kommission 'Aufarbeitung von Geschichte und Folgen der SED-Diktatur in Deutschland' (12. Wahlperiode des Deutschen Bundestages), vol. 9: Formen und Ziele der Auseinandersetzung mit den beiden Diktaturen in Deutschland,* ed. Deutscher Bundestag (Baden-Baden, 1995), 686–94.

95. Gabriel Motzkin, "Memory and Cultural Translation," *The Translatability of Cultures: Figurations of the Space Between,* ed. Sanford Budick and Wolfgang Isers (Stanford, 1996), 265–81, 276.

96. For an assessment of the historical significance of this period for American race relations, and the legacy it bequeathed to American society see Manfred Berg, "1968: A Turning Point in American Race Relations?" in *1968: The World Transformed,* ed. Carole Fink, Philipp Gassert, and Detlef Junker (New York, 1998), 397–420.

97. See Novick, *The Holocaust in American Life,* esp. 146–69.

98. See Alvin H. Rosenfeld, "The Americanization of the Holocaust," in *Thinking About the Holocaust: After Half a Century,* ed. Alvin H. Rosenfeld (Bloomington and Indianapolis, 1997), 119–50, esp. 127; James E. Young, "America's Holocaust: Memory and the Politics of Identity," in Flanzbaum, *The Americanization of the Holocaust,* 68–82, esp. 79–80.

99. Cole, *Selling the Holocaust,* 152.

100. Ibid., 155.

101. See Manfred Hennigsen, "The Place of the Holocaust in the American Economy of Evil," in *The German-American Encounter: Conflict and Cooperation between Two Cultures, 1800–2000,* ed. Frank Trommler and Elliot Shores (New York and Oxford, 2001), 198–211. Indeed, so successful has been the Americanization of the Holocaust that the latest twist in this mutual appropriation of each other's history saw Germany's most successful producer of historical documentaries, Guido Knopp, label his six-part series on the Holocaust—broadcast in 2000—"Holokaust" in an effort to reclaim from the Americans, through a symbolic act of spelling, what he considers to be German history. See Ole Frahm, "Von Holocaust zu Holokaust: Guido Knopps Aneignung der Vernichtung der europäischen Juden," *1999. Zeitschrift für Sozialgeschichte des 20. und 21. Jahrhunderts* 17, no. 2 (2002): 128–38.

Chapter 4

Topographies of Memory
The 1960s Student Movement in Germany and the US. Representations in Contemporary German Literature

Susanne Rinner

Introduction

This chapter explores the representation of the 1960s student movement in contemporary German literature. The theoretical frame for my analysis is informed by the discourse on remembering and forgetting, storytelling and silence. While my research is part of a larger project,[1] in this essay I am focusing on the representation of the United States and the American-German relationship within the literary representations of 1968.[2]

Told from the point of view of first-person narrators who participated in the events of 1968, the novels I am reading—*Frühstück mit Max* by Ulrike Kolb (2000), *Der Vorleser* by Bernhard Schlink (1995), and *Eduards Heimkehr* by Peter Schneider (1999)—construct the US as a geographical location as well as an imaginary space, allowing critical reflection on the 1960s student movement and on the transatlantic relationship.[3] I propose to read these literary texts as a contribution to the discourse on processes of cultural transfer and as an invitation to reflect on the construction of identities within a historical perspective.

1968 and Literature

The year 1968 as a historical, political, cultural, and social event enjoys a complex relationship with German literature. Many contemporary German authors played key roles during the German student movement. At the same time, 1968 marks the proclaimed death of literature. Hans Magnus Enzensberger, editor of the literary journal *Kursbuch*—one of the key publications of the 1960s student movement—published the widely read polemic "Gemeinplätze, die Neueste Literatur betreffend," boldly asserting the death of literature due to its inability to fulfill a political function in the struggles of the 1960s.[4] Sparking a heated public debate, Enzensberger's claim did not put an end to the publication of literature. In fact, in the same volume of the *Kursbuch* with the famous verdict, numerous literary texts and poems were published. The emerging debate over the function of literature led to a renewed interest in the possible topics that literary texts might address and in aesthetic questions. Thus, literary productivity and publication continued even after the proclaimed death of literature, and from this conflict emerged the later representations of the events of 1968 in German literature. In the immediate aftermath, texts such as *Heißer Sommer* (Uwe Timm, 1974), *Kerbels Flucht* (Uwe Timm, 1980), and *Lenz* (Peter Schneider, 1973) dealt with the '68ers' disillusionment about the failure of the movement to implement immediate fundamental change.

Since 1989, a continuously growing number of literary publications have dealt with the German student movement in the 1960s.[5] This renewed interest in 1968 expressed in literary texts coincided with the new political reality after the fall of the Berlin Wall and German unification, which initiated a debate over how to anchor the student movement within the history of a unified Germany. Current literary representations differ markedly from the novels published in the immediate aftermath of the student movement. Since they tell the story of the movement and its participants retrospectively, these current novels include reflective and self-reflective layers of recollections that shift meanings and challenge former approaches and attitudes.

Representation of the US in 1968 Memory Novels

I argue that remembering 1968, in the three novels by Kolb, Schlink, and Schneider, serves as the lens through which the American-German relations in the twentieth century are remembered and reevaluated. In fact, the texts seem to suggest that it is impossible to remember 1968 without also remembering the US and its importance for Germany in the twentieth century. The novels achieve this by structuring the remembered history as a history of three generations: the generation of parents who experienced and participated in the Third Reich, the '68ers who are narrating the stories, and their children, who constitute the third generation.

Distinguishing among three generations points not so much toward the actual birth date of the literary figures, but to "clusters of shared formative experience."[6] These experiences connect and divide the generations.[7] On the one hand, these experiences are passed on from one generation to the next. On the other hand, many protests of the younger generations take on the form of generational conflicts that create distance between the generations. From the viewpoint of the second generation, the first generation frequently passed on their experiences of the Third Reich as a form of silence. In the 1960s, the second generation protested against the way West Germany had dealt, or rather had failed to deal, with its Nazi past. The second generation spoke of the collective guilt of their parents and of the fascist environment their parents had created and raised them in, since the past had not ended yet. These second-generation West Germans considered themselves to be the victims of their parents, thus posing, in very problematic ways, as the historical victims of the Third Reich and replacing the actual victims.[8] In their literary memories, the second-generation narrators reflect on their failure to address their own responsibility or to investigate their own family histories by focusing on some abstract collective guilt.[9] Members of the third generation then turn away from their own parents because they disagree with their parents' attempts to fundamentally change the social structure of society during the 1960s and 1970s.

These generational experiences determine the representation of the United States and the relationship between the US and Germany. The novels construct the US as the land of exile for those members of the first generation who were forced to leave Nazi Germany and who were able to escape the Holocaust. The members of the second generation remember their ambivalent attitude toward the US during the 1960s, whereas their offspring do not seem to be burdened by history and view the US as the utopia of the globalized twenty-first century, albeit in problematic ways.

Temporalities and Topographies in the Discourse on Memory

Literary texts that are embedded in the discourse on memory create a meeting place for individual and culturally mediated memories. They connect personal experiences and historical events and shed light on the political ramifications of personal memories and the significance of historical and political events for the individual. Yet, literary texts differentiate themselves from autobiographies as well as from historiographies because they create possible worlds and thus are typically not confronted with claims or questions regarding their truth value or validity in terms of their representation and interpretation of the past. In fact, the interpretation of a literary text depends on the analysis of the specific qualities of the genre, its language use, the position of the narrator and the literary figures, and its intertextuality and historical context.

In this section I will outline and connect two theoretical considerations that form the basis for my claim that literary remembering is structured both temporally and spatially. The process of remembering constructs a three-dimensional palimpsest of layered memories that can be unearthed in the manner Walter Benjamin proposes in his short essay "Ausgraben und Erinnern," with the implications described therein.[10] On the one hand, literary texts as one medium among others (e.g., holidays, memorials, museums, art, films, music, and architecture) contribute to the continuous construction and deconstruction of cultural memory.[11] The model of the palimpsest thus visualizes the relations among literary texts that obtain additional meaning and significance through their reception and in literary histories. As outlined in the introduction, this is also true for the representation of 1968 in German literature. On the other hand, in certain literary genres, processes of remembering and forgetting often form the basis of the plot and structure the narrative. This is particularly true for autobiographies, autobiographical fiction, and fiction that is told from the perspective of the first-person narrator looking back at his or her life.

The Temporal Dimension of Memory

As a concept, memory refers to the past, the present, and the future. The word memory implies that the person who remembers refers to his or her own experiences in the past. Memories are shaped by the present in which they are remembered. Furthermore, memories determine which past is remembered and how the past is remembered in the future. As the analysis of the three novels shows, the narrators not only remember events that shaped their lives—mainly the student movement in the 1960s—but they also seem to "remember" the Nazi past, which they experienced only as very young children, if at all. Marianne Hirsch calls such memories, which are based not on one's own experiences but on transmission by others, whether via conversations, books, visual depictions of the past, or any other form of cultural representation, "postmemories."[12]

I propose to apply Hirsch's concept of postmemory to the analysis of the novels in order to shed light on the complex temporal dimensions they represent. Thus, the narrators tell stories based on both their own memories of the student movement and postmemories of the Nazi past. These memories and postmemories construct the temporal dimension in the novels. These layers question and critique each other and create problematic fusions and confusions. Their combination points to the constructedness of both memories and postmemories. While memories rest upon one's own experiences and construct those experiences from a present perspective, postmemories are removed one step further, since they are mediated by some form of cultural representation.

As former members of the student movement, the narrators revisit their memories of their involvement in that movement. This leads to a reassessment of their own roles within the movement and its function for Germany before and after the fall of the Berlin Wall. In particular, the narrators reevaluate their attitudes toward the Nazi past. While the students of 1968 protested against what they perceived as silence—the inability, and the unwillingness, of their parents' generation to confront their involvement in and with the Third Reich—and the continuation of fascism in West Germany even after 1945, thirty years later the narrators focus on their own shortcomings first, before condemning their parents and society as a whole.

These second-generation narrators emphasize the problematic aspects of their own engagement with the past, which was also marked by silences, in particular because of their inability and unwillingness to engage in a dialogue with their parents. In *Frühstück mit Max*, Nelly's parents are mentioned only in passing, described as the cliché family of the 1950s, focusing on the future, the "*Wieder-aufbau*" (reconstruction) and the "*Wirtschaftswunder*" (economic miracle). In *Der Vorleser*, Michael Berg seeks a conversation with his father, a professor of ethics, in order to find an answer to the question of whether he has the responsibility to reveal Hanna's illiteracy to the court. However, since the relationship between Berg and his parents is marked by emotional distance, he describes his dilemma on a very abstract level and avoids mentioning Hanna and his relationship with her; thus he receives only a very abstract answer from his father. In *Eduards Heimkehr*, Eduard Hoffmann only learns more about his grandfather, who bequeathed him an apartment complex, by talking with a Jewish survivor. His grandfather, who was excluded from the family memory, was not included in Eduard's interest in the past either, since as a member of the student movement Eduard was dealing with a general "*Vergangenheitsbewältigung*" (coming to terms with the past) and not with his own family history. Even his marriage to the daughter of Holocaust survivors does not spur a more personal engagement with Germany's past.

In addition, by posing as victims of the perceived fascist structures in West Germany, the students displace the historical victims of National Socialism, who did not find a space within the German discourse about National Socialism and the Holocaust in the 1960s. Literary texts bring to life memories as well as silences, absences, and voids that are often understood as forgetting. Revisiting their postmemories, the narrators question the sources that mediated them originally. Furthermore, they attempt to include voices that were previously forgotten, missing, absent, or silenced, in particular those of the victims of the Third Reich and their families. The narrators reassess their postmemories, which were often mediated through their own families, and complement them with the memories of the victims of the Nazis. I read this as an attempt to gain a more comprehensive understanding of the past and to give the victims a voice within the German discourse on National Socialism and the Holocaust as represented in German literature. These representations also stress the ongoing responsibility of the second and third generations for a past that will not go away.

The Spatial Dimension of Memory

The literary palimpsest of memories contains not only a temporal, but also a spatial dimension. Pierre Nora agrees with Maurice Halbwachs that individual memories are established within a social framework, from which they thus gain their meaning.[13] At the same time, the construction of memory within a society is based on a variety of individual representations of the past, which form narratives that are negotiated, accepted, and/or refuted by the public discourse. Nora argues that in premodern times societies experienced memory as a continuous reliving of the past through rituals, the passing on of traditions from one generation to the next, and the reliance on traditions that resisted modernization. Modern society, according to Nora, separates the past from memory. Due to this loss of the "milieux de mémoire," modern societies are forced to create "lieux de mémoire," specific locations and occasions of remembering in order to enable individuals and groups to gain access to the past. Nora concludes that this loss of the everyday experience of remembering as a lived and living tradition initiated the contemporary discourse on memory and remembering. Nora's definition of memory as a primitive or sacred form of accessing the past that is opposed to modern historical consciousness expresses a nostalgic longing for a past that has probably never existed in the proposed form. And while I do not agree with his fundamental critique of history and historiography as having destroyed the "milieux de mémoire," I find his concept of "lieux de mémoire" to be a useful analytical tool for analyzing the representation of space in literary texts.

In my reading, particular locations in the United States and Germany serve as topographies of memories that evoke the personal experiences of the narrators and the literary figures and point to questions of personal and national identity. Analyzing the literary representation of the United States and Germany as "lieux de mémoire" emphasizes their constructedness through processes of remembering and forgetting. These memories and postmemories evoke the geographical locations, their national boundaries, and the controversial images thereof. The representation of the United States after 1989 also evokes a displaced discussion about the German nation, national history, and national identity. In addition, the novels create the United States as a meeting place for the three generations and as a site of generational conflicts. While the second generation revisits its ambivalence toward the US in the 1960s, the importance of the country for members of the first generation who emigrated to the US in the 1930s and 1940s is recognized. The third generation places its dreams and hopes on a country that promises life, liberty, and the pursuit of happiness. The various representations of the United States do not offer access to historical, political, or social authenticity, yet the country serves as "lieux de mémoire" and thus adds layers to the palimpsest of memories and postmemories that structures these novels.

Remembering the United States:
A Site of Generational Conflicts

The three generations that mark the temporal structure of these 1968 memory novels evoke very different images of the United States. Furthermore, the United States serves as a site of generational conflict, both within a generation and among the generations. These projections onto, and appropriations of, the United States also point to the self-definitions of the three generations. I propose to read the three novels in light of their much differentiated constructions of the United States as a utopian imagination, as a land of exile and immigration, and as a country that often seems to entail political, social, and cultural extremes.

I am particularly focusing on the representation of the United States in the recollections of the second generation. The '68ers revisit their own past and their images of the US in the 1960s. During the time of the student movement, the '68ers' perception of the US as fascist often overshadowed their awareness that the US was also the country that initiated and inspired the worldwide protest movements. Revisiting this bifurcation allows the narrators to recognize the complexities of the transatlantic relation and to add a historical dimension that was often missing in the earlier debates, i.e., the important role the US played as the host to many emigrants and victims of the Nazi regime. In *Der Vorleser* and in *Eduards Heimkehr*, both narrators visit the United States in order to meet survivors of the Holocaust who emigrated there during the 1930s and 1940s. In addition, the third generation questions the second generation's ambivalence toward the United States. The third generation is now able to emphasize the utopian opportunities of a country that does not burden its inhabitants with the demands of a long history and promises individual freedom and the limitless pursuit of happiness.

The US during the 1960s: Country of Extremes

All three narrators remember their contradictions and ambivalences toward the United States in the 1960s. Even though the United States was a member of the Allied forces that liberated Germany from National Socialism—something the Germans had failed to accomplish themselves—and supported the democratization of West Germany, the members of the student movement did not perceive the US as a liberating, but rather as an imperialist and colonialist force. Furthermore, some of the characters fail to acknowledge that the movements on both sides of the Atlantic shared the same goals, such as the struggle against imperialism and colonialism and the fight for equality and peace, as well as the same methods of protesting, initiated by the outrage against oppression and exploitation of the Third World and against US military involvement in Southeast Asia.[14]

Leggewie points to the fact that the anti-authoritarian movement in the United States determined the themes—Vietnam and racism—and gave shape to spontaneous forms of action, such as teach-ins, sit-ins, and happenings that were extensively adopted and imitated on the other side of the Atlantic.[15] Gassert calls the anti-Americanism of the New Left an anti-Americanism "with America against America."[16] Thus, in their recollections, the narrators acknowledge that what looked like an outright rejection of the US in the 1960s was a much more complex process of rejection and appropriation that did not juxtapose Germany and the US but rather unified the younger generation in both countries against the governments in power.

In addition, many of the former German protesters moved to the United States. As the German government enacted laws banning radical activists from civil service employment, the so-called "*Radikalenerlass*," many of the protesters could not find work in their home country but found opportunities in the United States, which seemed more capable of reintegrating the protesters into mainstream society. This is indicated in *Eduards Heimkehr*. Eduard works as a professor of genetics in California, emphasizing that he did not leave Berlin on his own account but rather was denied an academic career in Germany because of his political past. Thus, the United States is able to confirm its image as the country of personal freedom and opportunities for everybody, even those who previously challenged American politics.

The US as the Land of Exile and Immigration

Despite the many shared aspects of the student movements in various countries, they were still distinct in their historical, cultural, and local situatedness. In Germany, this was marked by the engagement with the Nazi past. Michael Berg, the narrator in *Der Vorleser*, reconsiders the critical engagement with the German past by the members of the 1960s student movement. Feelings of guilt, shame, embarrassment, and complicity accompany him his whole life. Since Hanna Schmitz, his former lover and a convicted concentration camp guard who kills herself on the day she is to be released from prison, has named him as executor of her will, he travels to New York City to deliver Hanna's possession, an old tin can and some money, to the daughter of a survivor of the concentration camp where Hanna was a guard.

Even though Berg recounts the visit to New York only briefly, the visit receives a prominent place at the end of the novel and gains significance because it is the only overseas travel described by the narrator. During the meeting the atmosphere is cold, and Berg and the woman remain rather distant, a feeling emphasized by the fact that the woman's name is not mentioned. The street where she lives consists of modest and orderly apartment buildings, leaving a rather clinical impression that is mirrored in the description of the woman as matter-of-fact. Her neighborhood does not evoke the Manhattan that is often described in German novels that concentrate on its energy, fast pace, and diversity.[17]

The conversation focuses on Berg's relationship with Hanna. Prompted by the woman, Berg describes his relationship with Hanna. This is the first time he is able to admit his relationship with her. Neither during the time of the relationship with Hanna, nor during the trial, nor long after the trial, when he meets a former fellow-student at the funeral of the professor who taught the seminar accompanying the trial, was Berg able to tell either his parents or any of the other students about Hanna. Thus, it is surprising that Berg readily tells a stranger about Hanna. The survivor's daughter attempts to interpret Berg's experiences in light of her own experiences as a victim of National Socialism. She insinuates that Berg suffered throughout his life because of Hanna. Even though Berg rejects this interpretation, the fact that he decides to tell his story to someone who is connected to Hanna through historical events remains puzzling. While his confession could be seen as yet another attempt by a '68er to align himself with a historical victim of the Holocaust, it also points to the importance of the United States as a place where the individual is not burdened by German history, by the many attempts to come to terms with it, or by a specific perspective of and approach to history that is determined by being German. Instead, Berg is free to tell his life story. Furthermore, Berg seems to trust the survivor to understand the complexity of the emotions he is struggling with.

Even though this is an important step in working through his own life and a sign of dissolving identity constructions previously fixed by essentialist notions of national identity, it is still problematic that this is the main topic of conversation between a German and one of the victims of National Socialism, in particular since this is their first encounter. It seems symptomatic of the contemporary German approach to the past that the German perspective—often expressed as German suffering, which seems to relativize the suffering of those who were persecuted by the Nazis—is emphasized. At the end of the visit, the woman refuses to accept the money because she does not want to exchange money for redemption. However, she does accept the tin can, which replaces the one she lost in the camp.

This visit in New York is Berg's first encounter with a Jewish survivor. This is surprising, since the generation of the student movement emphasized the need to come to terms with the past. However, this generation's approach did not include a dialogue with those who suffered most during the Third Reich.[18] Instead of talking with survivors of the Holocaust, Berg visits a concentration camp twice during the time of Hanna's trial. On one of his trips to a camp, he angrily engages in an argument with a male member of his parents' generation. The conversation ends rapidly, signaling the breakdown in communication between the first and the second generation.

Berg is disappointed that visiting the concentration camp neither gives him access to the past nor allows him to engage in a dialogue with the past. Historical locations do not contain significance because they were the locations of historical events; rather, they gain significance because meaning is attributed to them by remembering. Since the Holocaust had not been publicly discussed in Germany for a long time, the historical locations are associated with few post-memories that Berg could refer to in order to access the past. For Berg, the sites of the Holocaust are neither "lieux" nor "milieux de mémoire."

In *Eduards Heimkehr*, a similar encounter between a survivor of the Holocaust and the narrator takes place, and the representation of the US and the transatlantic relationship play an even more prominent role. Peter Schneider tells the story of Eduard Hoffmann, a professor of genetics at a university in California who is married to the daughter of Holocaust survivors. After the fall of the Berlin Wall, Hoffmann accepts a position at a research institute in the former East Berlin. Even though Eduard is originally from Berlin, his return to the city is not a homecoming but a confrontation with a city that has changed as fundamentally as the political situation changed after German unification. Furthermore, Eduard is constantly tempted to compare the German and American ways of life.

Eduard inherits an apartment building in the former East Berlin that is occupied by squatters. To prevent Eduard from claiming his property, the squatters accuse his deceased grandfather of having acquired the house from the previous Jewish owners during the 1940s, thus profiting from the Nazi laws expropriating Jewish property. Eduard, who had not anticipated any of these difficulties when he accepted the inheritance, is not familiar with his family history and is determined to uncover the truth. He first consults the archives, which do not provide sufficient information. In an attempt to stress the importance of eyewitnesses, he discovers that the former owner's daughter lives in Florida.

Like the encounter described in *Der Vorleser*, his visit to Florida is characterized by an ironic distancing on the part of the Jewish woman called Edita Marwitz. She comments on the Germans' need to receive a pardon from Jewish survivors at a time when it is convenient and necessary for the Germans. She assures Eduard that his grandfather did not profit unduly from the political situation but in fact helped her father by buying the house at a fair price at a time when Jewish property was already being confiscated by the Nazis without compensation for the Jewish owners. She also adds her personal story to the mere legal facts and emphasizes that Eduard's grandfather did not help solely out of humanitarian reasons, but because secretly he was in love with her.

The encounters described in the two novels are similar not only in that they both take place in the US, but in that they also both involve a male narrator and an older Jewish woman. The women are the eyewitnesses who are asked to grant redemption and to lend their recollections in order to gain access to the historical events. Both women initiate a switch in the language that is spoken during the encounters. They greet their visitors in English and tell their stories in German—their mother tongue, as Edita Marwitz emphasizes.[19] I propose to read these literary representations of the meetings between the survivors and members of the second generation as an ironic inversion and a gendered critique of constructions of history and historiography traditionally dominated by male voices. As the narrators fail in their attempts to rely on "objective" representations of history, such as historical locations and documents, they need to seek out the female voices, which until that point have been forgotten. This adds female memories—remembering the public and the personal and their connections—to the historiography of the Holocaust, and emphasizes the necessity of storytelling in order to create a more complete and complex image of the past.[20]

These first attempts at a Jewish-German dialogue are problematic because they are seemingly self-serving. Without the obligation to pass on an inheritance in Berg's case or the need for information in Hoffmann's case, the Germans of the second generation would still not have sought the direct contact with the victims of the Third Reich. Both narrators comment on this failure and interpret it as a continuation of the problematic silence, neglect, and avoidance strategies inherited from the parents' generation, against all opposite assurances by the second generation to address the aftermath of the Third Reich in a different way than the previous generation.

Yet even though these encounters are problematic and characterize the Germans as naive at best or vicious at worst, they nevertheless give Jewish survivors a voice in contemporary German literature. The members of the second generation, who thought to differentiate and distance themselves from their parents' involvement in the past, reevaluate their behavior in the 1960s and change their approach via reflections and actions. The actual encounters take place in the United States, thus acknowledging the difficulty of the German-Jewish dialogue in Germany in the 1990s and the important role the US played in offering exile to refugees in the 1930s and 1940s. For this discourse, the US serves as the "lieux de mémoire," because only the distance from Germany and the visits in the homes of the survivors and refugees in the United States allow members of the second generation of Germans to remember their own life and to reassess their own approaches to the past.

The US as a Utopian Construct

Whereas in *Der Vorleser* and *Eduards Heimkehr* the United States serves as the meeting ground for the second generation and the survivors of Nazi Germany, the novel *Frühstück mit Max* tells the story of the encounter of Nelly and Max, members of the second and third generation respectively, in a coffee house in Manhattan. The chance meeting triggers the exchange of their memories. Nelly, who is visiting New York as a tourist, was Max's father's girlfriend and participated in raising Max, who now lives in Brooklyn and works in Manhattan as an architect. They remember the years they lived together in a communal living project in Berlin called "Mommsen" (named after the street where they lived, and invoking the renowned historian) and tell each other their life stories. Intertwined with and juxtaposed to the dialogue between the two characters are their individual memories. These reveal that Nelly and Max's experiences during the 1960s and their evaluations of those years differ greatly. Whereas Nelly remembers the dreams that inspired the generation of the '68ers and the attempts to realize them in the communal living project, Max emphasizes the chaos and neglect he experienced as a young boy, which he blames on the lack of a stable family structure. Even though Nelly's dreams have been shattered—she has separated from Max's father and battled alcoholism and depression—she still remembers the 1960s with fondness. Max, however, moved to the United States to distance himself from his father, the 1960s, and the historical burden Germany as a home imposes on its inhabitants.

In a book review of *Frühstück mit Max,* Reinhard Baumgart comments on the important function of New York City as the location of the novel.[21] He claims that the city enables the creation of balance between the past and the present and between the contradictory emotions triggered by the encounter between Max and Nelly and their memories. Baumgart stresses that placing the encounter in the US rather than in Berlin creates a distance and thus avoids any kind of nostalgic longing for the past. In addition, I would like to emphasize the importance of New York City as the seemingly appropriate background for Max's lifestyle.

Max's first visit to the city left such a strong impression that he decided to move there as soon as he had finished high school. Describing his emotions retrospectively, he refers to feeling high and being turned on by its atmosphere, using language that is usually employed to describe the effects of drug use. This attempt to free himself, and to live in a city that promises not only personal freedom but also liberation from the burden of having grown up in Germany, is at least linguistically overshadowed by implications of dependency and addiction. For Max, the burden of the past is not primarily the burden of national history, in particular National Socialism and the Holocaust, but of having grown up in a communal living project in Berlin during the late 1960s and 1970s. He detests the chaos he experienced there and is unable to forgive his father or to show any understanding for his father's attempt to raise his son in an anti-authoritarian manner.

The US seems to offer the third generation an opportunity to break away from the burden of family obligations and make a fresh start. In Nora's terms, immigration to the US leads to a loss of everyday experiences of remembering as a living tradition. However, in my reading of Max, this does not entail a utopian imagination of radical difference, since he limits himself to preserving or rather recreating a lifestyle that was already outdated in the 1960s. As his form of rebellion against his upbringing, he chooses to become an architect in an attempt to create order and impose structure, and he lives a neatly organized and regulated life within a nuclear family. Furthermore, Max does not settle in Manhattan, but in Brooklyn. Thus, he rarely experiences the rush of emotions that led to his migration to Manhattan; only if he has some domestic disagreement with his wife does he feel liberated on the Brooklyn Bridge on his way to work.

Nelly comments critically on Max's attempt to lead a self-determined life. When he describes his current life to her, in particular his obsession with his work, which actually leaves him very little time for anything else, including his family, she thinks that he is what they—the generation of 1968—used to call a "*Fachidiot*" (narrow–minded nerd), exposing him as a conformist adhering to the expectations of Western capitalist society. His rebellion gains significance as a rebellion only in light of his personal experience within his family's history. This rebellion will impact changes on the political level only in so far as such changes equalize historical and cultural difference, since his life lacks any engagement with specific historical events. This is indicated by the name of the coffee house—Space Untitled—where Nelly and Max meet. The design and atmosphere of the coffee house attract all generations despite their differences, foreshadowing the loss of any historical or cultural specificity due to processes of globalization. In that sense, Manhattan as a city full of contradictions, whose name means "heavenly earth," does indeed provide the space to reconcile difference, if only on the surface.[22]

Conclusion

Reassessing 1968 today means acknowledging that any attempt to deal with the Holocaust and National Socialism will turn out to be insufficient and only partially successful. As visualized in the image of the palimpsest, this is inherent in the problem, since this past will not go away and thus the only appropriate response to it is a constant process of remembering. Consequently, neither the parents' generation nor the '68ers learn how to explain and come to terms with the past; rather, each generation must find its own strategies, which will be contradicted, disputed, argued about, silenced, and expanded upon by the next generation.

At the same time, the contemporary literary representation of the 1960s student movement necessitates reconsideration of the impact and the significance of the movement. Some of the participants, as represented by the literary figures, paid a very high price for their political activism, ranging from death and injury to the exclusion from certain professions imposed by the German government, and to exploitation and self-exploitation by the various Marxist groups that formed in the 1970s.[23] Others were quite successful in their "*Marsch durch die Institutionen*," their march through the institutions, and achieved positions of considerable political, economic, and cultural influence. At the same time, all members of the 1960s student movement are confronted with the blame for current social problems. Rather than acknowledging the positive effects of a general liberation for a variety of formerly repressed groups, contemporary conservatives bemoan the loss of tradition expressed in essentialist notions of "Germanness," since the 1960s student movement ultimately supported the further democratization, Americanization, and globalization of West Germany.

The novels *Frühstück mit Max, Der Vorleser,* and *Eduards Heimkehr* contribute to the discourse on processes of cultural transfer and invite reflection on the construction of personal and national identities within a historical perspective. As literary texts, they emphasize the central role of storytelling within these discourses. As memory novels, they enable the study of the complex relation between the past, the present, and the future. They open poetic spaces that address remembering as well as forgetting. According to Umberto Eco, "forgetting" is impossible in language, since language always marks the absence and the void with linguistic signs that in turn make "forgetting" impossible.[24] Thus, different strategies of "forgetting" in literary representations can be interpreted as additional layers of recollections. This analysis entails a sense of play, since poetic spaces invite creativity and resistance to the demands imposed by everyday language use.

At the same time, some aspects of the novels I have been analyzing also entail an affirmation of the status quo. They seem to refer back to essentialist notions of identity, in particular with respect to what it means to be German, and they attempt to place contemporary literature firmly into a rather traditional German literary history. The narrator in *Der Vorleser* seems to suggest that in order to fill the vacuum left by the Third Reich one must construct a personal and national identity based on what is genuinely German and has remained unchanged over the last centuries: German language and literature. He sends Hanna sound recordings of German literature that he himself tapes. His choice consists of the traditional canon of German literature, since he claims that neither he nor Hanna needs any more experiments, and he does not include any literature outside the canon. Thus, he relies on the notion of *Kulturnation*,[25] the idea of shared literature, music, art, and philosophy that provides a cultural identity untainted by German history. That this in itself is a problematic notion, however, is made clear by the structure of the novel as well as its end: the narrator questions himself constantly, and every single assertion is contradicted by numerous considerations and rhetorical questions that are not answered. Furthermore, the attempt to rely on the canon of German literature cannot "save" Hanna or redeem her guilt or replace a dialogue between Berg and her—even after she is able to read and write and has listened to many tapes, she still decides to commit suicide the day before she is released from prison.[26]

In *Eduards Heimkehr,* the third generation as represented by the squatters draws on the moments of protest and revolutionary attempts in Germany in the last three centuries and appropriates these moments for its own purposes. However, the squatters' eclecticism and only fragmentary knowledge of history leads them to misrepresent Eduard's grandfather, whom they falsely accuse of having obtained the house illegally. Furthermore, their protest ends once they have the opportunity to purchase the apartment complex. The day they sign the contract is marked as their return into mainstream society: They cover the table with a white tablecloth, roll out the carpets, and offer coffee and homemade cake to Eduard. Like Max in Kolb's novel, who has already settled into a nine-to-five lifestyle with long work hours and rare meetings with his nuclear family, their future of a middle-class lifestyle seems predestined. One couple is expecting their first child and planning their wedding. Both novels seem to indicate that just like the chain of short-lived and failed revolutions in Germany, the revolutionary attitude expressed by a generation is only an adolescent phase, which the individual outgrows. Thus, many of the literary figures who participated in protest movements reenter a society that preserves the status quo of traditional definitions of identity and that is shaped by democratic and capitalist constitutions within a globalized world.

I suggest that the literary representations of the 1960s student movement add historical depth to the engagement with contemporary social movements. If the 1960s' critique of capitalism, imperialism, and militarism and its fight for equality, democracy, and peace foreshadow the contemporary critique of globalization, then perhaps the novels suggest that the fourth generation might learn from their grandparents in order to avoid the mistake the latter identified in the aftermath of the 1960s: "Wir sind nicht radikal gewesen!"[27]

Notes

1. I am currently working on a book manuscript, tentatively entitled *1968 and the German Literary Imagination. Literary Representations and Debates of the 1960s after 1989*.

2. I am using "1968" as the label for the events comprising the student movement, with the height of the German movement between 2 June 1967 (death of Benno Ohnesorg) and 11 April 1968 (Rudi Dutschke wounded by gunshots).

3. Ulrike Kolb, *Frühstück mit Max* (Stuttgart, 2000); Bernhard Schlink, *Der Vorleser* (Zurich, 1995), *The Reader,* trans. Carol Brown Janeway, (New York, 1997); Peter Schneider, *Eduards Heimkehr* (Berlin, 1999), *Eduard's Homecoming,* trans. John Brownjohn (New York, 2000).

4. Hans Magnus Enzensberger. "Gemeinplätze, die Neueste Literatur betreffend," *Kursbuch* 15 (1968): 187–97.

5. Among them: Sophie Dannenberg, *Das bleiche Herz der Revolution* (2004), Klaus Modick, *Der Flügel* (1994), Sten Nadolny, *Selim oder die Gabe der Rede* (1990), Robert Schindel, *Gebürtig* (1992), Elke Schmitter, *Leichte Verfehlungen* (2002), Peter Schneider, *Skylla* (2005), Leander Scholz, *Rosenfest* (2000), Franz Maria Sonner, *Als die Beatles Rudi Dutschke erschossen* (1996), Franz Maria Sonner, *Die Bibliothek des Attentäters* (2001), Heipe Weiss, *Fuchstanz* (1999), Ulrich Woelk, *Rückspiel* (1993) and Ulrich Woelk, *Die letzte Vorstellung* (2002).

6. Saul Friedländer, "History, Memory and the Historian," in *Gedächtnis, Geld und Gesetz: Vom Umgang mit der Vergangenheit des Zweiten Weltkriegs,* ed. Jakob Tanner and Sigrid Weigel (Zurich, 2002), 68. See also the following contributions to the discourse on generational history and memory: Heinz Bude, "Die Erinnerung der Generationen," *Vergangenheitsbewältigung am Ende des 20. Jahrhunderts,* ed. Helmut König, Michael Kohlstruck, and Andreas Wöll (Opladen and Wiesbaden, 1998), 69–85; and Christina Schneider, Cordelia Stillke, and Bernd Leineweber, *Das Erbe der Napola: Versuch einer Generationengeschichte* (Hamburg, 1996); and Sigrid Weigel, "'Generation' as a Symbolic Form: On the Genealogical Discourse of Memory since 1945," *Germanic Review* 77, no. 4 (2002): 264–77.

7. See the insightful essay by Salomon Korn who uses the term "geteilte Erinnerung" to point to the shared and separating aspects of the memory of the Holocaust for Germans and Jews. This concept is also applicable to the different generations con-

stituting the memory discourse: Salomon Korn, *Geteilte Erinnerung: Beiträge zur 'deutsch-jüdischen' Gegenwart* (Berlin, 1999).

8. This aspect has been well explored with respect to the "Väterliteratur" published in the 1970s. Furthermore, many 68ers comment on this aspect in their autobiographical and biographical accounts. Cf. Renate Siebert, "Don't Forget: Fragments of a Negative Tradition," in *International Yearbook of Oral History and Life Stories: Memory and Totalitarianism,* ed. Luisa Passerini (London, 1992), 165–77, 166: "'We are all Jewish', we used to cry in student demonstrations in Germany in 1968."

9. Mark Roseman, ed., *Generations in Conflict: Youth Revolt and Generation Formation in Germany 1770–1968* (Cambridge, 1995), 45: "It was a curious fact that although the 1968 generation wanted to break through the taboos and the silences it was not prepared to acknowledge its own vulnerability or to confront fully its own relationship with the past."

10. Walter Benjamin, "Ausgraben und Erinnern," in *Gesammelte Schriften,* 7 vols., ed. Tillman Rexroth (Frankfurt, 1981), 4.1: 400–401.

11. For further discussion see Peter Reichel, *Politik mit der Erinnerung: Gedächtnisorte im Streit um die nationalsozialistische Vergangenheit* (Munich, 1995) and James E. Young, *At Memory's Edge: After-Images of the Holocaust in Contemporary Art and Architecture* (New Haven and London, 2000).

12. Marianne Hirsch, *Family Frames: Photography, Narrative, and Postmemory* (Cambridge, 1997).

13. Pierre Nora, "Between Memory and History: Les Lieux de Mémoire" *Representations* 26, no. 1 (1989): 7–24; Maurice Halbwachs, *The Collective Memory,* trans. Francis J. Ditter, Jr., and Vida Yazdi Ditter (New York, 1980).

14. See Martin Klimke's contribution to this volume.

15. Claus Leggewie, "'1968': A Transatlantic Event and Its Consequences," in *The United States and Germany in the Era of the Cold War, 1945–1990: A Handbook,* 2 vols., ed. Detlef Junker (New York, 2004), 2:421–29.

16. Philipp Gassert, "'With America against America': Anti-Americanism in West Germany," in Junker, *Era of the Cold War,* 2:502–509.

17. For an overview of the subject in German literature after 1945 see Sigrid Bauschinger, "Mythos Manhattan. Die Faszination einer Stadt," in *Amerika in der deutschen Literatur: Neue Welt, Nordamerika, USA,* ed. Sigrid Bauschinger, Horst Denkler and Wilfried Malsch (Stuttgart, 1975), 382–97.

18. The only notable exception is the law professor who was in exile for unknown reasons and who teaches the seminar focused on the Nazi trials that Berg enrolls in as a law student in the 1960s.

19. All four characters are not completely comfortable using English, pointing to the importance of language for the purposes of identity constructions. In particular, both Berg and Hoffmann emphasize that, for them, texts written in English and conversations in English always create a distance and do not cause the same immediate affective reactions as those in German. In *Eduards Heimkehr* the language switch is not only talked about, but integrated in the text: The first couple of sentences of the dialogue between Hoffmann and Marwitz are written in English.

20. In particular in *Der Vorleser* the difference and complementary necessity of historical research, personal memory, and storytelling is emphasized: in the 1960s, the woman

whom Berg visits had published a book about the camp that the law students used in order to research the Holocaust.

21. Reinhard Baumgart, "Ferne Zeit, ganz nah," *Die Zeit,* 18 May 2000, 55.

22. Bauschinger, "Mythos Manhattan: Die Faszination einer Stadt," 396.

23. For the last aspect, see Gerd Koenen, *Das Rote Jahrzehnt: Unsere kleine deutsche Kulturrevolution 1967–77* (Cologne, 2001).

24. Umberto Eco, "An Art Oblivionalis? Forget It!" *Publication of the Modern Language Association of America* 103 (1988): 254–61.

25. For a discussion of that concept see Stephen Brockmann, *Literature and German Reunification* (Cambridge, 1999).

26. After the extremely successful initial reception of the novel in the US, mostly due to the enthusiastic review in Oprah's book club, the more recent reception by American scholars has been more critical.

27. "We have not been radical!" See "Wir haben Fehler gemacht." Rede von Peter Schneider vor der Vollversammlung aller Fakultäten der Freien Universität Berlin, 5 May 1967, http://www.glasnost.de/hist/apo/fehler.html. Accessed 17 August 2009.

Chapter 5

"We too are Berliners"

Protest, Symbolism, and the City
in Cold War Germany

Carla MacDougall

On 11 June 1982, US President Ronald Reagan visited West Berlin after a summit
meeting of the NATO Council in Bonn one day before. To the embarrassment of
the political elite, hundreds of thousands of peace and anti-nuclear demonstrators came out on the streets of Bonn and West Berlin to protest against Reagan's
foreign and defense policies concerning rearmament, and against NATO's security strategies.[1] The belligerent tone of the new Reagan administration, demonstrated by the president's explicit commitment to the military buildup already
begun under President Jimmy Carter, and the implementation of NATO's 1979
double-track decision to deploy intermediate-range nuclear missiles (INF) in
several Western European countries, had sparked an upsurge in anti-nuclear and
peace protests across the continent. Barely into the first year of Reagan's first
term as president, both Americans and West Germans perceived his administration as marking an important shift in the international power dynamics of
the Cold War, and especially of the complex relations between these two countries. Divergent interests between the Federal Republic and the United States
regarding military strategy and foreign policy, such as détente and arms control,
widened with the advent of the "Second Cold War," a second period of intense
rivalry between the superpowers depicted most clearly by Ronald Reagan's confrontational anti-communist rhetoric.[2]

In terms of West German and American relations, the new Reagan administration embodied an already visible estrangement between the two countries.[3]
This was a moment when the threat of nuclear war (augmented by anxieties that
it would take place on German soil) seemed closer than it had in decades. Peace
activists had been organizing throughout the 1970s in response to West German
defense policies, but mass protests of peace demonstrators first became animated
by the bellicose rhetoric of the Reagan presidency and the related concern that
the American president could quite possibly instigate a third world war.[4] The
salience of the peace protests in West Berlin, and more generally in West Germany, owed much to the country's vulnerable geostrategic position in Cold War

Europe. The growth of the peace movement in the early 1980s presented a domestic problem for Chancellor Helmut Schmidt, who, in the face of increased opposition within his own party and by protest groups, was confronted with the task of defending his support for INF deployment. Schmidt saw the modernization of intermediate-range nuclear forces as crucial to European security, yet this vision clashed with Reagan's arms-control policy, a policy focused instead on restoring American military superiority, which Reagan believed to be weakened during the era of détente. Schmidt's efforts to maintain a delicate balance between a strong alliance with the West (i.e., the United States) while endorsing an open policy of détente contributed to the rift between West Germany and the new US administration intent on abandoning this approach.

Despite diverging interests between the transatlantic partners, there was no doubt that a strong commitment to the alliance was a clear priority of the Schmidt government. Nonetheless, West German and US relations reached a low point in the early 1980s as the Schmidt government continued to assert West German interests independently of, and often in direct conflict with, the United States. In the context of uneasy transatlantic relations, this essay demonstrates how political elites relied on the symbolic function of Berlin to position West Germany as a "reliable friend" with respect to the Western alliance and Reagan's America. I focus on two official visits to West Berlin in the early years of the Reagan administration, a visit by Secretary of State Alexander Haig in September 1981 and a visit by President Reagan in June 1982, to suggest a more nuanced understanding of the symbolic use of Berlin during the tumultuous final decade of the Cold War. Significantly, a wide spectrum of peace and anti-Reagan protest groups mobilized in West Berlin in the weeks and months leading up to both visits. In a city that continued to be defined by early Cold War events, the Berliners who gathered to show President Reagan that he was not welcome did not simply choose to reject the policies of a specific American administration, but in so doing proposed a radical reformulation of a city whose laurels had rested on its ritualistic ties to the United States. The discourse of local peace and anti-Reagan protests was clearly part of a larger dialogue concerning American rearmament that extended beyond West Germany's borders, despite the absence of explicit transnational links between protesters in West Berlin and the United States.[5]

That West Berlin held a position of supreme importance to the West, militarily, economically, and perhaps most important symbolically, has been well established.[6] Beginning at least with the Berlin Blockade in 1948–49 and lasting throughout the Cold War period, continual acts of (re)constructing Berlin served West German and Americans alike. This shared understanding of the meaning and history of West Berlin served as a stage onto which a carefully crafted image of the German-American friendship could be projected and acted out. The flow of American dollars, as well as West German funds, rebuilt a new, capitalist democratic Berlin out of the rubble of the western half of the former capital of

Nazi Germany. This essay is based on a belief that the space of West Berlin is crucial for gauging the complex and shifting relations between the United States and the Federal Republic toward the end of the Cold War era. The tensions inherent in the wide-reaching and long-term changes in the West German and American friendship came to a head in the events leading up to and during President Reagan's 1982 visit to West Berlin. An analysis of these tensions is necessary in order to fully understand the history of the left in post-1968 Germany, and more specifically the role of German attitudes toward the United States.

By the latter years of the Cold War, American presidential visits to West Berlin, or more specifically the Berlin Wall, had established themselves as ritualized acts, as they both drew upon the historical importance of positive German-American relations and recreated it for television cameras, reporters, and crowds of enthusiastic onlookers.[7] In 1982, confronted with Reagan's confrontational global politics, the massive protests of a sizeable number of West Berliners, and specifically how they were staged, offered an explicit challenge to this traditionally positive history; in doing so, these protests reflected the growing cracks in the long-cherished model of positive West German–American relations, challenging a central narrative of postwar Europe and the United States. Ultimately these challenges, which were rekindled in the relatively small context of West Berlin local politics, were to continue throughout the 1980s, and went on to redefine the meaning of the German left, as well as the contours of the German-American "partnership."

The peace marches of 1982 were but one element in a wave of protests between 1979 and 1983 that both confronted West German and US political leaders. In fact, in sheer numbers of participants this wave of peace and anti-nuclear protests surpassed the protest activities of the 1960s.[8] An undeniable element of anti-American rhetoric, long a mainstay of German protests on both the left and right, became clearly visible during the protest activism of this period, and indeed assumed a greater role in West German protest culture than it had in previous decades. Although this general trend was also true of other protest movements elsewhere in Europe at the time, the intimate involvement of the US in West German politics, culture, and society since 1945 bestowed a more complicated meaning on anti-American sentiments in West German protest movements.[9] The anti-Reagan demonstrations in West Berlin in 1981 and 1982 took place against this backdrop of fraught German-American relations, during a time when the US first began to develop concerns over West Germany's commitment to the security of the Atlantic Alliance. The purpose of this essay is not to enter into the discussion of West German (leftist) anti-Americanism, but rather to examine the ways in which both official and alternative discourse utilized the symbolic power of West Berlin in a key turning point in the history of West German–American relations.[10] Through an analysis of these tense years of the early 1980s, I will argue that these protests by the West German left were central signposts of a larger shift in international relations.

Of course, the discernible symbolic power of Berlin is not unique to the Cold War period. Berlin enjoyed an iconic status nationally and internationally during Imperial, Weimar, and Nazi Germany, when the erstwhile capital held a central place in the political, cultural, and social debates that have shaped our understanding not only of Germany itself, but of the nature of European modernity. For example, as the *"grösste Mietskasernestadt der Welt"*[11] (world's greatest tenement city), Berlin was emblematic of the social extremes of the nineteenth-century industrial capital; as the home of modern architecture in the 1920s it became a symbol of modernity in the twentieth century. Most vividly, in 1945 the city marked the global ambitions and then absolute defeat of Nazi Germany. However, in the period between 1945 and 1989 the western half of Berlin not only constituted the social identity of its residents as "good" capitalists, in opposition to their unfortunate brothers in the city's other half: as *the* symbol of the Cold War, the divided city with its western section embedded deep inside of the Soviet sphere, it also represented both the threat of communism and the vital importance of Western capitalism as a counterbalance and bulwark. Berlin ultimately came to embody the political and moral superiority of the West, and above all the United States, the most extreme example of both capitalism and democracy. Already in the immediate postwar period the Marshall Plan and the Berlin Blockade succeeded in firmly displaying to an avidly watching world this economic, moral, and political superiority over the Soviets, at the same time, of course, capturing the devotion of the West Berliners.

After surrendering its political status as the capital of Germany and losing its economic vitality as a result of the division, Berlin's symbolic power became all the more crucial to the dynamic process of reinventing an identity for the western half of the city, the country, and ultimately the "Western world." The image of West Berlin that was projected to the world in the first decades of the Cold War was one built on the idea of the city as an outpost of Western democracy in a divided Europe, a site that served as grounds for the US to continue investing in the city. During reconstruction, the role of the US political establishment in packaging West Berlin as a countermodel to communist societies and, in turn, into a partial remaking of itself, cannot be underestimated. In this process of creating a "new" Berlin in postwar Europe, America, as Andreas Daum has argued, clung to a perception of the city as a place that mirrored specific historical myths and political visions of the United States.[12]

According to Daum, the dissonance between how Americans imagined West Berlin, and Berliners' perception of themselves and their city grew steadily wider throughout the Cold War, reaching new heights during the anti-Vietnam student protests of the 1960s.[13] As is now well documented, the mid to late 1960s saw the first fractures in the idealized view of America that West German students had grown up with.[14] The expectations of a benevolent and morally credible America clashed with the reality of the civil rights movement and Vietnam. Yet as Mary Nolan notes in her detailed analysis of anti-Americanism and Americanization in Germany, the protests against the Vietnam War led by West German students did not mark a definitive worsening of German-American relations.[15] She argues instead that the political anti-Americanism of the '68ers found little resonance in broader discourse, remaining essentially a fringe phenomenon.[16] Nolan, along with contemporary observers, considers the early 1980s to in fact be the transformative phase in the ever more conflicted relationship between West Germany and the United States.[17]

To be sure, the loaded symbolism that defined the character of West Berlin did not operate with equal intensity throughout the four Cold War decades. The 1971 Four Power Agreement, which marked an international acceptance of the division of Berlin, deescalated the fear of imminent conflict within divided Germany. For the West, both the FRG and the US, the agreement also marked a gradual decrease in popular and political interest in West Berlin, its status no longer tensely ambiguous. In a practical sense, the agreement also "normalized" the lives of West Berliners, as access in and out of the city, as well as more casual dealings vis-à-vis daily amenities, became easier.[18] In the domain of politics, throughout the course of the 1970s and early 1980s Berlin was gradually transformed from a site of heightened political tensions on an international scale where the world believed a war could erupt, to a city that, politically, commanded little attention.[19]

It is at first glance ironic, then, that the increasingly depoliticized West Berlin became, beginning in the 1960s and increasing through the 1970s up to the fall of the wall, a refuge for *Andersdenkende*, those who sought an escape from the perceived social, political, and cultural conformity of the West German provinces. The anti-NATO and anti-Reagan demonstrations I focus on in this chapter drew a broad segment of their support from this leftist-alternative milieu or "scene" (*linksalternative Szene*). This "scene" does not lend itself to easy classification, being made up of ecological and political groups of various grades of dogmatism, local grassroots organizations, punks, and a growing faction of militant autonomous groups (*Autonomen*). During the 1970s, the main pulse of the "scene" had moved, albeit briefly, from the politicized West Berlin of the 1960s to the West German provinces. It was here, in the rural and sparsely populated countryside of Schlwesig-Holstein, Lower Saxony, Bavaria, and Baden-Wuerttenberg, where militant protests and attempts to block the sites, or potential sites, of nuclear power stations led to the emergence of alternative camps "occupying" sites in Wyhl, Brokdorf, and Gorleben (*Republik Freies Wendland*). By 1980–81, however, West Berlin became once again a hub of alternative protest as a center of the squatting movement.[20] The year 1981 signaled the emergence of a new generation of leftists who were eager to show that their antipathy toward NATO's missile policies extended beyond just the policies of a particular administration and represented a larger system critique.

Starting in the 1960s, the extraparliamentary left in Germany and throughout much of the world began linking the United States with the excesses of market capitalism, modernism, and consumerism. West German '68ers joined students around the globe in opposing US capitalism and imperialism and, like future generations of activists, held critical views of American foreign policies. However, by specifically focusing on President Reagan's first visit to West Berlin, we can clearly see the crystallization of a specifically German anti-Americanism that departed from the West German '68ers' essentially political criticism of American domestic and foreign policies by its visible opposition to the American presence in West Germany and West Berlin, American foreign policies, and American society as a model to be emulated.[21] It is of course unsurprising that these political shifts and tensions expressed themselves within the walled-in city of West Berlin. The perception of West Berlin as pivotal to measuring West German–American relations fed both conservative and leftist discourse at the time. Beginning with the visit of Reagan's Secretary of State Alexander Haig in September 1981 and continuing with fervor to the 1982 presidential visit and beyond, a struggle ensued between the left and the mainstream over the image and symbolic value of the city. There emerged a passionate struggle to claim Berlin, official discourse insistently clinging to a vision of the city as closely tied to the US while the discourse of the alternative movement promoted a vision of the city that rejected "American" values both symbolically and literally. For the young radicals of West Germany, reclaiming the city as a physical space was crucial to demonstrating their own definition of their national identity, a definition that was deliberately negotiated in the city traditionally understood as reflecting the visions of West-East relations and German-American relations.

The Secretary of State in West Berlin

Before the demonstrations in West Berlin that greeted Ronald Reagan's Berlin visit in 1982, which was his first visit overseas since taking office in January 1981, his Secretary of State Alexander Haig paid a visit to the city on 13 and 14 September 1981. This visit was a crucial predecessor to the presidential visit the following year. Although it was not explicitly linked to Reagan's visit, it triggered an immense outpouring of hostility from left-alternative protest groups toward American policies that is crucial to understanding the developing shift in German-American relations.[22] During his four-day trip to Europe, Haig met in Bonn with West German Foreign Minister Hans-Dietrich Genscher, and then, on 14 September, he addressed the Berlin Press Association in West Berlin. In his speech to the Press Association, Haig defended a military buildup regarding the East-West conflict by suggesting that there was evidence to show that the Soviet Union and its allies were employing illegal chemical weapons in Southeast Asia.[23] Haig went on to reassure Western European governments of the Reagan administration's commitment to arms reduction with a plea for an East-West military balance, and furthermore warned that without this precondition there could be no policy of détente.[24] Despite direct appeals by the West German government (the SPD and its coalition partner the Free Democratic Party or FDP) to discourage protest plans, the youth wings of both parties, in concert with West Berlin's Green Party, the Alternative List, the Protestant Students' Association of the Free University and Abroad, the Socialist Unity Part of West Berlin, and the Youth Initiative against Rearmament, along with a remarkable fifty-two other organizations, successfully organized a demonstration on the day of Haig's visit.[25]

The demonstration caused a great degree of embarrassment for West German and West Berlin political leaders. Raised with a deep belief in the affection that linked Berlin with the US, the political elite of the established parties was deeply disturbed by the growing atmosphere of anti-American sentiment, fearing that the protests would send the wrong message not only to the Reagan administration but to the American public as well.[26] Rejecting official pleas for order and restraint, the protest organizers mobilized under the general slogan "There is nothing more important than peace!" turning on its head an alleged comment by Haig in which he declared: "There are more important things than peace." Protest groups rallied participants by characterizing the Reagan administration as promoting a reactionary politics, one that was "deluded by its superpower status and as a result, show[ed] ruthlessness vis-à-vis anyone who dare[d] to stand in the way of Washington's interests."[27] In the same flyer, distributed in the days before the demonstration, the organizers explained their decision to protest Haig's presence in the city: "A man whose country only knows war as something that happens in other places is trying to obscure the fact that our country could become a battlefield for the second time this century. This man is a provocation to us all! And we must show him this by taking to the streets."[28]

The expectation was that Haig would try to defend the US's position on rearmament by framing these issues as a defense strategy. The organizers of the protest cautioned against "their" city becoming a battlefield for "the second time this century" in the name of a country that "only knows war as something that happens somewhere else."[29] One co-organizer of the protest, West Berlin's Alternative List, expressed its opposition to Haig's visit in a full-page editorial in West Berlin's daily *Der Tagesspiegel* titled, "Do something for security in Berlin and elsewhere – Rid Europe of nuclear arms!" The Alternative List promoted the stance that Germany, and in particular Berlin as the "symbol of East-West confrontation in Europe," was the most important starting point of the peace movement. Only in embattled Berlin would signs of any willingness to disarm be not only the most urgent but also the most believable.[30]

On the day of the demonstration, West Berliners gathered in front of city hall in the West Berlin neighborhood of Schöneberg, where John F. Kennedy had delivered the first, and more memorable, of his two West Berlin speeches almost twenty years earlier, in order to receive US Secretary of State Haig.[31] As he gave his speech, a demonstration involving between 40,000 and 60,000 participants marched through the neighborhood carrying homemade placards with anti-Haig/USA slogans painted on them. Contemporary observers noted that the demonstration was the largest protest in West Berlin since the anti-Vietnam protests in the late 1960s.[32] Violence broke out after several hundred of the protesters exited the demonstration and made an attempt to demonstrate closer to the city hall. In part due to the 1979 assassination attempt on Haig in Brussels in his role as commander of NATO, and to the attacks on US military bases in southern Germany, the police deployment in the city was significant. Haig glimpsed neither the protest nor the riot, yet he defended the demonstrators' right to protest, once briefed on the afternoon's events. Just as the announcement of a planned protest had stirred public debate in the days leading to Haig's visit, the actual day, and especially the brawl between police and radical protesters, was to generate even more heated discussion.

In the days after the visit, SPD Executive Director Peter Glotz responded in *Die Zeit* to criticism by West Germany's national daily the *Frankurter Allgemeine Zeitung* (*FAZ*); the *FAZ* editorial accused the SPD of undermining the integrity of the rule of law (*Rechtsstaat*) by not banning the demonstration outright: "the whole thing is an alarming piece of today's reality. The rule of law has degenerated to such an extent that it is incapable of confronting threatening mass violence initiated by political extremists."[33] Warning against the danger of restricting the freedom of assembly in the name of protecting the rule of law, Glotz noted that "this city cannot simply stand by and watch as the right to demonstrate is smashed to bits."[34] He did not, however, throw his support wholeheartedly behind the organizers of the demonstration. In his rebuke of the Young Socialists and Young Democrats, Glotz criticized the organizers for losing their political perspective in their commitment to the protest:

> Of all places to demonstrate against the Americans, whoever would demonstrate in Berlin has to reckon with and take into account the inevitable support of the Moscow-loyal West Berlin Communist Party and a violent crowd of "professional demonstrators." With these two groups supporting the demonstration, even the most honest of motivations cannot be held free from blame. The demonstration then might win over a part of the youth generation, but will damage any semblance of sympathy and/or support from all others.[35]

The connection Glotz made here between the American presence in the city and the actions of a segment of the demonstrators of a city the Americans helped to protect was of course not coincidental, but pointed to a reweaving of a symbolic thread, held onto dearly by state officials, that had begun to fray. Glotz appealed to the fact that in *this* city, created and protected by the Americans, the implications of such a protest were profound. His comment inadvertently points directly to the tensions inside the city between, on the one side, a now large population of left-leaning alternatives, a militant *Autonome Szene,* and communist party members, and on the other side a political elite intent on maintaining a status quo relationship with the Americans.

The tensions surrounding the question of West Berlin–American relations were evident in much political discourse of the time. The new Christian Democrat mayor, Richard von Weizsäcker, confirmed a strong identification with the American presence in West Berlin in an interview he gave in *Die Welt* in July 1981, one month after the mayoral election and just two months before Haig's visit. Weizsäcker's remarks in the interview clearly articulate the symbolic role he assigned to West Berlin in European, and even more so in international, politics. In response to the question of whether or not he believed that Berlin was still the pressure point between East and West, Weizsäcker agreed that the city of West Berlin was no longer a place where the East would exert its military muscle to put pressure on the West; however, he added that Berlin was still a vitally important symbol. The mayor insisted proudly that in fact the very importance and multiple meanings of Berlin were present inside the heads of both the East and West more than the Berliners themselves were even aware of.[36] Weizsäcker's confidence in West Berlin's political centrality to the rest of West Germany was grounded in West Berlin's role as a unique indicator of German-American relations. He insisted that West Berlin's special status as an occupied city meant that "one is aware of things more quickly here [in Berlin] more so than in Bonn as to the kind of effect the actions of Germans or Europeans have on America. Berliners live with the Americans on a daily basis. To be sure, living in Berlin one cannot easily forget what the Americans have done for this city and one can also not lose sight of the fact that the freedom we gained and now enjoy would be impossible without the protection of the Allied powers."[37] According to Weizsäcker, an examination of Berlin was quite explicitly the only way to approach the question of German-American relations. Again, his emphasis on West Berlin's special relationship to the Americans was astutely grounded historically and implied the belief that any criticism of this kind, i.e., of the US administration, could only be read as a direct insult to one's neighbor (the US presence in West Berlin) and therefore had no space, either literally or figuratively, in West Berlin.

The fact that Haig's visit moved 50,000 people to demonstrate against American defense policies, and that the protest ultimately escalated into a street fight between the police and a segment of the protesters, prompted an immediate apology by a deeply embarrassed Weizsäcker. Dismissing the tens of thousands of protesters as not representing the "true face" of the city, the mayor declared West Berlin's deep-seated commitment to the Alliance and publicly invited Reagan to pay a visit to the city in order to get a glimpse of West Berlin's loyalty, and to hear the "true voice" of the Germans. Yet as *Die Zeit's* correspondent in Washington Michael Naumann aptly noted in an opinion piece four days after Haig's visit, both the audience and city had changed since in the past decade. Gone were the days of the city wholeheartedly welcoming early Cold War rhetoric that boldly positioned Western democratic ideals against Soviet communism, the sort of rhetoric that had made John F. Kennedy so dear to the hearts of Berliners nearly two decades earlier.[38] The debates that surrounded the Haig visit, and both the official and unofficial receptions he received in West Berlin, are significant for two reasons. On the one hand, the Haig visit would become a reference point for Reagan's visit to West Berlin months later, one used by both the left and the political establishment. On the other hand, Haig, alongside Bonn and Berlin's political elite, called upon early Cold War rhetoric in order to evoke an older tradition of mutual affection, an obvious attempt to temper emerging differences between the two countries on questions of policy. This appeal to emotional symbols, however, while it reinforced a particular and traditional image of West Berlin, was now being met with less and less resonance on the ground level.

President Reagan Visits the Occupied City

The visits by Secretary of State Haig and President Reagan signaled a new phase in the development of German-American relations after 1945. As I have suggested, both official visits, Ronald Reagan's most notably, marked the moment when it became apparent to both the American and German political elite that the now familiar Cold War references that defined the city as pro-American no longer resonated with a growing number of West Berlin's residents (i.e., no longer evoked the same sense of loyalty on the part of the West Berliners).[39] Before Reagan even set foot on German soil, the West German political establishment trumpeted the president's planned trips to Bonn and West Berlin as a "signal" of the German-American partnership.[40] Ironically, it had remained unclear until three months before the visit whether or not Reagan would ultimately bypass West Germany during this first, brief European tour. Apparently, Germany's significance to the US was more obvious to the Germans than the Americans. The prospect of his not visiting the Federal Republic, however, was entirely unacceptable to a West German leadership that was keen on reaffirming its commitment to the Western alliance.

In the face of Chancellor Schmidt's deep regrets at the prospect of Reagan passing over a German visit, Secretary of State Haig immediately moved to make new arrangements to relocate the planned NATO meeting from Brussels to Bonn. Yet it was only after talks between West German Foreign Minister Genscher and Reagan took place in Washington in March that the official announcement was made that Reagan would also visit West Berlin. Genscher was, among other reasons, in Washington to further discuss West Germany's plan to go ahead with a plan to build a natural gas pipeline that would run from Siberia to Western Europe.[41] The unwillingness of West German politicians to pay heed to Washington's misgivings about negotiations with the Russians caused a degree of tension between the two countries. Despite opposing positions over the pipeline construction plans in Siberia, Genscher left the meeting with the "reaffirmed view that the U.S., like the Federal Republic, are aware of the vital importance this relationship has for the efficiency of the Western alliance."[42] To this end, Genscher made his message clear in the weeks leading up to the much-anticipated Reagan visit: this visit was no ordinary one, but rather a chance to demonstrate West German solidarity with the United States.[43]

In *Die Zeit*'s coverage of the meeting, its Washington correspondent cited Reagan's decision to visit West Berlin as one of the more concrete results of Genscher's visit to Washington. In general the editorial reflects the belief on the part of the mainstream media and Bonn's leaders that it was vital for Reagan "to see first hand the German reality [*deutsche Wirklichkeit*] at the confrontation point between East and West, i.e., Berlin."[44] And of course, the reporter assures us, in order to ensure absolute security, the American president would be led through emptied streets in West Berlin, a vow intended to protect him from the harassment of demonstrators.[45] In light of the Haig visit that no one had forgotten, this promise was made a definite reality by the largest police deployment in West Berlin's history. The editorial hinges on the widely held view that only a visit to West Berlin could salvage German-American relations. After the White House formally announced the visit, Richard von Weizsäcker called on West Berliners to welcome President Reagan on 11 June by underlining that "the Berliners do not forget those friends who stand by them in difficult times." With his statement he evoked the historical ties between Germans and Americans, harking back to the airlift of 1948-49, when the Soviets closed off West Berlin from West Germany, and then to 1961, when East Germany divided the city with the Berlin Wall.[46] Weizsäcker's appeal to the citizens of West Berlin drew attention to their supposed astuteness: "they know who protects their freedom."[47] His rhetoric asked the people of West Berlin to identify their own lived memories with the city as a whole, to remember the literal and metaphoric protection from the Soviet threat that Americans have represented since the blockade.

The repetition of this by now tired Cold War rhetoric reminding West Berliners of the debt they owed to American generosity was designed to mask what was, for the political elites, a worrisome development: a new generation of West Berliners, both born and imported, who were attempting to redefine the relationship between America and West Berlin. At the most basic level, members of this generation of Germans simply did not possess memories of American goodwill, e.g., the chocolate and the chewing gum, but instead were part of a different global generation. Not the children of the postwar years of suffering, these youth had come of age in a postwar world that was defined by the debacle of the Vietnam War and the horrors of Hiroshima, events that rendered impossible any uncritically positive attitude toward the United States. Unsurprisingly, as soon as the official announcement had been made that Reagan would visit the city, a passionate response emerged on the left, one committed to making obvious to the American president that his presence in the city was not welcome.

For the alternative scene in West Berlin, Reagan embodied the threat inherent in what was perceived as a dangerous round of NATO rearmament, something that was feared could lead to a nuclear war on the European continent. Reagan's own belligerent rhetoric, as well as the administration's policy toward Latin America (i.e., Nicaragua and El Salvador), augmented these fears.[48] Although antipathy toward Reagan's foreign and defense policies was a common sentiment more generally among peace activists and the Greens, its manifestation took a particularly hostile form in the alternative scene in West Berlin. Here, in the city that had once loved the US above all else, Germans gathered together to express an outright rejection of the United States. As anti-Americanism reached new heights in West Germany, the one place where the political elites above all feared its presence was West Berlin.

Ultimately, of course, nowhere in the Federal Republic was anti-Americanism to be as eminently visible as in West Berlin. In the weeks leading up to Reagan's visit, whole sections of the city were adorned with anti-Reagan slogans draped out of apartment windows and balconies, nailed to rooftops, spray painted on apartment façades and on public edifices, most notably on the Berlin Wall itself. Such slogans included "Here's where the American sector ends," "Ami go home," "On June 11 it's going to rain" (*Am 11. Juni fällt Reagan*), and "All of Berlin will stink when Reagan waves" (*Ganz Berlin stinkt, wenn Reagan winkt*). The consistent reaction of the West Berlin authorities to the very public display of anti-Reaganism escalated into what the alternative media came to term the *Lappenkrieg* (rag war). It was named in honor of the protest banners swaying off of balconies and out of windows, which were made from old or tattered bed linens.[49] The heart of the this anti-Reagan campaign was found in the two West Berlin districts where the squatting movement was its strongest, Kreuzberg and Schöneberg, although banners were also displayed on apartments not "occupied" by squatters. The police systematically moved through the city to confiscate the banners and paint over the slogans found on the façades of apartment houses. After the first round of raids resulted in the confiscation of fifteen banners with "punishable" content and several arrests on the grounds of insulting a foreign state official, the *Besetzerrat* (Squatters' Council) organized a response on 24 May, just two weeks before the visit, in which West Berliners were encouraged to simultaneously drape their balconies, windows, or rooftops with anti-Reagan banners in order to show solidarity with those arrested, and to demonstrate their right to freedom of expression.[50] This game of cat and mouse went on for days leading up to Reagan's visit. By the fifteenth day of the "war," Berlin's interior minister wearily declared that 616 banners had been confiscated for "safe-keeping."[51]

The busy weeks prior to Reagan's arrival illustrated above all the public reclaiming of the city by a vigorous protest culture, one that had been cultivated in West Berlin since the student protests of the 1960s. The *Lappenkrieg* was significant in that it literally projected a message onto the face of the city, and this message was a resounding rejection of how the city had and still was being officially defined. What was specifically at stake for the alternative scene was a re-definition of the relationship "their" city had with the United States. This would find its expression not just in a two-hour demonstration or ten-hour brawl with the police, but rather more in the spectacularly visible rejection of the rhetoric applied by politicians to describe the city. This visual claiming of the city repre-sented a physical assertion of the right to articulate the terms defining the role of West Berlin in German-American relations. To put it another way, the *Lappen-krieg* suggested an important shift in discourse: the ritualistic Cold War rhetoric conjuring up a formidable citadel of resistance to the Soviet menace was rejected once and for all. During the *Lappenkrieg,* the alternative scene used West Berlin not as a positive, but a negative site to define the relationship between Germany and the United States. These voices had been virtually absent from the public radar up to now; in the context of the Haig and Reagan visits, however, they thrust themselves literally onto every corner of the city.

Up to the day of the actual visit, it was still unclear whether or not Reagan would actually land in West Berlin or if he would just view the city from a helicopter. The decision was never disclosed to the general public, a desired con-sequence of which was that Reagan's convoy drove through empty streets on its way to the obligatory visit of the Berlin Wall, and finally to Schloss Charlotten-burg. Here 25,000 invited visitors were carefully inspected before being allowed to enter the grounds.[52] The high security measures were taken in fear that Reagan might be attacked; this fear had of course been compounded by the experience of the Haig visit, which still echoed loudly in the memories of both the political elite and the alternative scene. In a preemptive response to the planned anti-Reagan demonstrations, two weeks before the visit the Berlin Senate announced a prohibition of any demonstration on the actual day of Reagan's visit. This rul-ing followed on the heels of Chancellor Helmut Schmidt's statement to SPD party members that any expressed interest in participating in an anti-Reagan demonstration, be it in Bonn or West Berlin, would be grounds for expulsion from the party.[53] In order to avoid any conflict, the organizers of the West Berlin demonstration, the Protestant Students' Association (ESG), accordingly planned their protest for 10 June, one day before the official visit. However, the more radical opponents of Reagan's presence (autonomous groups and the Alterna-tive List) decided to go through with their original plan to demonstrate on 11 June, legally or not.[54] The co-organizers of the Haig demonstration, the Young Democrats, joined the autonomous groups and the Alternative List in going ahead with the plans for a protest on 11 June.[55] Both camps were intent on demonstrating, albeit under slightly different mottos, the ESG singling out a demonstration for peace and disarmament, while the protest planned on the day of Reagan's visit was explicitly anti-Reagan.

Given the obsessive attention to the planned demonstrations, it was not sur-prising that President Reagan expressed an interest in the brouhaha surrounding his visit. The West German daily *Frankfurter Rundschau* quoted Reagan from a television interview broadcast out of Washington as saying that he was "curious about whether or not these people [demonstrators] know what I really stand for." To underscore his commitment to peace, Reagan then evoked the symbolism of West Berlin as a place where "much more is at stake in the conflict between East and West."[56] Importantly—for the peace that Reagan was offering was protection from a communist threat—he did not realize that this threat was no longer meaningful to these protesters, for whom American bombs seemed both more frightening and more plausible. These "people" he referred to, however, were mainly concerned with disrupting what they perceived would be a "Reagan and Schmidt propaganda show"; that is, a performance that used the symbolic power of West Berlin to accentuate a German-American friendship, a friendship the demonstrators were no longer interested in being a part of.[57]

The demonstrations proceeded as anticipated by both political establishment and radical left, the first with relative calm, and the second ending in a street brawl complete with riot police squad. The conclusion reached by West Berlin political elites was that the visit was a success. Weizsäcker confirmed this view in his assessment of the visit, and stated that the success of Reagan's visit to Europe rested in the president's recognition of Berlin's unique role for the effectiveness of the Alliance.[58] The character of the discussion on the left following Reagan's visit not surprisingly took quite a different tone. The alternative daily newspaper *taz* referred to the street fights as the worst the city had witnessed since 17 June 1953, noting that despite his official intentions, President Reagan had not brought "peace" but rather riots to West Berlin.[59] In addition, the left criticized the city's political elites and the conservative media for discrediting demonstrators' critiques by labeling all protesters as violent left-wing extremists, and thus in one broad sweep shutting down a space for legal, if militant, protest.

Conclusion

In the aftermath of the demonstration, the *taz* declared: "Women and squatters, anarchists and non-conformists, peace activists and left-leaning mentors, those beaten on the streets and the street fighter … We too are Berliners."[60] This proclamation challenged a supposed Cold War clarity, one in which the identity of West Berlin was understood primarily in relation to its postwar "protector." What Paul Steege has identified as a central tension in the early Cold War apparatus, the slippage between real places and the symbolic, also aptly captures the meaning of West Berlin in the 1980s.[61] The Haig and Reagan visits brought to a head a struggle of two visions of what West Berlin meant for German-American relations and revealed serious fissures in the decade-long crafting of West Berlin as a desired site of pro-Americanism. The myth of West Berlin still had symbolic power, and in crucial moments of discord in German-American relations the political elite engaged with this symbolism to bolster a sense of harmony between the two countries.

The city had lost its frontline status in the decade after the Wall was built, but its political elites continued to draw upon the city's symbolism as established in the early years of the Cold War. The official image of the city needed to be (re)created or (re)defined on the basis of a reality in which Berliners lived. Instead, city officials continued to reiterate early Cold War rhetoric in moments of crisis. In fact, I would argue that the vitality of the alternative movement, and West Berlin's function as one important space where political and cultural protest had flourished since the 1960s, sustained the spirit and practice of yet another way to define the city space.

Notes

1. The estimated numbers reported in the German press on the day after the respective demonstrations were over 300,000 in Bonn, 100,000 in West Berlin on 10 June, and between 2,000 and 3,000 on 11 June. I do not argue here that West Berlin was the center of the peace movement in the 1980s; rather, it is West Berlin's protest movements and alternative scene that interest me for the sake of better understanding German-American relations.

2. David S. Painter, *The Cold War: An International History* (London and New York, 1999), chap. 6; Fred Halliday, "The Ends Of Cold War," *New Left Review* 180 (March–April 1990): 5–24.

3. On the growing tension between West Germany and the United States in this period, see Harald Mueller and Thomas Risse-Kappen, "Origins of Estrangement: The Peace Movement and the Changed Image of America in West Germany," *International Security* 12, no. 1 (1987): 52–88; Matthias Dembinski, "Differences on Arms Control in German-American Relations," in *The United States and Germany in the Era of the Cold War, 1945–1990: A Handbook,* 2 vols., ed. Detlef Junker (New York), 2:140–47; and in the same volume, Michael Broer, "The NATO Double-Track Decision, the INF Treaty, and the SNF Controversy: German-American Relations between Consensus and Conflict," 2:148–54; Wolfgang Schlauch, "Reliable Partnership? Perspectives on Recent German-American Relations," *German Studies Review* 8, no. 1 (1985): 107–25.

4. See Klaus Schwabe, "Détente and Multipolarity: The Cold War and German-American Relations, 1968–1990," in Junker, *Era of the Cold War,* 2:1–17.

5. Carl Lankowski, "Social Movements in Germany and the United States: The Peace Movement and the Environmental Movement," in Junker, *Era of the Cold War,* 2:435.

6. For a detailed discussion of how Berlin became *the* symbolic capital of the Cold War, see Paul Steege, *Black Market, Cold War: Everyday Life in Berlin, 1946–1949,* (Cambridge, 2007). On West Berlin's strategic importance see Armin Grünbacher, "Sustaining the Island: Western Aid to 1950s West Berlin," *Cold War History* 3, no. 3 (2003): 1–23.

7. It is perhaps worth mentioning here that in the popular discourse it is Reagan's second visit to West Berlin in 1987 that is most often referenced. This is due largely to Reagan's speech at the Brandenburg Gate in which he uttered the infamous line, "Mr. Gorbachev, tear down this wall!"

8. Sociologist Ruud Koopmans's work confirms that new social movements (NSM) in West Germany were concentrated in two periods: the late 1960s and the 1980s. His analysis shows that at least quantitatively the protests in the early 1980s surpassed those of the late 1960s. For literature on the West German peace movement of the 1980s see Joyce Marie Mushaben, "Grassroots and Gewaltfreie Aktionen: A Study of Mass Mobilization Strategies in the West German Peace Movement," *Journal of Peace Research* 23, no. 2 (1986): 141–54; Alice Holmes Cooper, "Public-good Movements and the Dimensions of Political Process: Postwar German Peace Movements," *Comparative Political Studies* 29, no. 3 (1996): 267–89.

9. American and West German relations are often characterized as a love-hate relationship that intensified after 1945. For studies that demonstrate the complexities of the German American encounter in the postwar period see Uta Poiger, *Jazz, Rock, and Rebels: Cold War Politics and American Culture in a Divided Germany* (Berkeley, 2000); and Maria Höhn, *GIs and Fräuleins: The German American Encounter in 1950s West Germany* (Chapel Hill, 2002).

10. On the relationship between space and protest in the city, see in particular Belinda Davis, "The City as Theater of Protest: West Berlin and West Germany, 1962–1983" in *The Spaces of the Modern City: Imaginaries, Politics and Everyday Life*, ed. Gyan Prakash and Kevin M. Kruse (Princeton, 2008), 247–74.

11. This oft-quoted title is from Werner Hegemann's 1930 work *Das steinerne Berlin: Geschichte der größten Mietskasernenstadt der Welt*. His book is recognized as one of the most powerful critiques of Berlin's infamous "rental barracks" and has influenced generations of reformers and urban planners working in Berlin.

12. Andreas Daum, "America's Berlin, 1945–2000: Between Myths and Visions," in *Berlin: The New Capital in the East: A Transatlantic* Appraisal, ed. Frank Trommler (Washington, D.C., 2000), 49-73.

13. Ibid., 64.

14. Philipp Gassert, "With America Against America: Anti-Americanism in West Germany," in Junker, *Era of the Cold War*, 2:502–509.

15. Mary Nolan, "Anti-Americanism and Americanization in Germany," *Politics and Society* 33, no. 1 (2005): 88–122, 110.

16. Nolan defines political anti-Americanism as a form of German anti-Americanism that emerged in the late 1960s and early 1970s, which accepts capitalism and is accompanied by an extensive Americanization of West German society: "Anti-Americanism and Americanization," 89. That anti-Americanism in West Germany attained a qualitatively different meaning from that elsewhere in Europe, see also Andrei Markovits and Philip Gorski, *The German Left: Red, Green and Beyond* (New York, 1993); Andrei Markovits, "On Anti-Americanism in West German," *New German Critique*, no. 34 (1985): 3–27.

17. Nolan, "Anti-Americanism and Americanization in Germany," 110; Gassert, "With America Against America," 503–4.

18. Wolfgang Ribbe, ed., *Geschichte Berlins, vol. 2: Von der Märzrevolution bis zur Gegenwart*, 3rd rev. and exp. ed. (Berlin, 2002).

19. By politically I mean here the city's centrality in diplomatic relations. In national politics it certainly remained present in the minds of West Germans as subsidies continued to flow into the city to keep it alive.

20. Dieter Rucht points to two factors, continuity over time of West Berlin's protest scene and its extraordinary size, as a way to explain the perception of the city being the "capital" of the West German leftist and alternative movements in his discussion of the anti-Reagan and anti-IMF campaigns. See "Mesomobilization: Organizing and Framing in Two Protest Campaigns in West Germany," *The American Journal of Sociology* 98, no. 3 (November 1992): 570.

21. On the formal and informal networks of collaboration between activists in the 1960s, especially between West Germans and Americans, see for example Martin Klimke, *The Other Alliance: Student Protest in West Germany and the United States in the Global Sixties* (Princeton, 2010); Michael Schmidtke, *Der Aufbruch der jungen Intelligenz: Die 68er Jahre in der Bundesrepublik und den USA* (Frankfurt am Main and New York, 2003). For studies on the relationship between youth and consumer cultures in the 1960s and 1970s, see Axel Schildt and Detlef Siegfried, eds., *Between Marx and Coca-Cola: Youth Cultures in Changing European Societies, 1960–1980* (New York, 2006).

22. Haig signed The Golden Book of West Berlin at the City Hall in the name of President Reagan.

23. "Haig in European Trip Stresses Soviet Threat; Focus on Western Alliance," *World News Digest,* 18 September 1981, 667.

24. "Genscher und Haig bekräftigen gemeinsame Bündnispolitik," *Der Tagesspiegel,* 15 September 1981, 2.

25. Papiertiger, Archiv und Bibliothek der sozialen Bewegung, Flyer, "Demonstration, Sonntag, 13.9.1981." At least fifty other organizations ranging from the feminist magazine *Courage* to the West Berlin Homosexual Action Group to the Berlin Tenants Association supported the demonstration.

26. "Demonstration gegen Haig im Bundestag scharf verurteilt," *Der Tagesspiegel,* 11 September 1981, 1; "SPD-Landesvorstand missbilligt geplante Demonstration gegen Haig," *Der Tagesspiegel,* 8 September 1981, 1; and "Ruling Parties' Youth Wings Plan to Protest Haig's West Berlin Visit," *New York Times,* 9 September 1981, A8. The American Nuclear Freeze Movement was gaining momentum in these same years and provided a domestic challenge to Reagan's plan to increase nuclear weapons.

27. Papiertiger, Archiv und Bibliothek der sozialen Bewegung, Flyer, "'Es gibt nichts wichtigeres als den Frieden, Mister Haig!' Sonntag, 13.9.1981."

28. Ibid.

29. Ibid.

30. Papiertiger, Archiv und Bibliothek der sozialen Bewegung, Flyer, "Aufruf zur Anti-Haig-Demonstration." Also published by the Alternative List in *Der Tagesspiegel,* 12 September 1981.

31. On the discrepancy between John F. Kennedy's two 1963 speeches in West Berlin, see Diethelm Prowe, "The Making of *ein Berliner:* Kennedy, Brandt, and the Origins of Détente Policy in Germany," in *From the Berlin Museum to the Berlin Wall: Essays on the Cultural and Political History of Modern Germany,* ed. David Wetzel (Westport, CT, and London, 1996): 169–89.

32. "Besuch in einer besetzten Stadt: Demonstrationen der Loyalität, der Friedfertigkeit

und der Gewalt," *Die Zeit,* Nr. 39, 18 September 1981, 4; "Violence in Berlin marks Haig's visit," *New York Times,* 14 September 1981, A9.

33. Quoted in "Ein Lehrstück für die Deutschen," *Die Zeit,* September 1981, 5.
34. Ibid.
35. Ibid.
36. *Die Welt,* 7 July 1981, 8.
37. Ibid.
38. "Berlin-Bild mit Kratzern, Haig's Deutschlandreise- nur ein Teil Erfolg," *Die Zeit,* 18 September 1981, 4. On the reception of Kennedy's speech by West Berliners, see Prowe, "The Making of *ein Berliner,*" 172–74.
39. The *FAZ* reported in 2002, shortly before President George W. Bush's visit to Berlin, that according to representatives of the American embassy there, Berlin has held the rank of the foreign city most frequently visited by US presidents for the last five and a half decades. This regularity comes as no surprise in light of the historical relationship between Americans and "their" city, a relationship that many deem as "special" even seventeen years after the fall of the Berlin Wall. See the article in the *FAZ* in which Berliner Gesine Schwan (now president of Viadrina European University in Frankfurt/Oder and then a political science professor at the Free University in Berlin as well as a member of the SPD's Commission of Basic Values, from which she was removed in 1984 for her critique of *Ostpolitik*) defends her initiative in 1982 to post an advertisement in the newspaper signed by like-minded university professors in which they spoke on behalf of all Berliners by emphasizing their gratitude to the Americans for securing the existence of West Berlin and underscored that they knew who their friends were, despite not always being of the same opinion. "Noch mal abdrucken! 1982 wurde Ronald Reagan mit einer Zeitungsanzeige begrüsst: Eine Initiative von Gesine Schwan," *FAZ,* 22 May 2002, BS1. See also "Bin ich noch ein Berliner?" *New York Times,* 26 February 1982, A23.
40. "Das andere Deutschland," *Der Spiegel,* 29 March 1982, 30.
41. The relevance of this visit was that it was one confrontation in a series of decisions in Bonn to negotiate with the Russians and therefore put the Western alliance, and especially the US, at unease about where Bonn stood; see "How West Germans see détente," *Financial Times,* 17 June 1982, 21.
42. "Reagan likely to visit West Berlin," *United Press International,* 9 March 1982. See also Helmut Schmidt, "A Policy of Reliable Partnership," *Foreign Affairs* 59, no. 4 (spring 1981): 743.
43. "Das andere Deutschland," *Der Spiegel,* 29 March 1982, 30.
44. "Schwer zu überzeugen. Ist der Widerstand gegen Erdgasgeschäft überwunden?" *Die Zeit,* Nr. 11, 1982, 5,10, 34.
45. Ibid.
46. "Berlin to Welcome Reagan," *New York Times,* 9 May 1982, 1.
47. Der Senat informiert. "Der amerikanische Präsident besucht am 11. Juni Berlin. Darüber freuen wir uns von Herzen," in "Wir sind noch immer Berliner," Johann Legner, in *Stadtfront: Berlin West Berlin* (Berlin, 1982), 124–126.
48. Reagan's support of military dictatorships in Central America revealed to the protesters his attitude toward forms of political dissent when it directly involved US interests, and generally US hegemony around the world.

49. Ulf Mailänder, Ulrich Zander and Guido Ullmann, *Das kleine West-Berlin Lexicon: Von Hausbesetzer bis Zapf-Umzüge - die alternative Szene der 70er und 80er Jahre* (Berlin, 2003), 167.

50. See clipping,"Lappen-Krieg ausgebrochen," *die tageszeitung* (*taz* hereafter*)*, 26 May 1982, from Sammlung Berlin, File "Hausbesetzer"; Also, clipping in same file,"Anti-Reagan Aktionen-Alternative Beflaggung,"*taz,* 28 May 1982.

51. J. C. Wartenberg, *Kreuzberg K 36: Leben in [der] Bewegung, Kreuzberg inside bis zum Fall der Mauer* (Berlin, 2005).

52. These visitors were recruited from associations, administrative bodies, and companies, but in fact it was not until after Mayor Weizsäcker announced that public servants would be rewarded with a paid day off that the numbers of accepted invitations soared.

53. "Das andere Deutschland," *Der Spiegel,* 29 March 1982, 30.

54. See clipping, "Am 11.6. keine legale Demonstration?" *taz,* 3 June1982, from Sammlung Berlin, File "Hausbesetzer".

55. See clipping, "Demo am Vorabend des Reagan-Besuchs: Friedlich ohne Randale," *taz,* 1 June 1982, from Sammlung Berlin, File "Hausbesetzer".

56. See clipping, "US-Präsident Ronald Reagan ist 'neugierig' auf Proteste," *Frankfurter Rundschau,* 3 June 1982, from Sammlung Berlin, File "Hausbesetzer".

57. Sammlung Berlin,"autonome und anti-imperialistische gruppen, anti-NATO demo 11 June W.-Berlin," pamphlet, 1982.

58. See clipping, "Weizsäcker: Reagans Besuch hat die Stellung Berlins gestärkt," *Tagesspiegel,* 16 June 1982, from Sammlung Berlin, File "Hausbesetzer".

59. See clipping, "Wir sind alle Berliner," *taz,* 14 June 1982, from Sammlung Berlin, File "Hausbesetzer".

60. Ibid.

61. Steege, *Black Market, Cold War,* 288.

Part III

Protest and Power

Chapter 6

A Growing Problem
for US Foreign Policy
The West German Student Movement
and the Western Alliance

Martin Klimke

> I first encountered the problem of student unrest while serving
> as United States Ambassador to Germany—in connection with
> the Free University of Berlin. The three allies are responsible for
> Berlin. We are the government so we could not ignore it. The Free
> University became, perhaps, the most troublesome university in
> the world for a year or two, as a direct result of what happened
> at Berkeley, and which illustrates clearly the cause and effect rela-
> tionship of incidents in one part of the world to those in another.
> —George McGhee

Introduction

On 21 May 1968, George McGhee departed from his post as US ambassador
to the Federal Republic of Germany to take on the job of ambassador-at-large
in Washington.[1] Throughout his diplomatic career, McGhee had shown a substantial interest in the situation of international youth. When the Department
of State formed a "Student Unrest Study Group" in mid 1968 to come to terms
with the international implications of the events of the "French May" for US
foreign policy, McGhee seemed like the natural candidate for the chairman-
ship. In his report to the president, McGhee wrote that internationally, students
had "toppled prime ministers, changed governments, ruined universities and in
some cases harmed the economy of the country." They had become the trigger
of larger social transformations and in their protest would transcend traditional
categories of patriotism and nationalism. For McGhee, they were not "interested
in their country" but would "basically feel a camaraderie with other students
around the world who are doing the same thing." Instead of a formal, hierarchical
organization, the opportunities of international communication and travel had

enabled them to spur each other through mutual emulation. With respect to West Germany, McGhee argued, events at Berkeley, for example, served as a model for disorder at the Free University of Berlin. Berlin students "said why can't we do it. And so they merely copied what they read in the press or saw on the television and did it. They weren't told by somebody in Berkeley or somebody higher up."[2]

Other American officials assigned to the Federal Republic in the 1960s shared McGhee's point of view. Witnessing equally dramatic changes in the prevailing images of the United States, they faced serious difficulties resulting from the war in Vietnam and the growing domestic opposition against it. As Public Affairs Officer at the United States Information Services (USIS) Hans Tuch remembered, the city of Berlin became a particular focal point of student unrest:

> Life in Berlin took on a definite anti-American tone during the following three years [1968–71], related to the Vietnam War and the opposition to it by Germans and German youth especially. Our America House in Berlin was sacked, completely sacked, two weekends in a row. Every window was broken. In the second incident 60 policemen were hurt by students who were throwing rocks and Molotov cocktails.[3]

Due to the peculiar status of the city, any public criticism of, or attacks against, the hitherto highly regarded US protective power were met by an outraged citizenry willing to prove and defend the special bond they enjoyed with America. American diplomats thus had to assess the danger of student disorder and supposedly "anti-American" protest in terms of an even greater problem, namely a public counterreaction. Hence, the US faced a twofold problem in confronting student unrest in West Germany. On the one hand, the students posed a security problem to the American presence in the country that needed to be dealt with. Far more seriously, however, they challenged the transatlantic partner ideologically and could not, as the country's future elite who would soon occupy positions of influence in West German society, be disregarded without consequences. On the other hand, student disruptions also caused a substantial change in the political landscape and exposed generational fissures in the Federal Republic that the American government was hard pressed to influence. How the US government came to terms with this challenge and how this response was embedded in a larger framework responding to youthful unrest worldwide will be outlined in the following.[4]

Institutional Frameworks of Confronting Student Unrest: The Inter-Agency Youth Committee

The problems of international youth had been a major concern of the US government since the beginning of the decade. In January 1962, George McGhee, then under secretary for political affairs, argued that "we are not adequately at-tuned to the needs and desires of youth (ages 6–20) and youth groups in the free world and that we have no specific program directed toward capturing the minds of these individuals."[5] In response to McGhee's demands for a stronger integration of youth as a prime target group in US cultural diplomacy efforts, a discussion about how to reach out to the young generation ensued in the Department of State, which eventually resulted in the establishment of an Inter-Agency Committee on Youth Affairs on 11 April 1962. Dedicated to drafting and coordinating an adequate foreign policy response to Communist propa-ganda, the Inter-Agency Youth Committee (IAYC), as it was later called, was designed to centralize efforts toward the buildup of a deep understanding of the US among a foreign country's educated young leaders, whose knowledge and opinions would multiply and thus ensure a long-term gain for US interests. As Secretary of State Dean Rusk later summarized the need for a "new emphasis on youth" in the competitive bipolar world of the Cold War:

> I believe that we are witnessing in this decade of rapid and sometimes violent change, a phenomenon which, if not new, has at least taken on new and vast proportions: It is the dynamic impact of young people, individually and in the mass, on the course of current events. Young leaders have risen and are rising to power, political change is occurring, and the events with which the traditional arts of diplomacy must deal are moving with a breath-taking speed. ... [W]e must make a much more concerted effort to identify and exercise decisive influence on the attitudes and actions of the rising young leaders, those who are coming to power now and those who will lead the "government after the next," especially in the newly-independent and less-developed countries. Of-ten this is a great deal more important than some of our traditional diplomacy. This is what the "Emphasis on Youth" is about.[6]

Accordingly, and with presidential support, the IAYC from then on assem-bled representatives from various branches of the Department of State, as well as leading officials from the Department of Defense, the Agency for International Development (AID), the United States Information Agency (USIA), the Central Intelligence Agency (CIA), the Peace Corps, and the White House on a regular basis. Furthermore, a full-time special assistant for youth affairs was appointed in the Bureau of Educational and Cultural Affairs of the State Department to form the Executive Secretary of the IAYC and serve as a main link for infor-mation and coordination of government activities aimed at reaching foreign youth.[7] The committee's efforts gradually expanded to include US posts over-seas, and in April 1963 the IAYC was able to report the appointment of ninety-nine youth coordinators and many forthcoming country studies.[8] Together with this increasing institutionalization and establishment of a permanent office and staff, the president himself became an avid supporter of the committee's work.[9] Shortly before his death, John F. Kennedy once more underlined his support for reaching out to the young generation abroad: "I want to emphasize again how important I consider our efforts directed toward young people throughout the world, and therefore the particular significance I attach to the work of the Interagency Youth Committee. It is essential to the successful conduct of our foreign affairs that we reach young people abroad to obtain their understanding and support."[10]

Kennedy made clear that the emphasis should be on potential young leaders or capable persons from all parts of society, especially those whose behavior might be harmful to US foreign policy objectives. For him, this was "a priority activity both in the field and in Washington." Abroad, the ambassador, supported by his country team and youth coordinator, was responsible for this task in combination with the various American informational, educational, and cultural services. In Washington, the IAYC would be in charge of coordinating the overseas youth programs carried out by the various departments and government agencies. Thereby, existing government resources should be bundled and used to jointly solve emerging problems.[11]

In the years that followed Kennedy's death, the IAYC, with the support of President Johnson, transformed itself into a permanent body seeking to evaluate and improve the country's programs aimed at foreign youth. The situation of youth in the developing countries, foreign students in the US or American scholars abroad, the training of foreign military personnel, the initiation of supplementary country studies, and the establishment of an international infrastructure to secure the committee's objectives locally became the main points on the IAYC's agenda. A report from 1964 described these efforts to "identify and cultivate rising young leaders" as "a new dimension in diplomacy ... initiated by the Interagency Youth Committee," in which the embassies' local youth committees would be at the "front line."[12] However, the intensification of the war in Vietnam and the rise of domestic and international opposition drastically changed the framework the IAYC was operating in.

The Discovery of the West German New Left

In August 1966, the USIA had already grasped the division of public opinion in the Federal Republic with regard to Vietnam, detecting that "a noisy left-wing minority opposes everything we do and is impervious to any explanation of US policy."[13] Although discernible throughout the country, the most vocal expression of anti-war sentiment prevailed in West Berlin, where "Communist clichés and slogans" were spread by a small student minority who regarded the Vietcong as resistance fighters against American imperialists.[14] In January 1967, the US mission in West Berlin reported more extensively on these "Red Guards of Berlin," as this group had been labeled by the local press. In a lengthy assessment, it discerned a new quality of protest among them: "Radical activity by Free University students took a new turn during the 1966–67 winter semester. In November and December, a small group of anarchistic leftists, calling themselves Maoists, created several serious disturbances at the FU and in downtown Berlin. The Berlin Maoists do not limit themselves to protests against the FU administration or US Vietnam policy. Instead, they call for violent opposition to all forms of authority now existing in the West."[15]

The mission pointed out that the student group from the Free University (FU) followed a loose Maoist philosophy and embraced Marxism together with a rejection of the East German and Soviet variants of it. To fiercely oppose the society they lived in, they drew on "Viet Cong tactics" or revolutionary actions such as the founding of a commune or plans for an alternative university to counter society's authoritarianism. They were, however, "deadly serious when they talk of revolution" and numbered about 200–300 supporters dissatisfied with current conditions. The apparent leader of this group, Rudi Dutschke, was characterized by the mission as "chief ideologist of the SDS 'terror group'" and as "the citizens' terror incarnate," for the most part agreeing with the unfavorable image of Dutschke painted by the Berlin tabloid "BZ." Although most of the protesters in Berlin were students, their provocations should, according to the mission, rather be considered "a determined attempt by a very small group of fanatics to initiate a political movement against authority in general," their objectives being the Berlin and West German government. Because of the American engagement in Vietnam, the US simply happened to be "a natural whipping boy."[16]

The "Pudding-Attentat" and student demonstrations during the visit of Vice President Hubert Humphrey to West Berlin in April 1967 drastically confirmed this judgment.[17] Whereas the "assassination attempt" only led to a small article in the *New York Times,* the Department of State saw it as a final wakeup call announcing that the opposition to the war in Vietnam in the Federal Republic had reached a level that mandated further action and analysis.[18] In his report to President Johnson about his European visit, Humphrey himself considered the profound alienation and possible loss of European youth over the war especially troublesome, since they would be of great political significance for future American foreign policy considerations: "At the heart of our effort must be a special outreach to the younger generation of Europeans. From all indications, the younger generation of Europe – just as our own younger generation – is idealistic, restless, outward-looking, and willing to give far more than it takes. We must increase our contacts with this younger generation and do a far better communication job than we have done thus far. As in our country, the post-war baby crop is coming to political influence at the ballot box."[19] To strengthen the American effort directed at the young generation of Europe, Humphrey not only outlined concrete measures to the president, but also voiced his concern at other high-level discussions within the administration.[20]

The situation of European youth had also become a great concern for the IAYC, whose interest shifted markedly to the European scene in the second half of the decade. In May 1966, former chairman and then Special Assistant to the President Harry McPherson suggested a country survey on European youth. The need for such a study had emerged since a variety of sources had detected "a growing problem involving relationships with young European leaders," while at the same time there seemed to be a rich flow of transnational exchange among certain youth groups involved in protest activities.[21] The underlying concern was that American domestic dissent might replicate itself in a European context to the disadvantage of the US: "If there is a 'moving apart,' is it the same movement that may be taking place between outspoken American youth and the older generation of Americans? Are we talking about a generational problem, or is there a special European quality added? If there is in fact an international network of contacts that embraces the New Left, SNCC, etc., presumably it has a broadening, maturing effect on the Americans involved. But what does it mean, what function does it serve, in overall relationships with European youth?"[22] In other words, as Foy Kohler, former US ambassador to Moscow and now under secretary of state for political affairs as well as chairman of the IAYC, phrased it, "do contacts between America's New Left and European youth help or hurt, as far as the national interest is concerned?"[23]

To informally survey the attitudes of young elites in West Germany, the German-born historian Fritz Stern was contracted by the State Department. In his report of January 1967, Stern discovered a marked decline in positive identification with the US among all West Germans as well as "a tiny minority of radical left-wing dissenters among German students who are violently critical of existing institutions and skeptical of all adult authority."[24] Questioning the omnipresent cliché of an apathetic youth, he found this particular segment of West German students the most vocal example of political activism, arguing that "[b]y virtue of their organization and superior tactics, these left-wing groups exercise a disproportionate influence on student governments and university life."[25] According to Stern, the actions of the SDS were, however, only a reflection of the fact that German youth in general had lost interest in the United States and a feeling of growing apart had set in.[26] Stern saw the rise of the general criticism of the US as independent from the war in Vietnam, although the latter was the ultimate focal point that united youthful opposition across political orientations: "That war has become the most general target of attack. The left condemns it as an extreme example of American neo-colonialism, and the right, as an example of America's irresolute pursuit of its own ends. I doubt that either group would turn strongly pro-American even if the war ended, though there is no doubt that the vast majority of students, which is not yet anti-American, is deeply disturbed by the brutality of the war and unpersuaded of its necessity."[27] As far as the nationwide impact of student unrest in Berlin was concerned, Stern predicted that the movement would soon turn into a "spreading condition" not only in the West as a whole, but also in the Federal Republic.[28]

Local American missions soon reconfirmed Stern's assessment and began to report extensively on student disruptions and protest activities. By the spring of 1968, US officials were increasingly dedicating time and resources to an extensive monitoring of the West German student movement, whose reverberations reached into various areas of American interest. As a result, the efforts of local youth committees that had been formed at the initiative of the IAYC in the first half of the decade increased rapidly. Dennis Kux, political officer in Bonn from 1966 to 1969, for example, was specifically assigned the task of monitoring the political attitudes of students from the American embassy: "I spent time on university campuses trying to understand the student movement. However, dealing with the student 'Left' was rather a specialized thing. ... I went to some of the conventions and the offices of the student movement. I met with the leaders; I sought out what their ideas were – very much as a newspaperman would do. Then I would come back to the Embassy and write up a report."[29] On 21 December 1967, for example, Kux sat down with SDS Chairman Karl-Dietrich Wolff to discuss the SDS's view of West German society, its stance on university reform, the Socialist countries and the Middle East, and the war in Vietnam. For the embassy official, the environment in which the meeting took place was rather irritating: "When I called on the leader of the most radical group, the SDS, he was not too happy to meet with me. Finally, I just went to their office in Frankfurt. I said: 'Here I am. I am Dennis Kux from the American Embassy.' It was a little awkward talking to the head of the SDS. On the wall there was a scrawled sign, 'Fuck LBJ.' Still, we somehow got through the conversation."[30] Other US officials also covered local student activities and established contact with various youth organizations. In Hamburg, Foreign Service Officer Ronald Humphrey even joined an anti-Vietnam demonstration on 21 March 1968 in order to give an inside account of the demonstrators' tactics and strategies, as well as the police reaction.[31]

The Challenge of West German Student Protest

The efforts of the Department of State with respect to the West German student movement did not stop at the level of mere observation. Especially in Berlin, disturbances caused by the student movement were a major concern for American officials due to Allied responsibility for the security and government of the city.[32] The events surrounding the visit of Vice President Humphrey in March 1967 had already laid bare the public rift concerning the support of American policy in Vietnam and induced the US mission to closely examine the local student left. However, the first instance in which American and Allied officials considered prohibiting anti-war protest, thereby interfering with the civil government of Berlin, came in April 1967 when a group of Americans residing in West Berlin decided to openly protest the war in Vietnam using an oversize American flag in their demonstrations. Aimed at generating anti-war support among other US citizens living in Berlin, the "U.S. Campaign to End the War in Vietnam" planned to use the flag in their weekly protest marches in the American sector. Alarmed American officials, who feared this national symbol would be tainted by its own citizens for supposedly "anti-American" purposes in a city where the image of American protection and determination was essential, sought various ways to prevent this and eventually recommended a complete banning of the demonstration.[33] Although the other Allied powers even suggested a possible expulsion of the persons in question, the Department of State decided that "attempts at suppression of demonstration or denial of permission to carry flags would probably get even worse and longer-lasting publicity." For this reason, Washington determined that, unless there was a major security threat, any interference should be avoided.[34]

Despite the fact that the demonstration in question was conducted peacefully, anti-war protest and student disorder, whether imported from the US or locally developed, now became political and security issues the Allies were hard pressed to avoid in their administration of the divided city.[35] This became especially clear after the riots following the killing of Benno Ohnesorg by a Berlin policeman on 2 June 1967. In the monthly tripartite meeting of the Allies on 9 June, the French representative noted that the situation had reached a point where the Allied powers should start considering possible reactions and strategies to confront continuing student unrest.[36] Only two weeks later, the FU student government addressed the Allied commanders directly in their protest against the upcoming emergency legislation. Demanding that the Allied powers should safeguard the democracy and security of the city, the student body argued that it was not the existence of an extraparliamentary opposition and the exercise of their constitutional rights that were harmful to the democratic order of Berlin, but the actions of the Senate. These included, for example, the suppression of the right of free assembly and the assent to police brutality. As the resolution contended, "West Berlin lives from its claim and its mission to be a 'show window of freedom'. The Federal Emergency Legislation has the potential of shattering this window."[37] American officials, however, chose to ignore the open letter to prevent the opening up of a dialogue between students and Allied officials and thus even more public attention to student protest.

In the following weeks, the Allied Command extensively discussed student disorders in Berlin with the governing mayor as well as other representatives from the Berlin Senate. A draft policy paper prepared by the US mission listed various means of confronting the issue, which included, among other things, "an Allied ban on demonstrations, dismissal of civil officials, expulsion of undesirable persons, and the closure of the universities."[38] Asserting the right of the Allied powers to take any measures guaranteeing the security and maintenance of order in Berlin, these steps were, however, not yet considered necessary. Rather, any direct role of Allied control or operative involvement in dealing with the student unrest was circumvented at all costs. The Allies considered bilateral talks with city officials much more efficient.[39] This strategy also prohibited Berlin officials from publicly diverting responsibility for their actions to the Allies and would counteract already existing rumors of Allied concern over student unrest. In short, US diplomats agreed on a policy that was to govern their future actions with respect to student protest, namely that the Allies "should only intervene if the dispute reaches such magnitude that it clearly endangers the future of West Berlin itself. At that point, our intervention should be clear, unequivocal and publicly justifiable."[40]

The US mission in Berlin became, however, increasingly worried about the escalation in militancy on the side of the students on the one hand, and the growing impatience and even physical backlash of Berliners against students on the other. The Department of State itself was equally concerned about the growing polarization in the city: "Berlin today is a paradox. The city faces no readily apparent external threat and yet it is the scene of more internal trouble than any time in the last fifteen years."[41] The department particularly blamed bad leadership for the escalation of the disruptions after the killing of Benno Ohnesorg. As a consequence, it anticipated that the Allies would eventually be forced to interfere with the city's government to maintain public order: "The problem of student unrest is of some concern to us because we, along with the British and the French, continue to bear the ultimate responsibility for the security of the city. We have tried to avoid becoming directly involved. This may become difficult if the student demonstrations become more violent or if the students attempt to bring about confrontations with Allied personnel."[42]

In the course of 1968, the necessity of such an intervention frequently seemed to be imminent. An event that tested Allied and especially American reaction was the Vietnam Congress from 17 to 18 February. Particularly in light of the international participation and the use of the city as a platform for "anti-American" propaganda, the American embassy was extremely worried about the detrimental political effects and security problems this event would pose.[43] However, after long deliberation and in accordance with the French and the British, the US mission in Berlin argued that banning the congress would be largely counterproductive. Such a ban might direct criticism away from the students and toward the war in Vietnam and the US presence in Berlin. Furthermore, the US would lose the respect earned among students for its restrained reaction in previous months. The mission therefore concluded that the US could "lose more by trying unsuccessfully to ban the congress than we would by allowing the local authorities to deal with any disturbances it may create."[44] But despite their confidence in the local police, the American mission and the US army were on high alert during the event and, to avoid confrontation with congress participants, advised their staff to clear the American military and housing area in Dahlem, the supposed destination of a concluding demonstration.[45]

Although the Vietnam Congress proceeded relatively calmly compared to previous American expectations, the US mission emphatically welcomed the pro-American "Peace and Freedom" rally called by the Berlin Senate and other organizations on 21 February, which attracted 150,000 people.[46] It considered it "in keeping with Berlin tradition" and an avenue for Berliners frustrated by the students' actions and upset by the Vietnam Congress "to stand up for more positive and traditional political values."[47] In a congratulatory message, Ambassador McGhee thanked the Berliners for their expression of "confidence in the United States and of their determination to stand with us in defense of freedom." Arguing that Schütz had persuasively illustrated that "your government and Berliners will prevent an extremist minority, many from outside of the city, from conveying to the world a false and dangerous impression about Berlin," McGhee intentionally linked the pro-American rally to past efforts to resist communist threats to the city, such as the Berlin crises at the beginning of the decade.[48] Thereby portraying the student movement as another attack by external forces on the "joint pledge to maintain freedom in Berlin" between the US and the citizens of Berlin, the US ambassador only additionally fueled the tense atmosphere in the city.

Despite regrets about the incidents of violence against innocent bystanders and the wave of public criticism in the Federal Republic, American posts generally interpreted the rally as a necessary boost for the city's morale and rejected West German criticism and comparisons to officially sponsored mass rallies of National Socialism. The American consulate in Frankfurt argued that some critics "fail to realize the delicate situation that would result if an impression is created that Berlin opposes the U.S. This could have incalculable effects on the moral position of the U.S. as an occupying power in Berlin."[49] Interestingly enough, American officials, who were otherwise very much concerned about the mutual spiral of militancy and an increase in physical backlash against student protesters, held that the costs of the militant public overreaction in reconfirming pro-American attitudes were outweighed by its benefits, even though they noticed that the attacks on students had prompted the "Republican Club" to discuss forming its own security squad.[50]

The so-called Easter riots after the assassination attempt on Rudi Dutschke only further escalated the situation in the city, in the view of the Allies. Now the focus of protest activities shifted more toward internal issues, such as protest against the press monopoly of Axel Springer and the upcoming ratification of the emergency laws. The US mission in Berlin recognized a new degree in militancy, namely demonstrators' resort to arson as exemplified by the burning of Springer trucks or police cars. Despite the largely restrained response by the local authorities, US officials saw the gap between the students and the population as widening. Apart from the smashing of windows at the America House and the

RIAS Berlin (Radio in the American Sector), which the CIA in its daily reports saw as proof that the riots would take on an "anti-American character," the US mission was relieved that no American institutions were targeted during the riots and maintained its policy of strict non-interference.[51]

An issue that particularly alerted American officials was the suspected support given to the demonstrators by East Germany. Possible contacts between the SED or FDJ and the student movement were addressed in almost every longer report on student disorders from American posts.[52] The Department of State continued to emphasize that the students were fully aware of these indirect subsidies and infiltration attempts by East Berlin and were utilizing them for their own ends. Whereas in some instances the student and communist causes actually overlapped, in others they would be so disparate as to cause embarrassment to the communists, particularly when associated with Mao, Che Guevara or the infamous "Kommune I." As a result, East Berlin had largely kept its support low-key, which, in the Department of State's view, seemed to have changed only slightly during the Easter riots, when protesting students were given free rides on the East German–run tram (*S-Bahn*) and tightly rolled copies of *Neues Deutschland* were used as torches in the attacks on the Springer building. In any case, the department concluded, despite the GDR's aim for greater control and influence on student leaders, its identification with and exploitation of the students' causes had chiefly been in vain: "The SED does not as yet appear, however, to have captured anything resembling control of the student movement, or of its leaders. Working against them, among other factors, is the simple but devastating fact that most German students simply regard the East German and Soviet brands of communism as an anachronism."[53] Although a much higher degree of infiltration and observation of the student movement by the GDR has become evident since the opening of East German archives, the basic assumptions of the department's analysis are still valid today.[54] Even in the city of Berlin, where the protest movement was situated between the two ideological blocs, communist efforts were not able to control the direction of student protest.

As a result of the close proximity to the ideological enemy, student protesters were nonetheless tempted to play on the opportunity to challenge the West Berlin government and the Allies by interfering in larger political processes of East-West tensions over the city. Such a chance presented itself during the Berlin access crisis in the spring and summer of 1968, when the GDR once more sought to capitalize politically from its control of the city's transit by denying entry to NPD members, as well as ministers and high officials of the West German government.[55] In this situation, the SDS discussed a blockade of the Autobahn under East German control, for which it had, according to US intelligence, already secured the goodwill of the East German authorities.[56] The Allied powers were even further alarmed by the establishment of an SDS committee with the specific goal of provoking their involvement. The US mission saw this move in keeping with "the long range SDS goal to force the allies to assume a more direct day to day responsibility for city operations, thus lending strength to their claim that the senate is bankrupt and incapable of governing the city." For mission officials, this strategy was "the logical source of any student plans to involve Berlin access routes in demonstrations."[57]

In light of this new development, American officials instructed the Berlin Senate and police to devise plans for the rerouting of traffic.[58] Since existing laws did not provide sufficient legal basis to prosecute demonstrators for such a blockade, an Allied legislative amendment as well as strategies to prevent and confront possible student blockades were drafted, the latter involving a clearing away of any obstacles to unhindered transit by American military convoys.[59] The Department of State, however, alerted by the students' strategy to openly elicit an Allied response to their actions in an area where they had no jurisdiction, insisted on a passive policy of patient observance and did not allow "contact between blockaders and Allied authority outside of the Berlin city limits."[60] The dilemma the US administration faced was that American or Allied operations on East German territory would have serious political consequences that it was not prepared to risk carelessly. As Edward Fried summed up the situation in a memo to Walt Rostow, in the case of student protesters setting up a barricade in the area in question, "it would not be possible for West Berlin or allied authorities to remove students without going into East Germany or obtaining Soviet help." The department feared that this could be the first time that the US as one of the Allied powers would have to give up its restrained policy toward student unrest and interfere directly in opposing student demonstrations, which in this case could yield unforeseeable diplomatic problems as well as negative consequences for the overall image of the US in West Germany.[61]

Although the expected blockade did not take place, the Allies drew their conclusions from this incident and in September 1968 introduced legislation that made any disturbance of Western traffic to the city of Berlin illegal.[62] Having thus ensured an adequate legal framework in which to confront future student actions, the Allies continued to exercise restraint in the face of mounting student disorder, since no such direct challenge of their power occurred afterward.

American concern over West German student unrest was, however, not restricted to West Berlin. The contacts student protesters sought with the stationed US military, for example, turned out to be another issue challenging the American presence in the Federal Republic. West German students, especially the SDS and local student governments, contributed substantially to a European network of desertion support that helped American soldiers escape to France and Sweden.[63] By 1968, various activist groups in the country engaged in efforts to organize American GIs by involving them in discussion of their role in the Vietnam War and American foreign policy.[64] American officials gradually came to see the rise of student-GI contact in conjunction with anti-war actions as a problem and approached the Foreign Office in Bonn about continuous student solicitations to desertion.[65] US military installations also frequently offered the chance for students to deliver their criticism of American foreign policy directly to its executing branches. Although the military itself provided specific instructions to its personnel on how to deal with demonstrators in these circumstances, the problem of US military personnel being harassed by student protesters also came to the attention of American representatives and provided further arguments for troop reductions in Europe.

A basic problem for American officials dealing with the student-directed GI organizing was that the calls for desertions were often so carefully worded as to be completely within the realms of the legally admissible, which made prosecution almost impossible.[66] In Berlin legislation, the laws declaring the solicitation of desertion an offense in the Federal Republic had surprisingly not been adopted. However, as a reaction to these student activities, an Allied amendment of September 1968 finally made it illegal to advocate desertion in Berlin and ordered West German courts to prosecute the perpetrators, despite initial British and French hesitations.[67] Although US military and other American officials considered the desertion campaigns and GI organizing by the West German student movement a problem, they saw their actual impact on the operational fitness and morale of US troops as negligible. As a 1969 army study on the subversion of military personnel abroad emphasized, the efforts by the U.S. Campaign to End the War in Vietnam and the SDS, despite their international connections to the American SDS (Students for a Democratic Society), MOBE (National Mobilization Committee to End the War in Vietnam), or the French RITA (Resistance Inside the Army) had only little significance and posed no imminent danger.[68]

West German Student Protest and International Relations: Implications for US Foreign Policy

The reactions of the US government to the West German student movement were embedded in a much larger effort to come to terms with the international dimension of student unrest. The May events of 1968 in France dramatically confirmed the significance the Inter-Agency Youth Committee had assigned to European youth since 1966. As a result, inquiries concerning the Western European and international youth scene became a pressing issue for US diplomats. In a circular to all American overseas posts on 30 May 1968, Dean Rusk considered the events in Paris a "sobering lesson," pointing out to the local American representatives "how successful a handful of university students in France were in precipitating a crisis which has potentially very serious overtones for our foreign policy interests."[69] Rusk urged the close examination of national trends toward similar incidents, in order to better assess their repercussions on US interests: "But our concern cannot be solely with the crises such disaffection may generate. We must be concerned with the very existence of such undercurrents before they coalesce to force action on longstanding social problems. They are a part of the ambiance in which we operate today and, more importantly, may foreshadow future national policies. As such, they must be evaluated and reported."[70]

The response from the various diplomatic posts all over the world was so overwhelming that the Department of State had to institute a "Student Unrest Study Group" chaired by George McGhee and including Robert Cross, the current department's youth advisor and staff director of the IAYC. The group dedicated itself to a comprehensive evaluation of policy guidelines in reaction to student unrest worldwide, especially any attack on "the objectives of U.S. foreign policy, our relations with the country concerned or the worldwide functioning of our business interests and our free enterprise economic system."[71] It argued that the specific causes and consequences of student unrest had to be meticulously analyzed in order to adjust any US policy response to the local situation, which might also include a welcoming of protest activities if beneficial to American policy objectives. Taking into account the dynamics of protest movements, the group concluded that "this is a field in which we should seek to take advantage of the inevitable and to accelerate the desirable."[72]

The inherently transnational orientation of student protesters was, in the view of the group's chairman, one of the greatest challenges for any foreign policy assessment:

> We sense that the emergence of the attitudes associated with the New Left are indicative of a historical turning point in national attitudes. We are unable to understand the full ramifications of this intuition, but we suggest that a major contributing factor is the relative absence of broadly accepted national concerns that would foster a stronger "nationalism" or "patriotism," in their traditional sense. If there is any common thread underlying the New Left, it is a marked lack of such attitudes. Perhaps it was the prosperity of the sixties, the seeming recent decline in the Soviet threat, and disillusionment with their country's national purposes that have contributed most to this situation.[73]

Assuming that their motives would more often be part of a domestic power struggle than related to the actual issues at stake, McGhee underlined that students often only represented the "trigger" of long-term developments beyond their control, representing essentially valid claims of various social groups. For the Department of State, it was therefore crucial to closely monitor the students' situation: "Above all, we must not overlook the dangers of being out of touch with those who will certainly have an important effect on future events."[74]

For this reason, President Johnson himself was constantly kept informed of these efforts and early on requested reports from CIA Director Richard Helms on the international connections of the anti-war movement.[75] In September 1968, another report on the global dimension of student unrest reached the White House, this time causing fierce debates at the highest level of the administration.

In this most extensive single study produced on the issue, Helms had his agency analyze the student movements in nineteen countries in utmost detail.[76] The report on "Restless Youth" dedicated itself at length to the historical roots of student protest, the alienation of the young generation in modern society and from politics, and current conditions at universities, as well as the rise of the New Left. It laid particular emphasis on the global interconnectedness of protest, which provoked heated discussion between various cabinet members and the president, who showed a surprisingly narrow focus on communist conspiracies and a disregard for the underlying problems leading to student unrest as spelled out by Helms.[77] Despite these views, the work of the CIA exhaustively informed the highest levels of the US administration on details of global student protest and furnished them with ample comparative information to gear their local response.

Throughout the whole process of assessing the possibility of student unrest like that in France occurring in other countries, the IAYC functioned as the main center for debate and exchange among the various branches of government. It was here that the studies and memos mentioned above were discussed, guidelines drafted, and further plans for action presented. In effect, the IAYC served as an institutionalized forum on how to confront overseas student revolts at a very high level in the administration. By the beginning of 1969, the US government had thus exhaustively analyzed the potential threat that worldwide student unrest posed to its foreign policy interests. It decided to not only increase its monitoring of youthful protest, but also to react to this challenge through other diplomatic means, interpreting current sentiments among students as possible trends for the opinion of future elites. Attempting to incorporate these findings into their individual country programming, US officials sought to confront what they saw as an international problem on a local level. Along these lines, student protest affected American foreign policy considerations in a remarkable way, as can be seen in the resulting adjustments taken in the public diplomacy programs directed at West Germany.

The West German Student Movement in German-American Relations

The efforts of the State Department and its overseas posts to reach the young generation of West Germany and particularly protesting students were substantial, manifold, and adapted to the shifts in public opinion that became noticeable over time. As far as the organizational structure dedicated to youth affairs was concerned, the embassy's youth committee, established in the course of the 1960s as a result of the IAYC's efforts, was chaired by the deputy chief of the mission, Martin Hillenbrand, and included representatives from other branches. Furthermore, youth programs were operated by USIS, the Defense Attaché, the consulates general, and the embassy itself.

As has already become evident in the description of US reactions to student unrest in Berlin, the war in Vietnam posed the greatest problem for American programs directed toward German youth.[78] As a former USIS lecturer remembered,

> I arranged for a very extensive, almost continuous, on-going lecture program on Vietnam and Vietnamese problems and questions. I lectured at universities, at political clubs, at civic organizations. I remember very vividly being invited by the student body of the Free University of Berlin to talk about Vietnam. When I arrived, there were the police. There were police dogs. There was a huge banner of the Viet Cong. And there was a rowdy group of students who did not want to let me speak. … Eggs were thrown. Objects were thrown. I was ultimately rescued by the police and their dogs and went back to my hotel.[79]

Instead of these public meetings, many American posts increasingly favored the idea of walking toward West German students and conducting informal discussions in which a deeper and more subtle picture of the US could be presented. When in November of 1967 the US Mission in Berlin concluded that the ongoing student unrest contributed to low morale and had become detrimental to the city's liberal reputation, it restructured its program efforts and made the young academic generation one of its prime areas of concern.[80] This refocusing included social get-togethers in the consulate officer's home as well as the assignment of junior officers to this primary target group and an increase in training personnel in this area. In the face of further reduction of its personnel, the use of junior foreign service officers also proved to be particularly effective in the efforts of the American Consulate at Stuttgart, which likewise argued that "the post-war generation is becoming an increasingly important factor in German politics, and greater efforts must be made by American policy makers to know and understand the goals of this group."[81]

Along very similar lines, the embassy in Bonn announced in May 1968 that "its past programs and priorities are no longer adequate."[82] It argued that, due to the dramatic increase in political activity among West German youth and its considerable influence on the political spectrum in recent years, the embassy's programs needed to be completely overhauled. As a consequence, American priorities in country programming for West German youth from now on should concentrate primarily on university and advanced high school (*Gymnasium*) students. The embassy justified this shift by claiming that this group had become an independent political force that would be the almost exclusive pool of the future leadership for the country. It thus had to become the main focus of the embassy's attention: "German students must be given the highest priority, not only because they have become to some extent a political force in their own right. The greatest emphasis must be placed on reaching the student leadership, both radical and moderate."[83] In USIS-sponsored programs as well, youth should become the major target audience. Accordingly, the embassy's focus with regard to youth organizations and "radical" students sharpened, and coverage of West German youth and student organizations intensified in order to better adjust to their growing influence. Viewing student unrest as a nationwide problem, the embassy also sought to confront the problem by providing specific training and a greater coordination of its various posts across the country. For this reason, youth officers' conferences and European Youth Seminars frequently took place in the Federal Republic in the following years, often co-organized by, or in close cooperation with, the IAYC.[84]

The young generation of West Germany, due to the future influential role it was believed to play in its country's politics, was a prominent factor in American country programming from now on. In November 1967, a State Department Policy Planning Council report had already concluded that, ideologically, the German student movement's "anti-Americanism, largely over Vietnam, coupled to that of most of the FRG's leftist intellectuals, does present a growing problem for US policy," especially in a long-term fusion with the attitudes of the German public.[85] In addition, it soon took note of the possible influence the young generation could exercise on future West German foreign policy:

> Account should also be taken of the fact that a new generation of German leaders will be coming into power in the not-too-distant future. There is widespread disaffection among younger Germans with the present leadership and its policies, disillusionment with the prospects for West European unity, and a strong interest in developing new approaches to German unity without regard for ideological restraints. It is somewhat easier to imagine that, when this generation assumes leadership, the FRG might, with relatively little provocation by US policies, reassess its essential interests and undertake a basic policy departure.[86]

In other words, the threat of a neutralist Germany, an "all-German status" for West Berlin, and massive reductions of US forces, as well as the Federal Republic's withdrawal from the Common Market and NATO, were the consequences US policy planners feared most as long-term effects of student protest.[87] In their view, the problem primarily consisted of the fact that despite the gradual faltering of the New Left on an organizational level, the ideological challenge it posed was not absorbed by the dominant political or intellectual elites, who gradually adopted similar viewpoints. In this context, the fact that the New Left's criticism of American foreign policy with respect to Southeast Asia partially resonated with members of the established parties was only one example of its intellectual influence on the political landscape of the Federal Republic.

Yet another aspect was the actual influx of former student activists in official party ranks. When it became apparent in mid 1969 that the youth organizations of the SPD and FDP were still very much under the radical students' influence, the US embassy anticipated the survival of New Left ideology in the established party system as a permanent aftereffect of the student movement. Its overall effect on the political system of the Federal Republic was thus seen as both profound and multifaceted: "For the present there appear to be four principal consequences of New Left activity: a right-wing backlash, a strengthening of the left among youth organizations, a new leftist ideological challenge to the Bonn political system and a connected spur to reform efforts."[88] Despite campaigns to counteract the intellectual attraction of the New Left, the impact that this new generation of young West German leaders shaped by the turbulent political experiences of the late 1960s would have for the Federal Republic was hardly considered reversible by American officials: "As persons 'formed in the struggle' move into positions of responsibility in the decades ahead, the long-term effect will probably be as much intellectual as political."[89]

American officials thus eagerly observed the ideological transformations initiated by this political generation. The new Chancellor Brandt's move toward the student left and his initial efforts to integrate it into existing party structures were watched with particular care by American posts and politicians alike in the following years.[90] In 1973, USIS rather helplessly stated that it was hard pressed to counteract the substantial change in the attitudes of West German youth since the 1950s with existing cultural diplomacy efforts alone:

> In some respects, the U.S. is still reaping the rewards of its large exchange programs of the 'fifties and early 'sixties. E.g., of the 18 members of the Federal Cabinet, eleven are returnees … and their actions and words reflect that their views of America have been strongly shaped by their exchange experience. But gradually the grantees of those years are disappearing from the scene; the circle of returnees able to serve as influential, well-informed interpreters between the U.S. and Germany is diminishing since CU resources are far smaller today than they were during the reorientation period.[91]

The West German student movement thus functioned as a catalyst for a redefinition of the transatlantic partnership in the second half of the 1960s. As its most visible symptom, it was responsible for a readjustment of American cultural diplomacy to the Federal Republic. As USIS Public Affairs Officer Hans Tuch recalled,

> There was a difference of view on the part of young Germans vis-a-vis the United States, vis-a-vis their society, vis-a-vis the East-West conflict. There was a generational difference. We also realized that these young people who did not have the same experiences as their elders had in the 1950s and the 1960s, who had an entirely different experience in growing up and being educated, were about to take over leadership in the Ger-

man society. ... We recognized that changes had taken place, and that we had to readdress our ideas on our association with the Germans and how to deal with the problem, how to cope with it in order to be able to maintain the relationship that we feel is necessary to maintain.[92]

However, the student protesters fell far short of achieving their declared goals, among them the destruction of NATO and the disentanglement of the Federal Republic from the transatlantic alliance system. Even the stationing of Pershing II missiles on West German soil at the beginning of the 1980s did not seriously weaken the official German-American bond, even though it involved the opposition of far greater segments of society.[93] Nonetheless, the actions of the student activists of the late 1960s provoked the increasing attention of American foreign-policy makers toward their ideology and its influence on West German society and laid the ground for a gradual change in the nature of German-American relations, which would emerge in the following decades as a result of their arrival in the halls of power.

Conclusion

The reaction of the US government to the student movement in West Germany was diverse and differed according to the various branches of the administrations, but it has nevertheless occupied a permanent place in German-American relations since the second half of the 1960s. What was first perceived as an imitation of the Free Speech Movement at the University of California, Berkeley, and part of an international movement against the war in Vietnam, came to be considered a far more serious problem for American foreign policy. American officials soon discerned a growing process of cultural estrangement from the United States among Western European youth in general, which was further evidenced by the turbulence accompanying the reception of Vice President Humphrey in 1967. Worries about the geographic spread of the movement from Berlin to other parts of the country and the effect of student militancy on internal stability ran through the extensive reporting of American posts on student disruptions in West Germany.

Student protesters in Berlin occupied a special place in this monitoring. Student unrest there not only challenged West German domestic politics, but also the Allied authority governing the city. On a number of occasions, American officials had to devise adequate responses toward the burning of the American flag by American protesters, the consequences of student unrest on the city's morale, and the utilization of this symbolic city as an international forum for protest against the war in Vietnam. Although provoked to a considerable degree by student cooperation with East Germany, American political and military forces adhered to their strict policy of non-interference in student protest, fearing that attention would otherwise be unnecessarily diverted toward them. Thereby trying to avoid becoming a direct target of student actions, they instead closely consulted with and supported West German officials in dealing with student protesters.

Faced with growing internal unrest in the country of one of its closest allies during the Cold War, the US government rather decided to address the dissatisfaction of the young West German generation by making them the primary target of its cultural and educational activities in the country. The youth committees of local American consulates rapidly intensified their efforts to reach out to future leaders, engaging them in discussions to find out more about their attitudes and potentially influence them. Despite the fact that student protest never occupied a prime position in German-American relations, it nonetheless frequently played a part in the strategic deliberations of American interests with regard to the Federal Republic and, as such, was a factor very much present for American policy makers. The US government was acutely aware that a number of the protesting students of the late 1960s would become the future leaders of West Germany and soon occupy positions of considerable influence in society and the political system. For this new generation coming of age in the 1960s, the immediate war experience and the Cold War confrontations of earlier years, as well as Manichean rhetoric conjuring up a Soviet threat, had long been replaced by fundamental concerns over détente between the superpowers during the 1960s. Accordingly, their view of the United States was considerably different from that of their predecessors:

> While the recent sudden and widely-discussed concern with growing "anti-Americanism" in Germany is doubtlessly exaggerated, the fact remains that there is growing here into positions of influence a new generation of men and women whose attitudes toward the U.S., in contrast to those born before (say) 1930, have not been shaped by America's contributions to Germany's postwar recovery and the creation of a secure Western Europe. Rather, their attitudes have been shaped by the war in Viet-Nam, an America beset by serious domestic problems, the assassinations of John F. Kennedy, Martin Luther King, Malcolm X, and Robert Kennedy, and American self-doubts – elements all which have dominated German media coverage of the U.S. during their formative years.[94]

It was this markedly changed image of the US, together with a transcendence of geopolitical bloc confrontations of the Cold War, that connected students from various parts of the globe and spurred a concerted US government effort in the form of the IAYC to monitor and influence youth from the time of the Kennedy administration onward. As the Department of State suggested in 1967 with respect to protesting students worldwide,

For them communism is neither a threat to the nation nor an answer to their problems. They seem to feel, one suspects, that for the older generation communism has come to serve as a pretext for not coming to grips with the serious problems of our society in fields like civil rights, poverty, slum clearance, and the host of other difficulties that afflict mass urban life. Hence the policy priorities of youth may run counter to the requirements imposed on the US by its role as a world power.[95]

Precisely this ideological transformation, which American foreign policy crucially needed to adjust to, presented the more serious long-term challenge posed by the West German student movement and the global protest movements at the end of the 1960s.

Notes

1. This chapter is based on Martin Klimke, *The Other Alliance: Student Protest in West Germany and the United States in the Global Sixties* (Princeton, 2010), chaps. 5 and 6.
2. All quotations taken from George McGhee to President Johnson, "World Student Unrest," Report, George McGhee: Writings, vol. 2, 1960–1969, 1968, 332, 335, George McGhee Papers: 2001 Accession, I, 2, 1, Georgetown University Library, Special Collections, Washington, D.C. (hereafter GUL).
3. Hans N. Tuch, oral history interview, 4 August 1989, Foreign Affairs Oral History Collection, GUL.
4. Research on the "establishment" reaction to West German student protest at the end of the 1960s has only just begun. Promising beginnings are, e.g., Klaus Weinhauer, *Schutzpolizei in der Bundesrepublik: Zwischen Bürgerkrieg und Innerer Sicherheit* (Paderborn, 2003); Hellmut Brunn and Thomas Kirn, eds., *Rechtsanwälte - Linksanwälte: 1971 bis 1981 - das Rote Jahrzehnt vor Gericht* (Frankfurt, 2004); Christina von Hodenberg, "Der Kampf um die Redaktionen: '1968' und die westdeutschen Massenmedien," in: Christina von Hodenberg and Detlef Siegfried, *Wo 1968 liegt. Reform und Revolte in der Geschichte der Bundesrepublik* (Göttingen, 2006), 139–163; Katja Nagel, "Die Provinz in Bewegung. Studentenunruhen in Heidelberg 1964 bis 1974," Ph.D. diss., University of Heidelberg, 2008; Sandra Kraft, "Vom Autoritätskonflikt zur Machtprobe: Die Studentenproteste der 60er Jahre als Herausforderung für das Establishment in Deutschland und den USA," Ph.D. diss., University of Heidelberg, 2008. For a more international perspective see Jeremi Suri, *Power and Protest: Global Revolution and the Rise of Détente* (Cambridge, MA, 2003); Stuart Hilwig, *Italy and 1968: Youthful Unrest and Democratic Culture* (London, 2009); Kathrin Fahlenbrach, Martin Klimke, and Joachim Scharloth, eds., *The 'Establishment' Responds: Power and Protest During and After the Cold War* (forthcoming 2010).
5. George McGhee to Philip Coombs, Bureau of Educational and Cultural Affairs, "Goals for Free World Youth," Under Secretary of State for Political Affairs, 23 January 1962, Bureau of Educational and Cultural Affairs (hereafter CU), G IV, S4, 37: Youth Office, Early History, Box 161, University of Arkansas Libraries, Special Collections, Fayetteville, AR (hereafter UASC).

6. Dean Rusk to ambassadors, Letter, Secretary of State, Washington, 8 July 1964, 2, Aides Files, Harry McPherson, Youth Committee, Box 18 (1415), Lyndon B. Johnson Library, Austin, TX (hereafter LBJL).

7. Lucius Battle, "Report on Inter-Agency Committee on Youth Affairs," 6 March 1963, 3, CU, G IV, S4, 37: Youth Office, Early History, Box 161, UASC.

8. Alfred Boerner, "Emphasis on Youth," Memo, 15 April 1963, CU, G IV, S4, 37: Youth Office, Early History, Box 161, UASC.

9. Thomas Sorensen, *The Word War: The Story of American Propaganda* (New York, 1968), 194f.

10. Dean Rusk, "Emphasis on Youth: Presidential Memorandum," Airgram, CA-5966, Department of State, 10 December 1963, in: CU, G IV, S4, 37: Youth Office, Early History, Box 161, UASC.

11. Ibid., 2.

12. "The Interagency Youth Committee," 1964 (undated), 1, in: CU, G IV, S4, 37: Youth Office, Early History, Box 161, UASC.

13. United States Information Agency Office of Policy and Research, "Vietnam and World Opinion," Report, 000951, August 1966, 19, RG 306, Records of the U.S. Information Agency, Office of Research, Special Reports, 1964–82, S-15-66, Box 3, U.S. National Archives II, College Park, Maryland (hereafter NA).

14. Ibid., 21.

15. Wyman to Department of State, "Radical Student Activity in West Berlin," Airgram, A-321, US Mission Berlin, 11 January 1967, 1, RG 59, Central Foreign Policy Files, 1967–69, POL 23-8, GER W, 6/1/67, Box 2133, NA.

16. Ibid., 4.

17. In the so-called "Pudding-Attentat," West Berlin police arrested eleven students, predominantly members of the "Kommune I," for a planned conspiracy with the intent of assassinating the vice president. The students later had to be set free after pudding, yogurt, and ingredients for butter tarts were found among them instead of explosives. See Siegward Lönnendonker, Bernd Rabehl and Jochen Staadt, eds., *Die antiautoritäre Revolte: Der Sozialistische Deutsche Studentenbund nach der Trennung von der SPD* (Wiesbaden, 1999), 319–24.

18. Not only had local American officials been informed of the police action, but US intelligence had cooperated "in developing information leading up to the arrests." Morris to Secretary of State, "Vice President Visit," Telegram, Berlin 1336, US Mission Berlin, 5 April 1967, RG 59, Central Foreign Policy Files, 1967–69, POL 7 US / Humphrey, 4/1/67, Box 2614, NA; "11 Seized in Berlin in a Reported Plot to Kill Humphrey," *New York Times*, 6 April 1967, 1, 5.

19. Hubert Humphrey to President, "Western Europe, March–April, 1967," Memo, 10 April 1967, 4f., NSF, International Meetings / Travel File, Vice President-Visit to Europe, Report to the President, March–April 1967, Box 26, LBJL.

20. See "Summary Notes of the 569th Meeting of the National Security Council," 3 May 1967, *FRUS*, 1964–68, 13:572 (I am grateful to Jeremi Suri for this reference) and for Humphrey's appearance before the IAYC in 1968, "Minutes of the Inter-Agency Youth Committee Meeting," Department of State, 21 February 1968, 2, in: RG 59, IAYC Records, IAYC Meeting, 21 February 1968, Box 1, NA.

21. Foy Kohler, "European Youth and Young Leaders Conference," Briefing Book, Department of State, May 1967, 8f., Aides Files, Harry McPherson, European Youth and Young Leaders, Box 23 (1518), LBJL.

22. Ibid., 10.
23. Ibid., 5. For an overview of these contacts see Klimke, *The Other Alliance,* chaps. 1–3.
24. Fritz Stern, "German Young Elites," Report for the Conference on European Youth and Young Leaders, Airlie House, 14–15 May 1967, 9 January 1967, 19, Aides Files, Harry McPherson, European Youth and Young Leaders, Box 23 (1518), LBJL.
25. Ibid., 22.
26. "It is fair to conclude that the German-American honeymoon is over. ... The spontaneous good will and the former almost deferential attitude toward us have largely disappeared." Ibid., 18, 30.
27. Ibid., 34.
28. Ibid., 27.
29. Dennis Kux, oral interview, 13 January 1995, Foreign Affairs Oral History Collection, GUL.
30. Ibid. For the extensive report see Fessenden to Department of State, "Views of Radical Student Leader," Airgram, A-794, American Embassy Bonn, 2 January 1968, 5, RG 59, Central Foreign Policy Files, 1967–69, POL 13-2, GER W, 1/1/68, Box 2125, NA.
31. Kidd to Department of State, "Anti–Viet Nam Demonstration in Hamburg, 22 March 1968," Airgram, A-162, American Consulate Hamburg, 1968, 03/27, RG 59, Central Foreign Policy Files, 1967–69, POL 23-8, GER W, 1/1/68, Box 2133, NA.
32. For the special role of Berlin see also Diethelm Prowe, "Berlin: Catalyst and Fault Line of German-American Relations in the Cold War," in *The United States and Germany in the Era of the Cold War: A Handbook,* 2 vols., ed. Detlef Junker (New York, 2004), 1:165–71; Andreas Daum, "America's Berlin, 1945–2000: Between Myth and Visions," in *Berlin: The New Capital in the East. A Transatlantic Appraisal,* ed. Frank Trommler (New York, 2000), 49–73.
33. Morris to Secretary of State, "Planned Vietnam Protest By Americans in Berlin," Telegram, Berlin 1447, US Mission Berlin, 21 April 1967, 2, RG 59, Central Foreign Policy Files, 1967–69, POL 23-8, GER W, 6/1/67, Box 2133, NA.
34. Dean Rusk to American Embassy Bonn, "Planned Vietnam Protest By US Students in Berlin, April 29," Telegram, 180320, Department of State, 21 April 1967, RG 59, Central Foreign Policy Files, 1967–69, POL 23-8, GER W, 6/1/67, Box 2133, NA.
35. With little public attention, about seventy demonstrators marched behind the US flag on 29 April 1967 carrying a banner that read: "Neutralize Vietnam: End the bombing and withdraw all foreign troops – let Vietnam live." Morris to Secretary of State, "'US Campaign' Demonstration," Telegram, Berlin 1498, US Mission Berlin, 29 April 1967, RG 59, Central Foreign Policy Files, 1967–69, POL 23-8, GER W, 6/1/67, Box 2133, NA.
36. Morris to Secretary of State, "Student Demonstrations," Telegram, Berlin 1660, US Mission Berlin, 14 June 1967, RG 59, Central Foreign Policy Files, 1967–69, POL 23-8, GER W, 6/1/67, Box 2133, NA.
37. Morris to Department of State, "Berlin Students' Open Letter to the Allies," Airgram, A-31, US Mission Berlin, 15 July 1967, 4–6, RG 59, Central Foreign Policy Files, 1967–69, EDU 9-3 GER B, 1/1/67, Box 344, NA.
38. Morris to Department of State, "Allied Consideration of Berlin Student Problems," Airgram, A-30, US Mission Berlin, 15 July 1967, 3, RG 59, Central Foreign Policy Files, 1967–69, EDU 9-3, GER W, 1/1/67, Box 345, NA.

39. "There are existing laws and regulations which can be used by German authorities to maintain order, and for the Allies to supplement these with specific orders would be to publicly imply that civil officials are incapable of dealing with the problem." Ibid., 3.

40. Ibid., 4.

41. Department of State, "Visit of Chancellor Kiesinger, August 1967: Berlin," Briefing Book, Department of State, 11 August 1967, NSF, Country File Germany, Visit of Chancellor Kiesinger, I (8/67), Box 193, LBJL.

42. Ibid., 2.

43. George McGhee to US Mission Berlin, "International Viet Nam Congress," Telegram, Bonn 7886, American Embassy Bonn, 1 February 1968, RG 59, Central Foreign Policy Files, 1967–69, POL 13-2, 1/1/68, Box 2870, NA.

44. American Embassy Bonn, "Mission Views on Possible Ban of Vietnam Congress," Telegram, Berlin 0911, US Mission Berlin, 8 February 1968, Section 2, 2, RG 59, Central Foreign Policy Files, 1967–69, POL 13-2, 1/1/68, Box 2870, NA.

45. Morris to Secretary of State, "Vietnam Congress," Telegram, Berlin 965, US Mission Berlin, 16 February 1968, RG 59, Central Foreign Policy Files, 1967–69, POL 13-2, 1/1/68, 2870, NA.

46. See Siegward Lönnendonker, Tilman Fichter and Jochen Staadt, eds., *Hochschule im Umbruch, Teil V: Gewalt und Gegengewalt (1967–1969)* (Berlin, 1983), 76; Dan Morgan, "150,000 Berliner Cheer for U.S.," *Washington Post,* 22 February 1968, A15.

47. Morris to Secretary of State, "Berlin Demonstration Planned for February 21," Telegram, 979, US Mission Berlin, 20 February 1968, 2, RG 59, Central Foreign Policy Files, 1967–69, POL 23-8, GER W, 1/1/68, Box 2133, NA.

48. George McGhee to Secretary of State, "Congratulatory Message to Governing Mayor Schuetz," Telegram, American Embassy Bonn, 22 February 1968, NSF, Country File Germany, Cables, Vol. XIV, 8/67–2/68, Box 188, LBJL.

49. Johnstone to Department of State, "Local Press and Labor Officials Critical of Berlin 'Freedom Rally'," Airgram, A-247, American Consulate Frankfurt, 1 March 1968, 2, RG 59, Central Foreign Policy Files, 1967–69, POL – Political Aff. & Rel., GER, 1967, Box 2107, NA.

50. Morris to Department of State, "Berlin New Left forms 'Militia'," Airgram, A-525, US Mission Berlin, 29 March 1968, RG 59, Central Foreign Policy Files, 1967–69, POL 13-10, GER W, 1/1/67, Box 2126, NA.

51. Wyman to Department of State, "Berlin Demonstrations – Comments on the Easter Weekend," Airgram, A-567, US Mission Berlin, 18 April 1968, 5, RG 59, Central Foreign Policy Files, 1967–69, POL 23-8, GER B, 1968, Box 2109, NA.

52. In September 1967, the US mission, for example, informed the State Department about the visit of the Kommune I to the Chinese embassy in East Berlin. Wyman to Department of State, "Members of West Berlin Kommune I Visit Communist Chinese Embassy in East Berlin," Airgram, A-120, US Mission Berlin, 12 September 1968, RG 59, Central Foreign Policy Files, 1967–69, POL 13-10, GER W, 1/1/67, Box 2126, NA.

53. Thomas L. Hughes to Secretary of State, "SED Influence in the West German Student Demonstration: Uncomfortable Alliance," Intelligence Note 296, Department

of State, Office of Intelligence and Research, 23 April 1968, 5, RG 59, Central Foreign Policy Files, 1967–69, POL 23-8, GER W, 4/1/68, Box 2133, NA.

54. Unless further evidence to the contrary can be found, the CIA estimate still holds true despite the 2009 revelations about the Stasi-connection of West German police officer Karl-Heinz Kurras, who killed student demonstrator Benno Ohnesorg in West Berlin on June 2, 1967. See Wolfgang Kraushaar, "Ein inoffizieller Staatsakt der DDR?," in: Berliner Zeitung, 23 May, 2009. See also Hubertus Knabe, *Die unterwanderte Republik: Stasi im Westen* (Munich, 2001), 182–233; Bernd Rabehl, *Feindblick: Der SDS im Fadenkreuz des ,Kalten Krieges'* (Berlin, 2000).

55. Dirk Kroegel, *Einen Anfang finden! Kurt Georg Kiesinger in der Außen- und Deutschlandpolitik der Großen Koalition* (Munich, 1997), 229f.

56. The part of the Autobahn in question was the "2 ½ kilometer stretch in GDR territory between the E[a]st Berlin 'mainland' and the peninsula of West Berlin at Dreilinden (Checkpoint Bravo)." Morris to Secretary of State, "Demonstrator's Threat to Harass Berlin Access," Telegram, Berlin 1270, US Mission Berlin, 16 April 1968, RG 59, Central Foreign Policy Files, 1967–69, POL 23-8, GER W, 4/1/68, Box 2133, NA.

57. Morris to Secretary of State, "SDS Committee to Involve Allies in Demonstrations," Telegram, Berlin 1325, US Mission Berlin, 25 April 1968, RG 59, Central Foreign Policy Files, 1967–69, POL 23-8, GER W, 4/1/68, Box 2133, NA.

58. Wyman to Secretary of State, "Demonstrators' Threat to Harass Berlin Access," Telegram, Berlin 1283, US Mission Berlin, 18 April 1968, 2, RG 59, Central Foreign Policy Files, 1967–69, POL 23-8, GER W, 4/1/68, Box 2133, NA.

59. Morris to Secretary of State, "Demonstrators' Threat to Block Berlin Access," Telegram, Berlin 1347, US Mission Berlin, 27 April 1968, RG 59, Central Foreign Policy Files, 1967–69, POL 23-8, GER W, 4/1/68, Box 2133, NA.

60. Dean Rusk to US Mission Berlin, "Demonstrator's Threat to Harass Berlin Access," Telegram, 154588, Department of State, 27 April 1968, RG 59, Central Foreign Policy Files, 1967–69, POL 23-8, GER W, 4/1/68, Box 2133, NA.

61. Edward Fried to Walt Rostow, "Berlin," Memo, The White House, 29 April 1968, NSF, Country File Germany, Memos, Vol. XV, 3/68–8/68, Box 189, LBJL.

62. See "Allies Impose Curbs to Deter West Berlin Leftists," *New York Times,* 20 September 1968, 14.

63. Max Watts, *US-Army – Europe: Von der Desertion zum Widerstand in der Kaserne oder wie die U-Bahn zur RITA fuhr* (Berlin, 1989), 7–38. See also Alexander Vazansky, "'Army in Anguish': The United States Army, Europe, in the Early 1970s," in Detlef Junker and Thomas Maulucci, eds., *GIs in Germany: The Social, Economic, Military, and Political History of the American Military Presence* (New York, forthcoming).

64. David Cortright and Zoltan Grossman, "Die GI-Bewegung in Deutschland," in *Widerstand in der US-Armee: GI-Bewegung in den siebziger Jahren,* ed. Dieter Brünn (Berlin, 1986), 88–101; Dave Harris, "FORWARD – Geschichte eines GI-Projekts in West-Berlin," ibid., 104–25.

65. In February 1968, the US Army headquarters in West Germany demanded that the US embassy remind the federal government of its legal responsibility "to insure by appropriate legislation the security and protection of the forces within its territory, which includes protection against inducement or facilitations of desertion." George

McGhee to US Mission Berlin, "Solicitation to Desert," Telegram, Bonn 10225, American Embassy Bonn, 29 February 1968, 1, 5, RG 59, Central Foreign Policy Files, 1967–69, DEF 9-3 US, 3/1/68, Box 1666, NA.

66. Creel to American Embassy Bonn, "Desertion Campaign," Telegram, Munich 824, American Consulate Munich, 7 May 1968, 2, RG 59, Central Foreign Policy Files, 1967–69, DEF 9-3 US, 5/1/68, Box 1667, NA.

67. "Allies Impose Curbs," 14.

68. Assistant Chief of Staff for Intelligence to Carl Wallace, Special Assistant to Secretary of Defense, "Counterintelligence Study 'Revolutionary Protest Movements,'" 1969, L-3f., Nixon Papers, WHSF, Staff Member and Office Files, John Dean: Subject File: Demonstrations and Domestic Intelligence, Army, Box 78, NA.

69. Dean Rusk to all diplomatic posts, Telegram, 170648, Department of State, 30 May 1968, 2, NSF, Files of Walt Rostow, The likelihood of more French-style Eruptions, Box 13, LBJL.

70. Ibid.

71. "Generalizations on Student Unrest," 1, attached to Dean Rusk to all diplomatic posts, "Student Unrest," Airgram, CA-10592, Department of State, 3 September 1968, NSF, Intelligence File, Student Unrest, Box 3, LBJL.

72. "General Action Recommendations on Student Unrest," attached to Dean Rusk to all diplomatic posts, "Student Unrest," Airgram, CA-10592, Department of State, 3 September 1968, 1, NSF, Intelligence File, Student Unrest, Box 3, LBJL.

73. George McGhee to Secretary of State, "Report of the Student Unrest Study Group," Information Memorandum, Department of State, Ambassador at Large, 17 January 1969, 7, NSF, Intelligence File, Student Unrest, Box 3, LBJL..

74. Ibid., 12.

75. Central Intelligence Agency, "International Connections of US Peace Groups," Study, 15 November 1967, 1, NSF, Intelligence File, U.S. Peace Groups – International Connections, Box 3, LBJL; Richard Helms, "International Connections of US Peace Groups – III," SC-07248-68, 28 February 1968, ibid.

76. The report is about 200 pages long. "Restless Youth," Study, 0613/68, Central Intelligence Agency, September 1968, NSF, Files of Walt Rostow, Youth and Student Movement, CIA report, Box 13, LBJL.

77. The White House, "Cabinet Meeting of September 18, 1968," 18 September 1968, 4f., Cabinet Meeting 9/18/1968 [1 of 3], Box 15, LBJL. See also Tom Wells, *The War Within: America's Battle over Vietnam* (Berkeley, 1994), 143–50, 209 f., 220–22.

78. For a more general perspective, see also Nicholas John Cull, *The Cold War and the United States Information Agency: American Propaganda and Public Diplomacy, 1945–1989* (New York, 2008), 255–92.

79. Patrick E. Nieburg, oral history interview, 1988, Foreign Affairs Oral History Collection, GUL.

80. Morris to Department of State, "Morale in West Berlin – Psychological and Cultural Factors," Airgram, A-252, US Mission Berlin, 17 November 1967, 4, RG 59, Central Foreign Policy Files, 1967–69, EDU GER B, 1/1/67, Box 344, NA.

81. Bruce Lancaster to Department of State, "Germany's Iconoclasts – And Some of Our Own," Airgram, A-85, American Consulate Stuttgart, 7 February 1968, 1f., RG 59, Central Foreign Policy Files, 1967–69, POL 13-2, GER W, 1/1/68, Box 2125, NA.

82. Lodge to Department of State, "Youth in Country Programming," Airgram, A-1394, American Embassy Bonn, 31 May 1968, 1, RG 59, Central Foreign Policy Files, 1967–69, EDX, GER W, 1/1/67, Box 363, NA.
83. Ibid., 4.
84. See, e.g., "Bonn Conference Of Embassy and USIS Officers On Youth and Change in Europe," Conference Report, 11–13 June 1969, RG 59, IAYC Records, Conference of Youth Coordinators, 1966, 1969, Box 4, NA.
85. Department of State, Policy Planning Council, "U.S.-German Relations," November 1967, 4, NSF, Country File Germany, Box 188, Folder Germany Vol. XIV, Memos, 8/67–2/68, Box 150a, LBJL.
86. Department of State, Policy Planning Council, "Where can the Germans go?" Draft, 19 December 1967, 9, NSF, Country File Germany, Memos, Vol. XIV, 8/67–2/68, Box 188, LBJL.
87. Ibid., 10.
88. Fessenden to Department of State, "The German New Left – A Current Look," Airgram, A-334, American Embassy Bonn, 8 April 1969, 7, RG 59, Central Foreign Policy Files, 1967–69, POL 13-2, GER W, 1/1/69, Box 2126, NA.
89. Ibid., 12.
90. In Congress, Senator Lloyd argued that "we must recognize reality and unfortunately reality suggests that Chancellor Brandt's party is being influenced by a far leftist faction whose intentions do not coincide with those of the United States or our allies." Idem, "American Tragedy," 6 April 1971, in: Congressional Record, 92nd Congress, 1st sess., vol. 117, pt. 8, 10794.
91. McKinney Russell to USIA Washington, "Country Plan for USIS Germany," USIS Bonn, 20 June 1973, 20, CU, I,2, 25: CPP, Germany [FY 1974], Box 14, UASC.
92. Hans A. Tuch, oral interview, 4 August 1989, Foreign Affairs Oral History Collection, GUL. See also idem, *Communicating with the World: U.S. Public Diplomacy Overseas* (New York, 1990), 152–60.
93. See Philipp Gassert, "Anti-Amerikaner? Die deutsche Neue Linke und die USA," in: Jan C. Behrends, Árpád von Klimo, and Patrice G. Poutrus, eds., *Anti-Amerikanismus im 20. Jahrhundert: Studien zu Ost- und Westeuropa* (Bonn, 2005), 250–67.
94. McKinney Russell, *Country Plan for USIS Germany*, USIS Bonn, 20 June 1973, 20.
95. "Youth and Revolt – Depth and Diversity," Department of State, Office of Intelligence and Research, 17 November 1967, 5f., RG 59, IAYC Records, IAYC Meeting, 8 November 1967, Box 1, NA. See also the work of Special Assistant to the President Joseph A. Califano, Jr., *The Student Revolution: A Global Confrontation* (New York, 1970).

Chapter 7

Ostpolitik as Domestic Containment

The Cultural Contradictions of the Cold War
and the West German State Response

Jeremi Suri

The history of the Cold War in the 1960s is a history of disillusionment and
unintended consequences. Writing in the aftermath of this turbulent decade,
sociologist Daniel Bell observed that the promises of liberal capitalism in the
twentieth century—individual enterprise, extensive wealth creation, and technological progress—had produced their own internal detractors. Many of the
young beneficiaries of capitalist enterprise, wealth, and technology in the most
prosperous Western societies no longer wished to support this system of relations. Raised in privilege, Bell's students at Harvard and other universities felt
free to reject dominant political and economic institutions in search of cultural
alternatives that emphasized more transcendent values. The very successes of
capitalism undermined its hold on the minds of young men and women who
took their high standard of living for granted. Modern societies confronted, in
Bell's famous phrase, "the cultural contradictions of capitalism."[1]

Bell's analysis remains powerful, but it suffers from a neglect of the Cold
War context that framed the development of capitalist institutions after 1945.
Soviet-American rivalry transformed capitalism. Confronted by a communist
adversary that appeared capable of endless "crash" production programs, the US
government and its allies pushed for rapid advances in science and technology.
To stay ahead of Soviet slave labor, Americans emphasized innovation, with generous federal support. Recent studies of the US "military-industrial complex"
have highlighted this point, particularly as it relates to the ways American policymakers contributed to a culture of inventiveness rather than enforced regimenta-
tion in the industrial facilities, military institutions, and universities funded for
anti-communist purposes.[2]

The inventiveness financed during the Cold War gave the United States
a tremendous long-term advantage in its competition with the Soviet Union.
American society produced a string of qualitative leaps in computers, communications, and consumer products that outstripped the quantitative capabilities of
communist "crash" programs. Over time, Moscow fell far behind the technologi-

cal advances in the West. A consciousness of this shortcoming, as much as its material effects, contributed to the collapse of the Communist bloc by the end of the twentieth century.[3] As early as the 1960s Soviet leader Nikita Khrushchev understood this problem and sought to redress it with rapid—frequently erratic—action on many fronts.[4]

America's comparative advantage in international competition, however, had a complicated domestic side. The programs that encouraged US and Western European innovation also inspired rebellion against the leadership of these societies. Sophisticated citizens could build better cars and rockets, but they now desired better politicians as well. By the second half of the 1960s the residents of the United States and its closest allies—particularly the Federal Republic of Germany—felt secure enough from international dangers to turn their attention to far-reaching reforms at home. Bell lamented that this revolt of the privileged was a cultural contradiction of capitalism. Integrating the international context with the local experience of popular unrest, we can more accurately call this a cultural contradiction of the Cold War.

Higher education is a particularly appropriate place to look for evidence of this contradiction. Between 1955 and 1965 the number of students enrolled in higher education at least doubled in the United States, France, and West Germany. In Great Britain university enrollments grew by nearly as much: 98 percent (see Table 7.1). Through 1970 this dramatic growth continued.

Policymakers in Washington, Paris, London, and Bonn financed this massive expansion in higher education because they understood, correctly, that a learned citizenry would out-compete its Soviet counterparts. Leaders, however, overlooked the ways in which higher education would also provide a setting and a set of skills for dissident behavior. The newly educated citizens who challenged Soviet technological capabilities also took to the streets against the men who made expanded university enrollments possible. To the dismay of Lyndon Johnson, Charles de Gaulle, Harold Wilson, and Willy Brandt—as well as Daniel Bell—Cold War education undermined the domestic foundations of Cold War foreign policy.[5]

Table 7.1: Total Enrollments in Higher Education

	US	West Germany	France	Britain
1955	2,812,000	133,884	152,246	85,200
1960	3,789,000	203,335	216,426	107,700
1965	5,921,000	279,345	368,154	168,600
1970	8,581,000	386,244	602,712	228,000

Sources: U.S. Department of Health, Education, and Welfare, *Projections of Educational Statistics to 1975–76* (Washington D.C.: U.S. Government Printing Office, 1966); *Statistisches Jahrbuch für die Bundesrepublik Deutschland* (Stuttgart: W. Kolhhammer, 1956–1971); Alain Bienaymé, *Systems of Higher Education:France* (New York: International Council for Educational Development, 1978); WAC Stewart, *Higher Education in Postwar Britain* (London: Macmillan, 1989).

West Berlin and its famous institution of higher learning, the Free University, were a microcosm for all of these trends and contradictions. Located at the geographic center of the Cold War, the Free University symbolized the creative advantages of West against East. The violent protests organized by students during the late 1960s also revealed the threat that this institution posed to the cohesion of Western societies. The Free University was a Frankenstein that turned on its creators. Like the monster in Mary Shelley's novel, it pointed to a wider series of unintended local disruptions triggered by international political and social transformations.[6]

This essay will examine how the Cold War shaped the Free University and the West German student movement in the late 1960s. It will then interrogate the Federal Republic's responses to unrest at home and abroad. The essay will argue that the student movement triggered a conservative turn in foreign policy, embedded in Chancellor Willy Brandt's *Ostpolitik*. For all its progressive aspirations, *Ostpolitik* was also a form of domestic containment. The evolution of the policy reflects the contradictory political and cultural trends of the period.

The Cold War and the Founding of the Free University

The Free University emerged from a set of student-led initiatives in West Berlin. Unlike any other German institution of higher learning, this institution was founded, in November 1948, as a response to public demand among citizens who found themselves alienated from the Soviet-dominated Humboldt University in East Berlin. Contrary to the rigid administration of its counterpart, the Free University encouraged experimental courses and creative pedagogy. Students in the Western institution had extensive voice in admissions and curricular decisions. The Free University was, at least in its earliest years, an experiment in democratic education, within a hardening context of Cold War conflict.

The West German and American governments, as well as prominent anti-communist institutions (particularly the Ford Foundation), funded the Free University because they recognized its attraction for men and women in the East.[7] This institution was an integral part of the Western alliance's "magnet" strategy in West Berlin, and in Europe in general. Policymakers in Washington and Bonn expected that the dynamic and democratic environment created by the Free University would attract the most ambitious and innovative minds from both Western and Eastern Europe. Drawn to the vigor and excitement of this institution, citizens from Soviet-dominated nations would now reject the gray and regimented life they endured under communist authority. In this sense, innovative government-sponsored higher education in West Berlin was a sophisticated form of Cold War subversion.[8]

During its first decade, the Free University served the purposes of its Cold War sponsors with remarkable success. Between 1949 and 1961 more than a third of the student population at the university came from East Germany. East-West contacts in this setting allowed Western authorities a unique opportunity to exert informal influence over some of the best and brightest emerging from the communist milieu. The virtues of the relatively open and democratic society in West Germany became evident, even as many students remained critical of US foreign policy. Most significant, the fact that students from East Germany had to travel outside of the communist milieu for a dynamic intellectual and social discourse highlighted the shortcomings of the Soviet-dominated states.[9]

The East German construction of the Berlin Wall in August 1961 marked a turning point for the Free University, the Cold War, and the local experiences of West and East German students. The forced separation of the two Germanys turned the dynamic and cosmopolitan environment around the Free University rigid and tense, like the Soviet-American rivalry in Central Europe at this time. East German students could no longer travel by street car (*S-Bahn*) to the Western university. West German and American-sponsored anti-communist propaganda became more dominant within the Free University. The West German government began to discourage, and even repress, potentially dissident experimental ideas.[10]

The Free University no longer served as an environment where diverse political groups came together in a consensual and relatively open setting. Like the city of West Berlin, it suffered from a pervasive sense of social abnormality. Here were a city and a university surrounded by a wall, preaching open and democratic education. The Free University benefited from increasing sums of funding to showcase the virtues of freedom in the West, but it also was under increasing pressure to repress communist points of view. West Berlin and the Free University became social pressure cookers for anxiety, discontent, and, very soon, angry protest against the isolating structures of the Cold War.[11]

The Free University and the Revolt against the Cold War

In the context of tightening Cold War divisions during the 1960s, the Free University developed as the "Berkeley of West Germany."[12] It symbolized the remarkable political and economic accomplishments of the Federal Republic even as it cultivated radical dissent. Students in West Berlin revolted against the division of the city, the government in Bonn, and the Cold War in general. The Free University attracted many politically left-leaning men from across West Germany because residence in the city of West Berlin—due its unique Cold War status—offered an exemption from the Federal Republic's mandatory military service.

By the late 1960s "most active groups among the student body," according to West German philosopher Jürgen Habermas, "desire[d] the immediate overthrow of social structures." Radical students became "the backbone of an extra-parliamentary opposition that seeks new forms of organization in clubs and informal centers, and a social basis wider than the university."[13] The student opposition around the Free University criticized not only the content of current government policies, but also the silences about prior collaboration between West German political leaders and Nazi war criminals. For this new post-1945 generation, the structures of Cold War authority prohibited a fair and open reconciliation with past injustices.[14]

German youth dissent grew particularly disruptive in late 1966. Students blamed the US government for prolonging the division of Germany and supporting a "Grand Coalition" of the dominant West German parties—the Christian Democratic Union (CDU) and the Social Democratic Party (SPD)—that constrained political debate. In December groups of young men and women demonstrated throughout West Berlin, including in the crowded shopping area known as the Kurfürstendamm. One student leaflet pledged to restore "democracy, a socialist alternative, [and] a new left party" in West Germany. The protesters proclaimed their opposition to the "bankruptcy of the established parties."[15]

Altercations between students and law enforcement officers in West Berlin, including alleged incidents of police brutality, escalated through the end of 1966 and the early months of 1967. In January 1967 West Berlin authorities entered the offices of the *Sozialistische Deutsche Studentenbund*.[16] They searched through the organization's materials, confiscated membership files, and accused the group of conducting illegal anti-government activities. This heavy-handed police behavior had the contradictory effect of strengthening public support for the student protesters throughout West Germany. In addition, it contributed to a more confrontational climate, especially within West Berlin and around the Free University. The social tension in this old Prussian city now approximated the polarized atmosphere of Berkeley.[17]

The Shadow of the Right

West German authorities worried about the mounting protests of the New Left found themselves also confronting a resurgent nationalist right. In 1967 and 1968 the Nationaldemokratische Partei Deutschlands (NPD) won between 7 and 9.8 percent of the vote in local elections. Friedrich Thielen and Adolf von Thadden—the leaders of the NPD—called for a strong, independent, and reunited Germany, free of the "alien" interests that allegedly corrupted the states on both sides of the Berlin Wall. "Our nation" (*Volk*), the NPD Manifesto proclaimed, "is being merged into two antagonistic systems." "Territorially alien powers are assuming the guardianship of the peoples [*Völker*] of Europe and jointly maintaining the division of Germany and of Europe for their own political aims."[18]

Like the students on the left, the NPD attacked what it called the "unrestrained materialism" that harmed the people's spiritual and moral health (*Volks-*

gesundheit). The party's 28,000 members condemned the grand coalition for repressing traditional German family and community traditions. Instead of increased federal aid to universities, the NPD argued that the "youth want and need decent, clean standards to look up to." The NPD demanded a strong central government that would eliminate "public immorality."[19]

In retrospect, the challenge from the nationalist right appears quite tame. The NPD never crossed the critical 5 percent threshold in national elections required for seating in the West German Bundestag. During the late 1960s, however, worries about the party animated radical students and government officials responsible for protecting the social order. Protesters at the Free University renounced the alleged return of "fascists" to German politics. They blamed their leaders and their parents for failing to expunge Nazi influences.[20] Policymakers feared that continued student radicalism would inspire more counterdemonstrations on the right. Excessive police repression of left-leaning protesters could also legitimize the militant rhetoric of the NPD. Student demonstrations at the Free University posed a very difficult dilemma for a society scarred by memories of both the Weimar period of social disorder and the Nazi years of excessive state power.[21]

The Shah's Visit and the West German State

In June 1967 the Shah of Iran Mohammed Reza Pahlavi made a dramatic state visit to West Berlin. The Persian dictator and his glamorous wife traveled around West Germany in an attempt to foster closer economic and cultural ties between the two societies. Leaders in both states saw themselves as emerging "middle" powers, poised to challenge Soviet and American global dominance as well as growing Chinese power in Asia. During an extended discussion, the shah and West German Chancellor Kurt Georg Kiesinger emphasized new opportunities for joint projects in weapons development and industrial production. West Germany would provide technical know-how and some capital. The Iranians would supply their own capital, labor, and, of course, oil. Working together the two states hoped to escape the limits of the bipolar international system.[22]

For residents of West Berlin, however, it appeared that deeper relations with the shah would only prolong the injustices of the Cold War world. Within the Free University, a number of Iranian émigrés publicized the frequent domestic brutalities of the government in Tehran.[23] The shah's security forces beat, tortured, and often murdered critics at home. No one could challenge the authority of the absolute ruler. The shah and his close associates accumulated and flaunted ostentatious riches while the majority of the country's citizens were mired in poverty.[24]

The Iranian leader was an anti-communist and a modernizer who maintained friendly relations with the Western powers in an important strategic area, but he was hardly a democrat. In the rush to build deeper economic and cultural ties with the shah, the Federal Republic—like the United States and other Western nations—neglected the Iranian leader's grave domestic shortcomings.[25] "We Germans," one student leaflet proclaimed, "have, with the help of the other great powers, supported a dictator. We cannot legitimize such a dictator with assistance and heartfelt reception." "Through our demonstration," the protesters announced, "we want to direct your attention to the true conditions in Iran."[26]

The domestic brutalities perpetrated in Iran, with Western aid, were not isolated occurrences. Students in West Berlin recognized that communist containment, economic development, and concerns for international stability frequently led democratic leaders to underwrite domestic violence. In Southeast Asia and Latin America this was so common by the 1960s as to almost escape notice. In Europe—including West Germany—the widespread acceptance of the divided status quo on the continent reflected a choice for security over self-determination. "Iran is for us," the protesting students explained, "just one example of the difficult problems in the developing countries today." The "realities" of international politics appeared to smother real democracy. By demonstrating against the Iranian shah, members of the Free University hoped that they could inspire greater international concern for "basic democratic rights."[27]

The shah arrived in West Berlin on 2 June 1967. Throughout the day protesting students trailed his entourage, shouting "freedom for Iranians" and "Shah, Shah, Charlatan," as well as other, cruder epithets. In the evening, as the foreign guests traveled to the city opera house for a performance of Mozart's *Magic Flute,* more than 800 men and women attempted to block the streets. An army of police officers and the shah's personal bodyguards reacted to the aggressive crowd with brutal force. After the delayed dignitaries finally reached their destination, the Iranian personnel accompanying the entourage used large sticks and other projectiles to beat the protesters. The West Berlin police, according to reports in *Der Spiegel,* acted similarly.[28]

Amidst the disorder on the Berlin streets, a plainclothes police officer fired two shots at approximately 8:20 PM. Benno Ohnesorg, a 26-year-old Free University student, fell to the ground and died soon thereafter. By almost all accounts Ohnesorg was only a peripheral participant in the demonstrations. No one provided evidence that he had directly provoked the West Berlin police in any way. According to the bishop of his church, Ohnesorg was "not a fanatic" but a good citizen, active in the student religious community.[29]

Ohnesorg's murder threw the city into virtual chaos. According to a prominent newsweekly, the anguish exhibited by students and other sympathetic citizens after the incident rivaled the emotions unleashed by the construction of the Berlin Wall almost six years earlier.[30] West Berlin's Mayor Heinrich Albertz gave an address on television the next day, pleading for "security and order." He accused an extreme minority of "terrorizing" the population.[31]

This student minority only grew in size and unruliness during the coming days. More than 4,000 men and women gathered on 3 June 1967 to condemn the entire West Berlin city government for Ohnesorg's death. The angry protesters demanded the resignation of the mayor, the police chief, and other officials.[32] Accused of authorizing widespread brutality, Mayor Albertz soon resigned.[33] The city of West Berlin never regained the "security and order" that government and university officials demanded. A frustrated Chancellor Kiesinger lamented that the youth of his nation had fallen victim to an "international sickness" that infected all of the major states.[34] The West German government struggled to repress proliferating student demonstrations without provoking more radicalism, or an NPD-advocated reaction.

Rudi Dutschke and the West German State

In the second half of 1967 one fiery student emerged as the chief agitator for protest activity in West Berlin. Rudolf "Rudi" Dutschke came from the province of Brandenburg in East Germany. The Communist government had barred him from higher education when he refused to participate in mandatory military service during the late 1950s. As a consequence, Dutschke attended the Free University—the only postsecondary institution from which he was not barred. After the construction of the Berlin Wall he fled to the Western half of the city, continuing his studies in sociology, philosophy, and political science at the Free University.[35]

Unlike most other students in Western Europe and the United States, Dutschke understood the domestic cruelties of the Soviet bloc firsthand. In West Berlin, however, he found many of the promised freedoms unfulfilled. Dutschke took particular aim at the "manipulation" of power that allowed dominant political and economic groups to make policy without popular consent. He blamed government "bureaucracy" for prolonging Cold War divisions in Europe, supporting dictators around the world, employing violence in Southeast Asia, and neglecting inequalities between rich and poor. The established political institutions in West Germany "blocked" necessary reforms, according to this analysis.[36] "We must always make more people conscious and politically mobilized," Dutschke announced. Active students would harass established elites, creating the foundation for what he called an "anti-authoritarian camp."[37]

Sit-ins, demonstrations, and organized student heckling prohibited regular instruction at the Free University during late 1967 and early 1968.[38] Dutschke's followers did much more than voice radical rhetoric. At times, student activity became explicitly violent. Men and women began to identify themselves as members of an "academic proletariat" that, in Marxist terms, required the use of force against its oppressors.[39] During protest marches students hurled tomatoes, rocks, and even bricks at the police.[40] Dutschke was careful never to advocate student violence, but when pressed he refused to condemn it.[41]

Free University students saw themselves as players in a larger global revolution. In his diary Dutschke wrote with relish about the development of an international movement against both American and Soviet domination. He intentionally overlooked the domestic abuses of Mao Zedong, Che Guevara, and Fidel Castro because these figures publicly challenged the Cold War status quo. They were vanguards for radical change in image, if not reality. Following Mao's inspiration in particular, Dutschke called on students around the world to lead a "long march" through the institutions of society, overturning established centers of power from within and without. "[T]he third front is set up," Dutschke wrote in his diary. Like guerrilla fighters in Bolivia and South Vietnam, men and women in West Germany would wage a militant struggle to smash the existing order.[42]

In this context the Vietnam War provided both an inspiration and an opportunity for the student protesters in West Berlin. Dutschke and others saw the fierce fighting around the time of the Tet Offensive as overriding confirmation of the destruction that followed from Western attempts to foster "development" in the Third World. In South Vietnam, American bombs and guns protected an unpopular, corrupt government that looked more like the shah's dictatorship than a democratic state. America and its Western European allies had become "imperialists," according to this analysis. Vietnamese villagers and German students would struggle as a united "third front" to "revolutionize the masses."[43]

American setbacks in Vietnam opened the possibility of successful resistance from the periphery and from within. "Comrades, Anti-authoritarians, People!" Dutschke exclaimed, "[w]e have an historic opening." "Real solidarity with the Vietnamese revolution comes from the actual weakening and upheaval in the centers of imperialism." Students, natives, and guerrilla fighters had all become proletarians under the domination of repressive "fascists." The time for a global "emancipatory struggle and national self-determination" had arrived.[44] After Tet the tide of history appeared to move in favor of the weak and downtrodden.

On 17–18 February 1968, students at the Free University organized an international Vietnam Congress, using the war to bring 10,000 protesters and intellectuals together from all across Western Europe.[45] Reform through existing institutions had become "hopeless," Dutschke remarked in his diary. "We must do something else." "We will make the Vietnam Congress," he wrote, "into an international manifestation of solidarity with the bombed and struggling people."[46] Accordingly, Dutschke addressed the attendees of the congress, calling for "revolutionary struggle" against the domination of the great powers in Asia, Latin America, and other parts of the world.[47]

Demonstrations throughout West Berlin and the rest of West Germany grew more confrontational after February 1968. The government proposed a set of "emergency laws" allowing expanded police powers to control unruly crowds. Students besieged government buildings, foreign embassies, and the offices of university administrators. Instead of sitting in, men and women now staged "go-ins" that included physical harassment and deliberate property damage. Almost all institutions of authority came under attack, including communist-supported organizations that appeared hesitant to join the student radicals.[48]

On the afternoon of 11 April 1968 an unemployed worker, Josef Bachmann, shot Rudi Dutschke three times at close range. Dutschke miraculously survived, but he never fully recovered before his death in 1979. Students immediately blamed the government and the press for encouraging the attack.[49] That night more than 5,000 young men and women marched to the center of West Berlin, angrily condemning the entire "system." The next day another 5,000 students protested in front of the city hall. Demonstrations with even larger numbers continued, reaching a crescendo during the month of May. When the West German Bundestag passed the long-debated "emergency laws" for public order on 30 May 1968, protesters demanded popular "agitation" to undermine the existing regime. The student revolt had, by this time, become a self-conscious "guerrilla" struggle.[50]

The Political Influence of the Student Demonstrations

The men and women who took to the streets did not achieve the radical changes they sought. They did, however, reorient West German society. Before 1968 West Berlin was a Cold War frontier, an outpost of communist containment. The East Germans and the Soviets constituted the greatest threat to the city. After 1968 the most pressing danger to West Berlin and the Federal Republic came from within. Moscow did not want war but expanded trade and economic assistance from the West.[51] University students, who received more financial aid from the state than other citizens, were now the main enemies of order. They continuously attacked the government through words, demonstrations, and in some cases, acts of terror. Through the next decade, extreme "extraparliamentary opposition" would remain a source of violence and uncertainty for the West German leadership.[52]

The history of the Free University and the West German student revolt in the 1960s underscores the cultural contradictions of the Cold War. As Daniel Bell suggested, the successes of American-sponsored enterprise, wealth, and technology gave students in West Berlin the freedom to rebel. After all, the citizens of the more regimented, impoverished, and technologically deficient Soviet bloc could not even contemplate public protests on the order of those around the Free University. Policymakers in Washington and Bonn built a vibrant university community in West Berlin to showcase the superiority of their societies. The large cohort of bright-eyed students who came to West Berlin, however, matured into a combustible source of violent protest when they found that the international rhetoric of Cold War freedoms did not match the reality of Cold War isolation. The geopolitics of West Berlin made the Free University an important instrument of American influence in Europe, but the social life of West Berlin made the university a source of violent anti-Americanism. This profound cultural contradiction reshaped the foreign policy of the Federal Republic.

The Transformation of *Ostpolitik*
in Response to Domestic Unrest

As early as 15 November 1966, Willy Brandt's long-time aide Egon Bahr warned of an internal crisis within the Federal Republic. "Twenty-one years after the end of the war," he wrote Brandt, "there exists a new generation." Bahr worried about rising "extremism on the right" and "extremism on the left." Overtures to the Soviet bloc, "*Ostpolitik*," offered the opportunity for creating a new political middle between right and left, but they also risked unleashing unrealistic public expectations. Domestic dissatisfaction could jeopardize the basic stability required for any durable agreements with the East.[53]

This was exactly the difficulty that Brandt and Bahr confronted at the end of the decade. Their concept of *Ostpolitik* called for broader public connections between citizens in the East and West. Domestic radicalism in the Federal Republic and other European states, however, made leaders fear that young people, when given opportunities for more freedom and movement, would create new sources of disorder and conflict. The student protests throughout West Germany indicated that "change through reconciliation" between societies—if not properly managed—could spark increased violence.[54]

Speaking to a group of fellow politicians on 3 September 1968, two weeks after the Warsaw Pact invasion of Czechoslovakia, Brandt made this very point. "Young people in many of our countries," he lamented, "do not understand why we, the older ones, cannot cope with the problems of [our] age." Counseling against extensive public criticism of Soviet intervention in Prague or the US war in Vietnam, Brandt argued that leaders had to control "dangerous tensions" through pragmatism and "reason"—two qualities frequently absent from the naive behavior of protesters. Policymakers needed to temper popular urges for well-intentioned but reckless political change.[55]

In contrast to many domestic activists in West Germany, Brandt refrained from any significant condemnation of the foreign policies pursued by Moscow and Washington in the late 1960s. He feared that criticism of the superpowers would create new barriers to East-West reconciliation. West Germany pursued a more independent foreign policy than ever before, but Brandt remained acutely aware that the functioning of *Ostpolitik* was dependent on the consent of the more powerful states—the Soviet Union and the United States—that continued to dominate the European continent.[56] This was an accurate strategic assessment, but it alienated many of *Ostpolitik*'s strongest domestic supporters in the Federal Republic. Brandt's caution appeared to perpetuate the great power politics of the Cold War. Once again, it seemed that the people of Central Europe had to sacrifice their interests for the sake of international stability. Once again, leaders accepted repression in Europe instead of promoting resistance and change.

West German youths who traveled to East Germany and other parts of the Soviet bloc as participants in a series of cultural exchange programs supported by Brandt became his most vocal critics. They observed the repressive conditions in the East, but they also imbibed the radical condemnations of established political leaders circulating among protesters in the West. During one meeting between students from the two Germanys in East Berlin, speakers from both sides called for more attention to "our freedom," allegedly smothered by domestic institutions, East and West. Disparaging all German leaders, they demanded that power devolve from national figures to student groups.[57] Other meetings of Eastern and Western students inspired extensive discussions about the alleged absence of moral values in politics on both sides of the Wall.[58]

By 1969 *Ostpolitik* had produced some important convergences between East and West, as Brandt hoped, but in a form he found most threatening. Students, radicalized by protest and dissident movements in their respective states, now formed East-West networks of criticism against established authority. Citizens traveling from the Federal Republic to the East curiously neglected the issue of reunification for discussions about what many called a common "system" of repression throughout Europe.[59] Peace and national unity would come, one group of Eastern and Western students proclaimed, when "existing communists and capitalists can meet one another on the socialist road."[60] Another group explicitly condemned the great powers for prolonging the Cold War. Exchange students called for grassroots, all-German answers to political and social problems that state leaders, including Brandt, appeared unable to solve.[61] East-West connections supported by Brandt and Bahr for the purpose of improving internal conditions had the opposite effect. With more knowledge and human contact, Germans on both sides of the Berlin Wall grew more restive, disorderly, and violent. Increased interaction between the two German states did not foster reconciliation and reunification, as Brandt and Bahr hoped. Instead, *Ostpolitik* contributed to a set of new domestic dangers for the future of the Federal Republic.[62]

The members of the CDU, who had only reluctantly embraced *Ostpolitik* in the 1960s, took advantage of Soviet aggression in Czechoslovakia and domestic unrest in the Federal Republic to criticize Brandt's overtures to the East for excessive radicalism. Rainer Barzel and Franz-Josef Strauss (from the CDU's sister party, the Christian Social Union) claimed that concessions to Moscow would legitimize Soviet tyranny in the East and prevent future German reunification. They accused Brandt's SPD of undermining the stability of the Federal Republic by advocating an overly optimistic foreign policy. While the former mayor of West Berlin did too little for *Ostpolitik* in the eyes of social activists, he was reviled by conservative members of the CDU for doing too much.[63]

Embattled on both the political left and right at home, Brandt and Bahr shifted gears. Late 1969 marks the point when they turned their overtures to the East against their own citizens. As chancellor after 21 October 1969, Brandt made *Ostpolitik* more elitist, centralized, and secret than ever before. He emphasized political control and speed over public deliberation and debate. Through

Bahr, Brandt personalized his foreign policy to prevent interference from both established bureaucracies and allegedly irresponsible domestic groups. One historian has compared Bahr to a "greyhound" who moved so quickly in 1969 and 1970 that he left his detractors—young radicals and CDU conservatives—"spluttering with shock and indignation."[64]

As Brandt's "State Secretary"—the rough equivalent of the US national security advisor—Bahr opened an unprecedented channel between Bonn and Moscow. Frequent secret meetings with Soviet representatives in Berlin, Moscow, and Leningrad created what he describes in his memoirs as a "relaxed atmosphere" among the very small group of men participating in these privileged discussions.[65] Almost all other members of the West German government—including Foreign Minister Walter Scheel—knew little about what transpired during these meetings. The public remained almost entirely in the dark about their occurrence at the time.[66]

Bahr does not justify the secrecy and the haste of his negotiations through the Moscow "channel" along strategic lines. His memoirs emphasize how the informality of his meetings with Soviet counterparts fostered personal connections and encouraged a frank exchange of opinions on critical issues.[67] The main hindrances to progress on East-West relations came not from the leaders secretly gathered around a secluded negotiating table, but from the bureaucrats, political rivals, and angry citizens causing trouble within the Federal Republic. Domestic opponents, not foreign rivals, jeopardized Brandt and Bahr's hopes for stable, secure, and dynamic relations between East and West after 1968.[68]

The West German leaders pursued a speedy agreement on improved relations between Bonn and Moscow for the purpose of containing their internal opposition. Lingering public debate would only allow criticism to coalesce on both the right and the left. Instead of following the deliberative approach common to West German foreign policy since the Adenauer years, Brandt and Bahr rushed to create a fait accompli that assured a series of openings between East and West but also established limits on how citizens could use *Ostpolitik*. While diplomatic, economic, and cultural contacts would increase across the Berlin Wall, the two German states would remain firmly intact, further empowered to control activities within their respective borders.[69]

Bahr explained to President Nixon's National Security Advisor Henry Kissinger that the chancellor sought to "normalize" political authority in Central Europe through his overtures to Moscow. West Germans would interact more with their Eastern neighbors, though not in the free and uninhibited way that Bahr and Brandt had contemplated years earlier. The leaders of the Federal Republic no longer sought reunification, except perhaps over the very long term. In the context of growing domestic upheaval, they wanted to use *Ostpolitik* to improve living conditions throughout the region while reinforcing existing structures of state authority. Any new challenges to political leadership threatened to unleash dangerous forces within the societies surrounding the Berlin Wall.[70]

In 1970 Bahr extolled the virtues of coupling agreements for increased human movement between East and West with reinforced state boundaries. He called this a maneuver designed to increase the political flexibility (*Spielraum*) available for embattled leaders. West German families receiving more frequent travel passes to visit relatives in the East would react favorably. Businesspeople and social activists would also appreciate a softening in European divisions. At the same time, the strengthening of existing frontiers promised that the region would remain stable and orderly. *Ostpolitik,* in this form, promoted social and cultural change but only on the political and strategic margins.[71]

For those who remembered Brandt and Bahr's idealistic speeches about *Ostpolitik* at Tutzing in 1963, this was a more conservative vision of East-West relations than the two men had initially advocated.[72] Political stability, not progressive change or what Brandt had called "deconcentration," emerged from the Bonn-Moscow channel. Cold War divisions in Central Europe became less rigid while they also grew more permanent. Instead of eliciting new openings for popular initiative, *Ostpolitik* confined the activities of citizens within a very limited framework.

Bahr called this "respecting realities," but his unprecedented negotiations with Moscow revealed that many of the inherited East-West animosities had, in fact, dissipated.[73] Domestic unrest in Berlin and other cities had replaced recurring superpower crises as the greatest immediate threat to the leaders of the Federal Republic. They used the old reality of Cold War divisions to control the new reality of internal weakness. Brandt, Bahr, and their Soviet counterparts clearly preferred managed great-power conflict to the risks of fundamental political and social change in the early 1970s.

Conclusion

The Cold War contributed to the global revolutions of the 1960s by both enabling public mobilization, often through universities, and limiting the avenues for peaceful change within established political institutions. As a consequence, a young cohort of well-educated and idealistic citizens across North America, Europe, and other continents turned to radical alternatives. The students at the Free University in West Berlin were not unique in their perception that the very Cold War conditions that gave them access to higher education had to be overturned to make the realization of that education possible. This is the central contradiction of the Cold War, and the common source of domestic upheaval in the late 1960s. Government-supported pressures for innovation and achievement elicited discontent, dissent, and domestic violence.

Willy Brandt and Egon Bahr were not alone in recognizing, by 1969, the self-defeating nature of this dynamic.[74] The West German state, like its transatlantic and Eastern counterparts, pursued new measures to contain internal dissent. Public mobilization for idealistic aims like *Ostpolitik* now appeared too dangerous. This was especially true in the West German case, where students sent on cultural exchange visits to the East returned with stronger criticisms of the Federal Republic.

The West German state did not abandon its traditional Cold War anti-communism in the late 1960s. It did, however, pursue relations with its Eastern neighbors, particularly the Soviet Union, that emphasized stability, secrecy, and expediency during this period. *Ostpolitik* became a policy of elites rather than publics because elites no longer trusted their publics. Some of this policy conservatism was, of course, unavoidable when operating in a complex international matrix of states, interests, and ideologies. Before the upheavals of the late 1960s, however, Brandt and Bahr had articulated a program that was far less secretive and accepting of the geopolitical status quo. The presence of pervasive student unrest in West Berlin and other cities around the globe motivated these leaders to abandon plans for broad public mobilization. The early 1960s rhetoric of "new frontiers" gave way to a late 1960s rhetoric of stability and order. *Ostpolitik* mutated from a call for open politics to a form of domestic containment.[75]

Connecting domestic upheaval with foreign policy change is always difficult. The lines of causality are never clear. Leaders rarely articulate their inner reasons for pursuing a set of actions. Often, statesmen act from intuition and feeling rather than reasoned analysis. Daniel Bell's examination of the cultural contradictions in the post–Second World War world is helpful because it provides a structural insight about the relationship between domestic society and foreign policy. Foreign policy competition in the Cold War created domestic dislocations, which in turn transformed Cold War relationships between states and their publics. Internal unrest in countries like West Germany was both a product and a rejection of the Cold War. State responses both redefined and preserved the Cold War.

Notes

1. Daniel Bell, *The Cultural Contradictions of Capitalism* (New York, 1996, originally 1976), especially 33–84.
2. Michael Hogan, *A Cross of Iron: Harry S. Truman and the Origins of the National Security State, 1945–1954* (New York, 1998); Aaron L. Friedberg, *In the Shadow of the Garrison State: America's Anti-Statism and its Cold War Grand Strategy* (Princeton, 2000). This emphasis on inventiveness in American institutions does not, of course, negate the regimenting influences of Cold War culture within the United States. On this point see Hogan, *A Cross of Iron,* especially 1–22, 419–62; Rebecca S. Lowen, *Creating the Cold War University: The Transformation of Stanford* (Berkeley, 1997); Ellen Schrecker, No Ivory Tower: McCarthyism and the Universities (New York and Oxford, 1986). Science and technology were not free of regimenting influences in the United States, but they greatly benefited from unprecedented resources and encouragement for innovative research.

3. See Stephen Kotkin, *Armageddon Averted: The Soviet Collapse, 1970–2000* (New York, 2001); Jeremi Suri, "Explaining the End of the Cold War: A New Historical Consensus?" *Journal of Cold War Studies* 4 (fall 2002): 60–92.

4. See William Taubman, *Khrushchev: The Man and His Era* (New York, 2003), 507–77; John Lewis Gaddis, *We Now Know: Rethinking Cold War History* (New York, 1997), 261–66.

5. For a more extended discussion of the foreign policy aims behind Cold War education, and the statistics on student enrollments, see Jeremi Suri, *Power and Protest: Global Revolution and the Rise of Détente* (Cambridge, MA, 2003), 88–130, 269–71.

6. Mary Wollstonecraft Shelley, *Frankenstein, or, The Modern Prometheus,* ed. Marilyn Butler (New York, 1998). Shelley initially published her novel in 1818.

7. For an account of the Ford Foundation and its Cold War investments in Europe, see Volker R. Berghahn, *America and the Intellectual Cold Wars in Europe: Shepard Stone Between Philanthropy, Academy, and Diplomacy* (Princeton, 2001), 143–213.

8. On American attempts to attract Eastern European citizens and states away from Soviet control, see Melvyn P. Leffler, *A Preponderance of Power: National Security, The Truman Administration, and the Cold War* (Stanford, 1992), 235–37; John Lewis Gaddis, *Strategies of Containment: A Critical Appraisal of Postwar American National Security Policy* (New York, 1982), 65–71.

9. See James F. Tent, *The Free University of Berlin: A Political History* (Bloomington, IN, 1988), 1–176. See how even a staunch anti-communist like West German Chancellor Konrad Adenauer was careful to distinguish between the asserted evils of communism and the goodness of ordinary citizens, especially those suffering under Soviet domination in Eastern Europe. Adenauer Rede in der Freien Universität, West Berlin, 5 December 1958, 16.25, 1958/Band 2, Adenauer Nachlaß, Stiftung Bundeskanzler-Adenauer-Haus, Rhöndorf, Germany.

10. See Tent, *The Free University,* 277–320. On the politics behind the construction of the Berlin Wall and its consequences, see Hope M. Harrison, *Driving the Soviets Up the Wall: Soviet–East German Relations, 1953–1961* (Princeton, 2003).

11. See Alexandra Richie, *Faust's Metropolis: A History of Berlin* (New York, 1998), 770–78.

12. Jürgen Habermas, "Student Protest in the Federal Republic of Germany," reprinted in idem, *Toward a Rational Society: Student Protest, Science, and Politics,* trans. Jeremy J. Shapiro (Boston, 1970), 15. Habermas originally delivered this lecture in November 1967.

13. Ibid., 18.

14. See Wolfgang Kraushaar, *1968 als Mythos, Chiffre und Zäsur* (Hamburg, 2000), 37–41; Wilfried Mausbach, "Auschwitz and Vietnam: West German Protest Against America's War During the 1960s," in Andreas W. Daum, Lloyd C. Gardner, and Wilfried Mausbach, eds., *America, the Vietnam War, and the World: Comparative and International Perspectives* (New York, 2003), 279–98. The seminal text on this subject is Norbert Frei, *Vergangenheitspolitik: Die Anfänge der Bundesrepublik und die NS-Vergangenheit* (Munich, 1996).

15. "Protest!" circa November-December 1966, Folder: Berlin, 1966–67, Box 87, German Subject Collection, Hoover Institution Archives, Stanford, CA (hereafter German Collection). See also Rolf Uesseler, *Die 68er: APO, Marx und freie Liebe*

(Munich, 1998), 192–207; Gerhard Bauß, *Die Studentenbewegung der sechziger Jahre* (Cologne, 1977), 34–41.

16. For the circumstances surrounding this event in West Berlin, see Jacques Schuster, *Heinrich Albertz—der Mann, der mehrere Leben lebte: eine Biographie* (Berlin, 1997), 183–98. For an excellent discussion of the West German SDS and its relationship with the American Students for a Democratic Society, see Martin Klimke, *The Other Alliance: Student Protest in West Germany and the United States in the Global Sixties* (Princeton, 2010), chaps. 1–2.

17. See Schuster, *Heinrich Albertz,* 183–98; Tent, *The Free University of Berlin,* 321–22; Richie, *Faust's Metropolis,* 779.

18. *The Manifesto of the NPD,* first promulgated in 1965, reprinted and translated in Ivor Montagu, *Germany's New Nazis* (London, 1967), 127–31, quotation on 127. See also Fred Richards, *Die NPD: Alternative oder Wiederkehr?* (Munich, 1967), 126–29; David Nagle, *The National Democratic Party: Right Radicalism in the Federal Republic of Germany* (Berkeley, 1970), especially 35–122; David Childs, "The Far Right in Germany since 1945," in Luciano Cheles, Ronnie Ferguson, and Michalina Vaughan, eds., *Neo-Fascism in Europe* (London, 1991), 72.

19. *The Manifesto of the NPD,* 128–31; Patrick Moreau, *Les Héritiers due IIIe Reich: L'extrême Droite Allemands de 1945 à nos Jours* (Paris, 1994), 7–14, 76–78, 91–94; David P. Conradt, *The West German Party System: An Ecological Analysis of Social Structure and Voting Behavior, 1961–1969* (London, 1972), 38–42.

20. See "Akademisches Proletariat?," Folder: Berlin 1966–67, Box 87, German Collection; Uesseler, *Die 68er,* 65–84.

21. See "Stand der Deutschlandfrage," 24 May 1965, Band 5, IIA1 - 80.00, Politisches Archiv des Auswärtigen Amts, Bonn, Germany (hereafter PA/AA); Klaus Hildebrand, *Von Erhard zur Großen Koalition, 1963–1969* (Stuttgart, 1984), 202–18, 283–301, 365–83.

22. See Gespräch des Bundeskanzlers Kiesinger mit Schah Reza Pahlevi, 28 May 1967, *Akten zur Auswärtigen Politik der Bundesrepublik Deutschland* (hereafter AAPD), 1967 (Munich, 1998), 2:797–808. See also Aufzeichnung des Staatssekretärs Rolf Lahr, 4 January 1967, AAPD, 1967, 1:19–22. On the early development of post-1945 West German "Weltpolitik"—expansion of influence in the developing world—see Karl Carstens an Ludwig Erhard, 4 October 1963, Band 159, B2—Büro Staatssekretäre, PA/AA; Karl Carstens an Willy Brandt, 5 December 1966, Mappe 641, N1337—Karl Carstens Nachlaß, Bundesarchiv Koblenz, Germany.

23. See Tent, *The Free University of Berlin,* 323.

24. James Bill argues that the shah of Iran pursued a policy of controlled "reform from above." He sought to modernize the Iranian economy by encouraging land reform and industrial development, according to Bill, while also retaining tight control on political behavior. The growth of vocal opposition groups within Iran during the 1960s motivated the shah to use force against domestic reformers. The shah would not allow citizens to challenge his dictatorship. See James A. Bill, *The Eagle and the Lion: The Tragedy of American-Iranian Relations* (New Haven, 1988), 141–49, 161–69.

25. See ibid., 169–76.

26. "Warum Wir demonstrieren," in "Dokumente des 2. Juni 1967 und der Zeit danach," Folder: Berlin, 1967, Box 87, German Collection.

27. Ibid. See also Klimke, *The Other Alliance,* chaps. 3–4.

28. See the eyewitness accounts in *Der Spiegel,* 12 June 1967. See also Uesseler, *Die 68er,* 244–55; Schuster, *Heinrich Albertz,* 199–226; Tent, *The Free University of Berlin,* 323–24.

29. See *Der Spiegel,* 12 June 1967.

30. Ibid.

31. Heinrich Albertz, "Sicherheit und Ordnung müssen gewährleistet bleiben," in "Dokumente des 2. Juni 1967 und der Zeit danach," Folder: Berlin, 1967, Box 87, German Collection.

32. Anzeige, in "Dokumente des 2. Juni 1967 und der Zeit danach," Folder: Berlin, 1967, Box 87, German Collection. See also Rudi Dutschke's diary entry for 3 June 1967, in Gretchen Dutschke, ed., *Rudi Dutschke—Jeder hat sein Leben ganz zu leben: Die Tagebücher, 1963–1979* (Cologne, 2003), 39–41.

33. See Schuster, *Heinrich Albertz,* 227–32.

34. Gespräch des Bundeskanzlers Kiesinger mit dem iranischen Botschafter Malek, 15 June 1967, in AAPD, 1967, 2:911–17, quotation on 916. See also Philipp Gassert, *Kurt Georg Kiesinger, 1904–1988* (Munich, 2004).

35. On Dutschke's background, his emergence as a protest leader, and his subsequent decline, see Ulrich Chaussy, *Die drei Leben des Rudi Dutschke: eine Biographie* (Berlin, 1993); Gretchen Dutschke, *Wir hatten ein barbarisches, schönes Leben: Rudi Dutschke, eine Biographie* (Cologne, 1996); Kraushaar, *1968,* 89–129; Bernd Rabehl, *Rudi Dutschke: Revolutionär im geteilten Deutschland* (Dresden, 2002). Both Kraushaar and Rabehl emphasize Dutschke's indignation regarding the enforced division of the German nation.

36. See Rudi Dutschke, "Mallet, Marcuse 'Formierte Gesellschaft' und politische Praxis der Linken hier und anderswo," (1965) in Wolfgang Kraushaar, ed., *Frankfurter Schule und Studentenbewegung: Von der Flaschenpost zum Molotowcocktail, 1946–1995,* 3 vols. (Hamburg, 1998), 2:186–87.

37. See Rudi Dutschke interview in *Der Spiegel,* 10 July 1967.

38. Radical students formed a parallel "Critical University," offering their own seminars and ad hoc courses. See "Kritische Universität: Provisorisches Verzeichnis," Wintersemester 1967/68, Folder: Berlin, 1967, Box 87, German Collection; Bernd Rabehl, *Am Ende der Utopie: Die politische Geschichte der Freien Universität Berlin* (Berlin, 1988), 225–38

39. See "Akademisches Proletariat?" circa late 1967, Folder: Berlin, 1966–67, Box 87, German Collection; "Zur Situation an der FU," 6 December 1967, Folder: Berlin, 1966–67, Box 87, German Collection.

40. See Uesseler, *Die 68er,* 256–96; Tent, *The Free University of Berlin,* 328–32.

41. See Rudi Dutschke, "Professor Habermas, Ihr begriffloser Objektivismus erschlägt das zu emanzipierende Subjekt," (9 June 1967), in Kraushaar, *Frankfurter Schule und Studentenbewegung,* 251–53; Rolf Wiggershaus, *The Frankfurt School: Its History, Theories, and Political Significance,* trans. Michael Robertson (Cambridge, MA, 1994), 617–19.

42. Rudi Dutschke, Tagebuch, 17 June 1967, in idem., *Mein langer Marsch: Reden, Schriften und Tagebücher aus zwanzig Jahren* (Hamburg, 1980), 70; Gretchen Dutschke, *Rudi Dutschke,* 53–54. See also Kraushaar, *1968,* 81–88; Jeffrey Herf, "War, Peace, and the Intellectuals: The West German Peace Movement," *International Security* 10 (spring 1986): 172–74.

43. Dutschke, "Rebellion der Studenten," (1968), in AGAIN: idem, *Mein langer Marsch*, 68–69.

44. Ibid.

45. Students at the Free University organized the Vietnam Congress in conjunction with students at the Technical University in West Berlin. See Einladung 30 January 1968, Folder: Berlin, 1968, Box 88, German Collection; Erklärung zur Internationalen Vietnamkonferenz—Westberlin, 17–18 February 1968, Folder: Berlin, 1968, Box 88, German Collection; Bauß, *Die Studentenbewegung der sechziger Jahre*, 95; Rabehl, *Am Ende der Utopie*, 256–68.

46. Dutschke, Tagebuch, January 1968, in idem, *Mein langer Marsch*, 122.

47. See Dutschke, *Mein langer Marsch*, 71–72.

48. See Offener Brief an die Regierung der Volksrepublik Polen, 12 March 1968, Folder: Berlin, 1968, Box 88, German Collection.

49. "Freunde und Genossen!" 11 April 1968, Folder: Berlin, 1968, Box 88, German Collection.

50. See *Aktuell* 1 (12 April 1968), Folder: Periodicals, *Aktuell*—Berlin, Box 86, German Collection; Report from the Rector of the Free University, Folder: Berlin, 1968, Box 87, German Collection.

51. On this point, see Suri, *Power and Protest*, 245–58.

52. See Stefan Aust, *Der Baader Meinhof Komplex* (Hamburg, 1986), especially 103–320; A. D. Moses, "The State and the Student Movement in West Germany, 1967–77," in Gerard J. DeGroot, ed., *Student Protest: The Sixties and After* (New York, 1998), 144–49; Jeremy Varon, *Bringing the War Home: The Weather Underground, the Red Army Faction, and Revolutionary Violence in the Sixties and Seventies* (Berkeley, 2004). Jeffrey Herf argues that the youth revolt in the late 1960s gave rise to a West German peace movement that refused to acknowledge serious security threats from the Soviet Union during the 1970s and early 1980s. See Herf, "War, Peace, and the Intellectuals," 172–200.

53. Bahr an Brandt, 15 November 1966, Box 352, Egon Bahr Nachlaß, Archiv der sozialen Demokratie, Friedrich-Ebert-Stiftung, Bonn (hereafter Bahr papers).

54. A number of officials made this point to the West German government at the time. See Dr. Kassel an Archiv für gesamtdeutsche Fragen, 6 February 1969, B137/2291, Bundesarchiv, Koblenz, Germany [hereafter BA]; Aufzeichnung vom Treffen mit Mitgliedern der Katholike Studentengemeinde Halle, 19 July 1969, B137/2295, BA.

55. Speech by Willy Brandt at the Conference of Non-Nuclear States in Genf, 3 September 1968, Box 288, Bahr papers.

56. See Entwurf einer Antwort auf die sowjetische Berlin-Mitteilung vom 6. Januar 1968, Box 310, Bahr papers.

57. Aufzeichnung vom Treffen mit Mitgliedern der Katholike Studentengemeinde Halle, 19 July 1969, B137/2295, BA.

58. Bericht über das Begegungstreffen in Ostberlin am 18-19. Januar 1969; Bericht vom Treffen der Studentendgemeinden Dresden und Munich (und Aachen) in Ost-Berlin vom 17–20. Januar 1969; Bericht über das Berlintreffen mit useren Freunden aus Karl-Marx Stadt am 4-5. Januar 1969, B137/2295, BA.

59. Bericht über das Treffen der Studentengemeinden Dresden, Munich, und Aachen in Berlin am 18–19. Januar 1969; Bericht von Bonhöffer-Treffen in Ostberlin, 15 Feb-

ruary 1969; Bericht über das Treffen zwischen Studenten der Studentengemeinden Halle/S und Cologne anlässlich der Leipziger Frühjahrsmesse 1969, 14 March 1969, B137/2295, BA.

60. Bericht über den Verlauf der Fahrt 23. Juni bis 27. Juni 1968 in Ostberlin, B137/2291, BA.

61. Bericht über das Begegungstreffen in Berlin vom 19. September bis 22. September 1968, B137/2291, BA.

62. Tony Judt's excellent history of postwar Europe does not deny the domestic unrest that accompanied *Ostpolitik,* but he does remind readers of the many citizens who benefited from renewed contacts across the East-West divide. See Tony Judt, *Postwar: A History of Europe since 1945* (New York, 2005), 496–500.

63. See Arnulf Baring, *Machtwechsel: Die Ära Brandt-Scheel* (Stuttgart, 1982), 396–403; Karl Dietrich Bracher, Wolfgang Jäger, und Werner Link, *Republik im Wandel, 1969–1974: Die Ära Brandt* (Stuttgart, 1986), 54–67; Clay Clemens, *Reluctant Realists: The Christian Democrats and West German Ostpolitik* (Durham, NC, 1989), 59–66.

64. See Timothy Garton Ash, *In Europe's Name: Germany and the Divided Continent* (New York, 1993), 69.

65. Egon Bahr, *Zu meiner Zeit* (Munich, 1996), 297.

66. See Garton Ash, *In Europe's Name,* 69–70.

67. See Bahr, *Zu meiner Zeit,* 331–32.

68. Ibid., 322–24; Baring, *Machtwechsel,* 361–499.

69. Tony Judt observes that *Ostpolitik* contributed to the "virtual disappearance of 'unification' from the German political agenda." Judt, *Postwar,* 500.

70. Egon Bahr an Henry Kissinger, 19 November 1969, Box 439, Bahr papers.

71. Unterredung zwischen Bahr und Kissinger im Weissen Haus, 17 August 1970; Minister Horst Ehmke über meine Gespräche im Washington mit Henry Kissinger, Martin Hillenbrand, Helmut Sonnenfeld, und Botschafter Rolf Pauls, 21 December 1970, Box 439, Bahr papers.

72. Vortrag des Regierenden Bürgermeisters von Berlin, Willy Brandt, in der Evangelischen Akademie Tutzing, 15 July 1963; Vortrag des Leiters des Presse- und Informationsamtes des Landes Berlin, Egon Bahr, 15 July 1963, *Dokumente zur Deutschlandpolitik,* s9:567–75. See also Suri, *Power and Protest,* 216–20.

73. Unterredung zwischen Bahr und Kissinger im Weissen Haus, 17 August 1970, Box 439, Bahr papers.

74. On this point, see Jeremi Suri, *Henry Kissinger and the American Century* (Cambridge, MA, 2007), chap. 5.

75. For evidence of increased cultural exchange, despite the political containment that accompanied *Ostpolitik,* see Klimke, *The Other Alliance,* chap. 6 and conclusion.

Part IV

Power and Resistance

Chapter 8

Transformation by Subversion?
The New Left and the Question of Violence

Ingrid Gilcher-Holtey

> Starausch: Scherbaum is suffering from the world. The least
> injustice touches him. He thinks he lives next door to the Viet-
> nam war. He doesn't see a solution—or only one. He wants to
> burn his dog publicly and thereby send a sign to the world.
> Irmgard Seifert sharply: This is nonsense.
> Zahnarzt: Admitted: this is nonsense.
> Starausch: And still we have to try to understand the boy.
> —Günter Grass

"Take 2/3 part gasoline, 1/3 part sand and detergent." This was the recipe to produce "Le cocktail Dany (inefficace)," published in March 1968 in the report of the "Student and Workers Struggle" committee of the 22 March Movement at the University of Nanterre.[1] Designed as a joke to comment ironically on the installation of iron doors at the administrative building of the university—a measure designed to protect the university against further occupation by students, as had taken place in March—it was to lead to unexpected effects. Leading student activist Daniel Cohn-Bendit was arrested on the charge of having incited the production of Molotov cocktails.

Take two or three quotations from Dutschke, a few pictures of Andreas Baader in the apartment of Régis Debray, assemble quotations and pictures and mix them with the shadow of a theory of violence that pretends to be innovative, and you can come up with *Le Cocktail Reemtsma 2005,* or, as we shall abbreviate it, *R 2005.* This volume is a cocktail of contemporary history "light," mixed and printed under the sponsorship of the Institute for Social Research in Hamburg, with the intent to start a critical discussion about the past among former activists of the 1968 movement and to enlighten the public about the real objective of the 1968 movement: that is, violence. The plan worked. Just like the police in Nanterre, the "critical press" reacted promptly. The *tageszeitung* (or *taz*) itself, the national daily arising out of the alternative press of the 1960s and 1970s, decided not only to publish the *Cocktail R 2005* but also to serve as a forum for a weeklong debate in March 2005, open to all kinds of speculations about the consequences of the 1968 movement.[2]

The difference between the "Cocktail Dany (inefficace)" and the *Cocktail R 2005* lies in the fact that the Reemtsma group, unlike the 22 March movement, obviously did not know or at least did not practice in this case the principle of the "auto-destruction of one's own statement," which has a prominent place in the works of the historic avant-garde,[3] and which is hidden in the report of Nanterre in the tiny word "inefficace"—*ineffective*. Indeed, in this widely read and discussed volume, typical of a rash of recent work focusing on the presumed centrality of violence within the New Left, and on the centrality of violence also in its legacy, these authors demonstrate scant understanding of violent practice more broadly and the meaning of violence above all in the context of the New Left. The book *Rudi Dutschke Andreas Baader and the RAF,* a slim volume compiling three essays, does not come off as a piece of provocative playfulness. It presents itself as the result of serious archival research and brain work. It inscribes itself into the research on violence of the Hamburg Institute for Social Research (HIS), which has stood in opposition to mainstream research on violence for several years, and which defines the basic premises and perspectives of this research.[4] Even though the three authors do not consequently deploy the framework of the eight dimensions that social scientists have recently developed for research on violence[5] (with the result that one has to call their effort subcomplex even by their own measure), in one point they follow the line of thinking of these research "innovators." That is, like the latter, these authors no longer ask for the causes of violence and the subjective intent of those who deploy it. They claim simply, so to speak, that "violence has no motives, has no sense." They make no distinction among the cognitive orientations of individuals and groups. They do not acknowledge the change of ideas in the process of diffusion under changing contextual conditions. Therefore, French philosopher and activist Régis Debray, West Berlin student and extraparliamentary leader Rudi Dutschke, and Red Army Faction (RAF) cofounder Andreas Baader appear to be activists of the same breed: adventurers who struggle for authenticity, and who as an avant-garde paved the way for avantgardistic activists. In the Reemtsma book all cats are gray.

By declining to put a comma between the names Dutschke and Baader in the title of their book, the three authors underscore their thesis that there was an irrefutable connection between the 1968 movement and the RAF. The sole evidence presented for this claim in the whole book is a quotation from RAF cofounder Ulrike Meinhof: in other words, it rests on a self-definition of the RAF. Aside from that, the authors construct this connection via the "avant-garde," which, according to them, had propagated the project of armed struggle well before 1968. To demonstrate this, they concentrate on the stream of tradition of the European post–avant-garde, especially the group Subversive Action, which found its orientation in the International Situationists around Guy

Debord. Contradicting the claims of the innovators in violence research by not emancipating their research from the causal-finalistic thinking, the three authors thereby reintroduce the causal-final scheme. Thus, they draw this connection not to pose questions, or as a method of research; they rather claim it simply as the result of their study. Claiming the intention to initiate a historicization of the 1968 movement, this volume, published through the HIS, succeeds in dehistoricizing the movement. Neither taking into account the international character and coherence of the 1968 movement, nor posing the question of imputation (let alone applying it empirically), the book insinuates continuities, constructs identities, and reduces extremely divergent strategies of transformation to one common denominator: violence. It does not even systematically define what violence means.

Any discussion of the questions of violence within the New Left has to be preceded by a clarification of the term "violence" and the localization of the question of violence within the context of the strategies of action and transformation of the New Left. We begin by briefly examining this one text, and the context in which it was produced. We will then move on to examine the actual understanding of violence within the New Left. This chapter argues that the question of violence cannot be separated from the movement's alternative scheme of order, or from its method to alter society by subversion. To see this, we need to understand the contemporary, specifically transnational context that shaped the activists' own understanding. It is this broader context that I outline here. Following the premise that violent action is shaped by attitudes toward and perceptions of violence,[6] the subsequent remarks will first sketch the dimensions of the term "violence," which molded the imagination of the important groups of the movement, and then put the question of violence into the context of the strategy of action and transformation of the movement. Three conclusions regarding the consequences of the strategy of subversion of the 1968 movement with respect to the political culture of the Federal Republic of Germany will close the discussion.

Dimensions of the Term "Violence"

What is "violence"? What did violence mean in the 1968 movement? In today's public and scientific debate, the least common denominator defines violence as "infliction of intentional physical harm to human beings by human beings."[7] Bodily harm is therefore the central criterion of violence. The notion of violence in the 1968 movement does not coincide with this definition. For the latter, a broad and dual notion of violence is characteristic. We trace here three dimensions of understanding violence in this movement.

First, we examine the Janus-headedness of violence. It is especially difficult to translate the German nuances of the term *Gewalt* into the English language.

If one looks at the history of the definition, *Gewalt* has several dimensions. Unlike the Latin-derived languages, the German language does not differentiate between *potestas* and *violentia,* or between *pouvoir* (power) and *violence* (violence). Therefore, *Gewalt* on the one hand signifies the legally wielded state power to maintain public order, the so-called state monopoly of exerting physical constraint (*Gewaltmonopol*). On the other hand, it means violent acts, whether privately or politically motivated, including those that are aimed against this state monopoly.[8] According to the sociologist Friedhelm Neidhardt, the Janus-headedness of violence (*Gewalt*) exists because the monopoly of legitimate physical constraint causes the state to simultaneously be applicator and recipient of "violence" in times of inner conflict.[9] This dual characteristic, which the German-language term brings to light, helped to make "violence" a combat term in 1968, used on both sides to scandalize and delegitimize the actions of the respective opponent.

Secondly, we note the duality of the term "violence." This combat term was broadened by a third dimension of "violence," which had its roots back in the nineteenth century but was renewed and dramatized by the 1968 movement. I refer here to "violence" as a principle of structure, also known as "structural violence," as political scientist Johan Galtung characterized it 120 years after Karl Marx.[10] It was Marx who first extended the term violence as a mode of action (comprising the legal physical constraint by executive organs as well as private violence) to a notion of violence as a principle of structure, which designated a state of relations of societal and political dependence and permeated all political and social relations manifestly as well as latently.[11] The 1968 movement did not yet have this term at its disposal. However, materially, contemporary activists followed Marx's premise that violence stemmed not only from human beings but also from superindividual powers and structural relations. As a result, they adopted the thesis that the capitalist economic system generates violence. This had consequences with respect to the practices of the 1968 movement. The movement directed the violent potential of protest, to put it in legal terms, against property, or, as they phrased it, "violence against things." However, the material (objective) violence that, as Marx saw it, permeated all political and social relations was not only derived from property relations, but was also found by the 1968 movement to be a characteristic of language itself.

Finally, we consider the violence of language. German writer Peter Handke spoke of a "*Sprechfolterung*" (torturing by speech), concerning the violence in speech that set tight limits on the authenticity of the individual, insofar as it subjected individual imagination and fantasy to the suffocating constraint of terms and templates. Handke's play *Kaspar* premiered on 11 May 1968, the day of the biggest demonstration of the extraparliamentary opposition, when the second reading of the emergency law legislation triggered the March (*Sternmarsch*) on Bonn.[12] The premier took place simultaneously at two German theaters. In the eyes of theater critic Peter Iden, this play expressed what was at stake in society at that moment. It emphasized and dramatized the so-called second or cultural alienation, which, caused by language, irrevocably intervened in the lives of citizens and was more profound than economic alienation. As early as the late 1950s, the International Situationists around Guy Debord (a group of artistic avant-gardists who later contributed to triggering the 1968 movement world-wide) criticized the loss of a language of communication.[13] As they saw it, the criticism of society required a new language. They tried to create this new lan-guage by, among other things, reversing the established relations between terms. The "removal of terms" (*détournement*) was the name the Situationists employed for this concept. It was meant to alienate the content from the meaning of terms, and to recharge them subversively with new significance. When texts managed to let "removed" terms "work," to break through or penetrate old templates of significance, this was taken as a type of criticism of society.[14]

The "removal" of theoretical terms was also perceived as an act of violence that disturbed any existing order. This definition lay transversal to the other two dimensions of "violence." "The act of violence" with which the Situationists tried to revolt against the constraints of the language was based on a redefinition, or a "removal," of the term "violence" altogether. "Acts of violence" was a designation for the creative and nonconforming action of breaking up normal meanings and everyday situations, of rules of speech or games. Their objective was to intensify the authentic expressivity of the individual by breaking rules, to renew lost or broken communication, and to alter templates of classification and perception. This rather "symbolic" violence (this analytical term was not yet at the disposal of the 1968 movement activists) was connected to the term "subversion," which aimed at similar goals.

"Subversion" stems from the Latin *subvertere,* and is defined in German dictionaries (*Subversion*) as "an activity that aims at the revolution of the existing state order, and that is in most cases carried out clandestinely."[15] In the French Larousse under *subversion,* one finds "illegal action, often clandestine, aimed at undermining established values and institutions."[16] It covers a revolution of state as well as a revolution of values. This corresponds to the English use of the term, which perceives "subversion" in an "immaterial sense, as overthrow of a law, rule etc."[17] The subversion that the Situationists wanted to initiate was aimed neither at conquering the political power nor at changing the laws, rules, and values. The objective of the Situationist's subversive action was the alteration of the rules of the rules—that is, they aimed at changing those templates of classification and perception that precede the forming of laws and rules.

Thus, perceptions of violence are not identical with attitudes toward vio-lence and do not explain violent actions. The unfolding of the various dimen-sions of the concept of violence that governed the 1968 movement shows that the problem of violence, which the Reemtsma group reduces to the connection between the 1968 movement and the RAF, must be seen in a much wider scope, including specifically a transnational scope. Violence was not a strategy to conquer political power. But neither was it reduced to the execution of physical power to overcome resistance. This becomes especially clear if one takes a closer look at the concepts of actions and transformation that governed the New Left.

The Question of Violence within the Context of the Strategy of Actions and Transformation

According to a premise of social movement research, violence within the process of mobilization of protest movements is ignited by the process of interaction. It can develop an escalating auto-dynamic, even if violence is not intended by the protagonists.[18] If one tries to systematically approach the question of violence by looking at the action and transformation strategies of the movement rather than by concentrating on their practices, it becomes necessary to differentiate several constellations of problems, five of which can be applied to the 1968 movement in an exemplary fashion.

In part, this was a question of changing terms. According to a maxim of the New Left, criticism must eventually become practical. In executing this maxim, the anti-authoritarian wing of the New Left especially took recourse to strategies of the Situationists, and thereby to the tradition of the literary avant-garde of the twentieth century. The New Left put terms to work. The "stealing" and the alienation of words and terms was significant for the leaflets of the Kommune I in Berlin and of the "Enragés" in Nanterre. Herbert Marcuse noted the ways in which the 1968 movement borrowed from the surrealistic avant-garde, emphasizing in this context activists' "obscene language."[19]

Thus, parts of the New Left shared the surrealistic premise that the breach with the established political order would also mean a breach with their vocabulary, that new ways of looking at things and new sensibility would also need new forms of verbal expression. Members of Subversive Action (among them Rudi Dutschke), having just joined the leading student political organization in West Germany (SDS), introduced themselves with a "poster action," criticizing West German foreign policy toward the war in Vietnam. Thus they announced that West German Chancellor "[Ludwig] Erhard and the political parties in power support MURDER. Murder by napalm bombs! Murder by poisonous gas! Murder by atom bombs!"[20] The authors of the poster used a term of the penal law designating private violence—murder—to describe governmental actions within the context of international relations. With this "stealing" of a term they provoked not only the public but also fellow SDS members. The term "murder" as characterization of the US policy in Vietnam was, however, not invented by the Berlin poster-hangers. It had already been used in the "Position Paper: Vietnam," which the African-American Student Nonviolent Coordinating Committee (SNCC) published in January 1966.[21] A subversive structure of language was thus also a characteristic of the black militants.

The New Left and especially the anti-authoritarian wing within the SDS connected methods that had been borrowed from a variety of protest groups. Their interest was not, as Wolfgang Kraushaar claims, focused solely on the situationistic avant-garde, which stood in the tradition of dadaism, surrealism, and lettrism. The New Left also took into consideration the tactics of civil disobedience of the US civil rights movement, the "direct action" of the Students for a Democratic Society, and the transformed thinking of SNCC, which in the mid 1960s broke with the concept of nonviolent resistance. Founded in 1960 with the objective of coordinating the numerous and various direct actions within the framework of the American civil rights movement, this student association renounced the principle of nonviolence as *conditio sine qua non* of the political struggle. Under the influence of the Tricontinental Conference in Havana (3–15 January 1966), members of the organization started to view themselves as part of the international wave of freedom movements. Members adopted the premise that the objective conditions for a revolutionary uprising could in many cases only be created by guerrilla tactics, which would engender the necessary revolutionary consciousness. The tasks, role, and function of this guerrilla activity was described in a book entitled *Revolution in the Revolution?*, which French philosopher Régis Debray, who had also taken part in the Tricontinental Conference, wrote at the request of Fidel Castro. The title was programmatic, announcing the subversion of the Old Left. The book was translated into German in 1967 with the help of Rudi Dutschke.

SDS members also borrowed the notion of the "subversion of the subversion." Starting with the hypothesis that a sociopolitical struggle, in which "American imperialism would play its last and decisive match," was about to commence in Latin America, the book unfolds strategic considerations and rules for this fight, derived from the example of the Cuban revolution. Its central message calls for the establishment of groups of guerrillas ("foci") in Latin America to form the backbone of the armed struggle of an avant-garde. Out of this movement of foci a new political order would evolve. This call for the development of guerrilla movements was aimed against both the Communist parties in Latin America and the multitude of foundations of Marxist-Leninist parties.[22] The maxim to move from military "focus" to political strategy was designed thus to prevent the subjection of the guerrilla to the orders of any political party.

The German SDS leaders Rudi Dutschke and Hans-Jürgen Krahl also used "focus theory" at the SDS convention in 1967, as a means of delegitimating traditional strategies of action and organization in the Old Left. They applied the theory in order to win an intra-organizational dispute. That is, they hoped the guerrilla concept would win support for the establishment of a new organizational concept within the SDS, rather than the prevailing model of party-founding within the Old Left. Dutschke and Krahl called this a "revisionist model of a bourgeois party, which was based on membership." The new maxim was organization by action, and not action by organization. It was to be executed intra-organizationally, via the terminology of focus theory. These terms were suggestive more through their stimulating content than through any cognitive values they communicated.

Additionally, leading West German activists differentiated between a "propaganda of shots" and a "propaganda of action." Dutschke and Krahl argued in the name of a self-proclaimed avant-garde, so-called "revolutionary consciousness groups,"[23] which were supposed to set "enlightening countersignals" within the society as well as support the auto-enlightenment of the protagonists. The groups of reference in this concept were the "relevant others," including the broad public, and the protagonists, referring not only to themselves. This went beyond the "adventurer,"[24] who rejected the order of things in order to reinvent his life and who, while struggling for authenticity, renounced responsibility toward others because his only goal was to give his life meaning. They differentiated themselves by their reference as well as by their objectives: the dissolution of societal contradiction and the eradication of alienation in all spheres of society. Thus they (as well as Debray) had nothing in common with the "adventurer" or the type of "dandy" that Karin Wieland illustrates using the example of Andreas Baader. The actions they proposed did not center around "luxury and violence." They were not empty of any deeper sense.[25] The "subjective factor" that they emphasized did not dissolve in the longing for individuality for the "autonomous subject."[26] On the contrary, members of the New Left connected collective and individual strategies of emancipation, self-government, and self-realization, and emphasized transformation of the subjective, based on the premise that the objective conditions for the transformation of society were a given.

This emphasis overlapped with Castro's concepts, even though the conditions in Latin America were different. Castro had explained the Cuban experiment in July 1966 with the following words: "As for subjective conditions, there were possibly no more than twenty, at first no more than ten, people who believed that a revolution was possible ... what was important was not the individuals involved, but conviction; merit lies not in the individuals, but in conviction."[27] Che Guevara also followed this premise. His strategy, which prescribed that a minority of guerilleros multiply themselves in action and thereby spread over the borders of Bolivia[28] to gradually liberate a continent of 300 million inhabitants,[29] counted on "consciousness," "will," and "obligation": that is, they presumed a notion of voluntarism.

Dutschke and Krahl referred to this voluntarism when they proclaimed in the organization committee: "The 'propaganda of shots' (Che) in the 'Third World' must be completed through the propaganda of action in the metropolises, which historically enables the urbanization of rural guerrilla activities. The urban guerillero is the organizer of the irregularity, such as destruction of the system of repressive institutions."[30] The "propaganda of shots" was thus not identical with the "propaganda of action." The appeal of the anti-authoritarians was not a call to arms in Frankfurt or Berlin. The transformation of the focus theory was not meant to be executed 1:1. Rather, a character of significance (Enzensberger) was ascribed to the guerrilla in Bolivia to restructure the relation of theory and practice, action and organization, based on the premise, which Hans Magnus Enzensberger counted among his "Berlin common phrases," that even the "tiniest political action … can, under the conditions with which we have to cope, lead to a new understanding."[31]

West German activists also adopted and transformed the relation of *direct action* and *violence*. The practice of actions in the border zone between legality and illegality was characteristic for the strategy of actions of the New Left. This applies to the strategy of "civil disobedience," which the New Left adopted from the Indian liberation movement of Gandhi and the American civil rights movement, as well as to the concept of the "construction of situations," which they borrowed from the International Situationists. If one asks for the motives and intentions of members of the groups that applied these methods, the answer is that through the use of limited contravention of rules, they aimed at unveiling the contradictions within the society, that they wanted to overcome apathy and indifference, and that they wanted to change attitudes and mentality structures.

The unconventional direct action in the border zone between legality and illegality broke with everyday life, with the normality of things. It violated norms, rules, laws, expectations. It caught the attention of the public and called for a reaction, for taking a position. The constraint engendered by the direct actions of civil disobedience was more often than not interpreted by the criminal courts as illegal duress and subsumed under the term "*vis compulsiva*," by use of psychic violence. In many instances police, prosecutors, and courts reacted sharply and took to stern repression and penal sanctions, which, as a kind of chain reaction, enhanced the movement's readiness to apply violence. A consequence of this potential escalation, as well as of the dependence of direct action on the reactions of the other side, was that the strategy of direct action was a hardly predictable and, in its effects, hardly controllable instrument of protest.

Finally, West German activist leaders grappled with questions of armed struggle and the New Left. The armed struggle of the guerrilla in Latin America aimed at conquering political power. According to Régis Debray, the focus theory was not designed for Europe and the democracies of the West.[32] The New Left strove for and experimented with the building up of a counterforce within existing institutions. The guiding idea of the New Left was not the conquest of political power in the state, but rather the alteration of the power structures. Activists sought to carry this out by dismantlement of hierarchies, by democratization of the mechanisms of direction and decision-making in all sectors of the society, by self-government and cooperation, and by the abolition of structures of dependency, changing the structures of needs.

Distinct in their objectives, liberation movements and the New Left also differed from one another in their methods of fighting for them, especially regarding the question of the application of violence. Violence within the industrialized countries of the West was interpreted by the representatives of the New Left as "organized refusal." It was illustrated with these words inspired by Herbert Marcuse: "We oppose with our unarmed bodies, with our trained brains, the most inhuman parts of the machinery (government machinery, instruments of manipulation); we do not play by their rules any longer, but intervene intentionally and directly into our own history."[33]

Nevertheless, the New Left did not categorically exclude the use of physical violence, including the armed struggle. Its principle "solidarity must become practical" and its self-obligation, derived from this principle, to actively support the liberation movements of the Third World, as well as its solidarity with organizations (like SNCC) that propagated and applied the violent struggle, excluded a rigorous refusal of the application of violence. Therefore one can say that the New Left was not at all pacifistic. Still, the New Left differed from terrorists like the RAF in one central point: the future society was to be tried out experimentally within the existing society. By creating new models of cooperation, unfolding alternative artistic values, and forging new structures of relations, activists would install the basic elements of the future society. This excluded a "march into the future" society by means of underground illegality and the use of bombs and explosives.

Thus, called upon to join the so-called "Weathermen" in the United States, Tom Hayden withstood the temptation to go underground. The "Port Huron side" within him, he later explained, prevented this. The guiding ideas of "participatory democracy" and "self-organization" were incompatible with the violent actionism of the "Weathermen" group. The same holds true for Rudi Dutschke, notwithstanding the fact that, in the spring of 1968, he entertained the thought of a bomb attack against American ships carrying war goods to Vietnam.[34] He turned down a call by Ulrike Meinhof to join the RAF. Her slogan, "The act of liberation within the act of destruction," implied a break with the strategy and the objectives of the New Left. Non-action is equally a type of action, which can be situatively conditioned but can also be molded by the sense structure that guides the person who acts, through attitudes, dispositions, and criteria of perspective, as well as through partition of the social world. The militant groups of the urban guerrilla movement and the terrorist groupings—and this is my thesis—used the forms of actions of the 1968 movement but radicalized them, because they did not share the basic values of the New Left, and rejected its strategy of transformation.

Conclusion

In analyzing the 1968 movement, a movement of the New Left, we might take into account the definition of *Handeln* (action) given by Max Weber, "insofar as the acting individual attaches a subjective meaning to his behavior, be it overt or covert, of omission or acquiescence," and of social action, "insofar as its subjective meaning takes account of the behavior of others and is thereby oriented in its course." By these definitions, it is impossible to separate the problem of violence from the cognitive orientation or the collective sense structure of the 1968 movement.[35] Given this, one can say that the movement used violence not to conquer power, but rather as means to alter the modes of perception. We can characterize this use of violence, adopted from a global context of traditions and practices, in three ways, and then demonstrate how pervasive, accepted, and critically important these views have become in the German and Western context.

The first is the notion of violence as a strategy to alter modes of perception. The politics of changing perceptions is aimed at politicizing society from "below," at changing rules by rule-breaking, with the objective of altering the rules of the rules. These rule-changing politics of the New Left were based on a broad, external notion of violence. Through the deployment of "symbolic violence" and "violence against objects," activists transgressed limits in order to unveil societal contradictions as well as structures of dependency and suppression, and initiate communication and discourse about them. One could call a multitude of their actions "*vis ludens*" ("playful violence") or "*vis subversiva*" ("subversive violence"), thereby describing their tendency—and in this way likening them to the historic avant-garde—to force the public to take a stance, and to question the justification of attitudes that are deeply rooted in the thinking and the "habitus" (from Pierre Bourdieu, who talks of "*vis insita*") of the people.

We can speak, too, of the subversion of the attitude toward violence. The executive power and the judiciary in West Germany, as elsewhere, tried to define the deployment of the new forms of protest, such as civil disobedience and the "construction of situations," as illegal actions and thereby to criminalize them. The student New Left countered these efforts by attempting in turn to legitimize this transition from legal to purportedly illegal forms of protest, and the application of violent forms of action, by making reference to the fundamental human right to demonstrate, to a right to resistance based on *Naturrecht* (natural law) or the necessity of *Gegengewalt* (counterviolence) in a situation of massive suppression. If one tries to draw conclusions about the outcome of this fight concerning the limits between legality and illegality, one might note that, in the long run, the New Left actually influenced the perception of violence. Activists' strategy of direct action, which later was adopted by the diverse movements that succeeded the 1968 movement (the alternative, peace, women's, and environmental movements), gradually found its place in the 1970s and 1980s in the political culture of the Federal Republic of Germany. These were forms of demonstration that already had a firm place in the political culture of neighboring France at that time. Empirical data reveal that between 1974 and 1989, it was not only the degree of tolerance toward these unconditional forms of protest that grew, but also the number of such forms of protest. Manifestations of these forms nearly doubled. At the same time, the readiness to participate in actions of civil disobedience, as well as to accept them as legitimate, was enhanced among the population. According to a survey of the German "Gewaltkommission" held in 1989, while popular disaffection for violence was extremely high, as it had been earlier, only 23 percent of the population defined a sit-in that blocked traffic as "violence."[36]

Finally, we observe an emphasis on power beyond the "Leviathan." The New Left and its provocative forms of action triggered discussions about the terms of violence and power in the social sciences as well as in the field of political theory. Without knowing the term, the New Left had recognized what was later on coined "structural violence" by Johan Galtung and made it a focus of discussion. In doing so, they had furthermore paved the way for the depersonalization of violence. While the extended sense of violence was in practice used mostly for agitation purposes (scandalization/dramatization), it reflected at the same time a notion of power (might/*potestas*) that was not confined to the Leviathan. Corresponding with the extended sense of violence was a depoliticized and depersonalized sense of power, which was responsible for the fact that the movement did not strive to conquer the political power.

Aside from Hannah Arendt, it was mainly the French philosopher Michel Foucault who redefined the term *Macht* (power). Influenced by the 1968 movement, he began to emphasize the ubiquity of power relations in the 1970s. As he saw it, they profoundly and subtly permeated the whole society: "It is necessary to examine the power beyond the Leviathan," he demanded.[37] Defined by Foucault, power "in reality consisted of a more or less coordinated bundle of relations, which were more or less organized and structured more or less in the form of a pyramid."[38] The task of identifying relations of power and centers of power, and of developing adequate forms of combat to fight against them, gained overwhelming importance for Foucault. To accuse centers of power by talking about them in public already meant fighting against them. This could be construed as an initial evasion of power, which could already be seen "in calling things by their names" to reveal "who had done what."[39] In these quotations one can distinctly identify the premises of the International Situationists. The perspective toward the term "power," which Foucault puts at the center of his theory of power, reflects the sense of power adopted (and spread) by the New Left.

Foucault did not tackle the problem of the judiciary, which arose during the demobilization process of the May movement in France, as the confrontation of a radical movement within a system of repression by the executive power and the judiciary, as Jean-Paul Sartre had characterized it. He focused his view on the prison system as the "cellar or lumber room of the penal system." He started to uncover the "prison regime" and the structures of power within the institution, "seemingly lost out of sight of the society." According to Foucault, this was a consequence of a political philosophy that was inherent in the state, the sovereign, the law, in prohibition and in the representative system of power. What he was demanding was to dehierarchize the system, to "cut off the head of the king."[40]

The New Left had symbolically anticipated and transformed into action those demands of Foucault in uncovering power and violence beyond the Leviathan. Its decentered understanding of power and of an extended notion of violence led the New Left to criticize the relations of power and violence in everyday life, within the family and within relations among the sexes. Thereby it sharpened the focus onto new forms and definitions of violence: symbolic violence, cultural violence, ritual violence, and—last but not least—sexual violence, which became objects of research and discussion in the social sciences as well as in the study of law in the 1970s.

Translation by Dr. Dierk Helmken.

Notes

1. Jean-Pierre Duteuil, *Nanterre 1965–66–67–68 : Vers le mouvement du 22 mars* (Mauléon, 1988), 235–37, 237.
2. Klaus Meschkat, "Fantasievolle Überraschungen," *taz*, 1 March 2005, 15; Wolfgang Kraushaar, "Der Eskalationsstratege," *taz*, 8 March 2005, 19; Robert Misik, "Lob der Guerilla-Mentalität," *taz*, 15 March 2005, 15; Arno Widmann, "Auf dem Trip namens Revolution," *taz*, 22 March 2005, 15; Stephan Schlak, "Der Nicht-Anschlussfähige," *taz*, 30 March 2005, 15; Christoph Bautz, "Überholter Zündstoff," *taz*, 5 April 2005, 15; Isolde Charim, "Kampf um die Sehnsüchte," *taz*, 13 April 2005, 15; Jürgen Busche, "Der schwankende Hintergrund," *taz*, 26 April 2005, 15.
3. Walter Fähnders, *Avantgarde und Moderne 1890–1933* (Stuttgart and Weimar, 1998), 192.
4. Wolfgang Kraushaar, Karin Wieland, and Jan Philipp Reemtsma, *Rudi Dutschke Andreas Baader und die RAF* (Hamburg, 2005).
5. Birgitta Nedelmann, "Gewaltsoziologie am Scheideweg: Die Auseinandersetzung in der gegenwärtigen und Wege der zukünftigen Gewaltforschung," in *Soziologie der Gewalt*, ed. Trutz von Trotha (Opladen, 1997), 59–85. About the differences between "mainstreamers" and "innovators" see Joachim Hüttemann, "'Dichte Beschreibung' oder Ursachenforschung der Gewalt? Anmerkungen zu einer falschen Alternative im Lichte der Problematik funktionaler Erklärung," in *Gewalt: Entwicklung, Strukturen, Analyseprobleme*, ed. Wilhelm Heitmeyer and Hans-Georg Soeffner (Frankfurt am Main, 2004), 107–124; Peter Imbusch, "'Mainstreamer' versus 'Innovateure' der Violenceforschung. Eine kuriose Debatte," in ibid., 125–50.
6. "Ursachen, Prävention und Kontrolle von Gewalt aus soziologischer Sicht (Gutachten der Unterkommission III)," in *Ursachen, Prävention und Kontrolle von Gewalt: Analysen und Vorschläge der Unabhängigen Regierungskommission zur Verhinderung und Bekämpfung von Gewalt*, 4 vols., ed. Hans-Dieter Schwind and Jürgen Baumann (Berlin, 1990), 2:293–414, 311.
7. Ibid., 1:36.
8. Furthermore, *Gewalt* is also often used in cases where the English language would prefer the word "force." In the context of this essay, *Gewalt* is used to mean "violence" in almost all cases.

9. Friedhelm Neidhardt, "Gewalt: Soziale Bedeutung und sozialwissenschjaftliche Bestimmungen eines Begriffs," in Bundeskriminalamt, ed., *Was ist Gewalt? Ausein-andersetzungen mit einem Begriff*, vol. 1, *Strafrechtliche und sozialwissenschaftliche Deutungen* (Wiesbaden, 1986), 114; Roland Eckert, Max Kaase, Fiedhelm Neidhardt, "Ursachen, Prävention und Kontroille von gewalt asu soziologischer Sicht: Gutachten der Unterkommission III", in Schwind and Baumann, *Ursachen*, 2:299–414, 306.

10. Johan Galtung, *Strukturelle Gewalt* (Reinbek, 1975).

11. Karl-Georg Faber, "Macht, Gewalt," in *Geschichtliche Grundbegriffe: Historisches Lexikon zur politisch-sozialen Sprache in Deutschland*, 8 vols.,, ed. Otto Brunner, Werner Conze, and Reinhart Koselleck (Stuttgart, 2004), 3:817–935, 922f.

12. Peter Handke, *Kaspar* (Frankfurt am Main, 1967), 7. Over a number of years the West German parliament debated the need for a set of "emergency laws" permitting government suspension of basic rights in "crisis" situations. Passed in May 1968 despite massive and widespread protest, the laws necessitated a special change in the West German constitution or "Basic Law."

13. Guy Debord, *Die Gesellschaft des Spektakels* (Berlin, 1996), 160f.

14. Ibid., 174.

15. *Brockhaus, Die Enzyklopädie in 24 Bänden*, 20th ed. (Leipzig and Mannheim, 1996ff.), 333.

16. *Grand Dictionnaire Encyclopédique Larousse*, vol. 9 (Paris, l985), 9857.

17. "Art. Subversion," in *The Oxford English Dictionary*, 2nd ed., vol. 8, ed. J. A. Simpson, E.S.C. (London, 1989), 88.

18. Compare Ingrid Gilcher-Holtey, *Die Phantasie an die Macht: Mai 68 in Frankreich* (Frankfurt am Main, 2003), 194ff., 232ff.

19. Herbert Marcuse, *Versuch über die Befreiung* (Frankfurt am Main, 1969), 56, 59. Compare also Karl-Heinz Bohrer, *Die gefährdete Phantasie, oder Surrealismus und Terror* (Munich, 1970), 32–61; as well as Greil Marcus, *Lipstick Traces: A Secret History of the Twentieth Century* (Cambridge, MA, 1989), 163ff.

20. Siegward Lönnendonker and Tilman Fichter, eds., *Freie Universität Berlin 1948 – 1973, Hochschule im Umbruch, Teil IV: 1964 – 1967* (Berlin, 1975), 66.

21. Compare Judith Clavier Albert and Stewart Edward Albert, eds., *The Sixties Papers: Documents of a Rebellious Decade* (New York, 1984), 117ff.

22. Regis Debray, *Kritik der Waffen* (Reinbek, 1975), 136.

23. Rudi Dutschke and Hans-Jürgen Krahl, "Das Sich-Verweigern erfordert Guerilla-Mentalität," in Rudi Dutschke, *Geschichte ist machbar: Texte über das herrschende Falsche und die Radikalität des Friedens*, Ed. Jürgen Miermeister and Klaus Wagenbach (Berlin, 1980), 89–95.

24. Compare with the adventurer type in Jean-Paul Sartre, "Portrait des Abenteurers," in idem, *Plädoyer für die Intellektuellen: Interviews, Artikel, Reden, 1950–1973* (Reinbek, 1995), 9–21; Georg Simmel, "Das Abenteuer," in idem, *Philosophische Kultur: Über das Abenteuer, die Geschlechter und die Krise der Moderne* (Berlin, 1983), 25–37; Regis Debray, "André Malraux ou l'imperatif du mensonge," in idem, *Éloges* (Paris, 1986), 109–46.

25. Karin Wieland, "a.," in Kraushaar, Wieland, and Reemtsma, *Rudi Dutschke*, 51–99, 86f.

26. Jan Philipp Reemtsma, "Was heißt 'die Geschichte der RAF verstehen'?" in Kraushaar, Wieland, and Reemtsma, *Rudi Dutschke*, 100–142, 134ff.
27. "Gramma of 27 July 1966," here cited after Sebastian Balfour, *Castro* (London, 1995), 89.
28. Régis Debray, *La guerilla du Che* (Paris, 1974), 83–88.
29. Ibid., 88, 135.
30. Dutschke and Krahl, "Das Sich-Verweigern," 94.
31. Hans-Magnus Enzensberger, *Berliner Gemeinplätze*, in *Kursbuch*, no. 11 (1968): 151–69, 159.
32. Regis Debray, interview with the author. Compare also Debray`s "preliminary remark" to *Revolution in the Revolution*, in which it is said that the book was compiled out of discussions with Latin American Communist Party members, and that it first of all addressed them, not the "'professional revolutionaries a la mode de Paris', where every student of the Sorbonne, who knows his Clausewitz, leads his guerrilla war to an easy victory with a sweep of his hand," in Regis Debray, *Revolution in der Revolution* (Munich, 1967), 8f.
33. Rudi Dutschke and Gaston Salvatore, "Einleitung," in Ernesto Che Guevara, *Schaffen wir zwei, drei viele Vietnam: Brief an das Exekutivsekretariat von OSPAAAL* (West Berlin, 1967).
34. See also Bernd Rabehl, *Rudi Dutschke: Revolutionär im geteilten Deutschland* (Dresden, 2002).
35. Max Weber, *Economy and Society: An Outline of Interpretive Sociology,* ed.Günther Roth and Claus Wittich (New York, 1968), 4.
36. Compare Max Kaase and Friedhelm Neidhardt, "Politische Gewalt und Repression: Ergebnisse von Bevölkerungsumfragen," in Schwind and Baumann, *Ursachen,* 4:7–55.
37. Michel Foucault, *Dispositive der Macht: Über Sexualität, Wissen und Wahrheit* (Berlin, 1978), 88.
38. "Das Spiel des Michel Foucault (1977)," in Michel Foucault, *Schriften—Dits et Ecrits,* 4 vols. (Frankfurt am Main, 2003), 3:397.
39. "Gespräch zwischen Michel Foucault und Gilles Deleuze: Die Intellektuellen und die Macht," in Michel Foucault, *Von der Subversion des Wissens* (Berlin, 1978), 128–140, 136f.
40. "Gespräch zwischen Michel Foucault, Alessandro Fontana und Pasquale Pasquino (Juni 1976)," in Foucault, *Schriften,* 3:186–213, here 200.

Chapter 9

"From Protest to Resistance"
Ulrike Meinhof and the Transatlantic
Movement of Ideas

Karin Bauer

> *Protest is when I say I don't like this.*
> *Resistance is when I put an end to what I don't like.*
> *Protest is when I say I refuse to go along with this any more.*
> *Resistance is when I make sure everybody else stops going along too.*
> —Ulrike Marie Meinhof

With her characteristic talent for combining the poetic and the programmatic, Ulrike Meinhof introduced the German left to a slogan that had long circulated in the United States in her April 1968 column entitled "From Protest to Resistance." Although Meinhof attributed the phrase to an anonymous African-American speaker of the Black Power movement at the 1968 Vietnam Congress, the slogan can be traced back, according to a May 1967 article in the *New York Times*, to Students for a Democratic Society (SDS) leader Carl Davidson.[1] The slogan still circulates widely today amongst anti-globalization, postcolonial environmental, feminist, anti-war, and various other activist groups; in a campaign against the reelection of George W. Bush, Davidson himself made the move "from resistance to politics."[2]

In the context of the protest movement in the 1960s, the slogan "from protest to resistance" spoke—on both sides of the Atlantic—to a climate of dissent and to the resolve to find more successful means to effect change. It served as a call for the radicalization of various groups and initiated intense debates on political strategy and the use of violence as a political tool. However, while the slogan expressed a transnational dissatisfaction with the seemingly scant results achieved through various forms of protest, its precise meaning and aim remain ambiguous. Amongst the various activist groups there existed no consensus on what it meant to move from protest to resistance, which strategies this would involve, and which forms of resistance would be considered effective and appropriate. Within the evolution of radical political agendas, the slogan was used by militant groups on both sides of the Atlantic to justify the increasingly violent means of furthering their agendas.

In the following I would like to focus on the German appropriation of the slogan "From Protest to Resistance" and in particular the various uses and abuses of the concept of resistance by the student movement, Meinhof, and the Red Army Faction (RAF). As Friedrich Nietzsche argued in *On the Genealogy of Morals:* "the cause of the origin of a thing and its eventual utility, its actual employment and place in the system of purposes, lie worlds apart; whatever exists, having somehow come into being, is again and again reinterpreted to new ends, taken over, transformed, and redirected."[3] In looking at some of the transformations of the concept of resistance, it is possible to trace its varied and shifting functions within the discourses of the radical left. The focus on Meinhof's writings to explicate shifting notions of protest and resistance leads into the very heart of the left's debates on oppositional strategies and violence. Close reading of Meinhof's columns published in *konkret* in the 1960s, as well as the texts she authored underground in the 1970s, brings to the foreground the internationalism and the cross-cultural currents of the protest movement, and—in particular—the important transnational migration of ideas from the US civil rights, anti-war, and student movement to European movements. What also becomes clear is that the movement of ideas and concepts from one national context to another is a complex operation that may occasion creative conceptual transformations.

In their examination of "The Cross-National Diffusion of Movement Ideas," Doug McAdam and Dieter Rucht argue that the American New Left had a considerable impact on the development of the "embryonic German New Left."[4] The American and German left had similar goals, strategies, and self-perceptions. On both sides of the Atlantic, the movements conceived of themselves as "midwives to a nonviolent revolution."[5] Social movements, McAdams and Rucht maintain, "are nothing more than clusters of new cultural items—new cognitive frames, behavioral routines, organizational forms, tactical repertoires" that the German left borrowed from the US.[6] McAdam and Rucht's relational and nonrelational diffusion theory assumes that there have to be transmitters and adopters of ideas. According to this theory, the transmission of ideas may happen through an interplay of relational and nonrelational channels—though interpersonal contact as well as though impersonal channels such as the mass media. McAdam and Rucht account for several interpersonal relationships, including activists' visit to North America, and they examine the possibilities of nonrelational channels such as television, newspapers, and radical and scholarly writings.

The diffusion theory may appear straightforward, and in many instances my findings will seemingly confirm the interplay of both interpersonal and nonrelational channels in the diffusion of an idea. However, this chapter will contest the unidirectional model of the diffusion theory. Transmission and adoption, it will become clear, are complex processes of adaptation, transformation, and appropriation that can not be adequately described by models of patrimony or matrimony. My contribution will also contest McAdam and Rucht's claim of the essentially nonviolent nature of the ideas and self-perceptions that were transmitted from the US to Germany. The tactical repertoire negotiated in "From Protest to Resistance" is no benevolent midwifery.

The adaptation of the slogan by the militant left presented a concrete instance of cultural transfer, yet the transmission, adaptation, mutation, and instrumentalization of the concept of "resistance" betrays the complexity of transnational diffusion. The historical resonances of resistance vary significantly, and resistance functioned very differently in different cultural and historical contexts. The term resistance gained currency in response to the atrocities of the Vietnam War and the outrage many felt when faced with the brutality of the war and the seemingly incorrigible thinking responsible for its escalation. With its evocation of the German past, "resistance" carried with it a very different historical and emotional baggage, and as a politically loaded term, it resonated very differently within the context of postwar Germany versus the context of the North American student, civil rights and Black Power movements.

In the US, the student movement's discussions of the adoption of more radical political aims and strategies long preceded the coining of the slogan. While indebted in the early years to the tradition of nonviolent civil disobedience, the major groups of the US movement that were influential in the German movement, such as the Student Nonviolent Coordinating Committee (SNCC) and the SDS, were involved in a continuous process of radicalization. Fueled by internal struggles as well as the escalation of the Vietnam War, the Cuban crisis, the activities of the congressional Un-American Committee, and the civil rights movement, both SDS and SNCC began to shift from protest to more confrontational tactics. As one activist remarked: "We can demonstrate until we are in jail, but neither the inconvenience we cause nor the moral witness we present will alter the situation."[7]

Spurred by Davidson, the SDS moved away from the reformist stance of the 1962 Port Huron Statement toward the more militant stance expressed at the 1966 Clear Lake Convention. Tom Hayden's and the SDS's goal at Port Huron was to stimulate democratic social movements on campuses and in communities across the US, to forge ties amongst various social movements, activist groups, and the Democratic Party, and to work toward establishing a participatory democracy.[8] Although in need of reform, the state was viewed as an instrument of the people. Indebted to a social democratic tradition, the Port Huron Statement explicitly condemned violence. In contrast, four years later at Clear Lake, some members of SDS were wearing "I Hate the State" buttons. With a new generation of activists and leaders at the helm, the SDS now adopted more radical positions and moved toward the adaptation of the more militant strategies captured by Davidson's slogan "from protest to resistance." Under the leadership of Davidson, in December 1966 at its National Council in Berkeley the SDS passed an anti-draft resolution encouraging young men to resist the draft. "Resistance" became a key term denoting the move away from anti-war protests to an active opposition to the war. Desertion, draft-dodging, and public burning of draft notices signaled the willingness to resist the war while simultaneously adopting confrontational strategies aiming at broader social and political changes. Thus, the slogan "from protest to resistance" also suggested the hope that a radicalization of the student movement would bring about a radicalization of the public sphere.

The civil rights organization SNCC, which was formed in 1960 by black college students in support of the sit-in movement, underwent a parallel process of radicalization. While SNCC originally advocated nonviolent protests against racial segregation in the South, it, too, broadened its scope in opposition to the Vietnam War. Under Stokely Carmichael and the influence of the Black Panthers, SNCC was no longer content organizing sit-ins and voter registration campaigns. It modified its nonviolent stance and, moving from protest to resistance, began to promote urban guerrilla tactics. Advocating self-reliance and "Black Power," SNCC expelled its white members in 1966 and adopted more militant tactics and goals. It supported violent actions as a legitimate means of self-defense.

Meinhof's 1968 *konkret* column was written within this global climate of escalating discontent. Meinhof's adaptation of the slogan "from protest and resistance" captured not only a widespread sentiment of frustration and discord amongst the protest movement, but also the political will by some segments of the Extra-Parliamentary Opposition (APO) to adopt more confrontational tactics. Involved in her own process of political, professional, and personal radicalization, Meinhof began in the spring of 1968 to push the boundaries toward a more engaged and, finally, violent political strategy. Only one year later, Meinhof ended her ten-year career as columnist and editor for the leftist magazine *konkret* and went underground.

Meinhof came to *konkret* from the German peace and anti-nuclear movement—a movement heavily peopled by Protestant pacifists. As a student at the Universities of Marburg and Münster, Meinhof was active in organizing protests against Germany's rearmament and the development and deployment of nuclear weapons. She was engaged in writing leaflets, open letters, and articles for student newspapers. At the time, the anti-nuclear movement was by no means a radical or marginalized movement; it drew its support not only from students but also from mainstream organizations, such as segments of the Protestant church, and from the wider public. Signed by top nuclear physicists, including Otto Hahn, Werner Heisenberg, and Carl Friedrich von Weizäcker, and supported by leading Protestant theologians, such as Helmut Gollwitzer, Kurt Scharf, and Heinrich Albertz, the well-publicized Declaration of Göttingen of 1957 opposed the production and the placement of nuclear weapons on German soil. Meinhof's Protestant activism—instilled in her by Renate Riemeck, the woman who raised her after the death of her mother—brought her in contact with the Easter March movement and with the liberal Protestant theology of Gollwitzer, a former member of the anti-fascist Bekennende Kirche (Confessing Church). As a supporter of the German resistance against National Socialism and an outspoken proponent of social justice, Gollwitzer exerted moral authority in student and leftist circles. Although his dispassionate intellectual engagement with Marxism and his insistence on exploring the social implications of biblical messages may have impressed Meinhof and the students, it also put him at odds with the Protestant establishment. In the 1960s, Gollwitzer became a supporter of the student movement and a friend and ally to activists, such as Dutschke and Meinhof, at whose funerals he held eulogies. While Protestant roots are often mentioned in connection with Dutschke, Meinhof, Gudrun Ensslin, Hans-Jürgen Krahl, and other activists, the significance of Protestantism for the German peace and protest movement has thus far escaped adequate exploration and recognition.

Described by a fellow student as a "Protestant flute-girl" (*evangelisches Blockflöten-Mädchen*) who prayed before eating lunch at the cafeteria, the protest of the young Meinhof was clearly driven by a moral fervor that seems, in retrospect, to foreshadow the uncompromising dogmatic fervor that marked her later writings.[9] While her early *konkret* columns were sharply critical of Western politics and government policies, they revealed a Protestant ethos and a belief in good works. The urgent yet conciliatory tone advocated the individual and collective responsibility to work toward the moral, social, and political improvement of humanity. Meinhof's early columns had not yet reached the rhetorical incisiveness of her later writings. Although her tone appeared to grow sharper with each column, she still expressed hope for a political rationality that would bring together the opponents of the Cold War. She argued for a rapprochement of capitalism and communism and maintained a guarded optimism concerning the political trajectory of the German Social Democrats and the US government vis-à-vis the Soviet Union. Considering the extent of Meinhof's later radicalization, many of Meinhof's early statements might have appeared strangely naïve even for leftist-liberal circles at the time. In 1959, for instance, Meinhof celebrated Nikita Khrushchev's meeting with US President Dwight D. Eisenhower at Camp David as a turning point in Cold War politics. Peace, Meinhof maintained in regard to the meeting, "has become the decisive factor of political action."[10] Uncharacteristic of her later strategies, in her early years at *konkret* Meinhof balanced her political idealism with a utilitarian approach to government. She contended that the ultimate test for the viability of political ideas is their practical applicability, "very pragmatic, non-ideological, and unsentimental; politics is the art of the possible."[11]

Despite Meinhof's proclivity toward political utilitarianism, her impetus for political action throughout the 1960s and 1970s appears firmly grounded in the Protestant ethos that Max Weber describes as *Gesinnungsethik*. For Weber, political action is driven by two different orientations. First, there is political action that is primarily guided by a sense of responsibility (*Verantwortungsethik*) for the consequences and results of one's actions. Secondly, there is political action motivated by "inner conviction" (*Gesinnungsethik*).[12] This is, according to Weber, a predominantly Protestant and anarchist drive, in which the observance of external law is displaced by the need to express and act in accordance to one's own inner conviction and sense of justice. Within the moral universe of *Gesinnungsethik*, political action is legitimated by moral righteousness and good intention rather than the weighing of intended and unintended consequences of one's actions. This is not to say that action taken in accordance with inner conviction is void of a sense of responsibility. For the young Meinhof and others of her generation, the necessity to protest, for instance, the government's nuclear armament grew out of a sense of responsibility for the fate of humanity. Protest and resistance thus derived from the moral imperative to oppose policies that might endanger human lives.

For Meinhof and many of her generation, the heightened sense of moral responsibility to act arose from Germany's failure to oppose National Socialism. Germany's fascist past remained the central historical reference point for Meinhof's early and later writing, and throughout the 1960s, Meinhof's columns testified to her sense of moral outrage about the Federal Republic's inability to confront Germany's past crimes. Meinhof criticized the structural continuities of fascism within legislative, judicial, and institutional bodies, and she exposed those who worked within these institutions under National Socialism and who were now actively engaged in determining policy in the Federal Republic. Visible throughout her writings in the 1960s was also a growing disillusionment with the Federal Republic's foreign policy and its support of the aggressive politics of the United States. Meinhof soon gave up the hope that the United States and Germany would be involved or even interested in constructively defusing Cold War tensions. Her positions became increasing radical, and her tone grew sharper and more polemical as she spoke out on a broad spectrum of issues, including women's rights, union politics, media manipulation, consumer society, and high-profile trials. Like other members of what later became the RAF, Meinhof was a spokeswoman for the marginalized groups of society, such as foreign workers, low-income parents, and institutionalized youth.

Meinhof arose as one of the most influential spokespersons of the New Left. Her writing sought to facilitate communication between student protesters, various interest groups, and the larger public. At the height of the student movement, when students clashed with police and protests became increasingly violent, she brought to her audience questions of violence and counter-violence. Under the ambiguous title "Counter-Violence," Meinhof thematized the left's ambiguous and contentious position toward violence. On the one hand, the movement was in principle "against violence" (*gegen Gewalt*), while on the other hand, the violence exercised by the state and by police provoked protesters to resort to "counter-violence" (*Gegengewalt*).[13]

With its references to the violence exercised by National Socialism, Meinhof's text was symptomatic of the New Left's opposition to the perceived systemic or structural violence inherent in the state apparatus. The goal was to expose and resist the latent violence exercised by the state and its institutions. Confronted with the memory of the failed resistance against National Socialism and the state monopoly on the exercise of violence, many believed that it was the left's moral duty to oppose the oppressive tendencies of the system. The debates on violence demonstrate that neither side was able to divorce reflections on violence in the Federal Republic from the violence exercised by fascism. Fascism remained the central reference point of the debates—from Jürgen Habermas's famous *Linksfaschismus* (fascism of the left) to Theodor W. Adorno's claim that "the students have taken on a bit of the role of the Jews," on the one side, to the conservative call to law and order and the Springer Press's portrayal of the protesters as a serious threat to German society, on the other side.[14]

In her column, Meinhof responded to the equation of violence exercised by the right and violence from the left—an equation that is, she argued, based on the widespread trivialization of fascism. In Germany, Meinhof maintained, fascism was still perceived as a mere insolence, "an episode of hooliganism, a momentary lapse in the German spirit, a misfortune of German history, a stroke of fate that had no source in society, and maybe did somehow somewhere have 'a sublime purpose,' that was just pursued with the wrong methods."[15] In drawing parallels between fascist terror and the violent outbursts of student protesters, the establishment was—again—attempting to silence opposition. There was, Meinhof lamented, a general lack of recognition that the students' disruptive behavior was a response to the violence exercised by the system. The violence of protesters must be seen as legitimate acts of self-defense, Meinhof argued, as amongst the left self-defense (*Notwehr*) became a central term in the debate of the moral defensibility of acts of violence and resistance.

Meinhof's column "From Protest to Resistance" spoke to the radical German left at a decisive turning point. Protests were growing against the Vietnam War, the German emergency laws, and the fossilization of the universities. The brutality of police against protesters only strengthened the latter's resolve to fight against repressive policies. Fueled by the conservative Springer Press, the reactionary climate created amongst the APO a siege mentality lending further urgency to questions of strategy and political survival. Segments of the protest movement—including Rudi Dutschke, Hans-Jürgen Krahl, and Meinhof—began flirting with the idea of a militant urban guerrilla movement.[16] Confronted with the experience of violence on the streets, nonviolent forms were perceived with increasing skepticism. Yet there existed amongst the movement many divergent strategies to affect change.[17] Thus, the debate on violence must be seen within a complex net of arguments about the failures of the past and the evolving modes of resistance and self-defense.[18]

It was the violent protests against the conservative Springer Press in the wake of the shooting of Dutschke in April 1968 that occasioned Meinhof's "From Protest to Resistance" column. A frequent subject of the conservative press, Dutschke had become the target of resentment against the protest movement, and on 11 April 1968 he was shot by a young worker who had in his possession a copy of the *Nationalzeitung,* a neofascist newspaper carrying the headline "Stop Dutschke Now." Meinhof, a close political ally of Dutschke, participated in the protest against Springer in Berlin. Her adaptation of the resistance slogan was accompanied by her enthusiastic support for the protests, in which an estimated 45,000 people in more than twenty German cities took part. In their attempt to stop delivery of Springer Press publications, the students, Meinhof maintained, were not merely voicing their discontent and practicing rebellion, but were carrying out acts of resistance. Referring back to the Vietnam Congress held a few months earlier, where major debates on the strategies of opposition to the Vietnam War had taken place, Meinhof argued that it was now time to return to these issues and discuss again questions of violence and counter-violence. While protest was the expression of discontent on intellectual and theoretical grounds, resistance was seen as a revolutionary praxis, and gestures of resistance could cross the line into illegality and counter-violence.

Identifying him only as a "black speaker from the Black Power movement,"[19] Meinhof referred in her column to Dale A. Smith, a SNCC activist and speaker at the Vietnam Congress held in Berlin in February 1968.[20] Leaving Smith nameless enhanced his status as a representative voice of Black Power and emphasized the collective nature of his ideas. At the same time, by identifying Smith as a black man (*Schwarzen*) and by denying him a name and an individual identity, Meinhof seemed to exploit rhetorically an identity politics of race embraced by segments of the German left that romanticized the struggles of the "Other"—be it in Vietnam, Cuba, South America, or the US. Meinhof distilled Smith's speech in the first paragraph of her column into the poignant sentences cited above and then proceeded with her arguments without further reference to him. Justifying her claim that the movement had shifted from protest to resistance, she gave an account of the various tactics used by the Springer protesters. Essentially, she recounted—albeit without reference to him—the strategies outlined by Smith: to frighten those in power, so they may no longer feel safe to pursue their deeds, make their luxury cars drive over nails, break windows, overturn cars.[21] In his critique of the protest movement, Smith had dismissed protests as "pretty" and ineffectual "games" played by rules imposed by those in power. Resonating with the leftist strategy of *gezielte Regelverletzung,* Smith's speech defined resistance likewise as the breaking of rules. Smith announced to his audience in Berlin the radicalization of the Black Power movement—the radicalization that had led Black Power to depart from the tradition of nonviolent resistance and civil disobedience so influential in the US in the early 1960s.

Smith's breaking of rules was also an intensely personal expression of solidarity with the victims of US imperialism and a direct response to the perceived repression by and aggression of those in power:

> To exercise resistance means to frighten Johnson and his marionettes so that they no longer dare to leave their houses ... Resistance means:

> As long as the parents in Vietnam cry for their children, the parents in
> the US shall cry for their children. If the Vietnamese people can't bring
> in their harvest without the shadow of death, then no American shall
> bring in his harvest and no American shall live outside the shadow of
> death.[22]

Thus, resistance was seen as a step into illegality motivated by the moral obligation toward the victims of US aggression. Acts of resistance were connected
to concrete targets and goals and derived their legitimacy from solidarity with
the farmers, parents, and children. Smith's breaking of rules stood in an immediate relationship to the goals to be accomplished and in this way contrasted
with Meinhof's reflections on the bombing of a Frankfurt department store by
Gudrun Ensslin, Andreas Baader, Thorwald Proll, and Horst Söhnlein. In her
column "Setting Fire to Department Stores"—published in *konkret* just a few
issues after "From Protest to Resistance" —Meinhof diverged from Smith's direct approach to breaking the law in favor of a more abstract notion. While
she noted that the endangerment of human life and the bombing's inability to
disrupt consumer society were to be held against such actions, she argued that
the progressive moment of the bombing lay in the illegality of the act itself.[23]
For Smith, breaking the law came as a result of the need to resist. For Meinhof,
arguing from the point of view of *Gesinnungsethik,* it was the illegal act itself and
not its consequences that could be described as progressive.

In his speech, Smith claimed that protesters vainly attempted to exert moral
influence on people who have no moral conscience and that protest was a mere
intellectual act, whereas resistance was a moral-political imperative in this epoch of revolt.[24] Protest was theory and games, while resistance was action and
practice. Smith's speech emanated a sense of urgency and an optimistic promise
of victory—a victory rhetorically framed in moral and existential rather than
political terms. Acts of resistance, according to Smith, demonstrated the heroic
triumph of humanity: although resistance meant putting one's life at risk, it also
meant truly living and being alive for the first time.

This sense of self-actualization and moral-existential mission was symptomatic for many expressions of protest on both sides of the Atlantic. In Smith, it
arose from his identity as an African-American and from the recognition that
the war in Vietnam was not fought only against the Vietnamese: "we, too, are
its victims," Smith maintained: "This is not only a war against the Vietnamese
people. This is a war against us."[25] Those in power were murderers, and "it is us,
who is getting killed by these murderers."[26] For Smith as an African-American,
this assertion was grounded in the concrete experience of the draft, the death
of predominantly black American soldiers in Vietnam, the lynching and racial
discrimination in the South, and the police brutality against civil rights activists.
Thus there was a basis for Smith's claim that "it is us, who is getting killed." His
experience was vastly different from that of his West Berlin audience, for whom,

however, the identification with the victims of the Vietnam War provided a se-
ductive model of thought. Also circulating at the time was Che Guevara's call for
the creation of many Vietnams, and Vietnam was seen as but one symptom of
the aggressive imperialist expansion of power and capital. In other words, Berlin
was Saigon, and thus Meinhof argued that the repressive character of liberal
democracy brought to light "what Berlin has to do with Vietnam."[27] Wilfried
Mausbach has aptly described the spatial-temporal displacements and the German left's identification with the victims of aggression as the "Germanization of
the Vietnam War."[28]

In her column, Meinhof argued that the action against Springer had given
the movement a push toward practicing resistance: "now that the shackles of common decency have been broken, we can and must discuss violence and counter-
violence anew and from the very beginning. Counter-violence, as was practiced
over Easter, does not easily garner support; it does not easily attract frightened
liberals to the side of the APO."[29] Despite the hope for a reformation of the
movement, Meinhof did not celebrate the gestures of resistance—as exercised by
the demonstration against Springer—for their effectiveness, but rather for their
potential to radicalize the struggle against the existing order. She recognized that
the action against Springer did not change the relations of power, but she praised
it as a step from theory to practice. As was so for Smith and much of the protest
movement, action and practice became privileged over theory and discussion.

Although Meinhof picked up the concept of resistance from Smith's speech,
"resistance" was clearly a term hovering over and haunting the discussions within
the German left, and Meinhof seemed to evoke the term precisely because of
its historical resonance. In claiming a systemic continuation of fascism in the
Federal Republic, Meinhof evoked, by extension, the need, and indeed the duty,
of resistance. In contrast to the American context and its intellectual tradition of
civil disobedience, resistance in the Federal Republic first and foremost invoked
resistance against National Socialism—a resistance that could not be divorced
from violent means.

The right to resist unlawful regimes was written into the German constitution in 1968 as an amendment at the time when the German government passed
the contested emergency laws. As consolation for the passage of the emergency
laws, which were opposed by the unions and the left, lawmakers gave the public
the right—if all legal avenues were exhausted—to resist illegitimate attempts by
the executive or the legislative bodies to undermine the democratic constitution.
However, the right to resist the unjust exercise of power by legitimate and illegitimate regimes reaches back to ancient times. From the murder of tyrants to
various forms of rebellion and civil disobedience, there lurks behind the moral
and judicial legitimation of resistance the question of when and how resistance
may be enacted.[30] The moral right to resist injustice is also inscribed in religious
thought. In Protestantism—a tradition relevant to an understanding of the student movement, as well as the armed struggle in Germany—there exists a moral

duty to resist for reasons of conscience. Faced with the conviction that they must oppose National Socialism, the Protestant theology of Dietrich Bonhoeffer, Niemöller, and Gollwitzer was at pains to come to terms with concepts and modes of resistance. Although Bonhoeffer's participation in the assassination attempt on Hitler remained a source of controversy, liberal protest theologians concurred with Bonhoeffer about the right and duty to resist institutions and states that commit crimes against humanity. However, resistance does not end with the overthrow of National Socialism. As Michael Geyer points out, it is Bonhoeffer's legacy to have conceived of resistance as a continuous, ongoing project, "not to commemorate but to participate in the reformation of society. Resistance, instead of being the record of past events, thus becomes the defining mark for the ongoing and always contested struggle."[31]

Influential within the student movement, Herbert Marcuse's notion of "repressive tolerance" adds another dimension to the reflections and debates on concepts and means of resistance taking place in the 1960s. Marcuse argued for a natural right to resistance, and activists referred to Marcuse in their attempt to legitimize militant opposition. Differentiating the violence of the system from the violence against the system, Marcuse argued that when faced with the oppressive violence of the system, pacifism and nonviolence on the side of the oppressed serve "the cause of actual violence by weakening the protest against it."[32] In this view, nonviolent action was seen as ineffectual passivity. Nonviolence may only strengthen the system, and violence may well become the conscientious form of objection and opposition. Although tolerance is thought to be a precondition for the creation of a humane society, tolerance should not be extended toward repressive conditions and tyranny.

For Meinhof, as a clandestine member of the Communist Party of Germany (KPD)—which had been banned in 1954—the objection to repressive tolerance and the call to resistance was intertwined with the KPD's history of anti-fascism. Within the KPD there circulated many individual stories of persecution and of resistance against Hitler, and Meinhof was certainly impressed by the individual and organized acts of everyday resistance by members of the KPD. In conjuring up the ghost of the failed resistance against National Socialism that was—and still is—haunting West German society, Meinhof appealed to the moral conscience of Germans to overcome passivity and repressive tolerance in favor of a participatory political engagement.

Yet her push toward the move from theory to practice also signified her professional and personal loss of hope in the power of enlightenment and the word. Read together with "Columnism," a piece she published in *konkret* in December 1968, it becomes clear that Meinhof began to question fundamentally her role as writer and columnist at a time when, with the disintegration of the APO after the passage of the emergency laws in June 1968, she was beginning to lose an audience receptive to activist mobilization. Whereas she had once maintained that "[p]oliticization means: Enlightenment about relations of power, property, and violence,"[33] she now questioned whether this enlightenment could be achieved through words and rational arguments. Although still writing her columns, she had left her husband, Klaus Rainer Röhl, the editor of *konkret,* and their seemingly comfortable bourgeois life in Hamburg. She moved to Berlin and became an outspoken critic of the magazine. She founded a counter editorial board in Berlin, and after a failed attempt to occupy the office of *konkret* in Hamburg, Meinhof finally resigned from the magazine in April 1969. In "Columnism," Meinhof maintained that columnists functioned as pretext and alibi. They were "the Blacks of the State Department," tokens and ornaments giving the impression that independence of mind and freedom of expression existed.[34] Yet behind the liberal image maintained through columns lurked other motivations connected to prestige and profit. "Columns are luxury articles, columnists are stars and the big fish in their own tiny pond," Meinhof maintained.[35]

In reality, the independence of the columnist was a fiction, "a fraud for the readers, self-deception, a personality cult."[36] A columnist was "a powerless individual, an isolated individual," and the magazine employed a columnist in order to avoid moving from theory to practice.[37] Meinhof expressed dismay over the marketing of star columnists and cited Röhl's refusal to allow collective authorship as an example of the magazine's regressive editorial practices. By insisting on individual authorship for the articles published in *konkret,* Röhl upheld, according to Meinhof, the capitalist status quo and turned a blind eye to the systemic transformations that would be necessary to turn the media into an organ for progressive change. In this context, Meinhof also denounced the journalistic practice of objectification: "Good journalists," she wrote, "turn the topic into the object, and do what they want with this object."[38] Meinhof wanted to effect not only a rethinking of the structure and organization of print culture, but also of journalistic practice. She no longer wanted to write about people, but with them. She wanted those who had something at stake to have a say in what was being written about them. She wanted stakeholders to have a chance to negotiate their representation and participate in the process of writing. Meinhof's *Bambule* project about reform institutions for young women, which she pursued after her resignation from *konkret,* exemplified her concern with objectification and spoke to her aim to give a voice to the disenfranchised by allowing for their active participation in the writing and production process. Because of structural and journalistic constraints, Meinhof believed that her own writing no longer served the cause of the left and was instead potentially counterproductive.

In her conflict with *konkret,* Meinhof again appealed to resistance—this time not against the Springer Press, but against the magazine. In her estimation, *konkret* had become almost indistinguishable from the Springer *Bild-Zeitung,* and the attempted occupation of the *konkret* office was a move from theory to practice and an assertion of her right and duty to resist. Only one year later, Meinhof helped to free Andreas Baader from police custody, went underground, and became a cofounder of the RAF.

In the first extensive communiqué by the RAF in April 1971, entitled "The Concept of Urban Guerrilla" and showing the marks of Meinhof's authorship, resistance was no longer defined as breaking windows and overturning cars but was almost exclusively envisioned as "armed resistance."[39] A collage of Marxist, Leninist, and Maoist thought and Marighela's theory of urban guerrilla warfare, the RAF defined itself as an "armed resistance group"[40] that wanted to undertake actions of expropriation in the form of bank robberies, car and identity theft, bombings, kidnappings, and the freeing of prisoners. The communiqué asserted the "primacy of practice" and the need for "active resistance."[41] In contrast to the Black Panther Party, which, according to the communiqué, failed to prepare adequately for illegality, "the Red Army Faction organizes illegality as an offensive position for revolutionary intervention."[42] However, the RAF did not claim that illegality was the only position from which to resist. The group initially sought to maintain contact to legally operating leftist groups. This aim was also expressed by its name. "Faction" indicated that the group saw itself as part of an international struggle to be carried out through legal and illegal means. "Red Army" reminded readers of the Chinese Red Army and, more important for German history, it reminded them of the Soviet Red Army, which liberated the camps of Auschwitz-Birkenau in 1945.

In its liberation fantasy, the RAF saw its violent actions as a revolutionary intervention that would prepare the way for a larger movement to follow. The RAF acknowledged the student movement as its own prehistory, but contended that it had moved beyond it. The group saw its violent interventions as a form of radical enlightenment aiming to undermine the myth of the omnipotence and invulnerability of the system. Much in the way Meinhof reasoned about the protest against Springer, there was no expectation that the actions would have an immediate effect on the relations of power; rather, the aim was to make visible the vulnerability of the system and the potential for revolutionary change. The group thus remained indebted to an enlightenment project, albeit an enlightenment no longer undertaken through theoretical arguments and expressions of dissent, but through militant action. The aim was to unmask the latent violence and the contradictions of the system. Actions speak louder than words, or in Marshall McLuhan's terms, the medium is the message. Although the group attempted to define itself through revolutionary practice rather than words, theories, and arguments, they could not escape the problem of mediation. Since the RAF's actions were not immediately or intuitively understood by either the public or the left, and since the press sensationalized and misrepresented the group's aims, it came under pressure to explain itself. Much like a work of art or a happening, the group's actions were in need of mediation to get across their message, aims, and underlying motivation. Enlightenment through action must be mediated through language. Thus, in a reversal of Meinhof's dilemma in regard to her journalistic writing, it was no longer a question of theory needing to move toward praxis, but of praxis needing theory to explain and legitimize itself.

Like no other member of the RAF, Meinhof understood very well the internal mechanisms of journalistic politics and how to use them for the group's aims. Certainly her status as a prominent journalist and public intellectual lent a certain legitimacy to the RAF. But more importantly, she understood how to get the attention of the media. Because of the group's constant need to communicate its deeds and aims, Meinhof was unable to escape the role of "columnist" and "star" that she had despised and rejected earlier. The interaction of the group, the media, and the state precipitated what Guy Debord termed the society of the spectacle, i.e., "a social relationship between people that is mediated by images"[43] or, to speak in Jean Baudrillard's terms, the mass-mediated theater of cruelty, in which the excess of reality produced by the media nullifies the possibility of victory and defeat.[44] While the group itself would have disputed this, there existed no RAF outside of the myriad of narratives and competing images produced in the 1970s, first during the relatively short period during which the first generation RAF was active underground and then during its time of incarceration.

The RAF reduced the multiple possibilities for resistance, mentioned by Meinhof in her *konkret* column in reference to Smith, to "armed resistance." Other possibilities, too, were reduced to strict oppositions, either friend or enemy; there was nothing in between: "If our enemy fights us, it is good, because it is proof, that we have drawn a clear line between us and the enemy."[45] Fittingly, the "Urban Guerrilla" communiqué ended with a quote from Black Panther Information Minister Eldridge Cleaver, which later was famously cited by Holger Meins: "Either you are part of the problem or part of the solution."[46]

The logic of the either-or and the lack of nuance that already marked the RAF's first declaration became only more prevalent in the later declarations. "Abstractions running amok" was how Peter Brückner described the reductions, analogies, and short-circuiting of arguments, testifying to the RAF's increasing distance from the social and political reality of the Federal Republic.[47] The increasing analytical reductionism and rhetorical cruelty of the RAF, whose universe was populated by pigs, bulls, fascist character masks, and counterrevolutionary cowards, marked the group's withdrawal from a concrete engagement with the specific circumstances of the FRG. Significantly, this disconnection from both the social reality of the FRG and the German left went hand in hand with the deflation of the concept of resistance in the rhetoric of the RAF. While in "The Concept of Urban Guerrilla" "armed resistance" was a notion central to the group's self-representation, in the later communiqués "resistance" no longer played a defining role. As Meinhof had moved from protest to resistance, the RAF now moved beyond resistance. In "Dem Volke dienen" from April 1972, just months before the arrest of its core group, the RAF defined itself as "avantgardistische Bewegung"[48]—an avant-garde movement rather than a resistance group.

The changing vocabulary was symptomatic not only for the increasing rift between the RAF and the conditions under which it operated, but also for the shift in self-definition. Resistance (*Widerstand*) denotes an oppositional stance and actions aiming to obstruct and impede something with which one disagrees.

Resistance thus implies a defensive and reactive position rather than an offensive action. Resisting, taking a stand against a dominant position, implies a dialectical relationship to reality. Within this oppositional paradigm of a stance and position against something, "resi-stance," or "*Wider-stand*," contrasts with *Bewegung,* movement, which signifies a process of becoming, development, evolution, and change. In contrast to the implied stasis of *Widerstand,* the notion of *Bewegung,* movement, signifies motion, fluidity, and progress. Resistance is a response and reaction to that which it opposes and remains caught in the process of negation. Thus, with its shifting rhetoric, the RAF distanced itself from the reactive position of resistance and emphasized instead its seemingly offensive, affirmative, and avant-gardist character. As an avant-garde movement, the RAF sought to forge ahead with its own agenda—an agenda no longer constrained by the rules of the existing order.

It is not surprising then that the RAF reappropriated the concept of "resistance" when the arrests of the core group forced it into the defensive position of incarceration. With the arrests of Meinhof, Baader, Ensslin, Holger Meins, Jan-Carl Raspe, Brigitte Mohnhaupt, and Irmgard Möller in June 1972, the RAF's world view became increasingly self-referential and modeled after its experience of prison. *Die verknastete Welt,* the imprisoned world, became a central metaphor for the group's perception of reality, and with its arrest the concept of resistance once again gained currency. Faced with the concrete reality of the penal system and its own position of physical immobility and isolation, the focus of the RAF's struggle turned onto itself and the conditions of its confinement. In September 1974, the group declared that its hunger strike represented an act of resistance against the *Vernichtungshaft,* the attempt by the state to liquidate the possibility of all resistance, and, supposedly, the attempt to annihilate the prisoners. *Politische Gefangene, Isolationsfolter, Vernichtung, Widerstand* were the loaded terms used by the RAF to gain the ear of the public, and resistance became part of a discursive field that drew from terms and concepts related to German fascism.

Like no other, the image of the emaciated corpse of Holger Meins—weighing a mere 39 kg after a five-week hunger strike—furthered the association of the imprisoned RAF members with the victims of National Socialism. Resembling the image of a concentration camp victim, the photographs of the dead Meins were indeed shocking and served as the most effective recruitment tool for the RAF and other militant groups. Dressed in a white silk gown, his hands folded, with sunken eyes, and flowing hair and beard, Meins conjured up not only the image of a concentration camp victim but also the image of the martyr—a suffering Christ-like figure who had sacrificed himself for the fight against injustice and had died for society's sins. Meins's death confirmed the RAF's claim of abuse by the state and set in motion ambiguous discourses that, on the one hand, identified the RAF members as political prisoners and victims of the state and, on the other hand, asserted their identity as fighters and martyrs who—by using their bodies as weapons of resistance—were able to maintain their individual and collective agency against all attempts by the state to erase it. The concept of resistance was now absorbed by the discursive and historical reference to National Socialism and mutated into a resonant rhetorical device employed not to further the struggle for social and political change, but to gain support and sympathy for those who had once engaged in this struggle.

Examining and contextualizing Meinhof's utilization of the concept of resistance affords insight into the ways in which the concept of resistance was negotiated amongst the militant left in the Federal Republic in the 1960s and 1970s. Haunting German society, the term resistance hovered over the debates on political action, morality, and violence. The term marked a turning point in the radicalization of Meinhof from Protestant pacifism to armed struggle. Resistance took on a central role in the rhetoric of the German left. Meinhof's adaptation of Smith's call to move from protest to resistance points beyond the German context toward the importance of transnational currents and ideas. Meinhof's adaptation brings into focus the importance of the US anti-war and civil rights movement for the struggle of the German left. However, while these transatlantic entwinements emphasize the internationalism of the protest movement, they also shed light on and force us to recognize the specificity of each national context. A unidirectional model of diffusion like the one proposed by McAdam and Rucht fails to take into account the heterogeneous factors at play when ideas are appropriated, functionalized, redefined, reinterpreted, and/or held hostage.

The intertwinement of "resistance" and the RAF also brings to the foreground some of the shortcomings of recent debates about Meinhof and the RAF: firstly, the failure to ground the origins of the RAF in the protest movement without, however, using the RAF's violence to discredit the protest movement, and secondly, the tendency to historicize the RAF's foundation and ideas too narrowly as a German phenomenon.[49] However, to understand the legacy of the protest movement and the RAF—I hope to have shown—it is necessary to take cognizance of both the international and the culturally specific moments constitutive to its origin, transformations, and demise.

Notes

1. Paul Hofmann, "The New Left Turns to Mood of Violence in Place of Protest," *New York Times,* 7 May 1967, 1.
2. For Davidson, moving from resistance to politics apparently meant to move from anti-war protest to support of the Democratic Party in the 2004 US presidential election. http://www.net4dem.org/cyrev/archive/issue8/articles/Regime%20Change/RegimeChange1.htm.
3. Friedrich Nietzsche, *On the Genealogy of Morals,* trans. Walter Kaufmann (New York, 1989), 77.
4. Doug McAdam and Dieter Rucht, "The Cross-National Diffusion of Movement Ideas," *Annals of the American Academy of Political and Social Science* 528 (1993): 56–74, 69.
5. Ibid., 69.

6. Ibid, 60.
7. Michael Frey, "Shifting to Confrontation: Herbert Marcuse and the Transformation of the American Student Movement," *Bulletin of the German Historical Institute Washington,* no. 34 (2004): 99–111, 99.
8. The complete Port Huron Statement is available at several sites, for example: http://coursesa.matrix.msu.edu/~hst306/documents/huron.html (5 September 2005).
9. See Reinhard Opitz in Mario Krebs, *Ulrike Meinhof: Ein Leben im Widerspruch* (Hamburg 1988), 31. While Meinhof"s—and Gudrun Ensslin's and other RAF members'—Protestant background is often mentioned, the influence of the work of Gollwitzer on Meinhof"s political ethos remains to be examined.
10. Ulrike Marie Meinhof, "Der Friede macht Geschichte," in idem, *Die Würde des Menschen ist antastbar: Aufsätze und Polemiken* (Berlin, 1995) 7–13, 12. Translation is my own.
11. Ulrike Marie Meinhof, "Status quo Mauer," in idem, *Die Würde des Menschen,* 20–24, 20. Translation is my own.
12. Max Weber, "Politik als Beruf." http://www.mynetcologne.de/~nc-clasenhe/soz/lk/beruf.htm (15 September 2005).
13. Ulrike Marie Meinhof, "Counter-Violence," in idem, *Everybody Talks About the Weather,* 235–39.
14. Wolfgang Kraushaar. *Frankfurter Schule und Studentenbewegung: Von der Flaschenpost zum Molotowcocktail 1946–1995* 3 (Hamburg, 1998), 1:254.
15. Ulrike Marie Meinhof, "Counter-Violence," 236.
16. In an attempt to correct what he believes to be a distorted holographic image of Dutschke as a pacifist and ecologist, Wolfgang Kraushaar has recently argued that Dutschke was the first in Germany to call for the formation of an urban guerrilla. Citing Dutschke's and Krahl's posthumously published 1967 *Organisationsreferat,* Kraushaar examines Dutschke's indebtedness to various urban guerrilla theories and speculates that Dutschke, had he not been shot, might have joined the armed struggle. The trajectory of Kraushaar's overall argument—which can also be seen in his recent documentation of the bombing of the Jewish Community Center in Berlin in 1969—is to emphasize that there existed strong violent, and anti-Semitic, undercurrents within the student movement. In this way, Kraushaar constructs a causal link between the decline of the student movement and the rise of the RAF. See Wolfgang Kraushaar, "Rudi Dutschke und der bewaffnete Kampf," in Wolfgang Kraushaar, Karin Wieland, and Jan Philipp Reemtsma, *Rudi Dutschke Andreas Baader und die RAF* (Hamburg, 2005), 13–50. Also see Gerd Koenen, *Das rote Jahrzehnt: Unsere kleine deutsche Kulturrevolution 1967–1977* (Cologne, 2001), and a response to Kraushaar by Koenen in "Black Box RAF: Zur symbolischen und realen Geschichte des linken Terrorismus in Deutschland," at www.oeko-net.de/kommune/kommune02-05/kkoenen.htm. July 15, 2009.
17. Kraushaar's conceptualization of the protest movement runs the risk, Ingrid Gilcher-Holtey argues, of dehistoricizing it and reducing its divergent strategies of social transformation to violence. See Gilcher-Holtey's essay in this volume.
18. For an informative discussion on the German debate on political violence see Karrin Hanshew, "Militant Democracy, Civil Disobedience and Terror: Political Violence and the West German Left during the 'German Autumn,' 1977." *AICGS Humanities Volume* 14 (2003): 20–46.

19. Meinhof, "From Protest to Resistance," 240.
20. I would like to thank Wolfgang Kraushaar for pointing out Smith's speech to me.
21. Dale A. Smith, "James Jaho würde sagen…" in *Vietnam-Kongreß*, ed. Sibylle Plog-stedt (Berlin, 1968): 139–41.
22. Smith, "James Jaho würde sagen…" 140.
23. Ulrike Meinhof, "Setting Fire to Department Stores," in idem, *Everybody Talks About the Weather*, 245–49, 248.
24. Smith, "James Jaho würde sagen…" 139.
25. Ibid., 140.
26. Ibid.
27. Krebs, *Ulrike Meinhof*, 153. The reductionism of this equation has been criticized by Peter Brückner and others, who asserted that the comparison of conditions in Berlin with those in Vietnam did grave injustice to the victims of the war.
28. See Wilfried Mausbach's piece in this volume. Illuminating in this regard are also the speeches held at the Vietnam Congress, for example the contributions of Peter Weiss and Bahman Nirumand in Plogstedt, *Vietnam-Kongreß*, 89–90 and 62–65.
29. Meinhof, "From Protest to Resistance," 243.
30. For insightful explorations of political murder see Michael Sommer, *Politische Morde: Vom Altertum bis zur Gegenwart* (Darmstadt, 2005).
31. Michael Geyer, "Resistance as Ongoing Project: Visions of Order, Obligations to Strangers, Struggles for Civil Society," *Journal of Modern History* 64 (1992): 217–41, 217.
32. Herbert Marcuse, *A Critique of Pure Tolerance*, ed. R. Wolff (Boston, 1971), 103.
33. Peter Brückner, *Ulrike Meinhof und die deutschen Verhältnisse* (Berlin, 2001), 128.
34. Ulrike Meinhof, "Columnismus," in idem, *Everybody Talks About the Weather*, 250–55, 252.
35. Ibid., 250.
36. Ibid., 254.
37. Ibid., 253.
38. Ibid., 251.
39. Rote Armee Fraktion, "Das Konzept Stadtguerilla," in *Rote Armee Fraktion: Texte und Materialien zur Geschichte der RAF* (Berlin, 1997), 27–48, 28.
40. Ibid., 31.
41. Ibid, 36.
42. Ibid, 48.
43. Guy Debord, *The Society of the Spectacle*, trans. D. Nicholson-Smith (New York, 2002), 12.
44. Jean Baudrillard, "Our Theatre of Cruelty," in *Hatred of Capitalism*, ed. C. Kraus and S. Lothringer (Los Angeles, 2003), 51–56, 54.
45. RAF, "Das Konzept Stadtguerilla," 27.
46. Ibid., 48.
47. Brückner, *Ulrike Meinhof*, 172.
48. Rote Armee Fraktion, "Dem Volk dienen: Stadtguerilla und Klassenkampf," in idem, *Rote Armee Fraktion*, 112–44, 144.
49. This is true, I would argue, also for the exhibition *Zur Vorstellung des Terrors: Die RAF* held at the KunstWerke Berlin in 2005.

Part V

(En)counter-Culture

Chapter 10

White Negroes

The Fascination of the Authentic in the West German Counterculture of the 1960s

Detlef Siegfried

> If all the hippies cut off all their hair
> I don't care,
> I don't care.
>
> —Jimi Hendrix, *If Six Was Nine* (1967)

In 1972, Helmut Salzinger commented on the revolutionary potential of long hair among young men by quoting a lengthy passage from Jerry Rubin's manifesto "Do it!", which had recently appeared in German. In it, the American hippie revolutionary describes how he tried to explain the meaning of his hairstyle to his Aunt Sadie, who, as a communist, was the black sheep of the family: "Aunt Sadie, Long hair is a commie plot! Long hair gets people uptight—more uptight than ideology, cause long hair is communication. We are a new minority group, a nationwide community of longhairs, a new identity, new loyalties. We longhairs recognize each other as brothers in the street. Young kids identify short hair with authority, discipline, unhappiness, boredom, rigidity, hatred of life—and long hair with letting go, letting your hair down, being free, being open."[1]

This euphoria was well understood in Germany, for young Germans had been searching for the direct, the genuine, and the real since the beginning of the twentieth century. Back then, it was a countermovement against the consequences of industrialization, against urbanization, division of labor, and the isolation of the individual within a "mass society." After the First World War, it continued in the radical political movements of the right and left, which both confronted an estranged "society" with an ethos of "community." The sociologist Helmuth Plessner contrasted this against a mediated culture, a "social ethos" in which people confronted each other as strangers, and social intercourse was mediated through the assumption of varying roles.[2] In the 1950s, Theodor Geiger referred back to Plessner's social criticism from 1924 and related it to contemporary youth behavioral patterns: rational behavior should define the basic pattern of democratic cooperation within a postwar multifunctional society. Helmut Schelsky also referred back to Plessner when he looked at the younger generation of the 1950s and saw in their behavior, especially in their "skepticism," a guarantee that there would be no new wave of social radicalism.[3] A few years later, in 1972, Plessner's book from 1924 was reprinted, prompting the author to remark that his text was obviously "still or yet again current."[4]

In fact, the time from the late 1950s to the early 1970s was marked by an increasing criticism of rationalism and a renaissance in emotion and intuition. Quite justifiably, Herbert Marcuse and Daniel Bell saw a significant hallmark of the 1960s in a "new sensibility," in which a new directness—a "political and cultural radicalism"—emerged in opposition to the formalism of social relationships, conventions, and the pressure to conform to roles.[5] It was particularly the youth-influenced counterculture that rehabilitated the ideal of a community that distanced itself from the norms and conventions of the majority society. The following examines how rebellious young West Germans used blues music, long hair, and an identification with the Black Panthers to recreate themselves as "white negroes," thus symbolically merging themselves with the subjects of postcolonial liberation movements.[6]

"White Negroes"

In West Germany, jazz was seen as modern, democratic, and decidedly anti-racist. It was consumed and produced primarily by young intellectuals who saw in the black protagonists of their music, and in African-Americans in general, the positive embodiment of a life principle that was fundamentally different from that of the white world. For culturally deviant whites, Norman Mailer's concept of the "white negro" provided an attractive theoretical basis for developing an oppositional habitus through an alliance with blacks. It emerged within the context of the American beat movement as a reflection on the character and sources of a minority culture within the technocratic society of the United States. Published in 1957, Mailer's essay was discussed in West Germany as an attempt to challenge the elitist, rationalist concepts of the Frankfurt school. The German jazz godfather Joachim-Ernst Berendt wrote a detailed introduction to Mailer's concept in early 1962 in *Twen* youth magazine, even before a German translation of the central text "The White Negro" appeared in 1963.[7] Mailer analyzed the new social figure of the "hipster," which had emerged as a reaction to the menace of concentration camps and atom bombs. In light of these potential threats, Mailer held that the certainties under which modern Western society operated were purely chimerical. New modes of living had to be found, by which one could react flexibly to the fundamental uncertainty of human existence. For the "American existentialist" in the form of the "hipster," the role models were African-Americans, whose traditionally fragile living situations had led to corresponding behavioral patterns. One could escape the adaptational mechanisms of the "totalitarian society" of the "squares" only by completely disengaging from society.

Thus emerged the social and racial mix of white bohemians, young criminals, and blacks, from which the "hipster" arose as an idealized type of outsider. He was distinguished by a strong focus on the present moment; instead of the rationalism of technological modernity, he followed his feelings and the "needs of his body"—a significant aspect of the "cultural heritage" that blacks had brought to the figure of the "hipster." "So there was a new breed of adventurers, urban adventurers who drifted out at night looking for action with a black man's code to fit their facts. The hipster had absorbed the existentialist synapses of the Negro, and for practical purposes could be considered a white Negro."[8] This construction made Mailer's concept—the possibility of affiliating oneself closely with African-Americans through a specific habitus, to blend in, as it were—attractive to white outsiders. In this process of appropriation, specifically racial components played a central role, so that along with being "hip," even more black elements were being injected into the stylistic repertoires of white youths who wanted to set themselves apart from the conventions of tradition.

Twen had begun dealing with this field quite early on. In 1960 it featured an article by Mailer on youth gangs in Brooklyn, as well as several articles written by young African-Americans in addition to its regular reports from the jazz scene. However, the magazine's editors had reservations about Mailer's conception of the modern outsider: argumentation through racial stereotypes, and moreover postulating the intermingling of racially defined characteristics, was touching on a sensitive area, especially in Germany. Even *konkret* magazine, featuring a 1961 interview with Mailer in which the "hipster" played a prominent role, treated his theory with skepticism, particularly because he stressed the unconscious over the rational.[9] In contrast, Berendt was fascinated by the figure of the "hipster," who was at the "innermost secret circle of jazz connoisseurship" and whose insider status had not been gained by conforming to the criteria prevalent among the white social majority of the West.[10] Berendt stated that the "hipster" defied the pull of whiteness through a fascination with blackness, "in which ... maybe he does not want to become like blacks, but is nonetheless most strongly moved by all things black: coolness, nonchalance, a tendency to understand the environment unconsciously rather than intellectually, modern mysticism instead of the no longer so very modern rationalism, rhythmic confidence and of course the relationship toward sex."[11]

With the introduction of Mailer's "hipster," Berendt was anticipating a debate in the area of music that would first provoke open controversy in the establishment in 1968, when the American literary scholar Leslie A. Fiedler gave a lecture in Freiburg in which he declared the literary modern to be passé, calling for a broadening of literary conceptions to include pulp fiction and legitimizing pop mythologies.[12]

The "American Folk Blues Festival"

Using the example of jazz, Berendt had highlighted a mechanism that was a hall-mark of pluralistic societies. The "message" of jazz—tolerance, generosity, direct-ness, honesty, liberality, freedom—was gradually being watered down, precisely because jazz was not much under attack anymore but was instead tolerated and accepted. It was particularly through widespread dissemination by the culture industry that avant-garde forms and subjects lost their teeth. "*Therefore,* when it really matters, it has to be even *more* concentrated and even *more* intensively expressed."[13]

With the encouragement of his friend, the jazz musician and concert pro-moter Horst Lippmann,[14] Berendt made an attempt to reach this higher degree of concentration and intensity, an initiative that met with resounding success because it satisfied an emerging desire for authenticity. Berendt had spent four months in 1960 touring the US, researching the evolution of jazz for a book and a television program. It was during this time that he stumbled across the vibrant Chicago blues scene and came up with the idea of bringing some of the biggest names back to Germany for television broadcasts on *Südwestfunk* (Southwest Broadcasting) in Baden-Baden.[15] The goal was to have a blues party, like the one he had experienced in a Chicago club, on German television. Lippmann pro-posed tying it in with a tour and traveled around Lake Michigan in 1961 to seek out musicians and convince them to come for a European concert tour. Such an enterprise, organizing a festival series with the blues greats, had never happened before in either Europe or the US. The American Folk Blues Festival (AFBF) came to Europe for the first time in October 1962, presented by Horst Lippmann in association with Fritz Rau,[16] *Twen* magazine, and the Deutsche Jazzföderation e.V. (German Jazz Federation). Berendt was an advisor in the art-ist selection process and produced the preplanned recordings for his television series "Jazz—gehört und gesehen" ("Jazz—heard and seen").

The festival series continued annually until 1969, lay dormant through the 1970s, and was then revived in the early 1980s. The concept was to present an "authentic documentation" of blues artists, both known and unknown, to the European public. The first year featured Memphis Slim, T-Bone Walker, John Lee Hooker, Sonny Terry, Brownie McGhee, and Willie Dixon, among others. Berendt promoted the festival by calling the rediscovery of traditional blues the most important new development in jazz since Charlie Parker. However, the con-tinuing loss of avant-garde jazz listeners in favor of more popular music could not be stopped, especially among the younger generation. On the contrary, despite the best of intentions, the raw sound of the blues proved to be less than acces-sible to Berendt's jazz clientele.[17] Lippmann and Rau, whose actual specialty was European tours for American greats like Duke Ellington, Ella Fitzgerald, and the Modern Jazz Quartet, had expected a classical jazz audience and had therefore booked medium-sized venues; however, they attracted (in greater numbers than expected) an audience that was by no means limited to jazz fans.

In regard to the *Twen* audience, Berendt had previously pointed out that there was no discontinuity between popular hits and blues music, which in turn made it interesting for young people. This insight was actually the true moment of success in the enterprise, for it was precisely now that a young music scene was emerging in Europe. Beyond the increasingly rarified forms of jazz, it was experimenting with popular styles and was now coming in direct contact with its black idols for the first time, through the American Folk Blues Festival. Rau, who often tells how one of the early festival visitors was the then unknown Mick Jagger, remembers: "We made these blues festivals for jazz fans, and received only scorn from them. But for the kids in London, Amsterdam and Copenhagen, these concerts were a joyful revelation. We'd triggered something truly enormous, without even knowing it."[18]

In fact, Lippmann, Rau, and Berendt had created an institution that influenced the development of pop music all over Europe. Its success rested upon the image of presenting "authentic" blues, thereby embedding itself in the widespread contemporary notion of being able to break through the distortions of the culture industry and expose the structural elements of reality by presenting the image of an "original" through the strategy of "documentation." Of course, this preference for the unmediated was revealed in its artistic implementation to be itself a construct. The brochures, newly designed by the organizers for the concertgoers every year, radiated an aura of high culture. They were expensively produced program booklets that were intended to give an impression of the authentic character of the blues and its exponents. The artists figured as representatives of distant, exotic worlds, who had been brought in by the organizers direct from the cotton fields of the Southern states or from the slums of Chicago's South Side and were appearing for the first time in front of a European audience, "far from the environment which had formed them, and in which they were accustomed to living."[19]

Nonetheless, they also had a message to deliver that was of importance to Europeans: life was hard, and it expressed itself in a self-contradictory everyday life that was to be overcome through "*Menschlichkeit*" (Lippmann) or "humanity." An emotional message, it "does not speak first to the head, but instead penetrates straight to the heart."[20] Berendt explained the renaissance of blues music by claiming that European art was "too intellectualized" and had distanced itself from "*Volkskunst*" (folk art). From these kinds of statements, it can be seen how much even the European defenders and importers of blues music used well-established stereotypes of the "noble savage" in order to create a positive resonance among the public: blacks stood for naturalness, emotionality, and physicality, and blues music was seen as the purest form of African-American music, which had survived in the milieus of the excluded, beyond all the popular and esoteric counterfeits, and should now be exposed.

In the West Germany of the 1960s, this analysis could have expected some sympathy, especially since, in light of the Nazi past, racial unrest in the US, and worldwide decolonization, sensitivities toward racist oppression were increasing.

In the portrayals of artist biographies in the AFBF program booklet, existential uncertainties played a prominent role: vagueness around birth dates, familial ruptures, unemployment, criminality, and imprisonment. Insignia of dislocation were documented through photographs of beggars, prisons, cotton fields, train tracks, and desolate slums. The outsider position of the musicians was visible not only in their social exclusion, but also in the always only temporary nature of their escape from obscurity. Formerly successful musicians had to work again as manual laborers, for example as a janitor (Lonnie Johnson), before they could be discovered by Berendt, Lippmann, or one of their colleagues, in a shack in a cotton field (Sleepy John Estes), in prison (Robert Pete Williams), or in the slum of a big northern city. In essence, these musicians did not offer themselves to the European music experts; they were "discovered" by them, as if on an ethnological expedition.[21] They were outsiders not only to the white population of the US, but also to the small "high society" of African-Americans.[22] In this regard, it was mostly about blacks who were experienced, but not civilized and tamed. They were representatives of an existentially insecure race, exactly as envisioned by Norman Mailer. The target audience of this ethnological enterprise was young white youth in Western Europe, whose emergent need for "authentic" orientation had to be satisfied.

After the success of the AFBF, Lippmann and Rau broadened the concept of "authentic documentation" into other musical directions, in which they evaluated "underdeveloped" countries in terms of cultural potential. Lippmann traversed the slums of Europe and the Americas, seeking and discovering many hitherto unknown folk musicians such as Mercedes Sosa from Argentina. According to Rau: "The overarching theme was always ghetto music, the sounds and speech of underprivileged classes."[23] In addition, the organizers connected this style of music with an educational function: as in the case of blues music, it was about working against the leveling tendencies of the commercial hits industry and promoting the further development of popular culture in Europe through the use of unexploited materials.

The dedication of Lippmann and Rau was praised not only by the industry press, but also by mass media outlets like *Spiegel* magazine, which published regular, consistently positive articles; *Pardon* magazine too praised the personal initiative of these organizers, "who had done more for German cultural development than certain artistic directors with their phantom artist fees funded by the taxpayer."[24] Siegfried Schmidt-Joos, who had a considerable part in the theoretical foundation and popularization of this concept, later summed up how the tailor-made fusion between idea and zeitgeist underpinned the success of Lippmann and Rau:

> Within short order, these two names had been impressed into the minds
> of intellectual youth as synonyms for cosmopolitanism, genuineness,
> and honesty. Lippmann+Rau aren't pushing pap. Their concerts don't

smother the brain, they don't peddle assembly-line turntable fodder; instead, they offer soul food, the plowman's lunch of hardworking people. They produce an "image" which penetrates mainstream newspapers right through to the classified pages. There is a contact ad in the *Frankfurter Rundschau* which precisely illustrates what is meant: "Student, F, 25, Lippmann+Rau type, seeks like-minded companion."[25]

Over the course of the 1960s, the "authentic" image of black music became tarnished by its increasing market success, particularly with the soul craze in the second half of the decade, but also through the popularization of blues music. Starting in 1967, Lippmann+Rau, as their concert agency was known, also made the transition to popular music styles, which were of course marketed as "authentic" music too. Rau had attended a London appearance by the American "Godfather of Soul" James Brown in 1967 and committed the artist to concerts in Germany—despite the initial misgivings of Lippmann, for whom, in agreement with Schmidt-Joos, this direction was too commercial. Although this music was met by whites with some reserve (in any case, the audience of both sold-out James Brown concerts in Frankfurt in 1967 was said to be composed almost exclusively of black GIs), danceable black music would soon find a following among young West Germans too.[26] In 1967, the Metronome record company employed a gigantic advertising campaign to market the dozens of soul platters they had produced that year. By year's end, James Brown figured in the West German press as the unparalleled representative of a new black self-confidence, in whose shows the elements of blues and gospels were "fused together under incredible heat into something completely new and unique." *Spiegel* summed it up rapturously as "*wahre Neger-Musik*" ("true negro music").[27]

The blues became a popular as well as a commercially successful musical style particularly because it was being taken up by white musicians. Traditional blues music's power of attraction hardly suffered as a result; in fact, the cultural-industrial exploitability of this "authentic" style was also becoming more obvious. The process of taking it in and further propagating it was labeled a "rebirth" or "rediscovery" of blues music: a movement of renewal in popular music, lifting it above the artificiality of commercial hits. Blues was seen as the "world language of a rebellious youth," symbolizing moreover an "overcoming of class barriers."[28] Thus it was quite within character for the concert promoters to begin to focus more on rock music in 1968, organizing concerts for Jimi Hendrix, The Doors, and Canned Heat.

Berendt also saw the success of blues music at the end of the decade as a big plus, although commercial success frequently benefited the white performers instead of the black originators of this new music. In essence, Mailer's idea of projecting a specifically black habitus onto young whites had been realized. The racial "Maginot Line" was no longer being crossed by blacks but by whites instead, and now for the first time in great numbers.[29] This contributed to changing their worldviews and behaviors: "If young people today are thinking more differently than ever before, then it also has to do with their having black music and black 'messages' in the soul."[30]

Particularly for circles on the political left, blues music represented an unfiltered view into social misery in the Western world. More clearly than in other political circles, one can see here how the critique of "Western" values was emerging in Western societies themselves, and how they pulled in elements of African-American culture as orientation points for fixing their own positions: "Blues music speaks the truth which is uncomfortable and disturbing for whites," according to Carsten Linde.[31] With blues music, one could push through the thicket of consumer industry and get to the revolutionary roots—this was the idea, now being applied to rock music, that Berendt had claimed for jazz years ago. Gerold Dommermuth, board member of the Frankfurt Socialist Club, who had once declared Liverpool Beat to be unadulterated revolutionary music, now said in regard to blues music: "That a management, practiced in the arts of integration, was able to defang the protest, to absorb the feared revolution into the hit parades, and to set the manifest opposition of youth against the terrorism of manipulated consumption, does not change the fact that black music in the form of rock 'n' roll and R&B has become the voice of the resistance. By accepting this music as their own, protesting youth have, before even expressing any rational solidarity, already proven to their black brother that they belong to his class."[32]

From a specifically West German and specifically radical left perspective, the differences between black and white revolutionaries were dissolved. The defining feature of "race" disappeared completely behind the (in this case) less defined category of "class." Racial boundaries no longer played a part, because there existed an apparent commonality between oppressed classes. Young white revolutionaries in West Germany became "white negroes" by defining away racial differences in favor of a putative class identity.

"Differently Constituted": Perceptions of American Race Riots

The discovery of blues music among European youth cultures of the 1960s cannot be isolated from the race riots that had been convulsing the US since 1962.[33] Unlike other European countries like Great Britain, France, and the Netherlands, West Germany did not have a significant percentage of nonwhites in its population, so the West German discourse around race, racial difference, and racial equality became heavily dependent upon long-distance observations of the relations in the US and was further complicated by the issue of anti-Semitism.

For devotees of jazz, taking a position against racial oppression had always been a culturally distinguishing feature and a political statement. Social studies

research from the early 1960s showed that, of all the subjects concerning relations between different peoples and races, it was relations between blacks and
whites that provoked the greatest interest among youth.[34] While South African
apartheid and the relations of "Third World" countries barely registered on the
radar, interest in the race relations of the US was "overwhelming," according
to Werner J. Cahnman, who interviewed West German pupils of various ages
in various types of schools. They condemned racist oppression in the US vehemently.[35] However, this was not just an expression of racial tolerance, but also
one of self-superiority. This pattern was also to be seen in countries like France
and Great Britain,[36] but there existed a German peculiarity: West German pupils
frequently compared racist persecution in the US with anti-Jewish persecution
during the Third Reich, ignoring the efforts of US administrators and white
liberals to promote racial equality. For example, one student said: "If this racial
discrimination were to happen in Germany, people would say the Germans are
doing it again, they have prejudices and stuff, but it's still going on in America
and nobody says anything."[37] A sixteen-year-old schoolgirl opined in 1962: "In
history class we often hear about serfdom, witch-hunts, racial hatred, and so on.
Many things have already been improved in the world. But racial hatred still exists! Especially in the USA, which blares freedom out to the world."[38]

In September 1964, the Divo opinion research institute implemented a
detailed survey of the attitudes of West Germans concerning the racial unrest
in the US; the results largely confirmed Cahnman's observations.[39] The most
interesting result was in the response to the hypothetical question of whether it
was possible that Germany could also experience racial unrest under similar circumstances (such as having a large percentage of black people in the population,
comparable to the US): the majority of respondents answered in the negative. By
far the most dominant reason given (46 percent) was that racial disparity was unknown amongst Germans because they were "more moderate, tolerant, decent,
reasonable, peaceful, and in essence differently constituted" in comparison to
Americans. A much smaller number, but still in second place (16 percent), listed
the not-so-different reasoning that Germans had learned from the persecution
of Jews under the Third Reich. In view of these findings, Cahnman (who as an
American Jew observed this type of mindset with particular interest) interpreted
the vehement condemnation of American racial oppression as a specifically German suppressive reflex, one element in a social context that blended an ideal
of racial equality, an urge to assuage guilt about the past, and a virulent anti-
Americanism: "The students wanted to absolve themselves in regards to the Jews
by suggesting that 'persecution' was a thing of the past in Germany, but was still
a continuing reality in America."[40] This urge toward absolution was much more
clearly expressed among older students, aged 20 and 21, as opposed to 16- and
17-year-olds.

Even in the early 1950s, empirical studies showed that Germans had a positive image of African-Americans. This contrasted greatly with the generally much

more negative views held in the US itself, which led German researchers to interpret this finding as the result of a long-distance psychological projection communicated through the media: "a generalization of the image which had been widely disseminated through reading *Uncle Tom's Cabin* and which was only further informed by the conceptualization of primitive impulses."[41] There was no doubt that normative ideals such as nonjudgmentalness and racial equality were well known to West Germans and also shared by the majority of them, at least in the case of the "*Neger*," who barely figured in their own personal experiences.[42] The decline in open racism, however ambiguously it might have occurred, was an important element in approaching Western behavioral norms. It could be seen more clearly among youth than among adults. However, it often remained just talk: when it came to implementing anti-racism in everyday practice, the problems started accumulating. In their sympathies and antipathies, girls hardly differentiated between Jews, Israelis, blacks, and Italians. In contrast, young men greatly preferred blacks over Italians (let alone Jews and Israelis) when, for example, it came to choosing someone from these groups for a (same-sex) friend, classmate, or housemate. Among the boys interviewed, 87 percent wanted a black friend and only 21 percent wanted a Jewish friend; these preferences were much more equalized among girls, who reported 45 and 49 percent for these groups.[43]

The dialectic of attraction and repulsion was particularly precarious when it came to acquaintances and love relationships with the opposite sex, i.e., when miscegenation threatened. "*Mischehen*" (mixed marriages) were repeatedly mentioned and viewed with considerable skepticism.[44] In 1964 there appeared a study that examined the relations between West German students and their African and Asian classmates, with the conclusion that there existed a "considerable social distance," especially between German female students and their nonwhite classmates.[45] As a reason for their reserve around nonwhite men, 80 percent of young, educated women said they declined "personal connections" for fear of negative judgments by others.

The 1964 Divo survey found significant differences especially according to age and educational background. Younger age groups rejected racist statements approximately twice as often and more categorically than did groups over 30. An Allensbach survey in 1972 showed that the generational discrepancy could be seen even in age differences of just a few years. The youngest age groups were often much more prepared than older cohorts to attribute positive features such as intelligence, industriousness, and honesty to nonwhites, and to reject negative stereotypes.[46]

Black Panthers: From Race Struggle to Class Struggle

The attention focused by 1960s youth on the putative oppressed of the "Third World" was closely associated with a feeling of having unjustified privileges, in comparison to the much poorer living conditions of their parents during the war and postwar years (as repeatedly recounted in public and around the kitchen table), the situation of their brothers and sisters in the GDR, and that of people in the "developing world." While working-class youth enjoyed their leisure-time privileges with relatively little compunction, university-track pupils and university students exhibited stronger reservations.[47] The taste for jazz, blues, folk, and gospel combined a joie de vivre with a lucid awareness of "suffering in the world."

In contrast, politically radical subcultures were not propagating racial integration but were instead attempting to build up an opposition to the dominant whites, show hands-on solidarity with members of the oppressed black race, and symbolically merge with them. In essence, blacks were seen as already being potential revolutionaries, by virtue of their marginalization by white majority societies and colonial powers. Mailer saw it this way, as did Rudi Dutschke in early 1966: "Sometimes you have to wonder why the colonized man would prefer to buy a transistor instead of a dress for his wife. He lives in an end-of-the-world atmosphere, and believes that nothing should pass him by. The colonized, the underdeveloped human, has become a *zoon politicon* [political animal], in the broadest sense of the term."[48] For him, African-Americans represented a "radical negation, carried out to the final consequence."[49] In this context, "Uncle Tom," as constantly depicted in the press, embodied the idealized type of the pacified slave, in contrast to Malcolm X, Stokely Carmichael, and Angela Davis as urbane, intellectual leaders of a rebellious black youth who were "black and proud" (James Brown) and who, in their radical stance, were often more consequential than their West German admirers.[50]

Since a revolutionary subject was hardly to be found in West Germany, aspirations were commonly projected onto African-American ghetto dwellers, who, during the summer of 1967 in the great cities of the leading Western power, renewed their violent confrontations with the state, and who had in 1966 also formed a militant vanguard organization of mostly young black men, in the form of the Black Panther Party.[51] In the writings of the radical left, blacks figured as the better revolutionaries because of attributes ascribed to their race: they were poor (otherwise they'd be called "'white' blacks"[52]), impulsive, physically sensual—and militant.[53] This was particularly effective in provoking the political classes as well as the majority population of West Germany because the violent actions of radical African-Americans mobilized racist resentments, cracked open the silent consensus around a supposed nonjudgmentalness, and laid bare West German society's connections with the past.[54] This escalation was welcomed and amplified by those on the radical left because it more clearly exposed the contradictions that had only been concealed by the nonviolent strategies of Martin Luther King. The Nobel Peace Prize winner, who was murdered on 4 April 1968, was here seen as a man of integrity but also a naïve "Uncle Tom"[55] who had, according to the view of the Kommune I, "won a prize for creating peace, when he should have waged war" and who even, according to a cynical analysis in *Charlie Kaputt*, had to be seen as an "enemy of the blacks … because he had stopped them from fighting for their rights; but the dead King did redeem himself and his crime by proving that violence can only be conquered by violence."[56] It was the young revolutionary leaders who first turned African-Americans from a "passive and suffering"[57] race to a fighting one. They had also overcome the ideal of the "hipster," which, according to the views of West German student revolutionaries, merely symbolized African-American aspirations (as mediated through consumption) toward racial assimilation and therefore pacification, while black consciousness mobilized the revolutionary potential of the black race.[58]

At the end of 1969, local initiatives in support of militant African-Americans arose from the ashes of the SDS. They spread information about the concepts and activities of the Black Panther Party, initiated political actions, and made hands-on efforts toward revolutionizing black GIs stationed in the West German garrisons of the US Army.[59] They found fertile ground among troops who had been increasingly demoralized by race conflicts, and among whom a cultural and political opposition movement made up of black army members in Germany had already developed.[60] The organizational center for the German sympathizers was the Black Panther Solidarity Committee in Frankfurt, which was largely driven by Karl Dietrich Wolff, a former SDS chair. Supporting the Black Panthers and connecting with revolutionary African-Americans was also supposed to contribute toward smashing the West German political system. At times, white middle-class revolutionaries would see the development of a militant black power movement in West Germany as the "only real method for smashing the fascist state."[61]

A significant precondition for this solidarity movement was the Black Panther Party's rejection of "black racism" and its propagation of a class struggle in which "the emancipation of African-Americans was inextricably tied to the revolutionizing of white America," thus incorporating at least the racial alliance with white student revolutionaries.[62] From the point of view of Dutschke, among others, it was about a process of revolutionary civilizing: "At the center of the 'Black Power' movement was no longer the romantic harking back to Africa and the confinement of political struggle to the black race, but rather a direct solidarity with all the revolutionary forces of the world."[63] In West Germany, categories such as "*Fremdgruppe*" and "*Minderheit*" ("alien group" and "minority") created the conceptual umbrella under which white revolutionaries could gather with nonwhites and guest workers who were excluded from the social majority by criteria supposedly tainted with racism.[64] This is how, through habitual appropriation and with semantic assistance, nonconformist young whites became "white negroes."

In 1971–72, the solidarity initiatives focused their activities on the release of black philosopher Angela Davis, who had been active in the Black Panther movement and the US Communist Party after having studied with Herbert Marcuse in the US and Adorno, Habermas, and Oskar Negt in Frankfurt, and who had been arrested in October 1970.[65] It was particularly the (mostly male) conceptions about Angela Davis that reflected a "colonial desire" (Robert Young), which included more than the erasing of racial difference within a class solidarity but also extended to a sexual component. Angela Davis represented not only youth, intellectualism, and revolutionary consciousness of class and race, but also the feminine "black beauty" ideal that had emerged in the 1960s. Her mentor Herbert Marcuse pointed out the specific recipe that defined how one perceived her as a person: "She's black, she's militant, she's communist and she's pretty."[66] This was not only "more than the system could tolerate," as meant by Marcuse, but also the precise combination of race, class and gender that stimulated the sentiments of West German leftists.[67]

However, these exchange processes, in which black music, black rebellion, and black role models were imported into Europe and West Germany, attained their explosive power against the background of a still pronounced racism. Indeed, during the 1960s, a period of far-reaching material and cultural upheavals, it was less clear than ever before what was "one's own," which was to be separated from "the alien." West German modernity had to conceptually relocate itself against the background of losing a war and the necessity of self-critically confronting the Nazi past, international integration, and the explosive growth of media usage. In addition, there was increased social pressure toward dismantling "prejudices." In this relatively open-ended situation, there also existed a wider scope for the reception of African-American stimuli, which began to seem even more "authentic," as one's own world came to be seen as "alienated." The orientation toward African-Americans and their supposed attributes, such as naturalness, courage, spontaneity and revolutionary energy, was an "invented tradition" (Eric Hobsbawm) whose composition emerged from the spiritual backgrounds and problems of white upper- and middle-class youth in the transition toward a "reflexive modernity."[68] Revolutionary African-Americans appeared as the collective ideal of a morally defined authenticity that was not vulnerable to being corrupted by the allure of consumption but rather realized itself in the social radicalism of an efficient collective devoted to struggle.

Even before the student movement began, the consumer industry within the cultural sphere had, by importing black music, also prepared the ground for political radicalization. One of its catalysts involved an intellectual process of appropriation, which could be seen in the reception of Mailer's "white negro" by Berendt and its direct popularization by *Twen* and Lippmann+Rau. With the distribution of this music by the consumer industry, the need for new demarcations increased, so that freedom from manipulation by the culture industry became a central factor for "authentic" music.

"Call me Yigger!" Long Hair as the "Black Skin" of the White Outsider

Blues music was the most direct and culturally most comfortable way to emulate the disempowered of the world. Another possibility was to signify difference through hairstyle. In West Germany, it was once more Salzinger who showed how much this method of distancing oneself was tied to racial categories, by looking at it through the eyes of Jerry Rubin, who lectured his Aunt Sadie (who argued the propaganda value of short hair) on the unbelievable mutational power of the luxuriant mane: "Aunt Sadie, long hair is our black skin. Long hair turns white middle-class youth into niggers. Amerika is a different country when you have long hair. We're outcasts. We, the children of the white middle class, feel like Indians, blacks, Vietnamese, the outsiders in Amerikan history."[69] This interpretation was not as absurd as it might seem, in that long hair, depending on the time and circumstances, could catapult the wearer out of the social pale. Thus Frankfurt "*Gammler*" (hippies), who in 1966 were refused restaurant service because of their hairstyle, saw "associations with the color bar of the American South."[70]

This was somewhat out of proportion, in that this temporary performative act was being lumped together with social ostracism stemming from birth, in order to legitimize a self-chosen otherness and denounce the illegitimacy of its ostracism. In any case, the "struggle for every millimeter"[71] was played out in many families—where, as a rule, this was to be taken literally, for in the beginning, a truly long "Beatles haircut" was still out of the question for most young men and was not aspired to. At first, it was predominantly youth from the beat culture milieu who wore long hair, especially members of the numerous beat bands that shot up like mushrooms. It was first the *Gammler* and Provo scenes, which were especially prominent in 1966–67, that correlated long hair and a taste for beat music more clearly and visibly than ever before with notions of an anti-consumerist lifestyle and political protest.

It was only a minority of youth protagonists and adult observers who saw long hair as significant in crossing racial boundaries and expressing political opposition. Among the multiple signs of deviance that it sent out, the public saw first and foremost a will toward dissolving gender boundaries. As soon as long hair was perceived as a significant trait of the Beatles, the smoldering cultural battle around this topic shifted to the everyday world, and young men began in greater numbers to emulate this and similar media role models, not least to please the girls, who appreciated the feminine and easygoing appearance of these bands. Starting in 1966, this androgynous tendency, which was primarily about effeminizing young men, was widely negotiated in the media under the term "unisex." "Jürgen wants to be like Uschi" is how an article in *Twen* highlighted the direction of this shifting tide, in examining the disappearance of "textile orientation aids" in the increasingly obscured jungle of gender distinctions.[72] While some had a positive view of the effects of this extreme social shift of masculine roles in the workplace and the military, others found it threatening. The "anti-masculine antihero," whose ambition was "to be pretty and be loved," was turning the traditional masculine ideal on its head.[73]

Most defenders of longer hair for men were consistent in denying that such cultural preferences were connected to any sort of political statement. On the one hand, long hair was in this sense not "political," but on the other hand, it also represented attitudes that contained political implications. Long hair was therefore becoming increasingly accepted, because it was seen less as a revolutionary "protest" and much more as symbolizing the desire for freedom and democracy—and therefore as nothing other than an outward manifestation of basic constitutional ideas. It communicated casualness and civility, which also became influential as political behavioral norms. Other more rebelliously tempered contemporaries attached significance to their long hair as a protest against society. How much it had already become a central symbol of youth rebellion in 1968 could be seen in the success of the musical *Hair*, which, by combining various subcultural elements drawn from hippie-esque attitudes toward life, drug consumption, and political protest, represented the mood of the times better than most cultural events of that year.

Nothing more clearly demonstrated the breakthrough of long hair, and the sea change in masculine norms it symbolized, than its invasion of the most authoritarian institution of the state. It was not only the police who were letting their hair grow: the German army (as it itself admitted) also had to adapt to this trend, because it, "in regards to its appearance, could not discount the development of general tastes."[74] A court had decided that a "traditional look for soldiers" did not exist, but that hair and beard styles changed according to fashion, and Federal Defense Minister Helmut Schmidt conformed to this judgment with the declaration that, in his opinion, what went on under the recruit's scalp was more important than the situation on top of it. Starting on 5 February 1971, German soldiers were allowed to wear long hairstyles, which were expressly described as "feminine" according to military regulations. However, this short summer of anarchy lasted for only a little more than a year, until a new ministerial "hair decree" in mid May 1972 once again stipulated short hair.

Rolf Schwendter traced the counterculture's fashion for long hair, beards, and relaxed apparel back to purely "functional-practical" reasons, which significantly "[reduced] the number of required ceremonies," as the daily shave, trip to the hairdresser and laundromat, etc., were characterized.[75] The real and the unspoiled were presented as an ideal in contrast to the artificial grooming of the body through cleanliness, shaving, and neat attire. This harmonized with a practice that sought to undermine the illusoriness of consumption through a strict orientation toward the practical value of things. As shown in the Jerry Rubin quotation, this form of practical social criticism found its traditions and allies among African-Americans, as well as among other ethnicities that were excluded by the white originators of modernity, such as the American Indians and Vietnamese mentioned by Rubin. In the dynamics of the postcolonial new order, nonwhite ethnic groups also sometimes exhibited a political radicalism that coincided with the desires of white minority groups. Two elements—premodern communal idealism and militant revolution fantasies—combined in West Germany most conspicuously in tribalistic milieus, which merged alternative living in rural communes with propaganda geared toward armed struggle in the cities. In "Red Power: The Revenge of the Longhaired," the authors of the underground magazine *Päng* demanded redress for the centuries-old history of oppression against Indians and Roma (Gypsies), whose "legitimate heirs" they considered themselves to be.[76] In their magazine, historical reminiscences of armed Indians blended together with contemporary hymns about armed struggle in West Germany, producing an ideal of militant "self-defense."[77]

Intellectuals distanced themselves from the symbolic negational power of hair through their political radicalness. Since the culture industry had appropriated the formerly oppositional significance of long hair and worn it away, by the early 1970s it could hardly be taken as proof of a rebellious character anymore. Pier Paolo Pasolini came to this conclusion: "Your freedom to wear your hair according to whim is no longer defensible, because it is no longer a freedom. Instead, it's high time to tell youth that their haircuts are disgusting, because they're servile and vulgar. What's more, it's high time that they saw this for themselves and freed themselves from this inexcusable inner compulsion which drives them to follow the herd."[78] In some radical groups of the early and mid 1970s, there was the additional theme of outwardly resembling the working class that they courted, which was supposed to lower the mobilization threshold for this target group. Jerry Rubin had tried in vain to convince Aunt Sadie of the revolutionary potential of long hair, and of its destructive power with regard to the economic and political foundations of American society. "'God help you destroy it, Jerry', Aunt Sadie wailed, chicken-soup tears dribbling down her cheeks. 'But you'd be so much more effective if you would cut your hair and dress nicely'."[79] However, Aunt Sadie, just as much as Pasolini and the communist splinter groups, would have to learn from experience that their efforts were in vain. Only seldom could rebellious youth be dissuaded from their hairstyles. In the Maoist splinter parties there existed varying degrees of peer pressure to cut hair short, which in the long run contributes to the disintegration of their memberships, who regarded these kinds of rules as unacceptable limitations on the personal freedom to define their own styles.

Listening to blues music, identification with the Black Power movement, and long hair arose in response to contemporary desires for unspoiled authenticity, which was seen in opposition to the alienation of modernity. However doubtful this construction of naturalness might be, "authentic" was less the sought-after object itself, and more the mode of its appropriation toward the construction of one's own style. In this creative act of appropriation, which reacted to the conditions of contemporary society, totally heterogeneous elements were mixed into new "reflexive authentic" styles.[80] Blues greats were disseminated by agents of the otherwise maligned culture industry, and members of the radical left listened to blues music and placed their hopes in the working class and the liberation movements of the "Third World"—and were nonetheless tied into the material ensemble of the maligned culture industry. Reflexive authenticity made possible this divergence from a supposed mainstream, precisely because the culture industry, with its endless supply of styles and listening possibilities, thus accelerated the push toward individualization. It was outsiders themselves who continually supplied new stimuli to the media, which, due to the frantic pace of the commercial exploitation process, were permanently on the hunt for unused styles. In this shifting of mentalities, elements of nativeness from all corners of the world came into play, but aspects from one's own history also spilled over. In the creation of a reflexive authenticity, the social actors questioned differences based on class, race, and gender, but not always rationally, and sometimes with the outcome of bizarre manifestations.

Notes

1. Jerry Rubin, *Do it! Scenarios of the Revolution,* New York 1970, 93; quoted by Helmut Salzinger in *Rock Power oder Wie musikalisch ist die Revolution? Ein Essay über Pop-Musik und Gegenkultur* (Frankfurt am Main, 1972), 169.

2. Helmuth Plessner, *Grenzen der Gemeinschaft. Eine Kritik des sozialen Radikalismus,* 2nd ed., (Frankfurt am Main, 2002); Helmut Lethen, *Verhaltenslehren der Kälte. Lebensversuche zwischen den Kriegen* (Frankfurt am Main, 1994); Wolfgang Eßbach, Joachim Fischer, and Helmut Lethen, eds., *Plessners 'Grenzen der Gemeinschaft'. Eine Debatte* (Frankfurt am Main, 2002).

3. Helmut Schelsky, *Die skeptische Generation. Eine Soziologie der deutschen Jugend* (Düsseldorf and Köln, 1957). Concerning Schelsky's classic and its resonance see Franz-Werner Kersting, "Helmut Schelskys 'Skeptische Generation' von 1957: Zur Publikations-und Wirkungsgeschichte eines Standardwerks," *Vierteljahrshefte für Zeitgeschichte* 50, no. 3 (2002): 465–95.

4. Helmuth Plessner, "Selbstdarstellung," in idem, *Gesammelte Schriften* (Frankfurt am Main, 1985), 302–45, 322.

5. Daniel Bell, *The Cultural Contradictions of Capitalism* (New York, 1996), 120; Herbert Marcuse, *Versuch über die Befreiung,* 2nd ed. (Frankfurt am Main, 1972), 43.

6. Initial considerations of this topic can be found in: Detlef Siegfried, "White Negroes: Westdeutsche Faszinationen des Echten," in *Bye Bye, Lübben City: Bluesfreaks, Tramps und Hippies in der DDR,* ed. Michael Rauhut and Thomas Kochan (Berlin, 2004), 333–344. See also Detlef Siegfried, *Time is on my Side. Konsum und Politik in der westdeutschen Jugendkultur der 60er Jahre* (Göttingen, 2006).

7. The first German translation in Norman Mailer, *Reklame für mich selber* (Berlin 1963), 369; originally Mailer, *Advertisements for Myself* (New York, 1959).

8. Mailer, *Advertisements,* 315.

9. Richard Wollheim, "Leben wie ein Held. Gespräch mit Norman Mailer," *konkret,* no. 22 (1961): 12.

10. Joachim Ernst Berendt, "Hip. Von twen zur Diskussion anheimgestellt: die neue Philosophie der 'weißen Neger,'" *Twen,* no. 1 (1962): 41. The editorial page of this volume reveals its reservations.

11. Ibid., 44.

12. This debate is described and partially documented in: Ulrich Ott and Friedrich Pfäfflin, eds., *Protest! Literatur um 1968: Eine Ausstellung des Deutschen Literaturarchivs*

in Verbindung mit dem. Germanistischen Seminar der Universität Heidelberg und des Deutschen Rundfunkarchiv im Schiller-Nationalmuseum Marbach a. Neckar (Marbach, 1998), 367.

13. Berendt, "Hip," 46.

14. Horst Lippmann (b. 1927) came from an affluent family in Frankfurt and founded the Frankfurt Hot Club with Albert Mangelsdorff, among others. At age sixteen, when the war was still on, he produced an illegal jazz newspaper, which led to several weeks of incarceration by the Gestapo. After the war, Lippmann studied economics. He played drums in various jazz bands and began working in 1948 as a jazz concert promoter. In 1956 he became the Executive Advisor on Concerts for the German Jazz Federation.

15. The story of how the AFBF was founded is described in Kathrin Brigl and Siegfried Schmidt-Joos, *Fritz Rau: Buchhalter der Träume* (Severin, 1985), 130; Joachim-Ernst Berendt, *Das Leben – ein Klang: Wege zwischen Jazz und Nada Brahma* (Munich, 1996), 320; "Blues before Sunrise: Die Konzertveranstalter Horst Lippmann und Fritz Rau schrieben ein dickes Kapitel Popmusikgeschichte," in Rauhut and Kochan, *Bye Bye, Lübben City*, 323–32.

16. Fritz Rau (b. 1930) studied law in Heidelberg, beginning in 1950 and finishing (with breaks) in 1960, on a scholarship from the German National Academic Foundation. He frequented Heidelberg's "Exi" scene and, in 1954, cofounded the local jazz club Cave 54. He moved to Frankfurt in 1956 to organize jazz concerts with Horst Lippmann in West Germany and across Europe. In 1964 he became equal partner in the joint-operated concert agency Lippmann+Rau.

17. This and the following explanations by Berendt in *Twen*, no. 9 (1962): 12.

18. Brigl and Schmidt-Joos, *Rau*, 128. See also interview with Rau in "Blues before Sunrise," 323.

19. According to Lippmann in American Folk Blues Festival program booklet (1963).

20. Lippmann, AFBF program booklet (1964).

21. According to Berendt in AFBF 1963 program booklet, not paginated. See also *Der Spiegel*, no. 48, 21 November 1966, 186. For the transference and effect of black entertainers to and within Germany and Europe in the late nineteenth and early twentieth centuries, see Rainer E. Lotz, *Black People: Entertainers of African Descent in Europe, and Germany* (Bonn, 1997).

22. Heinz Werner Wunderlich in AFBF program booklet (1963).

23. Brigl and Schmidt-Joos, *Rau*, 149.

24. *Pardon*, no. 5 (1968): 34.

25. Written with Kathrin Brigl, in Brigl and Schmidt-Joos, *Rau*, 144.

26. Brigl and Schmidt-Joos, *Rau*, 153. See also Lippmann's comments in *Der Musikmarkt*, no. 7 (1968): 11.

27. *Der Spiegel*, no. 51, 11 December 1967, 169. The previous quotation comes from the jazz critic Werner Burckhardt, quoted in ibid. This contrasts with radical leftist groups who called Brown a "*schwarzes Schwein*" ("black pig") and claimed he aligned himself with the Black Power movement only in pursuit of commercial success. The "White Panther" group, a self-defined equivalent of the Black Panthers, obviously considered itself not only justified in using this name, but also immune from any suspicion of racism (Schwarze Zelle Neukölln/Kreuzberg, "White Panther, Schweine sind nicht immer rosa!" ["pigs are not always pink!"], Archiv "APO und soziale

Bewegungen," Fachbereich Politik- und Sozialwissenschaften der Freien Universität Berlin (FUB/ZI6/APO-Archiv), Anarchisten Berlin, flyer).

28. Quotation from a contemporary reflection in *Musik-Informationen,* no. 8 (1969): 10f.

29. Joachim E. Berendt, *Blues* (Cologne, 1970), not paginated, in reference to Eldridge Cleaver.

30 30. Quoted ibid.

31. *Elan,* no. 7 (1970): 39.

32. Quoted ibid. See also Jürgen Seuss, Gerold Dommermuth, and Hans Maier, *Beat in Liverpool* (Frankfurt am Main, 1965). It was no accident that "Blues" was the self-chosen label of the diffuse scene around West Berlin's militant "*Umherschweifenden Haschrebellen*" ("vagabond hash rebels"). According to one of their texts, blacks "had this feeling, which was the basis of the blues, and was transmitted almost in the mother's milk: they too are living in the biggest shit." Printed in *Der Blues: Gesammelte Texte der Bewegung 2. Juni,* 2 vols., ed. Bewegung 2. Juni (Dortmund, 2001), 1:137.

33. On race relations within the US in the 1960s, see Thomas Borstelmann, *The Cold War and the Color Line: American Race Relations in the Global Arena* (Cambridge, 2003), and as an overview Manfred Berg, "1968: A Turning Point in American Race Relations?" in *1968: The World Transformed,* ed. Carole Fink, Philipp Gassert, and Detlef Junker (New York), 397–420.

34. Werner J. Cahnman, *Völker und Rassen im Urteil der Jugend. Ergebnisse einer Untersuchung an Münchner Schulen* (Munich, 1965), 45f.

35. Evidence of this can also be seen in the results of research done in the autumn of 1962, where Frankfurt school students said that the preeminent characteristic of blacks was "love of freedom." Hermann Müller, *Rassen und Völker im Denken der Jugend* (Stuttgart, 1967), 55.

36. Additionally, Arthur Marwick, *The 1960s: Cultural Revolution in Britain, France, Italy, and the United States, c.1958–c.1974* (Oxford, 1998), 229ff.

37. Cahnman, *Völker,* 75.

38. Edith Göbel, *Mädchen zwischen 14 und 18: Ihre Probleme und Interessen, ihre Vorbilder, Leitbilder und Ideale, und ihr Verhältnis zu den Erwachsenen* (Hanover, 1964), 94.

39. Divo news service, March 1965 and March II 1965.

40. Cahnman, *Völker,* 47.

41. According to a 1953 publication on "national prejudices," quoted in Müller, *Rassen,* 56.

42. Elisabeth Noelle and Erich Peter Neumann, eds., *Jahrbuch der öffentlichen Meinung 1965–1967* (Allensbach, 1967), 467; Divo news service, March 1965. Müller's 1962 research had shown that the surprisingly positive characterizations given to blacks by schoolchildren had to be matched with the fact that, when asked about particularly suitable occupations for blacks, they largely responded with stereotypes of subordination: servant, shoeshine boy, and the like: Müller, *Rassen,* 78f.

43. Cahnman, *Völker,* 30.

44. Ibid., 35f. and 115. According to a 1968 Gallup poll, 35 percent of West Germans approved of marriage between whites and blacks, compared to 20 percent in the US and 29 percent in Great Britain, and in contrast to 67 percent in Sweden and 62 per-

cent in France: *Emnid-Informationen*, no. 11/12 (1968): 2ff. For the basics on this topic see Robert J. C. Young, *Colonial Desire: Hybridity in Theory, Culture and Race* (London, 1995); for details see Maria Höhn, *GIs and Fräuleins: The German-American Encounter in 1950s West Germany* (Chapel Hill, 2002); Heide Fehrenbach, "Of German Mothers and 'Negermischlingskinder': Race, Sex, and the Postwar Nation," in *The Miracle Years: A Cultural History of West Germany, 1949–1968,* ed. Hanna Schissler (Princeton, 2001), 164–86; and Peter Martin, "…als wäre gar nichts geschehen," in *Zwischen Charleston und Stechschritt: Schwarze im Nationalsozialismus,* ed. Peter Martin and Christine Alonzo (Hamburg and Munich, 2004), 700–710.

45. Dieter Breitenbach, *Das Afrika- und Asienbild bei deutschen Studenten* (Berlin and Bonn, 1964), 87ff. Similar findings in Cahnman, *Völker,* 34 and 45.

46. Elisabeth Noelle and Erich Peter Neumann, eds., *Jahrbuch der öffentlichen Meinung 1968–1973* (Allensbach, 1974), 495. This corresponds perfectly with Müller's 1962 findings (Müller, *Rassen,* 54ff.).

47. An impression of this kind of worldview can be seen in the 1959 statement of a sixteen-year-old female student: "We love going to balls, tea dances and parties, and don't worry ourselves with the suffering that reigns in the world." Göbel, *Mädchen,* 200.

48. Uwe Bergmann, Rudi Dutschke, Wolfgang Lefèvre, and Bernd Rabehl, *Rebellion der Studenten oder Die neue Opposition* (Reinbek, 1968), 69.

49. *Kursbuch,* no. 14 (1968): 155.

50. This contrast in *Die Welt,* 23 July 1965; *Telegraf,* 26 July 1967.

51. The revolts of the summer of 1967 were seen as "the end of the militant self-defense phase and the necessary beginning of offensive military actions against the power structure of the capitalist establishment": Dutschke, Hammer, Hoornweg, Jacob-Baur, and Petermann, eds., *Black Power: Dokumentation. Stokeley Carmichael, Rap Brown, Malcolm X* (Berlin, 1967), 11. "All that's missing is the spark, before the great cities burn from the East Coast to California," according to one author's excited fantasies in an article in *Ça ira* "wall newspaper," (spring 1968), FUB/ZI6/APO-Archiv, Berlin: Schüler I.

52. *Solidarität mit der Black Panther Partei,* no date, FUB/ZI6/APO-Archiv, USA: BPP.

53. See also Michael Schneider, "Revolution der Sprache, Sprache der Revolution," in *Malcolm X, Schwarze Gewalt: Reden* [= *Voltaire Handbuch,* 1] (Frankfurt am Main and Berlin, 1968), 5–47, 30f. Stereotypical perceptions at the intersection of race, revolution, and gender could lead to bizarre situations, as seen in this memorable episode from the reminiscences of Barbara Herrmann, a Berlin member of the SDS, who tells about her dance-floor encounter with Black Panther leader Ray Robinson: "[It was] a pleasure – not like with those pleasurehating SDS guys, who saw dance itself as a sin against the revolution." When Herrmann refused to obey her male SDS comrades' demand that she sleep with her dance partner (their reasoning: "otherwise he'll think leftist girls have something against negroes"), they called her a "racist"; see *Twen,* no. 4 (1970):10. Starting in 1968, sexual relations between blacks and whites became a frequently discussed subject in the topical press. See Moritz Ege, *Schwarz werden: „Afroamerikanophilie" in den 1960er und 1970er Jahren* (Bielefeld, 2007).

54. *Der Spiegel,* no. 21, 22 May 1963, 60ff.; *FAZ,* 17 August 1965; *Die Zeit,* 19 August 1966; *Der Spiegel,* no. 34, 14 August 1967, 156ff.; *Die Welt,* 2 August 1967; *Quick,* no. 33 (1967). This kind of resentment was especially articulated by the public after

it came to gunshots in Ramstein in November 1970, with the participation of Black Panther activists. See also Maria Höhn's contribution in this volume.

55. Dutschke et al., *Black Power*, 8.

56. Kommune I, "Kein schönrer Mord in dieser Zeit", 6 April 1968, FUB/ZI6/APO-Archiv, K 1; *Charlie Kaputt*, no. 1 (May 1968), not paginated.

57. This well-known anti-Semitic stereotype in Dutschke et al., *Black Power*, 12.

58. Schneider, "Revolution," 9ff. For the relationship between critiques of consumption and critiques of imperialism from the perspective of the West German radical left, see Uta G. Poiger, "Imperialism and Consumption: Two Tropes in West German Radicalism," in *Between Marx and Coca-Cola: Youth Cultures in Changing European Societies 1960–1980,* ed. Axel Schildt and Detlef Siegfried (New York and Oxford, 2006), 158–69.

59. For now, see on this subject primarily Ingo Juchler, *Die Studentenbewegungen in den Vereinigten Staaten und der Bundesrepublik Deutschland der sechziger Jahre: Eine Untersuchung hinsichtlich ihrer Beeinflussung durch Befreiungsbewegungen und -theorien aus der Dritten Welt* (Berlin, 1996), 245ff. On the practical cooperation between white student revolutionaries and black GI Black Panther sympathizers see the report in *Pardon,* no. 3 (1970): 68ff.

60. *Der Spiegel,* no. 26, 21 June 1971, 31ff.; David Cortright and Zoltan Grossman, "Die GI-Bewegung in Deutschland," in *Widerstand in der US-Armee: GI-Bewegung in den siebziger Jahren,* ed. Dieter Brünn (Berlin, 1986), 88–100.

61. Kommune Che, *Kille, kille, Weihnachtsstille!,* FUB/ZI6/APO-Archiv, K 1. The US was seen as "fascist" by many involved here. Eldridge Cleaver in particular (not very differently from Herbert Marcuse) proclaimed that the US "was following in the footsteps of Nazi Germany" (see also for various: JK der Roten Zellen, PL/PI, *Seize the Time – Power to the People,* no date, and *Solidarität mit der Black Panther Partei,* no date, both in FUB/ZI6/APO-Archiv, USA: BPP). "I see in America the historical inheritance of fascism," confided Marcuse to Horkheimer in a letter of 17 June 1967, printed in *Frankfurter Schule und Studentenbewegung: Von der Flaschenpost zum Molotowcocktail 1946–1995,* ed. Wolfgang Kraushaar, 3 vols. (Frankfurt am Main, 1998), 2:262. On how the West German *"Stadtguerilla"* (urban guerrilla) formations claimed to be inspired by the Black Panthers, see the preliminary abstract in Juchler, *Studentenbewegungen,* 376ff. and recently in detail Martin Klimke, "Black Panther, die RAF und die Rolle der Black Panther-Solidaritätskomitees," in *Die RAF und der linke Terrorismus,* ed. Wolfgang Kraushaar, 2 vols. (Hamburg, 2006), 1:562–82.

62. Quote: *Black-Panther-Info,* 10 February 1971, Hamburger Institut für Sozialforschung (HIS), KD Wolff. It was often brought up that this would allow the party to transcend white racism and make itself compatible with a Western revolutionary concept. Uwe Bergmann coined the memorable phrase that North American blacks were "an oppressed people as a social class": Uwe Bergmann, "Taktiken der Konterrevolution in den Gettos," in *Über die Organisation des Befreiungskampfes* [= Sozialistisches Jahrbuch 1], ed. Wolfgang Dreßen (Berlin, 1970), 107–17, 116.

63. Dutschke et al., *Black Power,* 12f. Almost identical in Schneider, "Revolution," 21. As a historical comparison see also the agitation for the "liberation struggle of oppressed peoples" around the Weimar era KPD (Communist Party of Germany): Michael Schubert, *Der schwarze Fremde: Das Bild des Schwarzafrikaners in der parlamentarischen und publizistischen Kolonialdiskussion in Deutschland von den 1870er*

bis in die 1930er Jahre (Stuttgart, 2003), 339ff.; Eve Rosenhaft, "Afrikaner und 'Afrikaner' im Deutschland der Weimarer Republik: Antikolonialismus und Antirassismus zwischen Doppelbewusstsein und Selbsterfindung," in *Phantasiereiche: Zur Kulturgeschichte des deutschen Kolonialismus,* ed. Birthe Kundrus (Frankfurt am Main and New York, 2003), 282–301.

64. As in *Black-Panther-Info,* 10 February 1971, 12, HIS, KD Wolff. This subsumed "nonwhites," migrant workers, hippies, and leftist intellectuals.

65. On the solidarity campaign for Angela Davis, who had studied in 1966–67 in Frankfurt, see the appeal from Oskar Negt in *konkret,* 28 January 1971, 52ff. See also also Kraushaar, *Frankfurter Schule und Studentenbewegung,* 1:501f.

66. Herbert Marcuse, speech at a rally for Angela Davis in Berkeley, 24 October 1969, in Kraushaar, *Frankfurter Schule und Studentenbewegung,* 2:688–89, here 689.

67. Such ideas could be seen even more prominently in the leftist infighting of the early 1970s. The 1973 World Youth Festival in East Berlin was described in retrospect by a Maoist participant: "And there she was, strutting everywhere, getting hugged everyday by Erich Honecker, turning the tribunes into catwalks, everyday in a new and even trendier velvet suit or draped maxi, that was Angela Davis. Her show-business pushiness, the darling of cameramen and photojournalists, stood in truly nauseating contrast to the friendliness and reserve of the Vietnamese delegation, who were met with a mixture of real interest and superficial ingratiation." "Von der 'Heerschau der Friedensjugend' zur 'friedlichen Heerschau der Jugend'. Erfahrungsbericht von Delegierten zu den X. Weltfestspielen der Jugend und Studenten," *Sozialistische Zeitschrift für Kunst und Gesellschaft,* no. 20/21 (November 1973), 197–210, 206.

68. See also Charles Taylor, *The Ethics of Authenticity* (Cambridge and London, 1991); Lionel Trilling, *Das Ende der Aufrichtigkeit* (Frankfurt am Main, 1989).

69. Rubin, *Do it!* 94. Even before the appearance of Rubin's book, Reimar Lenz was inspired by the symbolic darkening of the skin in yippie circles, and quoted Tuli Kupferberg in agreement: "The hippie yippie is the new nigger. Call me yigger!" Reimar Lenz, "Schluss mit den Hippies! Amerikas Underground hat sich für das politische Engagement entschieden," *Pardon,* no. 8 (August 1969): 48.

70. Hans-Christian Kirsch, "Gammler, Provos, Anarchisten," in *Deutsche Jugend* 16 (1968): 31–40, 35.

71. Roland Neuwirth, "Meine haarige Zeit: Eine Abrechnung," in *Beatles, Bond, und Blumenkinder: Unser Lebensgefühl in den sechsiger Jahren,* ed. Willi Resetarits and Hans Veigl (Vienna, 2003), 103–9, 104.

72. *Twen,* no. 12 (December 1966): 59ff., quotation on 59.

73. According to Fiedler, quoted in Dieter Baacke, "Die Andere Kultur: Idylle und Provokation," in *Jugend-Stil, Stil der Jugend: Thesen und Aspekte,* ed. Hermann Glaser (Munich, 1971), 26–56, 45.

74. *Der Spiegel,* no. 18, 26 April 1971, 202.

75. Rolf Schwendter, *Theorie der Subkultur,* 2nd ed., (Hamburg, 1993), 229f.

76. *Päng,* no. 1 (1970): 11. See also no. 4 (1971): 7.

77. "A generation is being forced into self-defense," according to a legitimization for the activities of the Red Army Faction in *Päng,* no. 6 (1972).

78. Pier Paolo Pasolini, "Die 'Sprache' der Haare" (January 1973), in idem, *Freibeuterschriften: Aufsätze und Polemiken über die Zerstörung des Einzelnen durch die Konsumgesellschaft* (Berlin, 1978), 19–133, 24.

79. Rubin, *Do it!* 97.

80. Alessandro Ferrara, *Reflective Authenticity: Rethinking the Project of Modernity* (London and New York, 1998); Georg Stauth, *Authentizität und kulturelle Globalisierung. Paradoxien kulturübergreifender Gesellschaft* (Bielefeld, 1999); Joana Breidenbach and Ina Zukrigl, *Tanz der Kulturen: Kulturelle Identität in einer globalisierten Welt* (Reinbek, 2000). See also Rob Kroes, "American Mass Culture and European Youth Culture," in Schildt and Siegfried, *Between Marx and Coca-Cola,* 82–105.

Chapter 11

The Black Panther Solidarity Committee and the Trial of the Ramstein 2

Maria Höhn

At the end of the tumultuous 1960s, a most unusual political alliance emerged, made up of German student radicals and African-American GIs serving tours of duty in Germany.[1] In the larger narrative of 1968 their collaboration has been mostly overlooked, even though such alliances flourished in all German cities that were home both to US military bases and German universities. The foremost center of this activity, however, was the greater Frankfurt area, where KD Wolff, the former head of the German SDS, connected the local anti–Vietnam War struggle of student radicals with a Black Panther Solidarity campaign that reached out to black GIs on military bases in Hesse, Rhineland-Palatinate, and Baden-Württemberg. KD Wolff and his fellow student radicals hoped that through an alliance with radicalized black GIs they could follow the example of the Black Panthers in the US and open another "front" against American militarism and imperialism, this time in the heart of West Germany.[2] The collaboration between German students organized in the *Black Panther Solidaritätskomitee* and African-American Black Panther activists working on the GI underground newspaper *Voice of the Lumpen* lasted for only three short years (1969–72), but during that time the collaborators engaged in an extensive campaign to educate the German public about the struggle of the Black Panthers in the US and to expose the connection between American racism and imperialism in the Third World.

A worm's eye exploration of the alliance between German students and black GIs illuminates a number of themes that are being raised in this collection of essays. Their transnational collaboration highlights the back and forth of ideas between the US and Germany, and how those ideas were put into praxis in and around US military bases in Germany. Closer attention to this alliance also demonstrates the degree to which the American race problem and (African-) American history had become globalized as a result of the US military base system. But a detailed study of this German-American encounter also suggests that much can be learned about German history by paying more attention to the "marginal border areas" where German civilians and African-American soldiers interacted. To highlight those themes, I will provide a short overview of how this most unusual alliance came about and what sort of propagandistic activities and demonstrations the students and GIs engaged in. I will then discuss in more detail the Ramstein 2 trial, which took place in June 1971 in the sleepy town of Zweibrücken. The trial of two Black Panther activists will serve as a case study to show how the students used the Black Panther Solidarity campaign to enact the international class and race solidarity they thought necessary in order to prepare first themselves and then the masses for revolutionary action. I will close with a discussion of how the students' frontal attack on American racism and imperialism failed to bring about revolution but brought about instead a society-wide debate about German forms of racism.

German Students and African-American GIs: An Unlikely Alliance

The collaboration between African-American GIs and German students between 1969 and 1972 was a most unlikely alliance, given the deep gulf that separated the two groups. Although African-American GIs had been stationed in Germany since 1945 and many had made an effort to experience Germany beyond the gates of their military bases, their distance from German society at large was perhaps even more pronounced than that of white GIs. For much of the 1950s and the early 1960s African-American GIs were noted mostly when German newspapers reported on problems associated with the American military presence.[3] German students were even less likely than the population at large to interact with black GIs, given the students' social and cultural distance from the US military. During the 1950s in *Diskus,* the Frankfurt University student newspaper, little interest was expressed in American GIs, let alone African-American GIs, despite the fact that every year some 30,000 African-American GIs were stationed in Germany. In the course of the late 1950s and early 1960s, students became interested in Third World issues through their interactions with students from non-Western countries, and as a result of this interaction also started taking a greater interest in the civil rights struggle of African-Americans in the US.[4] Until then, however, the black GIs in their midst remained for the most part outside the students' scope of experience.

This alienation would be overcome by the mid 1960s for two reasons. First, students became enchanted with the politics and ideology of the Black Power movement in the US, which offered them a novel theoretical model for revolutionary action.[5] Second, through their anti–Vietnam War activism students became more cognizant of the presence of African-American soldiers stationed in Germany, many of whom had become politicized and radicalized by the war in Vietnam and the failure of the liberal civil rights movement to overcome poverty and racial inequality in the US.

Beginning with the war in Vietnam, German students no longer assessed American racism as an incidental oversight of an otherwise admirable system but interpreted it as part and parcel of American capitalism and American imperialism in the Third World.[6] With that analytical shift, the German SDS also took note of the Black Power movement in the US but especially the Black Panther Party for Self-Defense (Black Panthers hereafter), founded by Huey Newton in Oakland, California, in 1966.[7] Students in the SDS were drawn to this particular expression of Black Power because the Black Panthers expressed most clearly the sort of revolutionary stance that radical German students aspired to develop. The Black Panthers' self-conscious identification as "Afro-Americans," or as America's "internal colony," expressed a solidarity with Third World liberation movements that German students espoused in their writings but could not enact, given their own privileged status in terms of race and class. In the eyes of the students, America's Black Panther activists had to all intents and purposes connected their own struggle against American capitalism and racism in the US with the international struggle against US imperialism in the non-Western world.[8] The fact that America's Black Panthers were willing to reach out to white revolutionaries, both in the US and abroad, fired up the imagination of many a German student radical in search of an "authentic" revolutionary subject and international allies.

The students' theoretical interest in the ideas and strategies of the Black Panthers transformed into concrete experience during the Desertion Campaign, decided on by the German SDS at its February 1968 Vietnam Congress. In that campaign, German students, just like their comrades in the American SDS, reached out to American GIs as possible allies, instead of denouncing them as war criminals. By encouraging soldiers to desert their units, students hoped to bring down the "American war machine" in Germany; thus contributing to the larger struggle against American militarism taking place in the US and the Third World.[9] By reaching out to disenchanted GIs in general, German students for the first time came face-to-face with the special revolutionary potential presented by black GIs—often after a tour of duty in Vietnam. While the war in Vietnam had politicized and radicalized both white and black soldiers, the contradictions of the "imperialist motherland," the students concluded, had been exposed most vividly to America's black minority. In their role as soldiers for the US military, black GIs had learned that "the only freedom they were defending in Vietnam, was the freedom to be exploited" and the freedom to "serve as the bull's eye for every racist police pig" once they returned home to the US.[10]

The ever more radical struggle of America's black minority had been brought to Germany through the American military base system, and black GIs who spoke up against the war confirmed much of the students' assessment of the situation. Black GIs stationed in Germany angrily denounced their country's violence in Vietnam, but also indicted the complicity of African-Americans who served in the US military. One soldier suggested that the "the same thing that is happening to our people [in the black ghettos] at home, well that is what the black man in the army is doing to other people around the world." As far as this GI was concerned it was time for African-American men to stop harassing and terrorizing the Vietnamese, because "they are common people, they don't got nothing … and most of the black men aren't doing a damn thing to stop it."[11] Other soldiers stationed in Germany were even more outspoken, telling military authorities that "because of the dirty stinking ghettos in Atlanta, Detroit or Jacksonville, [they] were no longer willing to fight a war for the Whites, and instead demanded weapons to liberate their brothers and sisters at home."[12]

The radicalization black GIs experienced because of the war in Vietnam was amplified by the pervasive and deeply embedded racism in a military where fewer than 3 percent of officers were black, while African-American GIs made up more than 50 percent of inmates in military stockades.[13] But African-American soldiers were equally angry over the racism they encountered in German society, when landlords refused to rent housing to them, or pub and discotheque owners declared their premises off limits.[14] By the late 1960s, the morale of the 30,000 African-American GIs stationed in Germany had reached an unprecedented low point, while racial tensions were boiling over. The 7th Army in Germany was close to collapse, as even the most ardent German supporters of the US military would later admit.[15] Many black soldiers dealt with their increasing anger and alienation through drug use, alcohol abuse, criminality, insubordination, or desertion. But many others chose a more political path to express their dissent. By 1970 and at the height of the racial crisis in the military, dozens of militant black organizations had been founded in military bases across West Germany.[16] It was GIs like these who became the primary hope for radical German student activists. An alliance or collaboration with these politicized and radicalized GIs, the students hoped, could bring about revolutionary action to unseat the centers of American empire in both Germany and the US, and thus push forward the struggle of liberation movements in the Third World.

The Black Panther Solidarity Committee and the *Voice of the Lumpen*

The collaboration between German students and African-American GIs between 1969 and 1972 was made possible by the efforts of KD Wolff, the founder of the Black Panther Solidarity Committee and cofounder of the *Voice of the Lumpen*, a GI newspaper aimed chiefly at black GIs. In late March 1969, KD Wolff, who had been the head of the German SDS from 1967 to 1968 and the preeminent student activist at Frankfurt University, returned from a six-week speaking tour of Canada and the United States. Wolff had been invited by the American SDS, and while in the US he met with SDS representatives Bernardine Dohrn, Tom Hayden, and Black Panther leader Bobby Seale. He also met with anti-war activists on numerous American college and university campuses.[17] Wolff had first become interested in the civil rights struggle of African-Americans when he spent a year as an exchange student at a high school in Marshall, Michigan (1958–59), and lived with a Quaker family that was involved in the civil rights struggle. This experience with American grassroots democracy and civic activism proved transformative for Wolff, as he later recalled. During his return trip to the US in 1969, Wolff was deeply impressed by the transformation that had taken place in the black liberation struggle and especially by the self-help programs of the Black Panthers in America's inner cities, as well as by their willingness to defend themselves against the brutality of white police forces in the black ghettos. During an interview with the *Frankfurter Rundschau* on his return from the US, Wolff reported "that the development of the Black Panther movement in the black ghettoes has led to a self-conscious class-struggle based movement and self-defense tactics, from which we have much to learn."[18]

After his visit to the US, Wolff was committed to supporting the struggle of the Black Panthers. To do so more effectively, he founded the Black Panther Solidarity Committee (Solidarity Committee hereafter) in late November 1969.[19] The Frankfurt-based Solidarity Committee, made up of just fifteen people from the Socialist Club in Frankfurt, became a model for other such committees founded in numerous German cities. The creation of the Solidarity Committee received an enthusiastic reception in the pages of New Left publications such as the *Berliner Extradienst*. The other main conduit to inform the German left on the Black Panthers and the activities of the Solidarity Committee was the *Sozialistische Correspondenz-Info*, a publication associated with the Socialist Club in Frankfurt and published by KD Wolff, his brother Frank, and Daniel Cohn-Bendit, among others.

Both of these publications printed extensive essays on the situation of African-Americans in the US, the program of the Black Panther Party, and what the Solidarity Committee wanted to achieve with its solidarity campaign.[20] Most importantly, the Solidarity Committee set out to correct prevailing misperceptions about the Black Panthers in the mainstream press and to forge international solidarity with the black liberation movement in the US and the non-Western world. Aside from exposing the "fascist terror of the ruling classes in the U.S.," the Solidarity Committee also pledged to provide material support for the Black Panthers, and to raise money for legal expenses and bail for its imprisoned leaders. To move the struggle forward, the Solidarity Committee also affirmed its goal to agitate and propagandize among white and black GIs stationed in Germany. By stressing the intrinsic connection between the anti–Vietnam War campaign and the Black Panther campaign, the Solidarity Committee hoped to create solidarity among those groups that could "open a second front in the metropolis of imperialism."[21]

Aside from educating the German public about the Black Panthers in the US and using their campaign to create new alliances, the Solidarity Committee also significantly expanded its efforts to reach out to collaborators in the US military.[22] This outreach was necessary because activists like Wolff believed that "political agitation became much more concrete in the face-to-face interaction" with the African-American GIs.[23] To make contact, students went to pubs, bars, and discotheques favored by black GIs. They also printed buttons and posters to be distributed in the bathrooms of those establishments. Contacts were often also made through German women students who dated black GIs. Furthermore, women students, also called "brides of the revolution," made contacts with black GIs at discotheques and then got them involved in political discussions on Vietnam and the Black Power struggle.[24] KD Wolff and his compatriots also joined black GIs on American military bases to participate in Black history study groups and reading groups focused on the Black Panther movement.

The concerted efforts to connect with black GIs clearly paid off. Both students and GIs participated in rallies and teach-ins held in December 1969 all over Germany.[25] During numerous demonstrations in the spring of 1970, Black Panther GIs marched with German students through downtown Frankfurt, protesting the war in Vietnam and calling for "Freedom for Bobby Seale."[26] On 4 July 1970, the US Independence Day, students and GI activists organized the "First Call for Justice Meeting" at Heidelberg University. The event was planned as a celebration to counter American Independence Day by indicting the United States' failure to grant freedom and equality to its black citizens. The protesters met at the assembly hall (*Aula*) of the university because the military had forbidden the GIs to hold the rally at the local military base, which was also the Headquarters of the 7th Army in Europe. Hundreds of Black Panther GIs and their German student supporters met to indict the war in Vietnam and American racism at home and abroad.[27]

In October, the Kaiserslautern "branch" of the Solidarity Committee followed suit and organized a huge rally at the Fruchthalle, the local convention hall. This was a critical event for this sleepy town of just 80,000 inhabitants, given that more than 40,000 soldiers were stationed in Kaiserslautern and the neighboring Ramstein air base and Landstuhl military hospital. The evening was advertised as a German American friendship happening that was to overcome the past year's rising tensions between African-American GIs and Germans. City officials and police were stunned when more than 1,000 Black Panther GIs and hundreds of their German supporters marched into the Fruchthalle to the shouts of "Right on, Brother" and "Black Power." The Kaiserslautern rally gained nationwide attention when the popular television news report *Panorama* devoted a whole segment of its show to the meeting and the activities of Black Panther GIs in Germany.[28]

To formalize their collaboration, the Solidarity Committee and some African-American activists living in Germany also founded an underground newspaper that was to represent the Black Panther Party in Germany in November 1970. The newspaper, *Voice of the Lumpen,* was another expression of the sort of international collaboration and solidarity that activists like KD Wolff had in mind. The paper was addressed to the GIs but was also to be read by interested German audiences. The name *Voice of the Lumpen* was chosen to acknowledge the contributions that the down and out of society, the *Lumpenproletariat*, long ignored by traditional Marxism, could make to the revolution. The editors stressed that soldiers interested in the struggle needed to educate themselves and read the writings of Mao, Che Guevera, Frantz Fanon, and Huey Newton.[29] The paper also informed the GIs about the Black Panther Party and its program, reporting on developments in the US and the non-Western world while also keeping the soldiers abreast of the struggle at military bases across the US military empire. In all their efforts, the editors wrote, they aimed at furthering "the GIs' capacity to deal with their situation in the military and to understand how it relates to the struggle being waged today inside Babylon (Amerikkka)."[30] The paper was published with the support of the Black Panther Solidarity Committee on the presses of KD Wolff's publishing house, Roter Stern. The usual press run was about 20,000 issues, with German subscribers subsidizing the press run so that copies could be made available to black GIs for free.[31]

The collaboration between privileged white German students from middle-class backgrounds and African-American GIs, often from disadvantaged backgrounds in America's inner cities or rural backwaters in the South, was indeed a most unusual alliance. Despite all the heady excitement and the constant reiteration of revolutionary class and race solidarity, much of the collaboration was fraught with problems from the beginning. Not all black GI activists believed in aligning with white activists, for example, and increasingly radical nationalist Blacks who espoused separatism from whites began to dominate the *Voice of the Lumpen*.[32] To many a black activist it must also have seemed deeply problematic that German students tried to identify their own "repression" in German society with that of black Americans in the US. Students, no matter how passionately they envisioned their solidarity campaign as an emancipating tool, were also not always able to rise above their own racial and cultural prejudices. An "instructional sheet" on how to interact with black GIs reveals that students were aware of that dilemma but not always able to overcome it. The flyer cautioned that students needed to approach the black GIs as "individuals" and not as "victims," and that the conversation needed to be conducted with "real humility" (*echte Demut*) that was informed "not by guilt but an understanding of injustice." Yet that same thoughtful document was completely oblivious to the sensibilities of the soldiers who wanted to be identified as "Blacks" or "Afro-Americans" and passionately denounced the use of the term "Negro" or "*Neger*" as racist. The document admonished fellow activists not to be arrogant in their conversations, "even though your English is probably better than that of the Negro (*Neger*)."[33]

At the same time, as the following discussion of the Ramstein 2 Trial shows, the collaboration between students and GIs lasted as long as it did because both sides benefited from the alliance. The material and logistical support from the

German students assured African-American GIs a political voice that they would not otherwise have had, given their cultural and social isolation in a foreign land. Thus, their grievances, as well as those of African-Americans in general, became known to a much broader audience, not only in Germany but also in the US.[34] Through the Black Panther campaign, and especially through their efforts on behalf of the Ramstein 2, German students were able to overcome their sense of disillusionment after the collapse of the European protest movements of 1968 and the dissolution of the SDS. Even more importantly, the activists relied on this alliance because they believed that only through their intimate, face-to-face encounter with African-American GIs could such abstract ideas as international class and race solidarity be made immediate and real. It was in enacting solidarity with the Black Panther GIs that privileged white students hoped to achieve the necessary transformation of consciousness for revolutionary action.[35]

The Trial of the Ramstein 2

Throughout 1970, the Solidarity Committee had expanded its activities and increased its outreach to black GIs, culminating in the founding of the *Voice of the Lumpen*. The escalation of the crackdown on the Black Panthers in the US and the October 1970 arrest of Angela Davis, who had been a student at Frankfurt University from 1965 to 1967, brought about a stepped-up level of the committee's informational and propagandistic activities. After Herbert Marcuse called for solidarity with Angela Davis in November 1970, KD Wolff and his fellow activist in Frankfurt, Daniel Cohn-Bendit, founded an Angela Davis Solidarity Committee in Frankfurt. They also planned a whole series of events and demonstrations for the last week of November 1970 to raise awareness of Angela Davis' plight and to call for solidarity with her and Bobby Seale.[36] Eldridge Cleaver was to be the key speaker, but the German Foreign Ministry, after calling Cleaver a "common criminal," rejected the Solidarity Committee's request to allow Cleaver to travel from Algiers to Germany. Since Eldridge Cleaver was not allowed to enter Germany, the Black Panther Solidarity Committee and the *Voice of the Lumpen* decided that his wife Kathleen Cleaver was to speak in his stead at the Angela Davis teach-in scheduled for 24 November at Frankfurt University. On 26 November, the American Thanksgiving holiday, she was also to speak at a "Progressive Blacks of the Military" rally, and on the 28th she was to appear at a large demonstration against US imperialism in downtown Frankfurt.[37]

While preparing for this busy week of events, the Solidarity Committee would get its own cause celebré when two of its American Black Panther activists were arrested by German police while advertising Kathleen Cleaver's visit to Frankfurt. The arrest came about when three Black Panther activists—former GIs who had taken a military discharge in Germany—drove to Ramstein Air Base on 19 November. They never made it into the air base to hang their posters because two of them, Edgar Jackson and William Burrell, were arrested for an alleged murder conspiracy while the third Black Panther, identified only as "Rich," was able to elude the police. What happened on that evening was never wholly made clear, but shots were fired after the German guard stopped the three activists and discovered Black Panther posters and a black beret on the back seat. The German civilian guard claimed that he ordered the driver and the two passengers in the car to show some identification. When one of them refused, the guard pulled the key from the ignition and stepped back. The guard claimed that one of the three shot at him after he pocketed the key, while the Black Panther activists claimed that they shot in self-defense only *after* the guard went for his holster. After allegedly being shot at twice, the guard returned fire, and the three fled on foot. A huge search party composed of American military police, German policemen, and some bloodhounds soon discovered Edgar Jackson and William Burrell hiding in the woods, soaking wet. No weapon was ever found, and no gunpowder residue was detected on their hands. Since the two activists were no longer in the military, they were to be tried before a German court in the provincial town of Zweibrücken, with the trial scheduled to begin in June 1971.[38]

Although the guard was only slightly wounded, the *Haftrichter* (committing magistrate) argued that the Black Panther materials that had been found in the car "openly called for murder" and thus initially charged Jackson and Burrell with "conspiracy to commit murder." That charge, however, was reduced to "attempted murder" by the state attorney who argued the case before the court.[39] An outraged Solidarity Committee responded quickly, calling both the *Haftrichter* and the state attorney racists, and charging that the two defendants could not expect a fair trial given the misinformation about the Black Panthers being spread by state officials and the media reporting on the case. To counteract this misperception, the Solidarity Committee, the *Voice of the Lumpen,* and their supporters rallied to the two defendants, providing them with excellent legal counsel and trial observers. The activists also insisted that an expert be heard who could speak to the horrific impact of US racism on African-Americans in general and on the two defendants in particular. Gerhard Amendt, who had spent time in America as a student during the 1967 ghettos uprisings and edited a collection of documents on Black Power after his return, was chosen by the Solidarity Committee to correct some of the widespread misperceptions of the Black Panthers within the courtroom.[40]

In their campaign to free Jackson and Burrell, the Solidarity Committee and the *Voice of the Lumpen* were able to connect their campaign to the one being conducted in the US to free Black Panther activists Angela Davis and Bobby Seale. Consequently, they made the case that Jackson and Burrell had, like the Black Panthers in the US, acted in self-defense. They had reached for their gun only *after* the German guard had reached for his. Furthermore, they argued that the trial against the Ramstein 2 was not a criminal trial for attempted murder, as the prosecutors insisted, but a political trial aimed at shutting out black dissent. The *Voice of the Lumpen* angrily made that case: "The puppet pigs in Zweibrücken have their orders: Forget justice, teach these niggers a lesson, the way we do in Amerikkka—Lock them up—or kill them, but shut them up."[41] The fact that in May 1971 the German police arrested one of the editors of the *Voice of the Lumpen* in Augsburg while he was selling the GI newspaper only increased the sense that German authorities were just as anxious to crack down on black dissent as were their counterparts in the US.[42]

The trial of the Ramstein 2 provides a wonderful case study of the tactics of grassroots organizing (*Basisarbeit*) that people like KD Wolff focused on after the disbanding of the SDS in March of 1970. Despite the martial rhetoric displayed by many of the posters and flyers of the Solidarity Committee and the *Voice of the Lumpen,* the activists believed foremost in collective learning experiences as a way to achieve critical solidarity and a transformation of consciousness.[43] But just as importantly, the arrest and imprisonment of the two Black Panther activists at the Ramstein air base and their trial six months later offered the Solidarity Committee an unexpected and much welcomed opportunity to make the struggles of the Black Panthers in the US historically concrete for large segments of society in West Germany. The trial also offered a tremendous chance to propagandize among GIs and Germans outside of university campuses, and to internationalize the Black Panther struggle beyond the US. To achieve that goal, Wolff and his supporters built a broad alliance of university students, high school students, young workers, and black GIs before and during the trial of the Ramstein 2, while also offering workshops and teach-ins for the local population.

To raise awareness about the trial among black GIs, the *Voice of the Lumpen* and the Black Panther Solidarity Committee held rallies and organized teach-ins on numerous US military bases.[44] The Solidarity Committee and the *Voice of the Lumpen* also held benefits featuring soul music, and handed out newspapers, leaflets, pamphlets, and buttons wherever black GIs could be reached: in bars, in front of the military barracks, and at rallies and demonstrations against the Vietnam War. May and June 1971 saw four large fundraisers for the Ramstein 2, organized by the Black Panther Solidarity Committee, *Voice of the Lumpen*, and Unsatisfied Black Soldiers of Heidelberg. At one of these events, the hall was decorated with Black Panther flags, guns, and a US flag in the shape of a pig.[45] The Solidarity Committee and the *Voice of the Lumpen* also convinced more than 6,000 black GIs to sign letters of solidarity, asking the German courts to free the Ramstein 2.[46]

Furthermore, the trial of the Ramstein 2 provided a unique opportunity to connect the city-based student groups and the socialist and communist groups in the Palatinate, who, according to the Solidarity Committee, were mostly inward-looking and concerned with their own regional issues. By being involved in the Ramstein 2 solidarity campaign, the students believed, those groups would be able to experience and confront "actual and real forms of racism and Imperialism."[47] For the campaign in the provinces, the Red Panthers, a study group of apprentices and high school students founded by KD Wolff, produced a series of posters to elucidate the political struggle of the Black Panthers. These posters aimed to educate Germans about unemployment and poverty rates of African-Americans and the stark differences in health care and education provided for black and white America. They made a special pitch to the German working class, insisting that the "comrades in the factories" needed to be educated about the struggle of the Black Panthers in the US as well.[48]

To bring together German and American, as well as urban and rural activists in an experiential rather than just theoretical solidarity, the Solidarity Committee and the *Voice of the Lumpen* declared 6 March the "International Day of Solidarity with Bobby Seale and the Ramstein 2." Activities were scheduled at university campuses across Germany. Students also arrived from all over West Germany and Berlin to participate in a teach-in about the Black Panthers at the Kreiskulturhaus Saarbrücken, and in a protest march in Zweibrücken, where the trial of the Ramstein 2 was scheduled to take place in June of that year.[49] The event in Saarbrücken played to an overflow crowd of some 700 participants, and more than 1,200 protesters participated at the rally in Zweibrücken. It must have been quite a sight to behold as hundreds of placards and banners bearing the images of Marx, Lenin, and Mao, as well as red flags and Black Panther flags and banners were carried through the sleepy town of Zweibrücken. According to the *Rheinpfalz*, KD Wolff, the "matador of the event," painted "the specter of fascism against a brilliant blue winter sky"[50] while an appreciative audience of university students, apprentices (*Lehrlinge*), and local high school students gathered at the Bismarck memorial in front of the courthouse. About 3,000 local onlookers from Zweibrücken and surrounding areas came to observe the activities, attracted, according to the *Rheinpfalz,* by the "giddy excitement" to have at long last the opportunity to "stare a living Red in the eye." To the dismay of the German organizers, the number of African-American participants was limited to about two dozen because American military commanders had ordered a lock-down at US military bases, and military police detachments were present to make sure that those orders were obeyed.[51]

Fearing for the worst, authorities had sent 500 policemen, three water cannons, and detachments of the US military police to keep order. The organizers need not have worried about violence, despite the martial language of the posters and flyers at the event. The demonstrators and police clashed only once, and according to the liberal newspaper coverage, the police provoked the scuffle as the march was coming to an end.[52] The organizers had clearly cautioned restraint, as was their tactic at previous marches where KD Wolff had called for restraint because, "breaking windows is not going to help" free Bobby Seale or the Ramstein 2.[53] When a Black Panther activist looked ready to come to blows, those around him settled him down by admonishing: "Peace Brother Peace!" The *Rheinpfalz* called the protest "*manierlich, wenn auch martialisch*" (mannered even if it was martial) and reported in an almost regretful tone that the clashes with the police at the end had cost the demonstrators the sympathies that some of the locals might have had for their cause.[54]

Although the 6 March rally was a protest about the Black Panthers and German solidarity with their struggle, it was the German past that hovered over the event. The *Süddeutsche Zeitung,* in a clear reference to the enthusiastic embrace of Hitler in this part of Germany in 1933, introduced its reportage by writing: "Since the days of Hitler, no political event … has been able to draw that many burghers, farmers and policemen on a Saturday afternoon in this neck of the woods as this demonstration excursion [*Demonstrationsabstecher*] of the extreme Left."[55] Not surprisingly, the "recent" German past was also center stage when students and some locals clashed over the town's Bismarck memorial. During the rally before the march, students had accessorized the Iron Chancellor with a banner that read "100 Years of Bismarck, 100 years of exploitation, 100 years of repression, 100 years of shit!" Having just commemorated the 100-year anniversary of the unification of Germany under Bismarck, that attack struck a nerve. The locals clearly did not agree with the students' embrace of Hans-Ulrich Wehler's 1969 bombshell essay, "Bismarck und der Imperialismus," which drew clear lines of continuity from the illiberal founding policies of Bismarck's Second Reich to the Third Reich. When some locals angrily jeered the students' "sacrilegious act" and the "defilement" of their Iron Chancellor, the students responded by painting "Freedom for the Ramstein 2" in bright red on the Iron Chancellor's pedestal. An outraged local farmer climbed the monument to pull down the banner attacking Bismarck, only to have students put it back up again. Control over the interpretation of German history changed five times, with angry locals finally destroying the banner and the young protesters chanting "Fascists! Brown Pest, Sieg Heil, you Nazis!"[56]

The events at the 6 March rally convinced the Solidarity Committee that the people of Zweibrücken needed to engage more closely with their country's history. During a "Day of Information" on the day before the trial, KD Wolff organized a history seminar in Zweibrücken's Festhalle to talk about the continuity in undemocratic structures in German history from Bismarck to Hitler to the Federal Republic. His talk, "Bismarck's Anti-Democratic Legacy and Us," attracted some 200 people, and even the state attorney took time from his busy schedule to attend. As part of the day's activities some thirty student activists occupied the auditorium of a Zweibrücken high school after the director refused them the opportunity to conduct a teach-in with the students.[57] To the great dismay of the local population, the Bismarck monument was again defiled; some audacious person, whose English was clearly not up to par, had crossed out the chancellor's name and replaced it in big pink letters with the word "PIK" (instead of pig).[58] Matters came to a head when some local hotheads attacked the students, throwing their posters and banners in the creek by the courthouse and trying to do the same with the students. This aggression, in turn, evoked chants of "*Faschistengesindel*" (fascist scum) from the students.[59]

The Solidarity Committee's strategy to build alliances and to use the agitation around the Ramstein 2 trial to energize the provinces proved quite successful. High school students from the Neusprachliches Gymnasium in Zweibrücken produced their own sets of flyers, cautioning their classmates not to be deceived into thinking that the trial of the Ramstein 2 did not concern them. The events of the day before had shown, the high school students argued, how the mere effort by the Solidarity Committee to discuss the trial with the local population had brought out a "fascist gang of thugs." Local high school students needed to be engaged, because "in the trial of Burrell and Jackson our situation in Zweibrücken, our media, and our way of life are at stake." They demanded, together with students from two other local high schools, that attendance at the trial be part of their social studies class.[60]

The Ramstein 2 campaign also shook up the certainties of the regional media. The *Rheinpfalz*, for example, had in its initial coverage of the events of November 1970 suggested a possible connection between a recent increase in criminal assaults by African-American GIs and the activities of Black Panther GIs in and around American military bases. The paper had also echoed the sentiments of the tabloid *Bild Zeitung*, which had belittled the Ramstein 2 by calling them common criminals and "whiskey smugglers."[61] In covering the activities of the Solidarity Committee during the trial, the *Rheinpfalz* was more thoughtful: no matter "how hard the court tried, the trial has long been infused with the political problem of a minority that has never been granted full freedom, and is now rebelling against white supremacy." The paper reported that the assessment of American racism by Gerhard Amendt—from the "War of Independence to today, and from ghetto life to school discrimination"—clearly impressed the court and the jury, but "one cannot help but conclude" that "this other view is not permitted" during the deliberations. The *Rheinpfalz* also reiterated an argument that had been raised by the defense lawyers: "Are German and American authorities making common cause in order to make it completely impossible for Black Panthers to educate [the public] about the civil rights struggle in US barracks and housing areas?"[62] Such sentiments were also echoed in other publications covering the trial.[63]

By the end of the trial and their campaign for the Ramstein 2, the Solidarity Committee and the *Voice of the Lumpen* had much to be proud of. In their campaign, they were able to mobilize a transnational alliance of student and GI activists. They overcame the existing urban-rural divide and involved a substantial segment of the local population in the political process. Through their efforts the activists were also able to convince some sections of the local press to be more thoughtful in their coverage of the Black Panthers and their demands in both the US and Germany. They failed, however, to convince the court of the probity of their larger cause. While Burrell was declared innocent of any wrongdoing, Jackson was less fortunate. Although he was declared innocent of the original charge of attempted murder, he still received a six-year jail sentence for attempted manslaughter, resisting arrest, and carrying a gun without a license. Amendt's testimony on the history of racism in the US seemed to have made some difference in lessening the severity of the sentence. In sentencing, the judge took into account that "perhaps [Jackson's] actions were influenced by the very special situation in which members of a non-white race find themselves in the US." When the case went into revision a year later, the Solidarity Committee again provided expert testimony on Jackson's behalf. The judge reduced the sentence to four years by addressing more forthrightly why the defendant might deserve special consideration. The judge ruled that Jackson's "reprehensible actions (*verwerfliches Verhalten*) might have been influenced by the fact that he, as a black man, has since childhood been confronted with the racial problems of the US and then came in contact with the Black Panthers as an adult."[64]

Black Panthers and Debates on German Racism

As my discussion has shown, the Solidarity Committee and the *Voice of the Lumpen* were not able to convince the court that the case of the Ramstein 2 was a political trial to shut out black dissent. Nor were the activists able to convince the courts that the activities of the Ramstein 2 were political acts to protest racial discrimination in the US *and* Germany, the country they were sent to protect. The state attorney was especially adamant in rejecting that point, and as the *Süddeutsche Zeitung* reported disapprovingly, he did so with a "tone of voice that tolerated no objections." He was this adamant "because we are here not in the USA, but in Germany, where there are—thank God—no racial conflicts." The inability to understand that the African-American GIs' protests of the past year were also an expression of frustration over the discrimination they experienced at the hands of German landlords or pub owners also came across in other statements made during the trial. When Jackson and Burrell were cross-examined, they were asked: "We sympathize with your lot … but why do you conduct your struggle on German soil? What do we have to do with it?"[65] Conservative newspaper coverage of the trial also reveals a stunning unwillingness to acknowledge the racism black GIs—as well as Afro-Germans, foreign students of color, and foreign-born guest workers—encountered in German society. The *Pfälzische Volkszeitung*, for example, haughtily rejected the educational activities of the Solidarity Committee as unnecessary because the "population stands united against racial discrimination."[66]

Liberal media observers of the trial were also not willing to equate the discrimination that African-American GIs experienced while trying to enter a discotheque or renting an apartment with the abject conditions in the ghettos of the US. Nor did they share the students' conviction that both the US and West Germany were on the brink of fascism. Still, the agitation and educational activities of the Solidarity Committee together with, and on behalf of, the black GIs alerted many of those publications to the impact of German racism on black GIs. As a consequence, German newspaper coverage, for example, no longer argued, as was often the norm in the 1950s and early 1960s, that racism against black GIs was an imported "American problem" because white GIs pressured German landlords and pub owners to keep black GIs out. Instead, newspapers stressed that the prejudices against black GIs had deep roots in German history. This shift in media coverage concerning the grievances of African-American GIs also meant that discrimination against "*Gastarbeiter*" or foreign students of color received more attention as well.[67] A short editorial in the *Frankfurter Rundschau* entitled "Nothing learned at all" (*Nichts dazu gelernt*) on German attitudes toward people of color in Frankfurt succinctly conveys the sentiments expressed in many of those articles.[68]

The Black Panther campaign thus helped to bring back "race" as a critical category into German public discourse. Surely, German students were not the first or even the only ones who reintroduced "race" into public debates in the course of the 1960s, but their sensationalist activities on behalf of and together with African-American GIs helped to broaden that discourse significantly.[69] In some sense, then, one can argue that the Black Panther Solidarity Campaign was a huge victory for the student activists. They had put the struggle of the Black Panthers front and center, while also alerting the German public to homegrown forms of racism. Given the Federal Republic's reliance on the American military alliance, the debate on German forms of racism against black GIs would therefore also have to be addressed at the highest level of government. As a direct response to the protest activities of the students and the black soldiers, Chancellor Willy Brandt, President Gustav Heinemann, Foreign Minister Walter Scheel, and Defense Minister Helmut Schmidt all made personal statements condemning the racism that black soldiers experienced in German society. Willy Brandt especially eloquently told Germans in March 1971 to stop criticizing other countries, such as the US or South Africa, for their racism and to take a hard look at the situation "at home" instead: "I am against self-righteousness which is often noticeable when foreign and far-away countries are being criticized. Charity begins at home, but also the rights of man start at home."[70]

While the Black Panther campaign had brought about a society-wide debate over German forms of racism, the student activists seemed to have missed out on some of their most trenchant lessons. The way the students framed and enunciated their arguments about racism in German society makes this all too clear. On the one hand, they argued that "racism was not a peculiarly American phenomenon but was inherent in all mature capitalist societies," and they faulted traditional Marxists for having ignored the "objective function" of racism by elites and "subjective function of racism" by the lower middle class in their analysis.[71] On the other hand, the students seemed to interpret the existence of racism in Germany society as emanating from the sorry "leftovers" of Germany's Nazi past. They repeatedly pointed out that the *Haftrichter* was a racist and that the presiding judge was a former *Divisionsrichter* (military judge). After the disappointing outcome of the Ramstein 2 trial, the students stepped up their language, calling the judge and the state attorney "desk murderers," the terms used for the faceless bureaucrats involved in the Final Solution.[72]

In both of these interpretative models the students were on the side of righteousness. But their stance also allowed them to remove themselves psychologically from their country's past and their parents' sins. Since the students had taken on the struggle against America's "racist crimes" at home and abroad, and against Germany's complicity in those crimes, they were fighting a fight their parents had never taken on. Furthermore, if racism was indeed indigenous to capitalism, as the students argued, the toxic German breed of racism that had culminated in the murder of millions of Jews was psychologically much more manageable. As KD Wolff reflected in an interview a few years ago, "in those days it was a relief for us to equate the US with the SS."[73] The second interpretative model exculpated the students as well, since their "anti-fascist generation" born in the waning days of the Nazi regime had taken on the struggle against the "old Nazis." As we have seen in the confrontations between the students and some of the locals in Zweibrücken, all too often the students' stance ended in labeling the older generation and present-day "reactionaries" as "fascist pigs" or "Nazi scum," culminating in what KD Wolff called in hindsight an "abstract morality" rather than a deeper wrestling with Germany's past and present.

In reflecting back on his activities during the Black Panther campaign, Wolff recalls that "debates on racism were central" to all their efforts, but that in many profound ways Germany's own racist past remained a "blind spot for us (*blinder Fleck*)."[74] Even though the students reiterated the illiberal continuities in German history from Bismarck to Hitler to the Federal Republic, Germany's own racist colonial past was absent in all their debates, and the racism of the Nazi past was obscured by overly abstract debates about past and present forms of fascism. It is only within this context that we can understand why the Black Panther Solidarity Committee believed, just twenty years after the defeat of Nazism, that the Black Panther campaign was essential so that Germans could experience and confront "actual and real forms of racism."[75] Perhaps it was also because of that *blinder Fleck* that activists like KD Wolff failed to reach out to Afro-Germans as possible allies. Admittedly, their numbers were minute, but Afro-Germans, often the children of African-American GIs, tended to live in and around the very US garrison towns where most of the protest activities took place. Perhaps it was also because of that larger oblivion toward Germany's own racist past and present that German students needed an alliance with black American soldiers to become sensitized to the plight of Germany's so-called *Fremdarbeiter* or *Gastarbeiter* in their deliberations on racism.[76]

Conclusion

To the great dismay and disappointment of German student radicals, the Black Panther Solidarity Campaign and the collaboration with African-American GIs did not overthrow the "American war machine" as many an idealistic student revolutionary had hoped in the heady days of the campaign. The students had overestimated their own strength, but also underestimated the ability of the United States to respond with comprehensive measures to address the grievances of African-American soldiers. As a response to the 4 July protest at Heidelberg University, the White House and Pentagon initiated a comprehensive investigation into racism in the military. That investigation was followed up by a NAACP visit to Germany in the spring of 1971. Their findings, *The Search for Military Justice,* as well as the Render Report coming out of the Pentagon investigation, led to unprecedented reforms and affirmative action programs within the military, which in turn have made the US military the most integrated institution in America.

But the students had also misjudged the state of affairs in Germany. The Federal Republic was not on the verge of fascism, no matter how adamant the students were in making that point, and responded with an extensive building program to help with the housing crisis that disproportionately afflicted black GIs in Germany's notoriously tight housing market. The federal government also instructed state governments with troops and garrison communities to set in place nondiscriminatory procedures for Germans who rented housing to Americans, and challenged pub and discotheque owners who discriminated against black GIs. The government also instructed the press to stop their practice of identifying the race of American soldiers in their news coverage. All these efforts had one goal, namely to tackle head-on the racial discrimination that black GIs encountered in West Germany, both within the military *and* in West German society.[77]

Once government officials in the US and West Germany took the grievances of black GIs seriously and thus deflated the racial crisis, the alliance between African-American GIs and white German students did not endure. The alliance also fell apart because the *Voice of the Lumpen* was torn by some of the same ideological divisions that tore apart the Black Panther Party in the US.[78] Furthermore, as the US military was under increasing pressure to satisfy personnel needs, a larger percentage of volunteers with criminal records or psychological problems entered the ranks. This in turn led to the introduction of gang structures and a serious increase in drug dealing, which did much to undermine the political activism of black GIs and that of the *Voice of the Lumpen.* The emergence of separatist black activists who rejected collaboration with white revolutionaries effectively ended the paper's collaboration with the students. Troubles also arose among the German alliance partners as debates over the use of violence deeply divided the Solidarity Committee. In the spring of 1971, three members of the

Solidarity Committee, Johannes Weinrich, Hans-Joachim Klein, and Winfried Böse, went underground and joined the armed struggle that would be responsible for violent attacks against US installations and US military personnel.[79] By the end of 1972, amidst much disenchantment, the Solidarity Committee ceased to exist. But for a few short years a tremendously optimistic sense had prevailed that an alliance between white German students, African-American GIs, and black GIs who had taken their military discharge in Germany could topple the US "military machine" in Germany and could thus aid in overcoming US imperialism in the non-Western world.

Notes

1. I would like to thank the National Endowment for the Humanities, The American Philosophical Society, and Vassar College for their generous support while I was conducting research for this essay. Thanks also to Martin Klimke, who has been most generous in sharing his thinking about this topic with me, my colleagues Judith Weisenfeld, Michael Hanagan, and Peggy Piesche, as well as my Ford Scholar Emma Woellk.

2. Martin Klimke, *The Other Alliance: Student Unrest in West Germany and the United States in the Global Sixties* (Princeton, 2010) and idem, "Black Power, die Black Panther Solidaritätskomitees und der bewaffnete Kampf," in *Die RAF und der linke Terrorismus,* ed. Wolfgang Kraushaar, 2 vols. (Hamburg, 2006), 1:562–82. Maria Höhn, "The Black Panther Solidarity Committees and the *Voice of the Lumpen*," *German Studies Review* 31, no. 1 (2008): 133.

3. Maria Höhn, *GIs and Fräuleins: The German American Encounter in 1950s West Germany* (Chapel Hill, 2002), chaps. 3 and 8.

4. A cursory reading of the student publication *Diskus* suggests that students completely ignored African-American GIs in Germany, even though a large number of GIs were stationed in and around Frankfurt. *Diskus* did start taking note of African-American issues in the US by the early 1960s. See, for example, *Diskus,* "Schwarz-Weisses Dilemma" (April 1960); "Aus besseren Familien. Eine Studie zur Situation der farbigen Studenten," and "The American Way of Life," (August 1962). On the collaboration with students from non-Western countries, see the important dissertation by Quinn Slobodian, "Radical Empathy: The Third World and the New Left in 1960s West Germany," (Ph.D. diss., New York University, 2008) and his "Dissident Guests: Afro-Asian Students and Transnational Activism in the West German Protest Movement" in Wendy Pojmann, ed., *Migration and Activism in Europe Since 1945* (New York, 2008).

5. See for example, "Fünf Formen von Black Power," *Diskus,* April 1969.

6. *Frankfurter Rundschau* (*FR* hereafter), 16 March 1963, "Gegen die Rassentrennung," reports on German students delivering a petition to the US consulate, imploring the American government to "overcome the sickness of racial hatred."

7. Students who had spent time at American universities and black exchange students from the US became important sources of information when they gave talks on Black Power and resistance struggles in America's inner cities. For advertisements of such talks, see *Berliner Extradienst* (*BED* hereafter), 31 January 1968 and 19 Novem-

ber 1968. See also *BED,* 23 April 1969, "Black Power in USA: Selbstorganisation der Neger." APO Archiv FU Berlin (APO Archiv hereafter), Black Panther folder, "Solidarität mit der Black Panther Partei."

8. See Martin Klimke's thoughtful discussion on the German SDS's reception of Black Power in chapter four of *The Other Alliance.*

9. Interview KD Wolff. For the Vietnam Kongress, see *Frankfurter Schule und Studentenbewegung: Von der Flaschenpost zum Molotowcocktail 1946–1995,* 3 vols., ed. Wolfgang Kraushaar (Hamburg, 1998), 1:298; Klimke, *The Other Alliance,* 84–86, 182–187 for the desertion campaign. Also, Dieter Brünn, ed., *Widerstand in der US-Armee: GI-Bewegung in den siebziger Jahren* (Berlin, 1986) and David Cortright, *Soldiers in Revolt: The American Military Today* (New York, 1975). See also "Die Arbeit in der US-Army," *Sozialistische Correspondenz-Info* (*SCI* hereafter), 25 April 1970; "Agitation in der US-Army," *SCI,* 23 November 1969. For contemporary reviews of dissent in the ranks and desertion, see "Wie Coca Cola," *Der Spiegel,* no. 35, 23 August 1971, 56, and "Wir mussten die Siebte Armee ruinieren," *Der Spiegel,* no. 17, 17 April 1972, 62.

10. "Aufruf zum Teach-In und Demonstration," *SCI,* 9 May 1970.

11. Archiv für Soldatenrecht, Berlin, "Transcript of interview with Bolden and Roberts." *Der Spiegel* interviewed Bolden and Roberts as well and published their story under the headline "Die Armee schafft sich immer neue Neger," in their 21 June 1971 edition (no. 26, 32). See also their article "Höherer Grad," ibid., 31. Also, "Schwarze GIs appellieren an Westberliner Bürger," *BED,* 23 June 1971, 1–2; "US-Kaserne McNair Rassendiskriminierung," *BED,* 29 April 1971; "Ein Schwarzer Soldat in Westdeutschland berichtet über den Krieg in Vietnam," *BED,* 10 December 1969. See also "Dokumente und Materialien zum antiimperialistischen Kampf der Völker Indochinas" published by the Komitee "Kampf dem Imperialismus," Frankfurt. *Der Spiegel* also reported extensively on Black Panther leaders in the US. See for example *Spiegel* interview with Stokely Carmichael, "Amerika niederbrennen, das wäre phantastisch," in *Der Spiegel,* no. 17, 21 April 1969, 124–32; and "Cleaver: Seele auf Feuer," *Der Spiegel,* no. 20, 12 May 1969, 189–92.

12. For quote see "Wir mussten die Siebte Armee ruinieren," *Der Spiegel,* no. 17, 17 April 1972, 72. For the radicalization of black soldiers due to Vietnam, see Terry Wallace, "Bringing the War Home," *Black Scholar* (November 1970): 2–18.

13. For a detailed discussion of the racism in the military see Höhn, "The Black Panther Solidarity Committees." For contemporary coverage, see "Neger – US-Veteranen – Wie gelernt," *Der Spiegel,* no. 17, 22 April 1968, 146, and "Neger – US-Streitkräfte – Sofort Aktiv," *Der Spiegel,* no. 37, 8 September 1969, 128. See also "Höherer Grad," *Der Spiegel,* no. 26, 21 June 1971, 31; "Die Armee schafft sich immer neue Neger," ibid., 32–33; "Wir mussten die Siebte Armee ruinieren," *Der Spiegel,* no. 17, 17 April 1972; Adalbert Weinstein, "Die Siebte Armee erholt sich von Vietnam," *Frankfurter Allgemeine Zeitung* (*FAZ* hereafter), 25 August 1972, 6; "Ku-Klux-Klan in Deutschland," *Der Stern,* 11 October 1970. For an overview of race problems in the military, see Brünn, *Widerstand* and Cortright, *Soldiers in Revolt.* See also Alexander Vazansky, "Army in Crisis: The United States Army, Europe, 1968–1975" (Ph.D. diss., Heidelberg University, 2009).

14. For the grievances of black GIs in Germany, see NAACP, *The Search for Military Justice: Report of an NAACP Inquiry Into the Problems of the Negro Servicemen in*

West Germany (New York, 1971) and Department of Defense, U.S. Assistant Secretary of Defense, Manpower and Reserve Affairs, Memorandum for the Secretary of Defense, "U.S. Military Race Relations in Europe – September 1970." For newspaper coverage see, for example, "'Modern und exclusiv': Zum Tanzen bitte weiße Haut/Rassendiskriminierung nach US-Muster/Geschäft vor Menschenwürde," *FR*, 3 May 1971; "Farbige Soldaten fühlen sich in Deutschland diskriminiert," *FR*, 28 April 1971; "Rassendiskriminierung in der Bundesrepublik," *Stuttgarter Zeitung*, 31 March 1971.

15. "Die Siebte Armee erholt sich von Vietnam," *FAZ*, 25 August 1972. On how bad the situation was with the 7th Army, see Congressional Record 92nd Congress, 1st Session, "Race Relations," 9 March 1971, 5650–51 and 16 July 1971, 25542–43. Also Congressional Record, 92nd Congress, 2nd Session, *Racism in the Military* 13–14 October 1972. For a contemporary American perspective, see Haynes Johnson and George Wilson, *Army in Anguish: The Washington Post National Report* (New York, 1971) and William Hauser, *America's Army in Crisis: A Study in Civil-Military Relations* (Baltimore, 1973). Also, Daniel Nelson, *Defenders or Intruders? The Dilemma of U.S. Forces in Germany* (Boulder, CO, 1987), 102–8.

16. "Höherer Grad," *Der Spiegel*, no. 26, 21 June 1971, 31. See also their coverage in "Wir mussten die Siebte Armee ruinieren," *Der Spiegel*, no. 17, 17 April 1972; "Schwarze Frustration," *Der Spiegel*, no. 5, 25 January 1971, 18; "Wie Coca Cola," *Der Spiegel*, no. 35, 23 August 1971, 56; Adalbert Weinstein, "Die Siebte Armee erholt sich von Vietnam" Kampfbereit trotz Haschisch und Rassenspannungen/ Besuch beim V. Korps (II), *FAZ*, 25 August 1972, 6. See also "Rassendiskriminierung in der US-Armee," *Süddeutsche Zeitung* (*SZ* hereafter), 19 August 1971; "Das Urteil das die Armeeführung schockierte," *FR*, 19 August 1971.

17. Kraushaar, *Frankfurter Schule und Studentenbewegung*, 1:407; "Black Panther Führer kommt," *FR*, 21 March 1969; "Mr. Senator, Sie sind ein Bandit," *Der Spiegel*, no. 13, 24 March 1969, 159.

18. Interview with KD Wolff, June 2002. See also "Black Panther Führer kommt," *FR*, 21 March 1969.

19. *SCI*, 6 December 1969, 11–12.

20. See for example *BED* issues 30, 34, 36, 46, 49, 50, 54, 61, 70/III and the extensive coverage on the Black Panthers in their 8 October 1969 and 26 March 1970 issues; also *SCI*, 13 December 1969, 9 May 1970, and 16 May 1970.

21. *SCI*, 6 December 1969, 11–12. Klimke, *The Other Alliance*, 120, shows that Agit 883 also published the founding documents of the Solidarity Committee.

22. In 1970, Wolff also founded the publishing house Roter Stern, which allowed him to considerably increase his educational activities and to raise money for the Panthers. See for example the last page of Eldridge Cleaver, *Zur Klassenanalyse der Black Panther Partei* (Frankfurt am Main, 1970), which lists all the ways in which the Solidarity Committee raised money for the party; Huey Newton, *Selbstverteidigung! Politische Essays* (Frankfurt am Main, 1971); Michael Cetewayo Tabor, *Harlem: Kapitalismus & Heroin = Völkermord* (Frankfurt am Main, 1970). Other publications from Roter Stern include: *Der Prozess gegen Bobby Seale: Das Gerichtsprotokoll* (Frankfurt am Main, [ca. 1970]); *Rassismus und politische Justiz in den USA: Der Prozess gegen Bobby Seale* (Frankfurt am Main, 1970); *Antiimperialistischer Kampf: Materialien & Diskussion*, no. 1 (1972).

23. Interview KD Wolff.
24. Interview KD Wolff. Klimke, *The Other Alliance*, 183.
25. Bundesarchiv Koblenz, B 106/39985 contains numerous reports by the BfV and the Ministry of the Interior on the pro–Black Panther meetings that took place all over West Germany in December 1969 and January 1970. Up to 1,000 people took part in each of these teach-ins.
26. See Kraushaar, *Frankfurter Schule und Studentenbewegung*, 1:474–92 for an overview of activities in Frankfurt.
27. "Ku-Klux-Klan in Deutschland," *Der Stern*, 11 October 1970; "Einmischung," *Die Welt*, 7 July 1970; "Treten farbige GI's in Aktion?" *Rhein-Neckar Zeitung*, 27 June1970; "Rassenstreit der Amerikaner in Europa," *FAZ*, 7 September 1970.
28. Stadtarchiv Kaiserslautern, Kulturamt, Akte Fruchthalle Vermietung. See also HIS, Sammlung Wolff, "Black Panther Info," booklet published by the Solidarity Committee Kaiserslautern (1971), 16. Archiv des Auswärtigen Amt, B 31/346, Bundesminister der Justiz report of 15 February 1971 to Auswärtiges Amt, "Black Panther."
29. *Voice of the Lumpen* (hereafter *VOL*), 6th ed., "The Trial of the Ramstein 2 Begins."
30. *VOL*, May/June 1971. The first issue of November 1970 has an extensive overview of how the *VOL* saw its role in the revolutionary struggle. The Archiv für Soldatenrecht in Berlin has copies of the paper.
31. Interview KD Wolff.
32. The problem of "cultural" nationalism bedeviled the collaboration from the beginning. See for example the flyer from the SDS and AStA of Mannheim University, which invited black GIs to a demonstration to express solidarity with the struggle of black Americans. The clumsily worded flyer expressed hope that the GIs would ignore the "suggestion by black power leaders not to join any action organized by whities" by assuring them that the "part of German youth sympathizing with black power is much more radical as [sic] those at home in the States." See APO Archiv, Black Panther Folder, flyer entitled "Black GIs."
33. APO Archiv, SDS Nachlass, "GIs." See Moritz Ege, *Schwarz werden: "Afroamerikanophilie" in den 1960er und 1970er Jahren* (Bielefeld, 2007) for a thoughtful discussion of these problems.
34. The *Süddeutsche Zeitung* wrote, for example, "that the voices of the minority soldiers could only be heard so powerfully because of the support they were getting from German leftist students, but especially from KD Wolff in Frankfurt." "Panther Sprung nach Europa," *SZ*, 18 December 1970.
35. Interview KD Wolff. Elizabeth Pfeifer, "Public Demonstrations of the 1960s: Participatory Democracy or Leftist Fascism?" in *Coping with the Nazi Past: West German Debates on Nazism and Generational Conflict, 1955–1975*, ed. Philipp Gassert and Alan Steinweis (New York, 2006), 199 makes this case for student protesters in general. See also Kraushaar, *Frankfurter Schule und Studentenbewegung*, 1:270 on Dutschke's thoughts on the urban guerrilla. Also see Wolfgang Kraushaar, Karin Wieland, and Jan Philip Reemtsa, *Rudi Dutschke Andreas Baader und die RAF* (Hamburg, 2005).
36. Kraushaar, *Frankfurter Schule und Studentenbewegung*, 1:501. See Klimke's discussion in *The Other Alliance* of the Angela Davis Solidarity Campaign organized by Oskar Negt in 1972 at Frankfurt University, 136–39.

37. Eldridge Cleaver was on the FBI's most wanted list and would have needed "diplomatic immunity" to avoid arrest in Germany. This Hans-Dietrich Genscher's Ministry of the Interior, responsible for matters of diplomatic immunity, declined to grant. Kathleen Cleaver was turned away at the airport as well, but the demonstrations and teach-ins proceeded nonetheless and were attended by large crowds.

38. "Starke Unruhen durch 'Schwarze Panther,'" *Rheinpfalz*, 21 November 1970; "Zum Schutz der Bürger alles tun," "OB; Mehr Schutz vor den 'Black Panthers,'" "Hat Black Panther erneut zugeschlagen?" all in *Pfälzische Volkszeitung*, 20 November 1970; see also their story of 21 November, "Black Panthers verübten Anschlag." See also Oberstaatsanwalt Zweibrücken, 29 Ks 3/71 Verdict of the Landesgericht Zweibrücken of 20 July 1971 and Verdict of the Schwurgericht Frankenthal of 13 July 1973.

39. APO Archive, Black Panther folder, "US Airforce-Posten schiesst auf Black Panther" and "Politische Justiz gegen farbige Genossen in der BRD" flyer. The *Haftrichter* sued Wolff for calling him a racist but lost the suit when the court ruled that Wolff, in his capacity as a spokesperson for the Solidarity Committee, had every right to make the statement. See Landeshauptarchiv Wiesbaden, 461/32149 Staatsanwalt gegen KD Wolff.

40. Gutachen in Landgericht Zweibrücken, 29 KS 3/71, Bd. VII, 74–75. See also "Küßchen, Zigaretten und Lange Pausen," *Rheinpfalz*, 2 July 1971, reprinted in *Antiimperialistischer Kampf*, no. 2/3 (1972): 66. See Gerhard Amendt, ed., *Black Power: Dokumente und Analysen* (Frankfurt am Main, 1970).

41. For the views of the *VOL* see their May 1971 issue. In another issue that deals with the Ramstein 2 trial, the *VOL* calls the defendants political prisoners while also insisting that "we are used to this from US," but having political [Black Panther] prisoners in Germany, "is a new step." "Political Prisoners in West Germany," *VOL*, May/June 1971.

42. APO Archiv, Black Panther folder, "Freiheit für die Ramstein 2." Larry Barnes was initially charged and jailed for undermining Germany's state security by urging black soldiers to resist their government, which was Germany's defensive bulwark against communism.

43. Klimke, *The Other Alliance*, 121f.

44. "The Trial of the Ramstein 2 Begins," *VOL*, 6th ed. (no month given). VOL was not consistent in identifying months or volumes.

45. *VOL*, May/June 1971 and *VOL*, 6th ed.

46. "Materialien & Diskussion, 'Ramstein 2 Prozess," *Antiimperialistischer Kampf*, no. 2/3 (1972): 34. For the petitions, see the trial records at the Landgericht Zweibrücken.

47. "Materialien & Diskussion, 'Ramstein 2 Prozess," *Antiimperialistischer Kampf*, no. 2/3 (1972): 34.

48. Stadtarchiv Kaiserslautern, Kulturamt, Akte Fruchthalle Vermietung. For the wide variety of posters produced see also the APO Archiv folder "Black Panthers" and the Johann Wolfgang Goethe University Archiv, "Flugblätter und Poster," Mappe 2. See also the 20-page informational brochure "Black Panther Info" produced by the Kaiserslautern Committee in HIS, Sammlung Wolff.

49. APO Archiv, Black Panther folder, Black Panther Solidaritätskomitee, "Aufruf!!" *Informationsbrief 2*, 71. See also flyers advertising the event in Saarbrücken at APO Archiv, Black Panther folder. Archiv der Johann Wolfgang Goethe Universität,

"Flugblätter und Poster," Mappe 2 has a flyer advertising a teach-in at Frankfurt University. The *BED* covered the events leading up to the trial and the trial. See for example 6 March 1971, 14 July 1971, 8 December 1971, 10 May 1972. See also the coverage in "You can't kill the Revolution," *Diskus,* 1 July 1971.

50. Quote from "Schwarze Panther: Sammetpfötchen und Krallen," *Rheinpfalz,* 8 March 1971. See also coverage of the event in *FR,* 8 March 1971, photo of protest in Zweibrücken; "Heiss war der Tag trotz Eiseskälte," *Pfälzischer Merkur,* 8 March 1971; "Linke Pilgerfahrt in die tiefste Provinz," *SZ,* 8 March 1971. See also Hessisches Hauptstaatsarchiv, Wiesbaden, 461/32218, "Staatsanwaltschaft gegen Unbekannt," folder contains a poster advertising the events.

51. "Schwarze Panter: Sammetpfötchen und Krallen," *Rheinpfalz,* 8 March 1971. The students reported 2,500 participants. Some papers talked of 1,500.

52. See the very critical coverage of the day's events in "Heiss war der Tag trotz Eiseskälte," *Pfälzischer Merkur,* 8 March 1971. Both the *Rheinpfalz* and the *SZ* blamed the police for provoking the clashes that did occur.

53. Stadtarchiv Frankfurt Sz Sammlung, A 9986 contains a number of newspaper articles dealing with protests in Frankfurt. See "Black Panther Freunde demonstrieren am Samstag," *Neue Presse,* 24 November 1979 and "Solidarisch mit Black Panther," *FR,* 24 November 1970. For other examples of how Wolff cautioned restraint at demonstrations, see for example "Demonstration in der Innenstadt," *FAZ,* 30 November 1970.

54. "Schwarze Panther: Sammetpfötchen und Krallen," *Rheinpfalz,* 8 March 1971.

55. "Linke Pilgerfahrt in die tiefste Provinz," *SZ,* 8 March 1971.

56. Ibid.; "Heiss war der Tag trotz Eiseskälte," *Pfälzischer Merkur,* 8 March 1971; interview KD Wolff.

57. "Black Panther Prozeß mit Zwischenfällen," *Rheinpfalz,* 17–18 June 1971.

58. Ibid. and "Schwarze Hinne," *Der Spiegel,* no. 26, 21 June 1971, 73.

59. Interview KD Wolff. See also "Black Panther Freunde beschworen in Zweibrücken neue Zwischenfälle herauf," *Pfälzische Volkszeitung,* no date, reprinted in *Antiimperialistischer Kampf,* no. 2–3 (1972): 67.

60. "Fordert den Besuch des Prozesses im Sozialkundeunterricht!" poster reprinted in *Antiimperialistischer Kampf,* no. 2–3 (1972): 68.

61. "Starke Unruhen durch 'Schwarze Panther'," *Rheinpfalz,* 21 November 1970. See also the even more derogatory coverage in "Zum Schutz der Bürger alles tun," "OB: Mehr Schutz vor den 'Black Panthers'," and "Hat Black Panther erneut zugeschlagen?" all in *Pfälzische Volkszeitung,* 20 November 1970. See also their story of 21 November, "Black Panthers verübten Anschlag."

62. "Küßchen, Zigaretten und Lange Pausen," *Rheinpfalz,* 2 July 1971, reprinted in *Antiimperialistischer Kampf,* no. 2/3 (1972): 66.

63. See for example "Wurden Vorfälle von Ramstein provoziert?" *Tageblatt,* 5 July 1971.

64. Oberstaatsanwalt Zweibrücken, 29 Ks 3/71, Verdict of the Landgericht Zweibrücken of 20 July 1971 and Verdict of the Schwurgericht Frankenthal of 13 July 1973. I want to thank Leitender Oberstaatsanwalt Bayer and Wolfgang Ohler for making the verdicts and trial materials available to me.

65. "Küßchen, Zigaretten und Lange Pausen," *Rheinpfalz,* 2 July 1971.

66. Quote from "Black Panther Freunde beschworen in Zweibrücken neue Zwischenfälle herauf. Statt 'Informationsversammlung' gab's Handgreiflichkeiten – Nächtliche

Schmiereien," *Pfälzische Volkszeitung,* no date, reprinted in *Antiimperialistischer Kampf,* no. 2/3 (1972): 67.

67. At the archive of the *Frankfurter Rundschau* the newspaper clipping file "BRD Neger" during that time was changed into "BRD Rassismus" and thus shows this shift aptly.

68. *FR,* 26 February 1971. The newspaper clipping files "BRD Neger" and "BRD Rassismus" at the *Frankfurter Rundschau* contain a wealth of articles dealing with this issue. See for example "'Modern und exclusiv': Zum Tanzen bitte weisse Haut. Rassendiskriminierung nach US-Muster/Geschäft vor Menschenwürde," *FR,* 3 May 1971; "Farbige Soldaten fühlen sich in Deutschland diskriminiert," *FR,* 28 April 1971; "Der Kommentar: Prügelknaben," *FR,* 4 May 1971. See also "Rassendiskriminierung in der Bundesrepublik," *Stuttgarter Zeitung,* 31 March 1971; "Panther Sprung nach Europa," *SZ,* 18 December 1970; "Die heile juristische Welt kam doch in Unordnung," *FR,* 28 June 1971.

69. Detlef Siegfried, *Time Is On My Side: Konsum und Politik in der westdeutschen Jugendkultur der 60er Jahre* (Göttingen, 2006), 154–58, shows how the Nazi past was discussed in youth magazines such as *Twen.* I show that transformation beginning in the early 1960s, as Germans debated the propriety of interracial love relations between German women and African-American soldiers. Those incidents, however, never rose to the level of high government intervention they reached in this case. See Maria Höhn, "'Ein Atemzug der Freiheit': Afro-amerikanische GIs, deutsche Frauen, und die Grenzen der Demokratie (1945–1968)," in Arnd Bauerkämper, Konrad H. Jarausch, and Marcus Payk, eds., *Demokratiewunder: Transatlantische Mittler und die kulturelle Öffnung Westdeutschlands, 1945–1970* (Göttingen, 2005), 104–28.

70. Archiv des Auswärtigen Amtes, B 86/1425 for text of 21 March 1971 speech. Still absent in any of these debates, and in Willy Brandt's speech, were Afro-Germans. This lack of attention to Germany's own racial minority confirms Heide Fehrenbach's finding how the denial of race as a critical category after 1945 had also erased the presence of Afro-Germans in German consciousness. Heide Fehrenbach, *Race After Hitler: Black Occupation Children in Postwar Germany and America* (Princeton, 2005).

71. "Zur Verhaftung von Angela Davis," *SCI,* 18 November 1970, 20. See especially "Black Panther Info," HIS, Sammlung Wolff.

72. *Antiimperialistischer Kampf,* no. 2/3 (1972): 64.

73. KD Wolff interview, June 2002.

74. Ibid.

75. "Materialien & Diskussion, 'Ramstein 2 Prozess,'" *Antiimperialistischer Kampf,* no. 2/3 (1972): 34.

76. See for example the "Resolution of the European Black Panther Solidarity Committees after their meeting in Frankfurt," reprinted in *SCI,* 2 May 1970, 6

77. For a more detailed discussion of the government responses to the racial crisis see my essay, "The Black Panther Solidarity Committees."

78. Wolff tried to save his organization after the breakup of the Black Panther Party in the US by insisting that the Solidarity Committee had never identified with the Black Panther Party unconditionally, but saw its main purpose in creating solidarity

with the struggle of the Black Panthers. See "Materialien & Diskussion, 'Zur Spaltung der Black Panther Partei,'"*Antiimperialistischer Kampf,* no.1 (1972): 1.

79. In his thoughtful discussion of the Black Panther Solidarity Committee and the emergence of the RAF, Klimke makes a powerful argument of how "the shadows of a past insufficiently overcome" and the infatuation with the ideas and tactics of the Black Panthers led some activists to turn toward terrorism after spring 1971. In their escalating rhetoric of resisting fascism in the US and at home, and of equating the war in Vietnam with the genocide in Auschwitz, they refused to be "good Germans" and took up arms. But Klimke also cautions, and I agree with his caution, that this turn to illegality should "neither be taken as direct or inevitable lines." Klimke, *The Other Alliance,* chap. 4, 132, 140. On the problematic association of Auschwitz and Vietnam, see also Wilfried Mausbach, "Auschwitz and Vietnam: West German Protest Against America's War During the 1960s," in *America, the Vietnam War, and the World: Comparative and International Perspectives,* ed. Andreas W. Daum, Lloyd C. Gardner, and Wilfried Mausbach (New York, 2003), 279–98, and idem, "'Man muss die ganze Wut diesen Herrenrassenbanditen ins Gesicht schreien': Die 68er und die nationalsozialistische Vergangenheit," *Deutschlandarchiv* 38, no. 2 (2005): 273–80; Gassert and Steinweis, *Coping with the Nazi Past.*

Chapter 12

Between Ballots and Bullets

Georgy Katsiaficas

Social movements in the 1960s provide astonishing evidence of the capacity of ordinary people to create participatory forms of popular power that contest the established system. In May 1968 in France, the entire country convulsed in near-revolution as organs of dual power sprang up everywhere. Two years later in the US, four million students and half a million faculty embarked upon a nationwide strike in May 1970 in response to the killings at Kent and Jackson State, the invasion of Cambodia, and repression of the Black Panther Party. No central organization brought together this strike—the largest in US history. (In the 1930s, the largest strike involved about 500,000 workers.) Despite the absence of centralized organization (or perhaps because of it), people were able to formulate unified national demands around political issues and to question the structure of the militaristic system that compelled universities to be part of weapons research and development. Although the movement fell short of its long-term goals, it provoked numerous political reforms and thoroughly transformed civil society.

In almost every country in the world, massive social movements intimately related to each other emerged in 1968. Sometimes the connections between these movements were quite visible. Between Germany and the US a veritable conveyor belt brought young Americans to Germany as part of the US military, and once in Germany many became politically active. Through rock 'n' roll and other cultural avenues, young Germans were greatly affected by American dynamics. In both countries, organizations with the initials SDS came to dominate student activist circles before both disintegrated for similar reasons at the end of the 1960s. (The German SDS was explicitly socialist, while its US sister organization was not—at least until its final days.)

Looking back at the history of the New Left and radical social movements since 1968, I am amazed at how distorted histories and conceptions of the past become when political ideologies come into play. What remains clearest to me is that the actions of millions of ordinary people continue to demonstrate a far more intelligent ability to govern society than those of entrenched elites, or even insurgent ones. Without centralized organizations or unified ideologies, peoples' unified actions intervene in history time and again, in positive ways. The unfolding logic of autonomous social movements presents a dynamic structure and content, gradually revealed in much the same way as we can discuss the ever-growing universality of vision found in eighteenth- and nineteenth-century German philosophy. In the twenty-first century, as the ever-expanding notion of People Power revolutions reverberates across the continents, so too does the superior capacity of millions of people to run society—and the reluctance of governments to use military force against publicly assembled citizenry.

Forms of direct democracy and collective action developed by the New Left continue to define movement aspirations and structures. This is precisely why the New Left was a world-historical movement. In 1980 in Gwangju, South Korea, people refused to accept a new military dictator and stayed in the streets for democracy. When the army brutally attacked the city, outraged citizens beat back a vicious military assault and held their liberated city for a week, using general assemblies and direct democracy to run their affairs. Soon thereafter, a chain reaction of uprisings swept East Asia—the Philippines in 1986, Korea and Taiwan in 1987, Burma in 1988, Tibet and China in 1989, Nepal and Bangladesh in 1990, Thailand in 1992.[1] Unlike the uprisings in Eastern Europe in this same period, the "eros effect" in East Asia was not precipitated by leaders at the highest levels of government seeking to shift power blocs but by the accumulation of experience in the hearts and minds of millions of people.

The "eros effect" was discovered during my empirical research on the global movement of 1968. As I sifted through my data on insurgencies in more than twenty countries, I had a Eureka moment when I realized that specific demonstration dates, issues raised, and tactics used from country to country were directly related to each other. As I developed the concept further, it came to refer to the capacity of ordinary people, acting together, to profoundly change the basic facts of social life. If we look at history, we can find moments in nearly every country when the activated population changed governments and economic structures—or even the way time and space are measured. In moments of the eros effect, love ties exist between people that are some of the most exhilarating feelings imaginable. This refers not simply to sexual ties, for love has many forms—love of parents for their children and vice versa; love for brothers, sisters, and other family members; love for a significant other; and most socially, love for one's fellow human beings.

When the eros effect is activated, humans' love for and solidarity with each other suddenly replace previously dominant values and norms. Competition gives way to cooperation, hierarchy to equality, power to truth. During the Vietnam War, for example, many Americans' patriotism was superseded by solidarity with the people of Vietnam, and in place of racism, many white Americans insisted a Vietnamese life was worth the same as an American life (defying the continual media barrage to the contrary). According to many opinion polls at that time, Vietnamese leader Ho Chi Minh was more popular on American college campuses than US President Nixon. Moments of the eros effect reveal the aspirations and visions of the movement in their lived meaning. Millions of peoples' actions define the movement's essential aspirations more than statements of leaders, organizations, or parties.[2]

The Invisibility of Autonomy

Almost without exception, revolutionary social movements in the twentieth century prior to the New Left sought simply to conquer national political power—either to take it over through elections or overthrow it through violence. Continuing in the New Left tradition of directly changing everyday life is the Central European autonomous movement, which built itself from the bottom up beginning in the late 1970s and sustained itself over several generations of activists. In 1981, tens of thousands of Germans marched for peace, and they helped bring an end to the nuclear arms race and the Cold War between the US and USSR. Among the participants were radical youth who had occupied hundreds of abandoned buildings and insurgent women who challenged patriarchy in governments' powers as well as in arenas of everyday life. Allied with farmers and squatters, German ecologists successfully stopped the country's nuclear power industry's attempt to produce bomb-grade uranium. The autonomous women's movement, the movement against nuclear power, and youthful squatters all became springboards for more generalized resistance involving militant tactics. As citizens' initiatives and new social movements followed their own internal logics, out of the crucible of all these struggles, the German autonomous movement, or Autonomen, was galvanized as a force resisting the corporate system *as a whole*.[3] More than a decade before the Seattle protests against the World Trade Organization, tens of thousands of people in Berlin confronted a global gathering of the most powerful wizards of high finance and compelled the world's bankers to adjourn hastily a day earlier than planned.

The goal of this autonomous movement is to transcend nation-states, not capture them. Unlike Social Democracy, anarchism, and Leninism, the main currents of the twentieth-century Left, autonomous social movements are relatively unencumbered by ideology. The absence of any central organization helps keep theory and practice in continual interplay. As one small group acts, another is inspired to rise up, and they in turn galvanize yet others. This chain reaction of social insurgency, a process I understand as essential to the eros effect, leads to the emergence of massive social movements capable of transforming civil society.

Direct actions speak for autonomists, not words, and the sheer volume of decentralized happenings generated by small groups acting on their own initiative often prohibits understanding of the totality of the movement. While Greens and guerrillas have been afforded high visibility by journalists, autonomous social movements have been largely invisible. Both in popular media as well as in scholarly accounts of the end of the Cold War, for example, political parties and politicians are highlighted, while peace initiatives in Europe, initially linked to a militant extraparliamentary youth movement, are overlooked. Through their attacks on nuclear power and weapons and their defense of squatted houses, a new generation of radicals helped to delegitimate the authority of national governments and NATO at a time when the postwar division of Europe into hostile zones of East and West had yet to lose its rationale in the minds of many Europeans. Within West Germany, the youth movement, at times violent and tempestuous, became a driving force that made peaceful marching an acceptable course for many people who otherwise might not have risked getting involved.

"The people make history," little more than an empty rhetorical device for both insurgent and entrenched political elites, clarifies the driving force behind the Cold War's end. The construction of a transnational civil society unanchored in any state or political party proceeded slowly at first. Long before nuclear disarmament developed massive support or Gorbachev considered *perestroika* and *glasnost,* grassroots citizens' initiatives against nuclear power galvanized locally based opposition movements, sometimes across national borders. As bottom-up initiatives proliferated, the electoral successes of the Greens encouraged Gorbachev to act, and Western leaders were compelled to respond because of the pressure of the peace movement.

In contrast to the centralized decisions and hierarchical authority structures of modern institutions, autonomous social movements involve people directly in decisions affecting them every day. They seek to expand democracy and to help individuals break free of domineering political structures and inherited patterns of behavior imposed upon them. Their subversion of politics would mean a complete reorientation of our understanding of the role of nation-states, the power of political parties, and individual obedience to unjust laws. In place of massive systems of representative democracy and majority rule, they live according to principles of direct democracy and self-government. They do not seek to create mammoth structures of power, nor are they interested in participating in existing ones. Although their numbers may be small, their actions often have significance beyond what quantitative analysis would indicate.

Autonomous social movements have no unified ideology and central organization; they fight "not for ideologies, not for the proletariat, not for the people" but, in much the same sense as feminists first put it, for a "politics of the first person." In various internal documents, they indicate they want self-determination and "the abolition of politics," not leadership by a party. They want to destroy the existing social system because they see it as the cause of "inhumanity, exploitation and daily monotony." No doubt autonomous social movements are difficult to define. Neither a party nor a movement, their diffuse status frustrates those who seek a quick and easy definition for them. Their more militant members appear as the "black block" at demonstrations. They gather in "autonomous assemblies" that are regionally organized or oriented around specific campaigns, but they have no fixed organizations or enduring spokespersons.

In the past three decades, they have manifested themselves within peace movements and anti-nuclear movements, and today they help animate the global justice (or anti-corporate globalization) movement. From below, the actions of millions of people around the world have formulated a focus for international mobilizations, that is, to confront elite meetings of the institutions of the world economic system—practical targets whose universal meaning is profound. No central organization dictated this focus. Rather, millions of people autonomously developed it through their own thoughts and actions. Similarly, without central organization, some thirty million people around the world took to the streets on 15 February 2003 to protest the second US war on Iraq, even though it had not yet started. As this global movement becomes increasingly aware of its own power, its strategy and impact are certain to become more focused. By creatively synthesizing direct-democratic forms of decision-making and militant popular resistance, the self-movement of social movements, contained within a grammar of autonomy and the eros effect, embodies what I call "conscious spontaneity." Key tactical issues facing the global justice movement are contained in microcosmic form in the development of the European Autonomen.

The European Autonomous Movement

As the twentieth century ended, many Germans were relieved to read continuing press accounts of the demise of the Autonomen. Berlin was in the midst of its post–Cold War building boom, and old Autonome neighborhoods were increasingly gentrified. Many middle-class people hoped the movement had finally succumbed to the untiring corporate onslaught. Although something of a legend in American activist circles, the Autonomen never grew beyond the marginality they embraced as proof of their righteousness, and they finally seemed on the verge of extinction. Yet Autonomen brought on their "rebirth" after years of invisibility in the anti-G8 protests near Rostock in 2007. Apparently, although the fires of autonomous resistance had died down, its embers were quickly fanned back into a conflagration that continues to burn beneath the façade of middle-class acceptance of world leaders' neoliberal agenda.

As I discuss below, varying levels of parliamentary, armed, and extraparliamentary actions depend on each other, and each should be evaluated primarily according to its efficacy in building insurgency from below, of strengthening and broadening popular movements. In an age of sound bites and instant-coffee consciousness, the propensity for quick fixes of fragmentary factoids has often led the media to use (erroneously) the term "anarchist" to refer to autonomous social movements. In Germany, their political terrain lies somewhere between parliamentary participation and guerrilla struggle (between ballots and bullets), and they were especially successful in the 1980s and 1990s. The Autonomen have never been eager to define themselves precisely. In the 1983 issue, *Radikal*, one of their more important magazines, commented that "Autonomy was a notion that overnight gave our revolt a name … Previously we understood ourselves as anarchists, *spontis,* communists or had diffuse, individual conceptions of living freely. Then we were all Autonomen."

Unlike communists, autonomous movements do not believe in the need for one true revolutionary party, a single guiding ideology, or one revolutionary sector of society. They believe in diversity and continuing differentiation. Nowhere written down, this principle emerges in the actions of thousands of people in their everyday lives. They believe in self-management and the need for individuals and groups to take responsibility for their own actions. While these notions may be contradicted by the actions of some, they materialize in enduring patterns of movement activity seeking to change governments as well as everyday life, to overthrow capitalism and patriarchy. Their decolonization of everyday life prepares the ground for the future transformation of the totality of global society.

Resistance to centralized leadership and to uniform theory is often regarded as weakness. Many people in the autonomous scene think of the movement's decentralization as a blessing, however, making it more difficult for police to infiltrate and easier for grassroots initiatives to develop. As the magazine *Radikal* put it: "The Autonomen movement is not a party and it consists of a minimum of organization if we make an historical comparison. This fact can be an advantage as the jailers search for structures and leaders which are not to be found." For more than thirty years, this movement has been able to regenerate itself by bringing in new strata of youth—precisely because of its decentralized character.

International associations link movement groups in many countries, including Germany, Norway, Denmark, Sweden, Holland, Russia, Poland, the Czech Republic, Belgium, and Switzerland. Communication at the grassroots is facilitated through a variety of conferences, meetings, public events, 'zines, friendships, and demonstrations. In many cities, squatted and legally purchased movement centers provide further space for movement networks to expand. The horizontal—even circular—collective structure of the Autonomen facilitates discussions and actions whose sources are numerous and diverse and whose approval depends upon the agreement of others, not directives from above. The "scene's" structure enhances individual decision-making and political development. With initiative coming from many sources, collectives are able to act immediately and decisively without waiting for a central committee to deliberate and approve ideas.

Militant opposition to nuclear power and the squatters' resolve to seize and defend houses were crucibles for the galvanization of the Autonomen. Their ability to provide a confrontational cutting edge to larger movements helped radicalize thousands of people and was crucial to stopping the Wackersdorf nuclear reprocessing plant (and Germany's possession of bomb-grade plutonium). Noteworthy here was their fighting alliance with Bavarian farmers. Confrontational politics invigorated Germany's political debates, compelled the established parties to change policies and programs, and deepened many people's commitment to fundamental social transformation.

Militant resistance to local instances of the system's encroachment upon previously autonomous dimensions of life propelled many people to resist the system as a whole. Within broad campaigns, the role of the Autonomen was to extend the critique enunciated by single-issue initiatives. In their 1989 annual report, the German federal police recognized this crucial role within movements against nuclear power and genetic engineering: "As soon as protest movements develop, above all Autonomen and other 'New Leftists' press for 'direct resistance' against 'the system.'" By raising the level of discourse from specific institutions to the system as a whole, a radical critique of the entire system of capitalist patriarchy was widely discussed and was sometimes transmitted to new sectors of the population.

Apparently, a Leninist-style party is no longer needed to transcend the reformism of spontaneously formed movements, since these movements by themselves develop a universal critique and have autonomous capacities for self-government. As a diffuse collection of militant counterculturalists who assemble sporadically and whose identity is far from fixed, the autonomous movements do not find their strength in their overwhelming numbers. In June 1987, for example, when US President Ronald Reagan visited Berlin, the autonomous "black block," identified by their black ski masks and collective discipline, numbered only about 3,000 out of 50,000 anti-Reagan demonstrators, but their militance and ability to intervene in the streets had great impact. In 1988, when 75,000 protesters gathered at the meeting of the International Monetary Fund and the World Bank in Berlin, only a small fraction could be counted as Autonomen. Once again, however, the initiative of Autonomen resulted in the larger actions taking form, and they were the militant organizers creating a context in which other forms of participation (signing petitions, attending programs and rallies, publishing informational leaflets, etc.) generated interest and impact.

For many people, radicals' rejection of traditional ideology implies the elevation of pragmatic values and the isolation of activism from theory. Neither of these appears to be a necessary consequence of autonomist politics. Theory is contained within the actions of autonomists rather than being congealed in rigid ideologies that precede action. Preparations for actions, the actions themselves, and the inevitable (and often prolonged) soul-searching afterward involve intensive theoretical reflection. Flexibility of action means the Autonomen are capable of lightning-swift responses to public events. Seldom can centralized organizations organize with the speed of autonomous movements. In the early 1990s, when neo-Nazi gangs went on a rampage and the police failed to respond in places like Hoyerswerda and Rostock, the Autonomen were able to mobilize hundreds of people within a few minutes, providing immediate assistance to Vietnamese, Turks, and Angolans. (Once the pogroms had been stopped the police finally did react, but they arrested anti-racist street fighters—not the neo-Nazi attackers, as might be assumed.)

After German reunification, a wave of squatters engulfed more than 130 buildings in the old eastern part of Berlin. Despite being defeated after the mammoth battle of Mainzer Street and generally rebuffed by a public anxiously awaiting the advent of consumer society—not the radical politics of the counter-culture—the self-directed action of hundreds of people (tens of thousands, if we include the concomitant student strike at the universities as well as other solidarity demonstrations) provides a model for political organization and action. As racist attacks on immigrants continued to intensify, the movement redirected its energies to confront neo-Nazi groups. Autonomen formed at least four different anti-fascist publications that provided quality exposes of the New Right and closed down Nazi demonstrations permitted by the police.

The Autonomen seek to live according to a new set of norms and values within which everyday life and all of civil society can be transformed. Beginning with overt political beliefs, they want to change isolated individuals into members of collectives within which egalitarian relationships can be created, relationships that subvert the traditional parent-child, husband-wife, couples-singles patterns that characterize patriarchal lifestyles. In place of the hierarchies of traditional political relationships (order-givers/order-takers, leaders/followers, media stars/media consumers), they strive for political interactions in which these roles are subverted. At their high point in the 1980s, their collective forms negated atomization, their activism transformed the passivity of consumerist spectacle, and their daily lives included a variety of people (immigrants, gays, lesbians, "others")—thereby negating the reification and standardization of mass society. Put another way, their self-determination negated the all too prevalent alienation from products of work. Even for most Greens, the Autonomen were regarded as "other." For their part, most Autonomen regard the Greens not as the movement in the government but the government in the movement.

Once the Green Party spawned by grassroots movements became part of the national government, their foreign minister (and former radical *sponti*) helped get German troops stationed outside the country for the first time since Hitler. With the Greens' help, Germany finally enjoyed a long-denied status that any "normal" European power takes for granted. While abstaining from the Anglo-American attack on Iraq, Germany played an active role in the war on the Taliban and cooperated with the world's great powers in the Balkans. (To their credit, the Greens were able to broker a legislative ban on construction of new nuclear power plants in Germany.)

If Germany has indeed qualitatively transformed itself from a militaristic imperialist power into a nation supporting peace and justice, we must certainly thank the Autonomen for their leadership. When these young Germans embarked upon their march *against* institutional power, they suffered terrible repression from the entrenched forces of state repression as well as from their former colleagues (like the Greens) who were engaged in the "long march *through* the institutions." With the apparent demise of the Greens through their incorporation into the liberal wing of the established power structure, the wisdom of marginality might better be comprehended.

The Guerrillas and the Movement

At the end of the 1960s, the German New Left discovered rock 'n' roll around the same time that the Kreuzberg Hash Rebels came into existence, and guerrilla groups like the Red Army Faction (RAF) and the 2 June movement began their armed attacks and bombings. These developments transformed a highly intellectual movement whose everyday life had reflected the cultural conformity of Germany. Feminists became increasingly autonomous as currents of sexual liberation and cultural revolution clashed with the dogmatic ideology of cadre groups and stern disapproval of parents and authorities—as well as their movement colleagues.

In May 1968, while France convulsed in near-revolution, German activists desperately fought against new repressive emergency laws (*Notstandsgesestze*) and attacked the conservative Springer press, which had targeted Rudi Dutschke (who was shot by a would-be assassin in April).[4] By way of comparison, the US movement's high point was reached from May to September 1970, when in a remarkable five-month upsurge, the movement produced the political strike on the campuses, the National Organization for Women's call for a general strike of women, the eruption of Vietnam veterans, the first Gay Pride week, the Chicano Moratorium, and the culminating event of the Black Panther Party's Revolutionary People Constitutional Convention in Philadelphia, in which 10,000 to 15,000 people were involved in writing a new constitution for the US.[5]

The German movement's relative isolation can be described numerically: there, the SDS never had more than 2,000 members.[6] Even though the New Left created quite a stir, it never attracted the widespread participation so essential to larger movements in France or the United States. In Germany, the ratio of SDS members to population was 1:30,000 whereas in the US it was 1:4,000—and that figure does not include members of the Black Liberation Movement or any of the other streams of rainbow resistance in the US.

By the 1980s, when a Punk Left reached a higher level of struggle in Germany than ever attained in the 1960s, most members of the New Left had become part of the university "establishment" and filled other professional positions. The most public examples of New Leftists who were not absorbed into the middle class were imprisoned members of guerrilla groups, some of whom were incarcerated in sunless, constantly videotaped isolation cells. Solidarity with these prisoners became an important rallying point within the movement, despite severe legal sanctions against writing or even publicly speaking in favor of "terrorists."

In 1977 (when Italy reached a boiling point), West Germany suffered through its "German Autumn," a time of both armed attacks on the country's elite by the RAF and intense political repression. Even after nearly all of its original members were dead or in jail, the RAF was able to regenerate itself in at least two more iterations. In 1979, RAF activists tried to kill Alexander Haig when he visited NATO headquarters in Belgium, but their bomb exploded after his car had passed. In 1981, a RAF bomb wounded twenty people at the NATO air base at Ramstein and a RAF rocket hit the car of Frederick Kroesen, US commander in Europe.[7] In 1982, over 600 bomb attacks were recorded in West Germany, many of which were tied to RAF and the autonomist Revolutionary Cells.[8]

After the demise of East Germany, many RAF members gave themselves up and others were arrested. Newly released information showed that the group had received aid for years from the East German *Stasi* (secret police). Although reported by the police to be nearly finished, the armed struggle continued to haunt the country's elite in the 1990s. On 31 March 1991, the head of Treuhand, the government agency overseeing the economic transition of East Germany, was shot and killed in his home in Düsseldorf. In 1993, a few days before a new $153 million prison was scheduled to open, RAF bombs were so precisely exploded that four cell blocks and the administration building had to be razed, adding a cost of over $60 million to the project and delaying its opening for years. Finally in 1998, the RAF announced the end of the armed struggle.

Although the most notorious, the RAF were not the only armed formation to appear in Germany. In the early 1970s, after nearly every single member of the original RAF had been killed or imprisoned, the Revolutionäre Zellen (Revolutionary Cells or RZ) initiated a quieter and less deadly series of attacks.[9] In contrast to Marxist-Leninist ideology and the centralized structure of the RAF, the RZ consisted of independently organized groups who selected their targets and tactics according to specific conditions, particularly as defined by popular struggles. One estimate placed the number of RZ members at about 300 in the early 1980s. The RZ were organized in autonomous groups, each of which was responsible for its own actions—a structure on a parallel with Italy's Prima Linea.

A part of the RZ consisting solely of women was the Red Zoras, autonomous feminist guerrillas who formed within currents of feminism and anti-imperialism. They took their name from a popular novel in which young girls steal from the rich to give to the poor. It is not uncommon for autonomous groups to borrow images from the life-world of children to describe themselves. In a popular squatters' song, the Hafenstrasse (residents of an occupied house in Hamburg) long relied on Pippi Longstocking to help explain how the houses miraculously remained occupied. In some sense, autonomous groups refuse to grow up: they refuse to shed their dreams of a better world or to conform to existing cultural norms like marrying, living in nuclear families, and taking on a career. Their affinity for the pleasure principle—or at least their negation of the reality principle—is a salient part of their identity.

Since 1974, when they bombed the Supreme Court building the day after it overturned the abortion law, the Red Zoras have conducted militant campaigns against pornographers international traders in women (those who profit from importing Asian women as "brides" for German men), the Doctors' Guild ("We see the Federal Doctors' Guild as exponents of rape in white trench coats."), and drug companies (notably Schering, which produced the birth defect–causing drug Duogynon). In conjunction with the RZ, they launched over 200 attacks on selected targets. Their most successful campaign was won in the summer of 1987, when they compelled the Adler Corporation, one of Germany's largest clothing producers, to agree to the demands of South Korean women textile workers. Adler had initially fired twelve South Korean women union leaders, but after the Red Zoras and their sister group in Berlin, the Amazons, firebombed ten Adler outlets in Germany, causing millions of dollars in damages, the company rehired the twelve and agreed to meet the textile workers' demands. In a recorded interview, the Red Zoras explained: "We do not fight for women in the Third World, we fight alongside them." The anti-authoritarian structure of their groups—a decentralized decision-making process for choosing targets and a lack of uniform politics or spokespersons—made it nearly impossible for German authorities to find them.

In contrast to guerrillas' direct attacks on government that aim to diminish its sovereignty, autonomous popular movements seek to choke off the legitimacy of government among the citizenry, to undermine its popular support while building new sources of dual power. Guerrillas go for the jugular, while popular movements aim to clog up the capillaries by creating nonhierarchical organization forms as part of a political culture that has little to do with parliamentary policy and elected representatives. Guerrillas prematurely pose the question of power, attempting to take over the central government themselves, rather than to dissolve its powers and make room for autonomously constituted forms of self-government. In contrast to a system that produces politics as spectacle for citizens who are little more than powerless spectators, autonomous movements seek massive participation in self-governance.

This same tactical division (guerrilla warfare vs. popular movement) was one of the dynamics spelling the end of the New Left in the US. The curtailment of public space for protests drove many activists underground, thereby intensifying further the government's use of force. Police provocations, aimed at depoliticizing the movement by ending the involvement of hundreds of thousands of people, began to succeed. Police repression and internal ideological splits wrecked havoc on the movement's centralized organizations (like the SDS and the Black Panther Party), sapping their strength and making them unable to act on their own initiatives.

Some activists welcomed the intensification of the struggle with the government, believing that we—not the forces of order—would win a civil war. Their shortsightedness is now evident in retrospect, although at that time no one could have been sure of the validity of such a judgment. Caught in a vise between the police and gun-toting radicals, the popular movement was denied the public space so vital to its existence. Squeezed between the violence of the police and the small-group actions of armed militants, the popular movement came to an abrupt end, and the drama of guerrilla warfare between a "righteous" elite and an evil one played to an increasingly empty house.

What remains most problematic is how a movement hoping to create a more democratic society can defend itself from armed police attacks while simultaneously strengthening popular participation. On the one hand, the legal imperative of those involved in parliamentary struggles distances them from insurgencies, and on the other, the underground actions of the guerrillas deprive popular movements of some of their finest activists and the public space to grow. Between the cooptation of parliament and the depoliticization of guerrillas, the movement is left with few avenues to maintain its popular resonance.

Of course, there are important exceptions. The RZ actions against Adler, coupled as they were with a popular movement, took no pains to tutor other activists nor made any claim to lead anyone, and the action enhanced the popular movement's power. The RZ neither understood themselves as a vanguard nor had a central organization—unlike the RAF and Weather Underground. Whenever the Weatherpeople published their communiqués, from action explanations to "Changing Weather" and *Prairie Fire,* they sought to lead the popular upsurge.

Many former Weatherpeople today walk the streets and freely practice professions, unlike the RAF or members of the Black Liberation Army, nearly all of whom are dead or in jail. Unlike these other guerrillas, the Weatherpeople were able to "invert" themselves, partly because German and US authorities have had very different relationships to former members of the undergrounds, partly because of race and class issues, partly because of illegal tactics used by the FBI that made subsequent prosecutions untenable, and partly because the groups' actions were quite different. Weather's morality dictated no assassinations—unlike the more working-class RAF, which murderously targeted the rich and powerful.

After so many dead and so much sacrifice, at least one thing is certain: the equation of one bombed banker plus (or minus) one dead industrialist and two dead generals (added to a few elected progressive parliamentary representatives) does not surpass the autonomous movement's transformation of civil society. Time and again, insurgent movements have shown a wisdom and intelligence that surpasses even the best organizations and parties.[10] What is needed for revolutionary change is a vibrant spectrum of actions emanating from a diverse popular movement. Specific tactics and actions should be primarily evaluated in relation to whether or not they help to build such movements.

At their best, autonomous movements pose a species-solidarity that transcends ethnic exclusivity, patriarchal power, and class divisions.[11] In Germany in the 1980s and 1990s, they critically pointed out the failure of even some of the most progressive Germans to go beyond their Germanness. They took the feminist universal to a higher level, interweaving it with class oppression on a global scale, and they similarly sublated the workerist imperative of orthodox forms of Marxism in their actions. While guerrillas and parliamentarians are inherently elitist groupings, autonomous popular movements insist on a global egalitarianism. Their vision and actions portray new species universality, and they are a source today of activism aimed at transforming the capitalist world system through the global justice movement.

Notes

1. See Georgy Katsiaficas, "Remembering the Kwangju Uprising," *Socialism and Democracy* 14, no.1 (spring-summer 2000): 85–107.

2. In George Katsiaficas, *The Imagination of the New Left: A Global Analysis of 1968* (Boston, 1987), I develop the notion of the eros effect. I locate the actions of millions of people as defining the movement's meaning in mass strikes in France in May 1968 the US in May 1970.

3. See George Katsiaficas, *The Subversion of Politics: European Social Movements and the Decolonization of Everyday Life* (Oakland, 2006).

4. H. J. Giessler, *APO-Rebellion Mai 1968* (Berlin, 1968).

5. See George Katsiaficas, "Organization and Movement: The Case of the Black Panther Party and the Revolutionary People's Constitutional Convention," in *Liberation, Imagination and The Black Panther Party*, ed. Kathleen Cleaver and George Katsiaficas (New York, 2001).

6. Tilman Fichter and Siegward Lönnendonker, *Kleine Geschichte des SDS: Der Sozialistische Deutsche Studentenbund von 1946 bis zur Selbstauflösung* (Berlin, 1977).

7. Richard Clutterbuck, *Terrorism, Drugs and Crime in Europe* (London, 1992), 50.

8. Tom Vague, *The Red Army Fraction Story, 1963–1993* (Edinburgh, 1994), 97.

9. See Redaktionsgruppe Früchte des Zorns, *Fruchte des Zorns*.

10. The most significant national revolutionary organization in the US in the latter half of the twentieth century was the Black Panther Party, but even in this case, its popular base was far more visionary than its leaders or organization.

11. I develop this theme more robustly in Katsiaficas, *The Subversion of Politics*.

Chapter 13

A Whole World Opening Up

Transcultural Contact, Difference, and
the Politicization of "New Left" Activists

Belinda Davis

In the first postwar decades, West Germans were on the move. As a function of influences as diverse as forced migration, economic fortunes, American culture, and a growing Europeanism, residents of the new Federal Republic moved around physically as no Germans had before, within the country and outside the country.[1] The broader world moved around them, too, in small towns as well as in big cities. For younger West Germans, this mobility engendered a challenge to shared assumptions, and even a seeking out of difference, a fascination for the idea of how things could be different. While not all who shared this experience became political activists, "New Left" activists consistently described this background as a factor in motivating their sense that things could and even should be other than as they were, and their conviction that they could change these things. This experience characterized not only the "stars" of the extraparliamentary opposition (APO), whose travels and transnational connections have long been acknowledged, but also hundreds of thousands of other activists who actively pursued such connections; it was pivotal to a sense of *Weltoffenheit*, openness to the world.[2]

Attention to these personal experiences and connections among so many, and across national and other boundaries, helps us first to understand one important fillip to the activism of this period. It aids secondly in broadening our understanding of 1968 as a transnational movement.[3] Thirdly, it contributes thereby to understanding the simultaneity of political action in the late 1960s, within European nations, the United States, and beyond. Many of the elements identified in West Germany (FRG) applied elsewhere as well (regarding transnational contact, this was de facto so), if in particular combination and sometimes with particular intensity in the Federal Republic. Fourthly, recognition of the importance of this experience across such a breadth of activists offers some challenge to recent assertions of activists' general dogmatic stance by the 1970s. Finally, it helps us to trace the effects of this broad activism in transforming West German political culture, and in understanding how change took place.

These assertions draw primarily on some fifty-five oral histories of activists (including West Germans spending time abroad and non-ethnic Germans likewise in the FRG) born between 1937 and 1957.[4] Looking at a range of life stories, and the vast variety of these contact points, this chapter highlights these activists' interactions with a wider world, in order to understand its effects on them—and vice versa. Scholars have discussed both 1968 and postwar political-cultural transformation in West Germany inter alia in terms of "Americanization."[5] This work has become one useful node of discussion on the broad question of "transnationalism."[6] At its best, such work offers a sense of overdetermined interaction at a variety of levels that both acknowledges the place of the "nation" and recognizes its limits in understanding the range of human contact and influence. Scholars have long characterized various forms of American influence specifically as central to the establishment of a new culture of democracy and of freedom in the FRG—at least as ideals that many embraced. Many speak too to a broader range of popular cultural and commercial influences. As still others have begun to emphasize, West Germans drew ideals and other notions not only from the United States, but also from elsewhere, including elsewhere in Europe.[7]

This chapter seeks to extend our understanding of trans- and cross-national influence, alongside other forms of "intercultural" contact, by looking more broadly at the range of forms of this contact and influence, and at how it produced specific effects in politicizing activists. In doing so, it emphasizes that while changing economic, political, and cultural conditions contributed to producing certain perspectives among activists and future activists, these changes in values (*Wertewandel*) were not "top down" only: these individuals also contributed to producing these changes—and to submitting themselves to difference—from early on. To contemporary inhabitants, "West Germany" marked the boundaries of a state, not a nation. But through such experiences, activists created and performed new ways to be (West) German.

A "West German" Childhood

Multiple elements contributed to this exposure to and, for many, embrace of the "new and different" among younger West Germans. The extraordinary postwar mobility was critical in this process. A shibboleth of postwar Europe, this character was particularly intense as applied to the Federal Republic. Members of the West German population were likely to have been born to mothers themselves displaced from other family members (including often husbands), and therefore "foreign" to their surroundings. Chances were good that these individuals moved house—most often several times and across long distances—in the first decade of life.[8] These experiences were as variable as the causes for this mobility. Rüdiger was born in 1942 in Bielefeld: authorities had ordered family members out of the surrounding countryside to work in the small city's armaments factories. When bombs fell on the city, he was evacuated to the countryside; he moved back and forth twice. Born in 1941, Wiebke walked with her mother from a village outside Breslau (Wrocław, Poland, after 1945) to the rubble of Berlin, one of millions of ethnic Germans expelled westward at the war's end. Jeanne's parents, avid pro-Nazis, had fled their native Belgium for Bremen just before her birth in 1945; because her father fled prosecution for his wartime activities, the family remained on the move for years, often split between different residences. Thomas was born in a refugee settlement in Schleswig-Holstein, moving several times thereafter; though he was not born until 1952, his parents' experience of displacement from East Prussia at the war's end strongly marked his childhood.

Despite this variability, these individuals' experience of such moves was surprisingly consistently salutary, at least as they recall it, in contrast with that of their parents.[9] Monika was born in 1950 in a Displaced Persons camp, with its rapidly shifting population, to Polish Jews who had survived concentration and death camps. She remembers delight in moving from Frankfurt am Main to the United States for a few years as a child, feeding a powerful sense of "nichts wie weg," a desire to get away to something new. Joschka Fischer, born in 1948 in Gerabronn to expellees happy to settle permanently, likewise remembers from early on that "I wanted to get away, I wanted out, I wanted to see the world." Kommune I activist Rainer Langhans, born in1940, remembers the excitement of his family's flight from East to West Germany in 1953, one of many moves his family made. It was "fantastic," "actually a great, great adventure." (Certainly it is possible there was also considerable anxiety that informants did not recall or did not share.) Many informants contrast this sentiment with that of their parents, who found such moves traumatic, despite or because of the various upheavals they had already undergone during the Third Reich and still earlier. This contrast questions recent assertions concerning a postwar longing for *Heimat*, or homeland; one might suggest that in some respects the concept met its demise in this period.[10] This difference of sentiment toward such major change between these populations may represent one marker separating '68ers from the "parents' generation," and even from the "skeptical generation," functioning more meaningfully than an emphasis a priori on specific birth years.[11]

But, as was the case for Thomas, parents' experience and their attendant responses influenced their children in many ways. Many activists claim to have learned a particular skepticism from their parents, possibly a function of the latter's own experience of disruption.[12] Thomas's parents did not automatically accept the legitimacy of the Federal Republic, even years after its founding in 1949, not least because of a sense that it represented a culture imposed from outside. He remembers drawing from this the sense that he need not agree to the conditions that governed him, simply because they were the prevailing conditions. Children also heard from their parents and others that a divided Germany was a temporary phenomenon (as was, in the eyes of some, the prevailing boundary between East Germany and Poland). Most of these household moves after the direct postwar period were "voluntary," on parents' part at least, once more communicating that one need not simply accept prevailing circumstances. Informants' parents emphasized to them too new opportunities for both travel and communications, a sense these parents may have learned themselves through bourgeoning opportunities in the Third Reich, as well as as a product of rising West German prosperity.[13] Well before the full flush of the "Economic Miracle," West German families began to travel regularly for pleasure, in and out of the country, often to visit newly dispersed family members.[14] Johannes's and Robert's families, who had relatives in the United States and Great Britain respectively, engaged in regular communication with these relatives and even exchanged visits. Johannes (born in 1948 in Hamburg) thereby heard intense political disagreement within this transnational family because his American cousins were far more conservative than his immediate family members, while Robert (born in 1949 in the Ruhr) came early on to admire the "glamour" of his English cousin, the inspiration for a lengthy independent visit to Britain as a young teenager. Many informants were in contact with close relatives in East Germany, Poland, and Czechoslovakia.

Many parents also sought actively to "bring the larger world in" to their homes, and several of the children from eight or nine years old onward regularly read newspapers and listened closely to news on the radio (along with American and British pop music[15]), discussing issues with their parents, and even creating clippings files on national and international issues. For some of these parents, informants understood, this was explicitly about inducing a critical and knowledgeable perspective in the new democracy. This avenue to a larger world should not be exaggerated. Gaby, born in 1946 into a farm-laboring family in the rural Rhineland, had no radio or newspapers at home; for others, the papers were most commonly the regional daily or weekly. Robert's father decried as "obscene" one of the early alternative newspapers Robert brought home as a teenager in the mid 1960s—even as Thomas's working-class father prohibited the boulevard daily *Bild* in the home. But many of these children felt they were exposed to a wider world through their parents and, further, politicized by and through them, including explicitly in connection with national and international issues. Anna's parents took her to peace demonstrations starting in her infancy in the mid 1950s (though this common commitment to politics made family relations none the more tolerable for Anna later on). Older siblings often also played such a role for their sisters and brothers. Robert was thrilled, on his first visit in the early 1960s, with the "foreignness" as well as the political liveliness even at the relatively sleepy University of Münster, where older his sister studied. He continued to visit her on weekends as often as he was allowed to.

Such encounters were not limited to informants' own travels. If so many individuals and families were displaced, it follows that others living in one's neighborhood and town were also often "from somewhere else," producing a heterogeneity in the early FRG that has perhaps been insufficiently recognized.[16] Inge Buhmann remembers her mother's discomfort with "the expellee families with their many children, who came one after another," billeted on her grandmother's farm, but for her brother and her, it was "more interesting than frightening."[17] Klaus Brandes found his north German town Lemgo suffocating, but it was his exposure to locally posted American GIs that led him to this assessment.[18] Beginning in the mid 1950s, ethnic Turkish, Greek, or Italian "guest workers" might be shopping at the local market, soon enough more dispersed than immigrant (and forced) laborers of earlier eras, even if immigrant communities remained relatively segregated.[19]

The likeliness of encounter with "difference" came from other sources as well. Migration, ruined cities, regime change, the Cold War, and other circumstances challenged the geography of class.[20] Karl (born in 1953), whose parents were both doctors, went to school in Hamburg with children from much poorer backgrounds, a contrast that struck him at a very young age. Conversely, Klaus's parents had little education—like the parents of many in this sample—and his father was unemployed. But Klaus was privileged to attend a *Gymnasium,* college-preparatory high school, in prosperous Zehlendorf, Berlin, in the mid 1960s. He left school at fourteen, and left home at seventeen—likely introducing a startling option in the eyes of many of his schoolmates, long expected to complete their *Abitur* (college-readiness examination) and continue on to university. This contact with difference that had been most often a characteristic of Berlin and a few other cities was also now far more widespread.

School was a site of young West Germans' exposure to new worlds through a range of sources. Although youth was a critical target of Allied High Command Occupation Government (HICOG) efforts, attempts to institute broad educational reform in the immediate postwar, promoting the "inculcation" of democratic values, were relatively limited and abortive. But other changes came to matter. West German–American teacher exchange programs had a strong impact, while widespread English language instruction had significant long-term effects for this mobile population.[21] Efforts to address a dire teacher shortage by the early 1960s brought tens of thousands of very young instructors into the classroom, alongside their older counterparts.[22] As early as the late 1950s, "radical democratic" teachers were influential in politicizing the children in their classroom; in this way, the earliest born of this age cohort began influencing those younger.[23] Martin, a "half-orphan" of the war born in 1944 in Munich, remembers two teachers in particular in the late 1950s "who influenced us all enormously, I think, and who also knew how to evoke a critical consciousness concerning National Socialism in us." Thus Martin was "politically sensitized through his history and German classes" even at twelve or thirteen, at least in some broad sense. As early as the first half of the 1960s, many teachers introduced pupils to contemporary world politics, from circumstances in Algeria to Vietnam to Chile.[24] But well into the 1960s schoolchildren were equally likely to sit in the classroom of an "old Nazi," or even just an older, conservative, authoritarian instructor who taught quite different lessons. Former activists suggest it was as often the striking contrast between such different teachers that provoked a questioning of how things should be. This questioning led to challenges quite early on in their own lives and in this period.

Pupil exchange programs, active between West Germany and the US, among other countries, were as important as those among teachers. These were often part of officials' efforts to promote good will and commitment to "common values." But former national German Socialist Student organization (SDS) chairman KD Wolff suggests that his exchange as a sixteen-year-old in 1959 to the small town of Marshall, Michigan, exposed him to some quite new values. At first he was suspicious. "I thought of myself as a socialist. So that meant I held myself at a certain distance, and [I] also noted of course that everything was conservative there." He was hardly unusual in arriving with advance expectations and judgments, despite an overall "openness." "And still," he noted, "it was really quite extraordinary, there was a kind of everyday liberality that was quite unlike anything I'd experienced at home." He remembers the gape-mouthed response when he asked who "allowed" an information stand for a local charity to be on Marshall's Main Street. "The question was simply without sense … So—simply the relationship to public space … Yes, it was, was simply astounding." His perception of this possibility might not have been entirely accurate, but the challenge to his expectations was the critical point. Years later in the early 1970s, Manfred's high school exchange brought him to keen awareness of the Vietnam War: his host family in conservative Virginia engaged in anti-war protest. A decade earlier in West Berlin, Harald, born in 1944, remembers his fascination with the "completely radical Christian politics" of visiting schoolmate "Randy" (Reinhard Lettau), an "American" pupil—who hailed originally from East Germany. It was such personal contacts that most effected such transformations in informants' thinking, as many remember it.

Community life across West Germany in the 1950s and 1960s might be ill characterized as cosmopolitan. But the range of factors we have identified created new opportunities and possibilities—and these young people sought in turn to create such opportunities for themselves and others. Susanne, born in 1950 in Oberharz to a mother from Switzerland, visited meetings of local neo-Nazis, among other groups, to expose herself to different ways of thinking. For Kerstin, living outside north Bavarian Hof, local meetings of the Anti-Imperialist League (to which her boyfriend had introduced her) as well as the town's new international film festival were critical markers for her of the possibilities as well as the limits of her hometown. Along with friends, she visited local bars (legal for German teenagers), seeking out those different in age, in class, and by other measures. She claims that although her parents had pegged her for the local hairdressing school, these experiences ultimately led her out of Hof, having first stood up to her father's beatings to insist on a different life for herself—or at least on the possibility of remaking herself. It may be that such experiences were on the whole even more significant for females than for males, relative to lesser initial expectations.[25] The willing challenge to "how things were" anticipated 1968, as well as the women's movement, the lesbian and gay rights movements, and the pursuit of alternative lifestyles. From the first half of the 1960s, many schoolchildren—college-bound and others—ventured onto the campuses of nearby institutions of higher education, attending lectures and participating in political meetings. Informants' narratives make clear that university campuses were not singular sites of the era's activism. Yet they were significant sites, for non-students as well as students. Their increasing heterogeneity, to which these individuals contributed, was a significant factor in the role they played.

Schoolchildren also traveled quite far afield without their families. Many informants emphasized the impact of trips they made outside the country, led by formal political organizations and other youth collectives.[26] Susanne traveled as a schoolgirl to Czechoslovakia with an SDS group in August 1968; her trip was cut short by the arrival of Soviet tanks. Her village in the Oberharz region may have felt cloying and constricting, but it was in part town funding that subsidized her trip to the "center of the world" at that moment. Still more important to this "opening up" were trips these young people made informally, on their own. This was the era of "Railpass" and "Autostop" (hitchhiking) travel; hitchhiking during school breaks, including outside the country, became an absolute norm. This kind of transnational exposure and experience, revolving around meeting people rather than touring museums or splashing on a beach, was a fundamental component in shaping the worldview of hundreds of thousands of young West Germans, which in turn became central in their politicization, the experience of informants suggest. While postwar and Cold War conditions rendered English a lingua franca in Western Europe, cultural differences even among Western Europeans (and among West Germans, for that matter) were in this era still quite substantial, regularly affording young travelers exposure to very different ways of doing things. West Germans frequently made more extended visits abroad too while still in high school. This was possibly still more commonplace for girls, who served as au pair helpers. Paradoxically, taking on such stereotypically female tasks functioned to open these girls to new experiences and perspectives.

The large numbers and varied demographic of individuals involved here, the regularity of the travel, the emphasis on personal contacts, and the often lengthy duration of visits all serve to augment existing frameworks of understanding of transnational protest movements and their sources. Such exposure undoubtedly did not elicit celebrations of difference in every instance, and assuredly rather often negative judgments at the time. One might at the same time examine more deeply the significance of a certain rejection of one's own culture for some. For present purposes, we emphasize that informants overwhelmingly stressed the "politicizing" nature of such travel. Harald's exposure to issues concerning the Algerian War came from a school trip to France: "that was political," he recalls simply. On her trip to Prague in 1969, Tulla, born in 1952 outside Stuttgart, "met the most remarkable people … many people who lived illegally in Czecho-slovakia, and who had tried to leave … That was an unbelievably formative political experience." Such experiences contributed to motivating young people to "activism" early in their lives, in their schools and communities, in a variety of more and less formal forms. Scholars have emphasized the role of more im-personal—or indirect—cultural contact, such as through music, and this too was important for these informants. Personal, sometimes lasting contacts (some, significantly, reaching across the "iron curtain"), however, provided an under-recognized basis for later transnational popular politics. Some have noted the ex-oticization and fetishization of difference, for example, of South Vietnamese and of Cubans.[27] Yet personal relations helped mitigate this effect. Susanne recalled a thrilling trip to London: "and there I saw [my] first Mao buttons and 'Mao bibles' [Mao's *Little Red Book*], and I was completely electrified, completely, I found it wonderful." But the thrill was in the newness of the ideas, rather than in the sense of having found a new absolute truth.

Young Adulthood

Most of these informants describe "politicization" during their younger years, drawing in part on these types of experiences and translating into an activism across a lengthy span of their own lives, and across the years preceding as well as succeeding 1968. The sense of, the excitement for, and the relative comfort with what was different led most informants to a clean and relatively early break with their parents' households and even with their "home" region: this was a move from "nothing like getting away" (*nichts wie weg*) to "nothing like getting to it" (*nichts wie dran*).[28] Edgar Reitz characterizes leaving home in his film cycle *Das zweite Heimat* as an attempt to establish a new "Heimat": one that one chose and made, and regularly remade, for oneself. Areas near universities and the variety of institutions of higher education were likely destinations (for young men, most often after their one-year military service), not only for students, and not least because of the admixture of cultures, ideas, and populations these campuses came in this period to represent.[29] Robert, who had visited his sister in Münster, found being at the University of Heidelberg, far from the Ruhr Valley, "crazily, crazily exciting," in the way it seemed to put him "in contact with the wider world." It made him feel "really terrific (*mächtig toll*), and adult, and … open-minded." Cities too drew broad younger populations, not least for the same rea-sons: as centers of imaginary geographies, as crucibles of widely varied elements, and in turn as sites for broad and deep opportunities for political involvement. Silke, an unemployed office worker born in 1954 in Oldenburg recalled a mo-ment in the late 1970s: "Then I realized things were really happening in [West] Berlin … Everything was possible. … I saw some kind of television report on housing occupations … it was about [protesting US involvement in] El Salvador. … It was such a catalyst: I thought, I gotta take a closer look at that. … So I just came here [to Berlin]. There was so much going on. There were lots of … that is, above all, lots of people from Italy … everyone." Cities and university towns did not constitute exclusive loci for "New Left" and wider popular political involvement, as the experiences described above make clear. But they are a focus here, specifically for the role both played in magnifying this experience of encounters with what was different.[30]

Universities and other institutes of higher education boasted a more heterogeneous population than at any time in the past. Postwar class "confusion," Cold War requisites, and other factors informed a certain "democratization" of higher education in West Germany. There were new forms of student aid for the broadening segment of *Gymnasium* graduates. While contemporaries decried the limited success of such programs, the great variability among informants' backgrounds is notable; it may be that those who "fit" the least easily—who encountered the greatest difference—were precisely most likely to become activists.[31] Because of the open-ended nature of matriculation and curriculum in comparison with, for example, the US, students could remain formally enrolled for extended periods while fundamentally practicing politics full-time. Often remaining enrolled was also a practical economic decision. Programs providing for an "alternative educational path" (*zweiter Bildungsweg*) too brought to student bodies diversity that became significant in spurring activism. The new willingness and even eagerness to move far from home also informed this relative heterogeneity. The explosive combination of prominent activist Dieter Kunzelmann's Catholic, middle-class, Bavarian "*Gaudi*" (fun) and extraparliamentary leader Rudi Dutschke's comparatively dour rural East German Protestantism is only one example among thousands. Deciding after some years to go to university as part of her activism, Kerstin spoke joyfully of the combination of politics and sociability she learned from and practiced with the small, ad hoc group she created with a few of her classmates in her first semester at the University of Regensburg: a Palestinian, an officer in the West German army, and a strong-minded, older, working-class woman pursuing the alternative educational path.

The role of ethnic non-Germans was critical in this context, although it is barely acknowledged in the existing literature.[32] For a range of political reasons, West German universities officially welcomed students from outside the country. Rudi Dutschke was himself a foreign student at the West Berlin Free University, having come from East Germany just before the Wall was built in 1961. Starting in the late 1950s, foreign students, often older, contributed to a particular diversity at West German universities. More than this, they introduced both political issues of concern and forms of protest that helped inform the broader West German extraparliamentary movement—among and beyond the student population.[33] Such protests were most often aimed at the regimes of the countries they had left—usually West German Cold War allies. The Iranian student group leader Majid Zarbakhsh (born in 1940 in Abadan, Iran) recalls from the time of his arrival in the FRG in 1960 growing interest among ethnic German students—and others—in protests against the shah of Iran. As the prominent national newspaper *Frankfurter Allgemeine Zeitung* reported, a demonstration against the shah in Frankfurt in December 1963 brought ethnic German participants from at least as far as Kassel, Saarbrücken, and Düsseldorf, over 200 kilometers away.[34]

University administrators panicked at the "infectious" nature of such protest, and they were not far from wrong in their estimation, even in these early years, during which FRG officials commented on the apolitical stance of West German students. While dramatic marches, demonstrations, and sit-ins on the scale of those that followed the shooting death of student protester Benno Ohnesorg on 2 June 1967 were rare before that point, the very protest in which Ohnesorg participated, against the state visit of the shah of Iran, took place across the country, in all the cities visited by the shah and well beyond. Critical moments in the history of the era's protest arose from the concerns of foreign students in West Germany, in West Berlin alone from the 1964 demonstration against visiting Congolese dictator Moïse Tchombé (in which police brutally attacked peaceful protestors), to the 1966 action against the screening of the perceived racist film Africa Addio, to the 1967 demonstration against the shah. In 1963, native West German students in Frankfurt, Mainz, and Giessen joined their visiting counterparts in demonstrations against racial discrimination in the Federal Republic—and against official threats of deportation against Iranian and Nigerian students, precisely as a consequence of their protesting.[35]

Certainly such demonstrations brought out only the smallest fraction of the local student population. But this was one site of protest among others, and it represented moreover a developing awareness of such issues. And in a logic created by university authorities themselves, native West German students came to identify with their non-German counterparts as "outsiders," which then spurred further protest.[36] This was the paradoxical counterpart to cultivating an ability to make oneself comfortable among people who did things differently. All told, more informal contact was at least as critical as the organizations co-sponsoring a demonstration; this offers too a sense of patterns of political involvement across many years. To the mind of Bärbel, born in 1957 in Jülich and coming to activism first in the mid 1970s, "the whole German student movement was actually initiated by foreigners, by foreign students." She added: "Really, it always revolved around personal relationships. I think it was that way with most of the people. You got to know someone, he joined a group, so you went along, and ..."

While there were relatively few South Vietnamese in West Germany (certainly in comparison with the number of North Vietnamese in East Germany), it was in part Americans in the Federal Republic—students, GIs, and others—who brought the issue of the Vietnam War to such widespread attention on West German university campuses and beyond. Johannes remembers the importance of Angela Davis's participation as an auditor in Theodor Adorno's seminar at the University of Frankfurt in 1966, well before she had become a "star."[37] This may have begun with students' fascination with her as an African-American, but exclusive focus on such "exoticism" ignores both a deeper and broader exposure and an interactive engagement with others' thinking that seems to have been surprisingly commonplace. (An exile to America during the Third Reich, Adorno himself represented a transnational presence, as did many "mentors" of the movement.[38]) Davis clearly also brought something home herself from this experience.[39] Johannes had close contact with many Americans, including GIs whom he met regularly at Frankfurt's "Mexicana" bar; this brought him to efforts to help GIs escape (re)deployment in Vietnam by fleeing to Sweden.[40] Susanne recalls her own friendship at the University of Frankfurt with an American who helped analyze her personal experience with the tools of feminism. "She brought the theoretical concepts and the models with her, as it were, from America." This was life-changing for Susanne, who came to realize "I really do well only in groups of women, and as long as men are around, it's just crap." Ed (born in 1949 to American parents), who spent his childhood in Washington, D.C., Munich, and Vienna, returned to West Germany on his own first in 1979 (via Japan—and a community of West German expatriates), drawn there by the new "Green" politics. He quickly came to play an important role in bringing individuals together as well as shuttling information and ideas between them in the US and West Germany during the peace movement of the early 1980s, contributing like so many others to the kind of contacts that made that movement transnational.

If high school–aged West Germans frequently crossed national boundaries themselves, they pursued these patterns still more actively after leaving school. Tobias, born in 1943 in a Lower Saxon village, dropped out of school and took off for Sweden to learn a trade as a welder before moving to Hanover, where, although not a university student, he helped build a local SDS chapter. For many who were students, travel abroad for extended periods of time was no longer epiphenomenal. It became central to pursuing one's research and politics both, bound together as they were for many. Gaby's experience provides a useful example. She left her isolated rural village, unpredictably, for the university at Cologne, then Tübingen's Eastern Europe Institute. A student in one of her study groups spoke Italian, and translated passages of Antonio Gramsci's work for the group. She herself learned Russian and studied the Eastern Bloc to give herself, a self-perceived ignorant daughter of rural workers, a chance to reflect knowledgeably on prevailing Cold War rhetoric. The Soviet Union was closed to her for study, so she pursued research instead in Paris, Amsterdam, and San Francisco. Her experience was not a purely intellectual one. Gaby soon took up work with the United Farmworkers on the grape boycott—and became romantically involved with a Black Panther. Her sense of different views of the world hit home in the most concrete sense. She vividly remembers looking at a world map produced in the US, oriented around that country. "That really knocked me out of my chair," she observed. Her "world view was totally changed. [I found] that Europe wasn't the center but rather that there were completely different perspectives."

It is in this broader context that we might understand the acknowledged transnationalism of the 1970s' "new social movements" and above all the women's movement. The West German women's movement had no sooner developed its nucleus in Helke Sander's kitchen than members established contacts throughout the country and abroad. It might come as no surprise that Sander herself had only recently returned to West Berlin in 1965 from several years in Finland, where she had married and had a baby. Alice Schwarzer initiated a piece of the movement in Cologne after returning from several years as a journalist in France. Inspired by the provocative French magazine article "I've Had an Abortion," Schwarzer and others organized a comparable West German piece, appearing in 1971 in *Stern* magazine. But these two "stars" were hardly the only ones to boast such experience. Leni, born in 1942 in Greifswald, remembered that, as a part of her feminist involvement, she made sure to know "what the Dutch were doing, and what they were doing in France, and so on, and to make contacts, and to consider, maybe I'll go to Amsterdam and then go in the women's library—and to the whole world." This was just "crazily exciting," a "beautiful departure" from the standards of how things "had to be done."

These exchanges and influences went in both directions. African students, Italian members of Lotta Continua, and American GIs took home with them—directly and via circuitous routes—lessons they learned through their contact with West Germans and others in the broad West German movement. Carla MacDougall has discovered evidence that the boxloads of literature that West German feminist groups sent to American counterpart groups went untouched, possibly because members of the latter did not speak German.[41] (Helke Sander claimed contemporaneously that she did not speak English, but as this was patently untrue, this claim was apparently a protest against the limits of some American feminists' ability to reach past their own national borders.) But West Germans clearly did affect their American counterparts, and vice versa. Former SDS President KD Wolff's well-documented return to the United States in 1969, visiting leading lights of the American movement as well as getting himself called before the US Senate, is one well-known example of this influence. As Martin Klimke has brought to new light, the SDS representative from Hanover Michael Vester was an important source of counsel for Tom Hayden in drafting the Port Huron statement in 1962—basing his recommendations on his experience in the SDS back home.[42] In Norway, the anticipation was so great to hear Rudi Dutschke speak that an audience packed to bursting waited some six hours for the SDS and extraparliamentary leader to arrive, until it became clear, soon after the talk was to have started, that the overwhelmed Dutschke had only just arrived back in his West Berlin apartment from another engagement.[43] But it was at least as often through the less "famous" that this exchange and influence took place. Shana, an American student who worked closely with Herbert Marcuse at

UCLA, first understood the value of his thinking for the protest movement in the US via contact with West Germans she had met. Martin, who co-founded a heterogeneous SDS chapter in Paris while pursuing a doctorate, organized a protest at the West German embassy after the April 1968 shooting of Dutschke. As increasing numbers of French people joined them, they decided to continue their protest on the Latin-Quarter Boulevard St. Michel. "That was," he claimed, "so to speak the first demonstration of the May movement," the "Paris May."

Certainly this was a significant event; Martin's very perception of his role is also notable. Of course, this was the stuff of broader West German fantasies as well. Just as Che Guevara had inspired many Congolese, and Frantz Fanon, West Africans (via Cuba and Algeria, respectively), so some West German activists imagined themselves in the roles played by Jeanne Moreau and Brigitte Bardot in Louis Malle's 1965 *Viva Maria:* as Europeans leading Mexicans to revolution (while satisfying themselves sexually). The movie played for months in particular West German film houses, inspiring the 1965 eponymous grouping founded by Dieter Kunzelmann and Rudi Dutschke, among others. Buoyed by his study of Spanish Republicans, 23-year-old Karl took off for Spain in 1976 in order to contribute his political experience, already quite considerable, to the role of youth in transforming post-Franco Spain. He returned home to West Germany with a Spanish wife. Monika left Frankfurt at eighteen, attending university and joining in protest groups in Israel. (She then moved back to the US, married an American, and moved with him to Amsterdam—and then back to Frankfurt, where she shared her experience with the others in the flat where she squatted.) West German activists played a role in Czechoslovakia, well beyond Rudi Dutschke's renowned speech in Prague's Wenceslas Square, in early spring 1968. Sibylle Plogstedt worked with local activists there for an extended period, before a two-year imprisonment in that country.[44] Others had active communications with Polish and East German activists. These communications and even visits lasted throughout the 1970s, and in the early 1980s blossomed into the largest transnational protests up to that time, over the threat of renewed nuclear build-up, and as the Eastern European reform movements grew. In this instance, as in others, the influences were bidirectional, and often circulatory, a complex and indirect set of movements. The Soviet crushing of the Prague Spring was a key element in the fracturing of the SDS, so invested were many West German activists in the Czechoslovak movement, and so inspired by it.

West Germany and Beyond

For those growing up and coming to activism in West Germany in the postwar decades, change and encounters with difference were critical pieces of their experience. This manifested itself in a desire for change and an interest in trying out new perspectives. Some of these activists became convinced of the singular "rightness" of one or another of these perspectives, adopting a dogmatic stance for shorter or longer periods, stalwart in the need to convince others of this rightness. Certainly most of these individuals developed strong opinions of how things might and even should be and, as activists, worked to advance such a vision. In turn, activists were not in every instance so open, nor were encounters with "difference" conflict- and pain-free. But the dogmatism of some and even the deluded-seeming nature of certain of these visions should not prevent recognition of the far more lasting impact that contemporary activists made on the political culture with this sense of "opening up to the world," a sense of multiple perspectives and multivocality. This is neither a question of heroizing nor defending the individual actors; rather, it is about acknowledging the broad range of these actors beyond a "tiny, radical minority" and recognizing in turn the significant and largely salutary role that informal activists played, drawing on the circumstances of their lives and interacting with them to create new circumstances. In the present moment of accelerating "globalization," in which things sometimes appear at least to be the same from one spot in the world to the next, when not incomprensibly different, these earlier efforts to embrace and to understand difference, and to use that experience to envision new possibilities, seem all the more important.

Notes

1. With acknowledgment that West Berlin was not formally a part of West Germany, or, the Federal Republic of Germany (FRG), for convenience I include it here in references to the FRG.

2. The terms "New Left" and even "activist" can both be unnecessarily limiting. I use "New Left" to relate to the larger, postwar, broadly extraparliamentary movement (also APO, extraparliamentary opposition) between ca. 1960 and 1980. I use "activist" to designate those politically active in a great variety of ways, and, in all cases here, over the course of several years at least. On the phenomenon described here, compare too Michael Vester et al., *Soziale Milieus im gesellschaftlichen Strukturwandel* (Frankfurt am Main, 1991).

3. On this see too Belinda Davis, "What's Left? Popular and Democratic Political Participation in Postwar Europe," *American Historical Review* 113, no. 2 (April 2008), 363–90.

4. Consistent with the broader movement, this source base includes some whose names were and/or are widely known and a majority who were less well known outside particular communities, but whose role was nonetheless individually and collectively critical. Informants in the latter category are identified by pseudonym. Informants were identified through a combination of written contemporary source material and snowball technique. Themes I identify among informants' interviews are corroborated by contemporary sources and memoirs.

5. There has been an explosion of historical literature on "Americanization" and related concepts. The most useful works have identified the complex and paradoxical effects, likewise the ambivalent reception, and the limits of its role. Compare with specific

reference to the Federal Repbulic, Kaspar Maase et al., eds., *Amerikanisierung der Alltagskultur? Zur Rezeption US-amerikanischer Populärkulture in der Bundesrepublik und in den Niederlanden* (Hamburg, 1990); Axel Schildt, *Ankunft im Westen: Ein Essay zur Erfolgsgeschichte der Bundesrepublik* (Frankfurt am Main, 1999); Ulrich Herbert, ed. *Wandlungsprozesse in Westdeutschland: Belastung, Integration, Liberalisierung 1945–1980* (Göttingen, 2002). Additional work spans the century and other parts of the continent.

6. Even the increasingly cosmopolitan and "global" character of the first third of the century was largely limited in Germany to a few cultural and/or industrial centers. Nazi Germany in turn represented no total cultural "autarky." But the spread of "outside" cultures to far reaches of (West) Germany society, if unevenly, was new. Among discussions of "global 1968," Ronald Fraser et al., *1968: A Student Generation in Revolt* (New York, 1988); George Katsiaficas, *The Imagination of the New Left: A Global Analysis of 1968* (Boston, 1987); Etienne François et al., eds., *1968—ein europäisches Jahr?* (Leipzig, 1997); Aldo Agosti et al., eds., *La cultura et i luoghi del '68* (Milan, 1991); Carole Fink et al., eds., *1968: The World Transformed* (New York and Cambridge, 1998); Ingrid Gilcher-Holtey, ed., *1968: Vom Ereignis zum Gegenstand der Geschichtswissenschaft* (Göttingen, 1998); Arthur Marwick, *The Sixties: Cultural Revolution in Britain, France, Italy, and the United States, c. 1958–c. 1974* (New York, 1998); Jeremi Suri, *Power and Protest: Global Revolution and the Rise of Détente* (Cambridge, MA, 2003); Andreas W. Daum, Lloyd C. Gardner, and Wilfried Mausbach, eds., *America, the Vietnam War, and the World: Comparative and International Perspectives* (New York, 2003); Martin Klimke and Joachim Scharloth, *1968 in Europe. A History of Protest and Activism, 1956–1977* (New York, 2008). Important correctives include efforts to elucidate variable influences in many directions as well as the notable interactions between Western and Eastern Europeans. On transnationalism, see the introduction to this volume.

7. Compare e.g. Coen Tasman, *Louter Kabouter: Kroniek van een Beweging 1969–1974* (Amsterdam, 1996); Donatella della Porta et al., eds., *Social Movements in a Globalizing World* (London, 1999); Bernd Weisbrod, "Eine ganz unamerikanische Tante: Die BBC und der nationale Mediendienst in der Nachkriegszeit," in *Alltag—Erfahrung—Eigensinn: Historisch-anthropologische Erkundungen*, ed. Belinda Davis et al. (Frankfurt am Main, 2008), 279-92.

8. The overwhelming majority of informants moved three times or more in childhood. Compare variously Axel Schildt, *Moderne Zeiten: Freizeit, Massenmedien und „Zeitgeist" in der Bundesrepublik der 50er Jahre* (Hamburg, 1995); Klaus J. Bade et al., eds., *Deutsche im Ausland, Fremde in Deutschland: Migration in Geschichte und Gegenwart* (Munich, 1992); Pertti Ahonen, *After the Expulsion: West Germany and Eastern Europe, 1945–1990* (Oxford, 2003). Family constellations were also highly mutable.

9. Jeanne was an exception, finding the constant moves traumatic because of the secrecy of the conditions.

10. Compare with Alon Confino, *Germany as a Culture of Remembrance: Promises and Limits of Writing History* (Chapel Hill, 2006).

11. There is considerable recent historical work on "generation," related to 68ers and others. Informants' testimonies corroborate the highly subjective nature of the concept, and therefore the liability of focusing too limitedly on birth year. One example

of this arose at the conference on which this volume is based, at which historian Detlef Junker characterized himself as a member of the "skeptical generation," while Rainer Langhans identified as a '68er. Both were born in 1940. See Belinda Davis, *The Internal Life of Politics: The "New Left" in West Germany, 1962–1983* (forthcoming). Within and beyond the birth cohort examined here there is evidence of younger activists taking their cue from older ones, and also vice versa.

12. This skepticism contrasts with findings in Ulrich Herbert, "Good Times, Bad Times: Memories of the Third Reich," in *Life in the Third Reich,* ed. Richard Bessel (Oxford, 1987), 97–110; compare also Helmut Schelsky, *Die skeptische Generation: Eine Soziologie der deutschen Jugend* (Düsseldorf and Cologne, 1957). Here too birth year is one significant but highly ambivalent indicator.

13. On travel in Nazi Germany variously Shelley Baranowski, *Strength through Joy: Consumerism and Mass Tourism in the Third Reich* (Cambridge, 2004); Elizabeth Harvey, *Women and the Nazi East: Agents and Witnesses of Germanization* (New Haven, 2003).

14. Among works on West German travel, Hasso Spode, ed., *Goldstrand und Teutongrill* (Berlin, 1996); Haus der Geschichte der Bundesrepublik Deutschland, ed., *Endlich Urlaub! Die Deutschen reisen* (Cologne, 1996); Christiane Keitz, *Reisen als Leitbild: Die Entstehung des modernen Massentourismus in Deutschland* (Munich, 1997); Friedrich-Ebert-Stiftung, ed., *Urlaub und Tourismus in beiden deutschen Staaten* (Bonn 1985). Tourism was hardly new; its importance in the period was a question of degree and of context.

15. Detlef Siegfried, *Time is on My Side: Konsum und Politik in der westdeutschen Jugendkultur der 60er Jahre* (Göttingen, 2006) (also his chapter in this collection); Inge Marßolek and Adelheid von Saldern, eds., *Radiozeiten: Herrschaft, Alltag, Gesellschaft (1924–1960)* (Berlin, 1999); also Gabriele Huster, "Ich habe Mick gesehen!" in *CheShahShit: Die sechziger Jahre zwischen Cocktail und Molotow,* ed. Eckhard Siepmann et al. (Berlin, 1984), 87–89; Hamburger Institut für Sozialforschung (HIS), File Kommune 1, 03.01, 03.10 Briefe. A majority of these families had no television until the early 1970s, by which point most of these activists were out of the home. But see Konrad Dussel, "Vom Radio- zum Fernsehzeitalter," in *Dynamische Zeiten,* ed. Axel Schildt, Detlef Siegfried, Karl Christian Lammers (Hamburg, 2000), 673–94.

16. To be sure, there was an enormous movement, above all of youth into cities, from the countryside and from outside the country, during the Second Empire and the Weimar Republic, which also produced regular "culture clashes" and generated political activism. Compare Derek Linton, *Who Has the Youth, Has the Future: The Campaign to Save Young Workers in Imperial Germany* (Cambridge, 1991).

17. Inge Buhmann, *Ich habe mir eine Geschichte geschrieben* (Frankfurt, 1988), 8.

18. Volkhard Brandes, *Wie der Stein ins Rollen kam: Vom Aufbruch in die Revolte der sechziger Jahre* (Frankfurt am Main, 1988); compare Maria Höhn, *GIs and Fräuleins: The German-American Encounter in 1950s West Germany* (Chapel Hill, 2002); Heide Fehrenbach, *Race after Hitler: Black Occupation Children in Postwar Germany and America* (Princeton, 2005).

19. Compare Jennifer Miller, "Postwar Negotiations: The First Generation of Turkish Guest Workers in Germany, 1961–1981" (PhD diss, Rutgers University, 2008); Miller emphasizes still that many of this population lived isolated from ethnic Ger-

mans. See also Karin Schönwälder et al., *Siedlungsstrukturen von Migrantengruppen in Deutschland* (Berlin, 2007); Rita Chin, *The Guestworker Question in Postwar Germany* (New York, 2007).

20. Class distinctions had been challenged for virtually the entirety of the twentieth century in Germany, including in the National Socialist era, but this was yet one more significant set of challenges in the postwar period.

21. Compare Hermann-Josef Rupieper, *Die Wurzeln der westdeutschen Nachkriegsdemokratie. Der amerikanische Beitrag 1945–1952* (Opladen, 1993); Brian M. Puaca, "Missionaries of Goodwill: Deutsche Austauschlehrer und –schüler," in Arnd Bauerkämper et al., eds., *Demokratiewunder: Transatlantische Mittler und die kulturelle Öffnung Westdeutschlands 1945–1970* (Göttingen, 2005), 305–31; also Jeremi Suri's essay in this volume.

22. Compare Georg Picht, *Die deutsche Bildungskatastrophe* (Munich, 1964); Carl-Ludwig Furck, *Das pädagogische Problem der Leistung in der Schule* (Weinheim, 1964); also historical work underway by Linde Apel and Monika Mattes.

23. Following the German, those in school are identified here as "schoolchildren" and "pupils" to avoid confusion; "students" refers to those in higher education.

24. There were undoubtedly increasing numbers of "left authoritarian" teachers, anxious to impose a specific political worldview on schoolchildren, but evidence suggests this was far less prominent than is often asserted.

25. The gendered dimension of this experience is further explored in Belinda Davis, "Transnation/Transculture: Gender and Politicization in and out of the BRD, 1950s–1970s," in Martina Ineichen et al, eds., *Gender in Trans-it: Transkulturelle und Transnationale Perspectiven/Transcultural and Transnational Perspectives* (Zurich, 2009), 51–67.

26. Hiking trips and other organized youth travel in Central Europe long predated the era. On youth tourism after the war, Alfons Kenkmann, *Wilde Jugend: Lebenswelt großstädtischer Jugendlicher zwischen Weltwirtschaftskrise, Nationalsozialismus, und Währungsreform* (Essen, 1996); Rainer Schönhammer, "Unabhängiger Jugendtourismus in der Nachkriegszeit," in Spode, *Goldstrand,* 117–28; Christoph Köck, "Mit dem Finger auf der Landkarte. Abenteuerurlaub für alle," in Haus der Geschichte, *Endlich Urlaub!* 59–64; Axel Schildt, "Across the Border: West German Youth Travel to Western Europe," in *Between Marx and Coca-Cola,* ed. Axel Schildt and Detlef Siegfried (New York, 2006), 149–60; and Anja Bertsch's dissertation in progress.

27. Compare Ingo Juchler, *Die Studentenbewegungen in den Vereinigten Staaten und der Bundesrepublik Deutschland der sechziger Jahre: Eine Untersuchung hinsichtlich ihrer Beeinflussung durch Befreiungsbewegungen und -theorien aus der Dritten Welt* (Berlin, 1996); Jennifer Hosek, "Cuba and the Germans: A Cultural History of an Infatuation" (PhD diss., University of California Berkeley, 2004); Quinn Slobodian, "Radical Empathy: The Third World and the New Left in 1960s West Germany" (PhD diss., New York University, 2008).

28. Brandes, *Wie der Stein,* 8.

29. The military requirement went into effect in 1956, affecting males born in 1938 and after. Those applying as conscientious objectors could perform "substitute duty," and eighteen-year-olds living in West Berlin had no military requirement, one factor in the draw to that city. On inaccuracies in the notion of "student movement" and on the universities' role, both broader and more limited than is often portrayed, see

Davis, *The Internal Life of Politics*. "University" is used here for convenience, but it is in part a misnomer: the broader range of West German institutions of higher learning served as foci for activism, from technical institutes to art schools to institutes of teacher training.

30. Compare Belinda Davis, "The City as Theater of Protest: West Berlin and West Germany, 1962–1983," in *The Spaces of the Modern City: Imaginaries, Politics, and Everyday Life*, ed. Gyan Prakash and Kevin M. Kruse (Princeton, 2008), 247–74. Activists away from cities and universities sought means such as women's and youth centers to emulate the density of activity and community. The chapter here emphasizes an increase in both heterogeneity and propensity to activism across the country, if not as intense as on university campuses and in cities.

31. Of the fifty-three informants ultimately pursuing any higher education (fourteen of these via nontraditional paths), nearly twenty, overlapping with the previous category, hailed from backgrounds that would have made such pursuits extremely unlikely if not impossible in earlier periods. There was some disruption of the traditional class divides in the Third Reich, as political allegiance took precedence; the general upheaval of that period contributed further to some breakdown of class norms, as I have suggested. Thus I include in my count those with parents who worked blue- or low-level white-collar jobs, but also more complicated cases, such as instances in which the parents were long-term unemployed, although the mother came from the intellectual bourgeoisie.

32. Compare the contemporary series of handbooks describing demographic breakdown at the University of Göttingen, a traditional university, Studentenwerk Göttingen, "Die soziale Lage der Studierenden," which shows foreign students at about 5 per cent in 1969, not negligible, and higher elsewhere.

33. Compare Universitätsarchiv Tübingen, File "Afrikanische Studentenunion (ASUT) 1963–1966"; ibid., File "Griechische Studentenvereinigung 'Aristoteles' 1959–1966"; ibid., 117E/1138 File "Iranischer Studentenverein, 1961–1967"; and in turn Universitätsarchiv Frankfurt, Abt. 413–5, File "Studenten-Demonstration 1959, 22.2.61, 7.11.61, 29.1.62, 13.2.63," including activities of the International Student Organization.

34. See clipping on the demonstration, *FAZ* December 1963, from Universitätsarchiv Frankfurt, Abt. 413–5, File "Studenten-Demonstration 1959, 22.2.61, 7.11.61, 29.1.62, 13.2.63."

35. Universitätsarchiv Frankfurt, Abt. 413–5, File "Studenten-Demonstration 1959, 22.2.61, 7.11.61, 29.1.62, 13.2.63."

36. Compare a Frankfurt University administration representative's claim at a demonstration (indeed off-campus) that "The only one with domiciliary rights (*Hausrecht*) here is me!," cited in "Eine Sekunde für die Toten von Persien: Studentendemonstration vor der Universität. Polizei griff ein," *Frankfurter Rundschau*, 12 June 1963.

37. Compare the memoir of American student Elsa Rassbach, "Aktivistin gegen den Vietnamkrieg," in *Die 68erinnen*, ed. Ute Kätzel (Berlin, 2002), 61–80.

38. See the contributions by Detlev Claussen and John Abromeit in this volume.

39. Angela Davis, *Angela Davis—an Autobiography* (New York, 1988).

40. Compare Maria Höhn's contribution to this volume.

41. Carla MacDougall, "Councils of Women," presented at Workshop "Atlantic Crossings? Transcultural Relations and Political Protest in Germany and the U.S., 1958–1977," German Historical Institute, Washington, D.C., October 2003.

42. Martin Klimke, *The Other Alliance: Student Protest in West Germany and the United States in the Global Sixties* (Princeton, 2010).

43. Cf. Gretchen Dutschke, *Rudi Dutschke: Wir hatten ein barbarisches, schönes Leben* (Cologne, 2006), 158.

44. Sibylle Plogstedt, *Im Netz der Gedichte: Gefangen in Prag nach 1968* (Berlin, 2001); compare Jürgen Leinemann, "Träume im Kopf, Sturm auf den Straßen," *Der Spiegel*, no. 20, 1988, 140-66, 146; also Paulina Bren, "1968 East and West: Visions of Political Change and Student Protest from Across the Iron Curtain," in *Transnational Moments of Change: Europe 1945, 1968, 1989,* ed. Gerd-Rainer Horn and Padraic Kenney (Lanham, MD, 2004), 119–36.

Part VI

A Retrospective

Chapter 14

"We didn't know how it was going to turn out"

Contemporary Activists Discuss Their Experiences of the 1960s and 1970s

NB: This chapter draws on several public discussions with contemporaries, which accompanied the conference from which this volume originated.[1] It is not an exact transcript of these discussions but rather a compilation that blends excerpts from different discussions and has undergone modest editing in transferring oral speech into written language, where we have nevertheless attempted to preserve both the flavor of the spoken word and the stimulating atmosphere of the encounters. The following pages have been authorized by all those whose voices are recorded here. For their active and illuminating participation in the conference as a whole we extend our enormous gratitude.

Bernd Greiner: OK, now we've all sat, and inadvertently you got a feel of the time, because there was hardly ever any SDS meeting starting on time, right? (*Audience laughter.*) So, welcome …

The questions I've written down are closely related to the discussions and deliberations we've had over the last two days of this conference. 1968 was a moment in history of simultaneous revolutions all over the world, not only in [West] Germany, but also in the United States, in Japan, in Italy, in France, in Great Britain. You name it. Now, my question would be, in your perspective, what were the driving forces behind this simultaneous outbreak, and how important were the transnational exchanges going back and forth in that case between the United States and Germany in bringing this movement to the fore?

KD Wolff: For me in a way the student revolt started in 1960. [As a high school exchange student in Michigan, o]n weekends I would go with friends from Marshall to Kalamazoo. In the mornings I would play at the Junior Symphony Orchestra and in the afternoons we'd go to a meeting of young people at a friend's home, Quakers. And the old man, probably he was thirty-five or something like that, who was leading that group, he was friends with the people who were organizing the first "freedom rides" down south. And he told us all about it.

And so when Greensboro happened, when the sit-in at the lunch counter took place, at a place where they didn't want to serve blacks, they called in the police and all kinds of rednecks and poured ketchup and mustard on them. And I saw it all on TV that night in Marshall. And the next day I had to go to the Boy Scout meeting, and it always started with the pledge to the flag, and, you know, the pledge to the flag ends with "liberty and justice for all." And when we sat down, I said quite loud: "Except for Jews, Negroes, and all other nasty foreigners." (*Audience laughter.*)

I was then called before the board of the Rotary Club in Marshall, because they were sponsoring my stay, and of course at that time they wouldn't realize that I would one day be president of Rotary Club Frankfurt/Römer (*audience laughter*). And the first question I was asked before the board was: "Karl, how can you say a thing like that, after all the Germans did to the Jews?" And I must tell you, when he said that, I thought it was just crazy. But I must tell you, the question has stayed with me, and the older I get, the more I am sure how good the question was.

Tom Hayden: I don't remember transnational networks then. I remember being very involved in New York, New Jersey, or Mississippi, in the United States, and very aware that there was a revolution going on in Mexico, in France, in Germany, in South Korea, and having no access to it, but a sort of comfort that there was this parallel development going on. But Michael Vester was the first German SDS person I laid eyes on and he came to the Port Huron convention. And he had a huge influence on one element of the work, which was to explain to us why from a German and a European point of view the Cold War should be ended.

We saw the Cold War only inside of the United States: United States versus Soviet Union. We weren't thinking of the people on the ground in between the superpowers. So if you read the Port Huron Statement, you'll see a German SDS influence on this long section about why the Cold War had to be ended and why it had to be ended with the involvement of European social movements. And I haven't seen him since.

Michael Vester: I think the great historical merit of what Tom Hayden coordinated in the Port Huron Manifesto was that it represented an integrated formula for either participatory democracy or *autogestion* [as in France] or autonomy as in England, a common value. And this integrative effort of Tom Hayden was most helpful to us.

I just brought one of these reading lists with me that we had at that time. There were several interrelated sources of the international New Left. From England, we were reading two books of Raymond Williams, *Culture and Society*[2] and *The Long Revolution*,[3] and also a sort of founding manifesto, the essays of the outstanding authors of the early English New Left, edited by Edward Thompson under the title *Out of Apathy*.[4]

The ideas reunited in this New Left have their historical roots in a long tradition of emancipatory popular *and* working-class movements, including socialist and communist dissidents, particularly but not only in Europe. These ideas may be deduced from three sources. First, there was an internationalist, anti-war strain, revived in the new movements for a "third way" beyond the political and military blocs of the Cold War. Second, the lost cultural dimensions of the working-class movements and a socialist humanism were recovered: women's emancipation, ethnic emancipation, alternative everyday culture, emancipatory psychoanalysis, educational reform, etc. Third, the traditions of workers' democracy and other forms of direct democracy, both suppressed by authoritarian and fascist as well as Stalinist and communist bureaucratic regimes, were rediscovered. The workers' councils in the revolutions of Russia of 1905 and 1917, of Germany 1918, of Spain 1936, of Hungary and Poland 1956—and Rosa Luxemburg— were important points of reference for "ouvrierist" groups supporting democracy, civic rights, and codetermination at the workplace in many countries.

In this context, it should not be forgotten that the two SDSes had their common historical roots exactly here. The American SDS originally was a student section of the League for Industrial Democracy, especially linked to the United Automobile Workers, the UAW, a union with roots in ouvrierist democracy. (And the very place Port Huron was a camp of the UAW in the state of Michigan.) The German SDS cooperated closely with the Industrial Union of Metal Workers (IG Metall), which had roots in the historical workers' councils' movements of 1918 and which successfully struggled for the German Model of workers' codetermination after 1945. Thus, the common orientations of the two student federations towards direct democracy and a dissident socialist humanism are not surprising.

Ingrid Gilcher-Holtey: There was a new strategy of transformation developing, which had an element of transcendence. You can find these new ideas first in France and Britain in the circle around E. P. Thompson and Raymond Williams in 1958–59, and in the pages of the *New Left Review*. In parallel, and somewhat more philosophically, you can find them in the pages of *Socialisme ou barbarie* and *Internationale Situationniste*. Everything is there and then it comes to the United States, and Tom Hayden reads it, and he adopts its central ideas. And afterwards we [in Europe] adopt participatory democracy because of Michael [Vester], who gives us an idea what direct action is.

Bernardine Dohrn: I used to have a talk where I'd start with January 1968 and just spend the first five minutes reminding us of what happened that year. You begin the year in January with the Tet Offensive, and the indictment of Dr.

Benjamin Spock and five others for conspiracy to incite resistance to the draft. In February, the siege at Khe Sanh began. In March, the massacre at My Lai took place and the president, LBJ, announced that he was not running. In April, Dr. Martin Luther King was assassinated and the National Guard occupied twenty-two cities in response to a massive uprising. Students occupied the administration and three other buildings at Columbia University. And it just keeps going like that. Every month is filled with twenty-five events that would in normal times be just overwhelming, if you said them out loud all the way through, through December, through Mexico, through the whole thing. So it seems to me that you always want to step back and try to locate yourself in at least some of the historical events that were happening around the world, to know all the complex forces that were at work, because otherwise you are just in danger of reducing it to something interesting as a theory, but not as complex as the richness of the world.

The Vietnamese provided a transnational network because their liberation struggle had roots, across Europe, across the globe. They had a sense of internationalism, with people located everywhere except inside the United States. So the anti-war movement's connections with the Vietnamese had to be outside of the United States, whether it was Canada, France, Cuba, or Eastern Europe. In many ways it was that travel to meet with "the enemy," so to speak, the breaking of the notion of us and them, the humanizing of the Vietnamese, that also connected us with Europe, with Germany, and with all of you. One of the triumphs of the anti-war movement was to humanize the Vietnamese people, to put a face on their suffering, to argue against the notion that they're not like us, that they don't value human life as Americans do, that they are different, fanatics, willing to die by the millions. I think it is important to remember that the Vietnamese themselves created a powerful, transnational network before '68.

For me, the ability of that year, 1968, to bring a delegation to meet with the Vietnamese, was life-altering. It happened to take place in Budapest. It was supposed to take place in Prague. The day [in August] that we were supposed to meet up in Prague, the Soviet Union invaded Czechoslovakia. The conference was hastily moved. It followed immediately upon a meeting of the New Left in Ljubljana, in which many people from all over Europe and North Africa were present. This incredible meeting in Ljubljana took place the same week as the Democratic National Convention demonstrations in Chicago, the same week that the Soviet Union invaded Czechoslovakia. This convening of New Left forces, who consciously came together after the spring 1968 uprisings in both the US and Europe, including Eastern Europe, was hugely transformative because it helped us locate where we were in history and define more clearly the challenge for people inside the United States in that particular moment—as we used to say, inside the belly of the beast.

So that experience of spring/summer of '68 stands for a kind of specific engagement, not just intellectual engagement and not just exchange students, but a New Left conversation with revolutionaries from other countries, but most particularly the Vietnamese. I see the Vietnamese as the organizing force that brought us into contact with other revolutionaries from around the world. They had the most extraordinary global network ever, because they were located in so many places, and they were extraordinarily deft at educating, at bringing in the broadest possible coalition and engaging people with each other. So I see, strangely enough, the New Left connections with Europe and with Germany in particular developing in ways highly connected to the Vietnamese struggle and their unbelievable resistance to imperialism.

The last thing I just want to say about '68 is, as Rainer [Langhans] said it the first day [of the conference]: We didn't know how it was going to turn out. You're now looking at it as young historians. You're going to describe how it turned out so far, and then your work will be revisited over and over again by other historians and rejected. But when you hurl yourself into these kinds of struggles in history, you don't know. I certainly thought, by the end of 1968, that we were in a revolutionary situation. I think that if most people were honest who were active at that time, they would recognize that as familiar, no matter what choices they made subsequently. I think that the liberation struggles of the Global South, then defined as the Third World, put armed struggle and militancy on the agenda. That doesn't mean everyone decided what to do based on that, but it was on the plate of worldwide revolution and we wanted to be part of it.

Tom Hayden: I'd like to frame my own experience at this conference with acknowledgement of the friends on the panel, and make four points. First, I'm very sorry that Bernardine was not in Chicago [in August, 1968], because she could have been the Chicago Ninth. She could have taken me into the Weather Underground, straight from the courtroom, if possible. Secondly, Michael Vester I have missed for forty-two years or so, but I credit him with conceiving and writing the entire Cold War section of the Port Huron statement. And it was imported, along with one quotation from Pope John XXIII, directly into the Port Huron statement, and I thank you. And, KD, what can you say? He set the standard [at his 1969 hearing] for defiance of US senators … (*Audience laughter.*)[5]

Now, my four points are these: in this conference about the 1960s and 1970s, I have felt uncomfortable, because I am in a social movement now. It is the global movement against [the war in] Iraq, which could consist of leafleting the soldiers I saw in the streets of Heidelberg today. And it is the global justice movement against neoliberalism, expressed in my work around sweatshops. My question there is, when will scholars like ourselves begin to interview *these* activists, and put the story together as living history?

My second point is that, in five years, believe it or not, we will begin the fiftieth anniversary of everything that happened in the 1960s. We should be ready to resist those who are trying to impose amnesia, and we should be supportive of efforts to reclaim and restore the memory. This conference is a great start, and I thank you and hope that you continue.

My third point is that there is an underestimation of how close we came to winning significant victories in the 1960s, and more thought has to be given [to that]. I've written a paper on the subject that can be summarized in two quick points. Usually the assassinations are removed from the scope of analyzing the '60s. But John Kennedy was murdered when I was twenty-three. Robert Kennedy was murdered shortly after Martin Luther King. There were many other murders, but those three represented at least two opportunities to achieve a disengagement from Vietnam, and an effort, somewhere between token and serious, to confront poverty and racism in the United States: to end the Cold War and focus on poverty and racism. And no one can say with certainty how that would have turned out. All my research leads me to be certain that that effort would have happened if it was not for those murders. We should not leave abrupt and unexpected circumstances like assassinations out of our inquiries into history and how things happened.

And, finally, my one long sentence is my "Tom Hayden theory of social movements" that I've been working on for some time. But in trying to talk to younger generations or students, I try to make it simple, and I try to start as many words as possible with an "M". Reform and revolution result from the interaction between social movements and Machiavellian systems of power. The social movements began at the margins out of mysterious origins, before a moment comes that enables them to march to the mainstream, where they become political majorities, and allow the Machiavellians to then try to moderate their achievements, through demobilizing the movements in exchange for moderate progress. The backlash then begins. The final phase—and this is the end and the beginning—the final phase of the movement model is the stage of memory in museums. What is remembered and what is forgotten and who does the remembering and who does the forgetting is all-important in how movements end and how movements begin. And this conference is a wonderful laboratory for that kind of thought.

Bernd Greiner: Well, Tom, this was a terrifically elegant way to evade a question.

Tom Hayden: I know. I have been in politics for eighteen years.

Michael Vester: I think there was a very specific constellation of simultaneous influences [behind these simultaneous revolutions]. On the one hand, there was a radical change of everyday culture, especially in the young generation. I think it was first observed in the United States by a social democratic economist named Galbraith in this book on *The Affluent Society*.[6] And, for us, the change of everyday culture, the end of economies of scarcity, the possibility of emancipation, development of everybody, this was also a product of capitalism in its contradictions. And this gave rise to a young generation, whether political or not, whether intellectual or working-class, that had the feeling that the old rules of social order, of discipline and of nonparticipation, of hierarchies, were outdated, because now there were these possibilities. And this was, of course, part of the American Dream, but this was not taken in this ideological way, but as a new possibility. And this gave rise to these strong tensions, starting from the young generation in the early 1960s. 1960, for me also, was the start of this, I think because it was symbolized by the presidency of Kennedy, that there was an opening of social space, and this translated into politics, too. And it was also very, very important to feel this. And you could feel this every day when you opened the journals: you saw that things became possible that were unthinkable before.

And there was a second development. First, the young generations in everyday culture, second including also culture at the workplace. There was especially in Germany a strong degree of more rights for the working class, in that they were no longer slaves in the workplace. It is often forgotten, but they were really subjects of their work. But the leaders of the ruling class developed new factions, which wanted to modernize. And these new factions, intellectuals [who] were also technocrats, came into conflict with the more conservative parts of the ruling classes. You could well observe this in Czechoslovakia. Those who came to power for a short time in '68 were symbolizing a new faction of a new idea, and they were able to make coalition with the young movements, and with the popular movements transcending the youth. And so it is not true that the ideas created this or politics created this, but it was a collusion of these influences. And this is a very classical development, which happened in all revolutions. But whether a revolution becomes a political revolution does not depend on your wanting it or not, but … [rather] on the capacity of the political powers to manage such transitions.

And seen from now, the 1968 change was not the end for us. In '68 it seemed that a great disillusionment [had taken place]. The powers were stronger in France, the professional politics of [Charles] de Gaulle were very well managed, to get the thing down. And it was not so very well managed in Prague, and so on. But it was the beginning of an opening, with many small struggles, until the late 1970s, when we had these huge movements of peace, and so on, to change everyday culture. And the rollback really came in a very different way, the neoliberal rollback later.

Rainer Langhans: We felt that the kind of revolution that some of the refugees from East Germany within the movement, meaning Rudi Dutschke and Bernd Rabehl for example, envisioned was not radical enough, not really radical, because it aimed only at changing the [socioeconomic] system. And we felt that this was not enough, because the hearts and minds of the people would still be the same. As we could see at the time in the so-called socialist countries, it is not enough to change relations only on the surface. It is much more important to revolutionize what is a priori to politics, namely the private sphere.

We were, in that regard, following the Frankfurt School, which was in New York at that time, and its work on the authoritarian personality.[7] And we believed that that authoritarian personality was prior to and consequently shaped politics, which were made by these personalities who, therefore, had to be revolutionized. Otherwise we would be treating the symptoms instead of curing the causes. After all, the system is shaped by persons according to their basic socialization—social experiences they have made within the nuclear family.

We also had this really unique problem in the world, being the children of murderers. All other countries and peoples had been the good ones and had freed the world from the bad ones, from these really wicked people, which were the Germans. So we as the children of these parents, of these murderous parents, we felt that we had to do anything against that—that is, not only the system but also the personality of the people responsible for the system. And therefore we felt it was not enough to analyze the system or fight the system in one way or another, but that we had to change ourselves. If we changed ourselves, we would also change the world. And therefore we said: We need to live in quite another way, in a radically different way than our parents did, meaning we had to search for the new man, inventing a new kind of, I don't know, humanity in a way.

Changing ourselves meant we wanted to love, we wanted to be free, we wanted to really have fun. Because revolution has always been a very serious, very earnest thing. You cannot have fun with it, you cannot be full of joy about it, but it's always really serious and without shedding blood it's not a real revolution. So at that time we did something, which made us capable to be very different, and very un-German, being free and being colorful. And we believed that was the possibility to get rid of this fascism inside of us, inside of our parents, and especially inside of the system in which we were living at the time.

At first it all seemed possible. In fact, we didn't think of ourselves as a counterculture at first. That was a later development when the whole movement collapsed and we retired into small niches, countercultural particles, where people hoped to be able to prolong that new life a bit. At the beginning, however, there was a real, a holy experience of the possibility of a full life to be lived, not only in small circles but as a whole, as a global experience with all men. And when you had that feeling for a short time, for, I would say, one year, about one year only, then you will not be able to return to your earlier small sad existence. And we seemingly were forced to do that. So we were desperately thinking of ways to hold on to this experience, when we felt that the window of opportunity was closing. And then people say, of course, "Oh no, not without resistance." And there were different modes of resistance. Some of them were violent. I was not inclined to go down that road, because I had been in the [German] Army and I had learned to destroy and to shoot people and so on. And at that time, very unconsciously and unpolitically, I said, that won't work. I knew that the people who had the arms would never let us prevail.

Of course, we didn't succeed, but more than thirty years after that, some people are coming to me and saying for example, "You don't know me, but you have changed my life, because when I saw you, I changed my life." So it worked in a way, but it worked not as fast as we'd hoped. Back then we were young people who didn't know what was happening, and the question is—and I would like to put it to you, too—what was that '68 feeling or unrest, which all of us seized or grasped? Where was it coming from? Because, as far as I know, there is nothing similar in history.

Greiner: How do you explain that violence was perceived at the time as a means of political change? And, looking back after forty years, how do you perceive this legacy?

KD Wolff: Sometime in the 1960s, the Bundesgerichtshof, the highest German [criminal] court, passed a sentence on the people who had sat down on the tracks of a tram, and denounced that as violence. They had sat down and blocked the tram. In a legal situation like that, any kind of civil disobedience is violence, and perhaps that kind of debate in the early 1960s already helped obfuscate the real problems for the movement from within, of where to draw the line and where not to draw the line. And, looking back now at those questions, I find it very strange that, at least in Germany, the whole question of violence—violence against things, violence against persons—was always discussed in very moral terms and with very little historic perspective. We all know that revolutions can turn violent, and sometimes have to turn violent, but there was hardly any historic perspective in that debate, in Germany at least.

And afterwards, the way the Red Army Faction developed, and the West German media jumped on them and portrayed them as *pars pro toto* of the movement as a whole, we felt crippled for years, [torn between the dilemma] to separate us from them and their political goals, and at the same time not to support the kind of hysteria that the bourgeois press and the *Bildzeitung* in particular were propagating. When I look back on it today, sometimes I think we should have been more open in the debate. During the conference there was some talk about misconceived allegiances. These are debates that for years and years we would not have entered into in public. Now, I think that was really a mistake. In a way we didn't trust the wider public, and we thought some debates would have to be made out within the groups and within the movement. And that is not really possible in a mass movement with a democratic aim.

Bernardine Dohrn: I found the discussion of our three days extraordinarily helpful and interesting. A lot of the things that came up, learning about Germany, for example, throws us back on ourselves, and is a way of refracting the differences in a new dramatic way. So, I mean, I'll have to think about some of these things.

For the United States, I think, I would single out two characteristics that frame the discussion of how far militancy goes. One is what H. Rap Brown said in 1968: "Violence is as American as cherry pie." In other words, throughout American history, the colonizing violence, the presence of guns, the vigilantism, the genocide of the Native Americans, slavery and the lynching history, remain alive and well. You can see this legacy of state violence and racialized justice in the death penalty today. So, the facts are that America is soaked in violence—but, as James Baldwin said so famously, it is the innocence that is the real crime here. The deeds are bad enough, but it is the insistence on innocence that is the truly unforgivable crime. And of course America demands that innocence, so that kind of blood-soaked history of violence and continuing romance with violence through the culture is a recognizably dramatic characteristic.

Second is the profound history of American exceptionalism, which proclaims that whatever happens in the US, it wasn't going to be subject to the same dynamics as everybody else in the world. In contrast, the particular history of an expanding US empire, the combination of the civil rights movement and the increasingly insurgent nature of the Black Freedom movement throughout the country, in the army, around the world connecting the United States with the history of Africa, with the national liberation struggles in Africa, with South Africa, [were critical]. There was a sense of extraordinary breakthroughs in the suffocating history of America that we'd all been taught, and [of] recovering some real history for us. Of course, John Brown became part of that.

The increasing escalation of militancy and insurrection on the left, as it played out, occurred in that framework. And I find it interesting that, at least in the Weather Underground, we catapulted ourselves up to that brink—and then stepped back and took a different course than what took place here [in West Germany]. And, I would argue, we remained more in harmony with the mass movement. The mass movements and the underground movements and the armed movements, that continuum of militancy was more cohesive. ... there were less abrupt jumps in the level of militancy. For example, there were some 10,000 political bombings each year in 1970, '71 and '72, widely dispersed across the US, not led by any organization. These actions were decentralized, anarchistic, and they were almost all directed at known and recognizable military targets: research labs on campuses, entities that the military had financed that we had long agitated against. Or [against] repressive police forces that were murdering Black Panther Party members. I look back in most instances and am amazed how restrained these activities were, not how violent it was. With the exception of the Madison bombing that went awry and killed an anti-war researcher who was working at the Army math research lab in the middle of the night, this widespread campaign was directly solely against property, against symbols of state violence. People were not killed by these thousands of actions—with the one exception—and they were not killed deliberately, and consciously.

We never terrorized even the government except as a kind of a specter, an image that they built up of us. Terrorism involves an intentional infliction of physical harm and violence on civilian populations. Perhaps we scared the authorities, surely we took them by surprise. Oddly enough we became ridiculously reliable. When the Weather Underground carried out an action and called in a warning, the state knew when it was the Weather Underground and when it was somebody else. And law enforcement responded based on those warning calls in multiple cities and multiple contexts. So the predictability of it became an important factor in terms of minimizing harm.

I'm going leave to all of you historians and younger people the question of effectiveness. We failed to end the war; we failed to end racism and white supremacy. We certainly failed to make a revolution. Those were our major goals, so we failed. I don't think that's the end of the story, because the dynamic of social change and social justice is endlessly more complex. Many of the legacies of the "sixties" would not have emerged but for the anti-war and Black Freedom struggles—progeny such as the feminist struggle, the environmental movement, the gay, lesbian, bisexual and transgender movement, the rights of the disabled, the struggle for a living wage, homeless movements, immigrant rights—these are changes that define our world today. I don't particularly claim any advantages to the existence of the Weather Underground, but it was a part of a broad resistance that included people organizing in communities and factories, in anti-war mobilizations or in anti-racist activities, in feminist communes or gay and lesbian communities, as environmental activists and those forging the disabilities rights movement. No single sector of the movement was responsible for the flowering and diffusion of struggle; the initial freedom movements served as a catalyst and inspiration for new forms of liberation.

So I look back and I think we were restrained. The American war in Vietnam went on for over ten years. Two thousand people a day were being murdered across Southeast Asia. We were compelled to object, to resist, to try to bring the war home. Overall, you look at the grave crimes of the United States. I don't think we were brilliant. We came out of a tradition that was separate from a leftist tradition and ideology. It was both a strength and a weakness. We were reinventing things. But overall, I look at it and I think: We were on the side of freedom, peace, and justice and we were restrained, not excessive.

They were the terrorists, state terrorism, there's just no question about it. It gives me a modicum of pleasure to think that they, some of the people from that era such as Henry Kissinger, don't feel safe enough to travel to Europe, because they could be arrested as war criminals. It would be much easier to take responsibility for what we did wrong, if responsibility were apportioned to [Robert] McNamara and [Henry] Kissinger and Dow Chemical, then I'd be happy to step up.

KD Wolff: Thank you, Bernardine. When I saw the movie [*The Weather Underground*], I was really moved, because situations developed so differently here. In the 1980s, together with Wolfgang Pohrt, I showed the earlier Weather [Underground] movie, [directed] by [Michelangelo] Antonioni.[8] And by showing the movie and talking about you surfacing we tried to talk the West German public into an amnesty campaign.

We failed utterly. Almost all the leftists thought we were traitors. So we are back at the question: How German is it? And how militaristic the Red Army Faction was and decided to stay? And what you do when you lose a battle and how to retreat and how to surface and how to continue?

Germany is full of ghosts. The Nazi ghosts and the Shoah ghosts and also the Red Army ghosts. And any resistance group inside Germany is noticing it all the time. That question of what happened in the 1970s has not been resolved. There has been no debate, no true public debate. And there are still leftists who think when you want that debate to come to a certain peace that you are just traitors. I thank you again.

Bernardine Dohrn: I just want to comment on it for a minute, KD, if I may, because I don't think that we in the US have had a reckoning either, although activists have had a large measure of accommodation with each other. All you have to do is see this Swift Boat campaign against John Kerry to know that we're pretty easily confused in America about the history of the Vietnam War. The idea that a presidential candidate who in his finest moment came back as a decorated veteran and told the truth to Congress and to the public about the Vietnam War could be discredited by a couple of people who sleazed their way out of the draft through their parents' connections—I don't mean, nobly resisted the draft, I mean sleazed out of the draft—is an ultimate irony.

Before 9/11 there was a large group of us, both military veterans and anti-war and radical activists from the 60s and 70s, discussing plans to convene a truth and reconciliation inquiry in the United States, because the ghosts of Vietnam are very deep with us, too. And 9/11, you know, made that sense of being open and honest about that history virtually impossible. You're for us or against us, you have to wear the American flag pin and fly the American flag. The whole discourse coming from the authorities changed so dramatically that it's still on our "to do" list. I think it's still our obligation to have some honest and open accounting of state and corporate accountability, which might clear the way for organizational and individual responsibility.

Wilfried Mausbach: In keeping with the transatlantic motif of this conference, and prompted by this letter of October 1977, quoted in the film, which speculated about a return from the underground, I was wondering whether, while you were underground, you were following what was going on in this country in that very same month.

Bernardine Dohrn: We were aware of course of the Red Army Faction when we were underground, but really only from the newspapers. And I can't say we were more aware of it than we were of ETA and the Basques or the IRA or the Tupamaros in Uruguay; these were phenomena that were taking place in numerous countries. So, on some level we identified, on some level we didn't. We made a decision early on that we would not leave the United States. We made a collective group decision that we would not take money from anybody outside the United States. We wanted to illustrate that all of the US military and counterintelligence technology could not find us or destroy the resistance networks inside the United States. That became part of our point. So, our connections to other struggles outside the US were symbolically in solidarity, but functionally distant at that point.

I don't know enough to compare. Armed struggle was happening all over the world during that period of time, from South Africa and the Portuguese colonies, to Palestine and Latin America. It was on the agenda for people to contemplate. It wasn't necessarily the right thing to do, but anybody who pretends that it was outside what everybody had to consider is just in a fantasyland about history. It had to be a consideration. National liberation struggles all over: Africa, Latin America, and Asia were engaged in armed struggle for their independence from colonialism. And the Cuban revolution had happened because of an organized, armed insurgency, and the ANC was openly engaged in armed struggle against apartheid and capitalism.

From our point of view, we found in American history a whole strain of militancy becoming armed conflict and armed resistance: through the Wobblies (the International Workers of the World), Emma Goldman, and John Brown. How was slavery going to be ended? Was slavery ended peacefully? Slavery was not ended peacefully, you know. Would it have been worth another 400 years?

Someone broke the locks of the FBI office in Media, Pennsylvania, seized the FBI files, and began leaking them to the *New York Times,* discovered a massive illegal and secret program know as COINTELPRO that lead to the indictment and conviction of two top FBI officials and constraints on domestic spying that lasted until 9/11. We still wouldn't know about COINTELPRO today if somebody hadn't broken into the building in the middle of the night. Was that violent? I don't know if that was violent, but it was surely illegal. And so I insist on some continuum of militant activity that acknowledges that the line between civil disobedience, direct action, and violent crime is complicated. It's an ethical conundrum; it's a complexity that you never want to let go of.

Michael Vester: I also think militancy, armed struggle, violence is a phenomenon of a certain historical constellation. The youth movements have their right and their prerogative of an immediacy and personal style of expression, and they don't have a sense of institutional mediation of conflicts, actually. And the institutional rules, which governed [in the] 1950s and also the 1960s, were authoritarian, militaristic, governed by secret services and information, and by a press which used to dramatize and just waited for provocations allowing authoritarian initiatives. That's the German perspective, the European perspective also. In Italy it was very similar to Germany; in France it was a bit different. And if a capitalist system has a regulation system which is not able to deal with these conflicts, it is inevitable that there are energies of conflict, which include anomic types of violence, and this cannot be avoided. But it is not the fault of these persons who do that, but of the whole field situation.

And what we learned in Germany, there I come to the second part of your question, was that, during the 1970s, we had to digest all these experiences. We had very new international experiences. We had revolution in Portugal and Nicaragua. We saw the things [that] were going on. It was quite important, but they were not going on without the institutional dimension. We could not rely on spontaneity and immediacy, not totally, but we had to think about how institutions of democracy had to be organized to get these social tensions regulated. So, the second big movement we had in Germany, the peace movements and also these numerous grassroots movements, which are rarely mentioned nowadays but were very important new social movements of the late 1970s, had a totally different style. They were "*koalitionsfähig*," able to build coalitions; they were adaptable to the values of a large part of the intelligentsia, and to large parts of the population. The outright violence presented by the RAF did not evoke any sympathy from anybody, because it violated values also of the humanistic part of the population in a very offensive way.

And these new movements were able to build a big popular coalition of the intelligentsia and the working classes. I went to the First of May [anti-war demonstration] in 1980 or '81 with just a sheet of paper against these [Pershing II] missiles, and I had 1,200 signatures of workers, of just ordinary workers. Then we had numbers of demonstrators in Germany in the early '80s that we [couldn't have imagined] in the '70s. It's like an iceberg: under the surface we have a radical change of everyday culture. And that's what the neoliberals didn't grasp. They think they can go back to these deregulated systems. And these deregulated systems, destroying the institutions to regulate social conflict, this is an attempt to call back this spirit of anomic conflict. And neoliberalism is organized anomie, actually. And in a way that tries to start a war of everybody against everybody.

Therefore, I think, at present we are eager to observe any movement to return to these institutions, go back from a militant anti-Keynesianism, to go back to solidarity movements, [and to see] that in the ruling class there is a shift coming about. In Germany, that's what we observe. This militancy, armed struggle, and violence were a warning for us to recapitulate historic lessons: how immediate action and personal action can be translated into reasonable, institutional mediation of conflicts. And this is what, while growing older and surviving, could be our contribution also to political culture in our countries. This fits into what you say, when fifty years will be over soon, this will be the answer, this will be the harvest, this might be the harvest, that we could give an answer to this relation of the immediate and the mediation.

Bernardine Dohrn: Can I disagree with Michael [Vester] in [response to] your terms about mediating conflict and institutionalizing reform?

We don't claim very many victories, but I think the broad anti-war resistance was the cradle for numerous subsequent social movements. And we had our versions of institutionalizing reform. In the United States, the War Powers Act constrained the ability of the US to invade another country, and forced them to resort to more limited though deadly proxy wars—and to a terrorist strategy in Africa, and in Central America, and ultimately Afghanistan. I think the development of international law and human rights comes in part out of these struggles. I think the Watergate impeachment was a direct result of the anti-war struggles. It was a sort of an impeachment before we had impeachments. The abolition of the draft, the constraints on the FBI and the CIA which lasted until the Gulf War, were part of this legacy. Not perfect, but significant, worth noting. The incredible success of the conspiracy trial meant that the next ten conspiracy indictments and the grand jury strategy and massive effort to make some people untouchable didn't really work in the United States and solidarity prevailed.

And, as to the hearts and minds, they were not able to win the American people to the war in Vietnam. And to some extent we were able to challenge racism. However, in place of that kind of sense of government as benign, we've ended up with the legacy of cynicism, rather than a clearly defined, analytical left. Nobody expects government to be anything other than lying and corrupt.

Michael Vester: What's the difference with my position? I didn't …

Bernardine Dohrn: … I'm trying to understand how the most virulent empire maybe in human history, the US today, my government today, how do we mediate that conflict into institutions? It seems to me that the momentum of empire, the grab for resources, the control of oil and natural resources and waterways and labor on markets, is only going to play itself out in confrontation, with whatever the next one is, China, India, whatever is next. So, how do you, I don't even understand the language of mediation in this context, that's what I'm saying.

Michael Vester: I think what I'm relating to is a discussion introduced by [Gøsta] Esping-Andersen and others, talking about certain paths, institutional paths, which capitalist countries [take]. A large part of the discourse is that you can distinguish the capitalist countries by the way of institutional mediation. And you have the sort of democratic path, which was developed especially in Sweden, and there you have people like [Gunnar and Alva] Myrdal and others, who [figure] the working class as being economic citizens in a society. Then we have the Central European model, of conservative, patriarchic, hierarchical [society], but nobody is thrown out. That is, the Italian, or French, or German conservative model of regulating is that we have patriarchy, but we don't have outcasts in the society. And that's how they bribe the population, because everybody gets his place. And then we have the liberal path, which is in the Anglo-Saxon countries, which I before called anomic, which is the sharpest criticism I can make. We call this the anarchy of war of everybody against everybody. And it really is an almost civil war situation into which you are forced. And therefore I said before, I cannot talk about the United States, because I'm talking [about] the two European paths, the Mediterranean-conservative and the North European, which is more egalitarian. And if you look to the North European, it's not all social democratic bureaucracy. You have a very strong female and woman position in the whole institutional system and, and this is integrated into a progressive equilibrium of forces. Of course there are other paths; in Eastern Europe, this is even also different. But it is that we have a sort of regulation.

Tom Hayden: I think that we're in a very similar situation. Instead of the Cold War, we have the war on terrorism, and instead of the US-Soviet relationship, we have the World Trade Organization. In response to that, we have a global movement that is rarely studied, that involves many millions of people. I've been to many of these demonstrations. At the Seattle demonstration, there was a network of anarchists who have something kindred to the European consciousness about their anarchism. And they targeted the windows and property of Starbucks and other facilities that were consumer outlets that they perceived as exploiting youth culture. You would think that it was Leningrad. For months, the media and the FBI and local police featured the Seattle anarchists as the symbol of the new revolution that was coming. And the result of that was precisely what the establishment wanted: to try to sow fear into the middle class and into the moderate voters, and divert attention away from the fact that this was an unrepresentative body of world trade ministers, who were losing jobs in America, supporting sweatshops, supporting repressive police, here and especially in Latin America, South Korea. But when you look back on the anarchist terrorists, [they] are sort of forgotten. And my point is that there will always be a moment of like disturbance in the middle-class social order and in the media—and then things move on.

In Cancún, at the next big meeting of the World Trade Organization, I was at the fence. I'm too old for this, but I tried to watch it and record it. And there was a South Korean farmer that committed suicide in front of my eyes. There were fifty to a hundred so-called anarchists from several countries, who came to attack the fence. It was, ideologically, "don't fence us out." The Mexicans, the government gave the orders to deescalate the violence, because they had apparently a different agenda than the American government. They did not want to make it appear that the Mexican security forces were repressive and were shattering the skulls of young people, because Cancún is a tourist resort perhaps, because the Mexican police have a worse image. But I sat there, stunned at how the United States security forces would have to learn from Mexico: that there is a way to handle radical civil disobedience without gassing people, batoning people, locking them up. And the people who were arrested were asked by the Mexican police if they wanted to go back to the demonstration side in an air-conditioned bus to make plans for the next day, instead of beating them up, gassing them, torturing them and scandalizing themselves.

So what I learned is that violence can be turned on and off by the situation, the field of energy that you're in, including what the media wants, and what the powers want. A last point, for example. I agree with Bernardine that the apparent differences between here and the United States, the 10,000 bombings in the United States were in that case not widely reported all the time, because that would be too scary for the image of a government that claims to monopolize the use of force. So they had a devastating effect on the morale of the institutions, because it represented a cost, the alienation of the future generation, as Martin [Klimke] said. They were very worried about what the next generation of leaders would be like in America, if they all grew up feeling that violence against the state was legitimate sometimes, if they all grew up believing in extraparliamentary opposition and so on.

But my point is, this [is] where it started. In 1964, the key moment for me was [when] the civil rights movement tried to rupture and reform the Democratic Party by organizing poor people in Mississippi into a Democratic Party, a state party. They started having to risk their lives to vote. Then they went to parallel institutions. They had 90,000 people sign votes as if they counted. This was on the same day that John F. Kennedy was murdered. They then organized in precincts, and organized delegates, and followed the rules, and they qualified as a legitimate Democratic Party, and they came to the [Democratic National] Convention [in Atlanta], playing by the rules, testifying in front of the Democrats. And the declassified documents from the White House show that President Johnson said: "They had to be stopped, because if their issue ever got to the floor of the convention, they would win." The Democratic Party chose the Mississippi Freedom Democratic Party. This happened at the same time that the United States government, under that same Democratic leader, bombed North Vietnam for the first time, on the false, fabricated pretext of the Gulf of Tonkin. The bodies [of civil rights workers] were buried in Mississippi as the planes went to Vietnam. The rejection was felt on all levels. Civil rights movement, youth movement rejected, rejected. Black people from the South rejected, rejected, in favor of a war and in favor of a segregated party.

There is nothing worse than the disillusionment of young idealists with their liberal elders who are caught in a compromised moral situation. That was for me the turning point. The choice was made that we would not look at poverty and racism. We would invade Vietnam. And that is the historical point when the Black Panther Party was founded. And if you inflict shame and disillusionment and violence on young people deeply enough, their violence is an inevitable psychological response and political response. I just don't know why administrators of power don't understand this, or whether some of them want this, because it's as clear as purified crystal to me how violence is created. And once it starts, you know, like many things in social movements, it's governed by its own dynamics and laws. It can't be switched off by moral decisions by individuals. Those who want to end their own violence need help from those who are instilling the violent feelings.

And so we went through a six- or seven-year period of acute violence, where it was just in the air. Did you start as a violent person? Did I start as a violent? Do we look like violent people? We became sort of violent. And then now we're here. We're sitting here with you, commenting, but I could still be provoked to violence. I could be. I know exactly what the authorities would have to do. It would be harder this time, but I know they could do it, because I know it's in me. And I can't stand a system that tries to inflame the need of violence rather than contain it and modify it and, you know, treat it as a danger to both parties.

Wilfried Mausbach: OK, I think I have a question that refers to this transition that was obviously made from the discourse of the civil rights movement, and on to the Vietnam War, as a major issue with all its consequences. In Lyndon Johnson's daily diary there is this entry of 4 August 1964 when two things happen. LBJ has a meeting and decides to bomb North Vietnam, and at the same time he gets this message about those three civil rights workers (Michael Schwerner, Andrew Goodman, and James Chaney), whose bodies are found in Mississippi. And then you have these letters from Freedom Summer volunteers in Mississippi saying, we can't have this war now, because then our cause here will suffer. So it seems that at that point the war seemed to be kind of an indirect problem in that it negatively affects the civil rights movement. But then that obviously changes, and I was wondering whether any of you can elaborate a little bit more on how you made this transition?

Helen Garvy: With difficulty. I got involved mainly because of the civil rights movement. I'd gone on peace demonstrations before that, but the civil rights movement was the center for me and Vietnam was very far away. When things were starting in Vietnam I really didn't understand how important it was going to be and I resisted taking that on as an issue. Then it soon just kind of cascaded on us and you just couldn't avoid it. I think at first we thought maybe it was going to go away, if we just kept doing the civil rights work we were doing, which we thought was incredibly important. We didn't ask for Vietnam, but we couldn't avoid it.

Robert Pardun: You remember some members of SDS took the position in 1964, "Part of the Way with LBJ." We knew that President Johnson was lying. He kept telling us that he was not going to send any Americans to a land war in Southeast Asia. This was important because the people elected him by a landslide on a platform of peace and his "War on Poverty." He could have continued his token progress on civil rights and poverty and stayed out of Vietnam. SDS recovered quickly and had an anti-war march in early 1965. SNCC had a harder time but they put out a statement against the war. We all knew that war in Vietnam would be the end of the civil rights and anti-poverty movements as we knew them.

Bernardine Dohrn: Yes and no. Maybe the end of the Southern one, because I first got involved by going to work also in the civil rights movement with Dr. King when he came to Chicago in 1965. He moved his whole operation to Chicago at that point. I went to work in the West Side of Chicago, when the focus was segregated and substandard housing and racial discrimination. By the end of the year I was being asked more and more, as a law student, to do draft counseling on the West Side of Chicago. We were demonstrating at 5 a.m. every morning as the draftees came in to the armory. We're imploring them to not step forward and telling them about the Vietnam War. So, to me, by the spring of 1966, winter '65/spring of '66, you know, the civil rights movement had come North to become the Black Freedom movement, the urban rebellions and military occupations were happening and the Vietnam War was in full play.

Helen Garvy: And there were a lot of complex things. I was working in a community organizing project in Hoboken, ten miles from where Tom [Hayden] was, in a primarily white community that was very urban but felt like a small town. We were working on a lot of economic issues that were important in the community. And we had long and very difficult discussions. What do we do about this war? I mean, we were working in this community. The US in the 1950s had gone through a whole period of McCarthyism and a lot of anti-communism and anybody who stood up would get attacked. We were afraid that all the work we were doing in these communities was going to just go down the drain if we stood up and started opposing the war. We would get red-baited and attacked for being communists.

And so for us, personally, it was very difficult. I remember the first time in Hoboken, which was right across the river from New York City. People in Hoboken didn't work in New York—now they do, but they didn't then. But there was a commuter train. People got off the train, got on a ferry and crossed to New York. We decided we were going to take leaflets and go down and leaflet both around the town and at the train station. People knew us by that time and we knew we were making a decision that we were then going to have to deal with the war from then on. And it turned out fine. I mean, the people in the town that we were working with didn't reject us, but it was very scary. It seemed to us that it might be an either-or proposition.

Robert Pardun: I moved to Texas in the fall of 1963 for graduate school. I knew nothing about Vietnam at that point. I had just gotten to Austin a month before and had gone to hear a speech by Madame Nhu who wanted to get our support for the coming war. As I walked out the door there were several guys handing out literature. Everyone was avoiding them because nobody in Texas really wanted to be confronted with something like that. So I went over to talk with them and discovered that these guys and lots of other people had been involved in the civil rights movement in Austin for the past two or three years. I got involved in this civil rights activity by organizing an SDS chapter and then I went to Mississippi during the summer of 1964. Following that I was hired by the SDS national office as a regional campus organizer. I was to get some virtual hundred dollars which never showed up (*audience laughter*).

I dropped out of school and was traveling full time organizing SDS chapters. Not being a student meant that I was eligible for the draft, so there was a whole series of communications between me and my draft board about whether my working in the civil rights movement was more important than going to Vietnam. I expected that most students would be interested in the civil rights movement, but the question that kept coming up over and over was: "What's happening in Vietnam?" "What do you know about the dynamics?" "Who are the Vietcong?" Before I could go on I really had to learn a lot about the history of Vietnam, and it became obvious to me that the United States was on the wrong side. That's what I told the draft volunteers. That set off a small skirmish (*audience laughter*).

Helen Garvy: We were very committed to the idea of issues being interconnected, and when the war came on us, we also decided we were going to use that as an entryway to radicalize all the people who were coming into SDS because of the war, people who weren't necessarily radical in a very deep way. They were against this war, they were afraid of being drafted—and our job was to explain how everything was connected and try to get a deeper radicalism out of that gut reaction about Vietnam.

Tom Hayden: Just like the movement against Vietnam started out of a movement around civil rights and it felt like the movement was being hijacked by Johnson's decision to go to war, the global justice movement against the WTO started just like the movement in Mississippi, except it was the whole South of the world. There was an anti-poverty, anti-neoliberal movement and we were in our country a small part of it. But Seattle then of course became a huge media thing.

So when the Iraq invasion came I thought it would obviously be necessary to oppose Iraq, but it meant that the movement would be really strained. Because the same hundred or two hundred or three hundred thousand people that we needed to work on global justice felt an obligation to work on the street demonstrations against Iraq. The good thing about that is the numbers were good. Fifteen thousand in Seattle was just an average number, but the movement against Iraq was very big, as you know, globally. You had 500,000 people in Berlin. We had 500,000 in New York and probably a million or more around the United States, and 600 places around the country. And it was significant, because it was the largest entire war demonstration before the officials were going to war that I think ever happened on earth, but certainly in United States history.

Jeremi Suri: What is it like for you to sit in here, with a bunch of historians, like many of us, who didn't live through this period?

Tom Hayden: I'm a professor at a couple of universities, so I'm somewhat compromised. But I've had some fear and anxiety about this conference and about the institutionalization in the university of the study of social movements. I have problems with the return of an ivory tower quality, resulting in a clique of insiders who use very, very strange language that could never be taken to the mass media, that could never be taken to the public. But at this conference and in my own work I've modified my position. I feel that, if it's properly understood, the activists can give something to the academic, the academic could give something to the activists. It's kind of like approaching a scholarly career the way we would have approached community organizing, because a lot of us were graduate students and we left the university, not to join the Red Guard or, you know, to have crazy expectations about the working class. But because we learned in Mississippi at the very beginning the power of people who were said to be unqualified and uneducated, and that lesson from the real South among the African-Americans was a completely revolutionary lesson. And the job was to create a context for discussion until what they knew could be manifest in some kind of tactic or some event or a rally or a voter registration campaign.

So that's stuck with me and that's why I'm really upset and obsessed with the need now to begin interviewing the young activists of this generation's social movements. Because we were never interviewed. There is no record. We have no photographs on these days. We have fragmented memories.

Belinda Davis: I wanted to just pick up on one piece of what you just said, Tom, regarding moving beyond the workerism of the past. I'm wondering if the same might be said about youth. I mean, is there a reason to focus specifically and single-mindedly on youth? Is there something special about youth here?

Tom Hayden: No, I meant the new movements. [They are youth movements] in part. Not only.

Bernardine Dohrn: I think that the youth movement of today, as I meet up with it, is way too generous with us. They want us to be ancestors in their circle and they want us to talk to them and they want lessons and think they need to know lessons. But I think it's time to get us off the stage. I'm stuck in a frame that still seems valid to me, but probably isn't. And I want to come along with young activists, but I don't want them to defer to us. It was never only young people, of course, you can overstate the issue. But in Little Rock, Birmingham,

Selma, Soweto, Tiananmen, Seattle, without the motor force of young people literally walking out of school and hurling themselves into their historical moment on the side of justice, identifying with other people, coming at it with a humanist sense that you can identify with other, without that, we wouldn't know the world that we know today, we wouldn't have a South Africa that has a majority rule. I never thought I'd see that in my lifetime.

So, back to Jeremi, I must get twenty e-mails a month from junior high students in Texas or Iowa who are going to be me in a history fair. And, you know (*audience laughter*), [they] want to know what to wear ...

Tom Hayden: As you said, we didn't know how it was going to turn out.

Bernardine Dohrn: ... but we have been part of struggles where people died, where people's bodies or minds were broken, where people were imprisoned and remain incarcerated. For many, heavy prices were paid. Ironically, a generation of women become professionals around feminist theory—impenetrable in many ways to the ordinary reader unless you've got the code—without recognizing that they became academics to some extent on the backs of millions of women who got them there. The same for critical race theory, the same for Black studies, and so on. This appropriation of struggle for careers is perhaps inevitable, but maybe it would be good to be self-conscious about it in a more inquisitive, interesting way.

Detlef Junker: All of you have made it. You live a life as a bourgeois. You have marched through the institutions. Do you think it has corrupted you, or is it a compliment to the institutions? (*Audience laughter.*)

KD Wolff: That fits nicely with what I wanted to talk about anyway. Because, let me first say, that I enjoyed to sit with my friends here. And I haven't met Tom since the spring of '69, and I'm very grateful for the opportunity of this conference to meet again. But also when I'm listening, I have a strange feeling that they are still movement leaders somehow and apparently in a certain way I never was, perhaps.

Because I've had a life after the movement. And the fights that I'm engaged in, they are quite different, but I think they are worthwhile. And I must say there is a certain kind of talk about youth culture that I detest. Since more than ten years ago now, I'm working on publishing the complete works of Franz Kafka, and it seems like the German language libraries don't even want it. The workers want it even less. And I must say, without my experience in the States and without my connections to the American movement, the civil rights movement, probably I wouldn't even be publishing Kafka like that.

And one thing that wasn't mentioned at the conference, and I've been thinking about it again and again, and that is where Michael Vester comes into the play. Because, without him, I might at the time not even have heard about [what was going on in the US]. He wrote about stuff going on in the States, in the movement, the civil rights movement. He wrote in the magazine *Neue Kritik*. And he was the first to write articles where I read about the Free Speech Movement at Berkeley. And we talked about SDS and SDS and "the other alliance" and everything. But the existentialism of Mario Savio: to put your body on the line, because you would not want to lead a life anymore where you would just function for the machine, and the machine would be so heinous that you would decide this machine had to be stopped. Well, that's where we come from.

And, one thinks, you get ten e-mails and you're being invited as a historical witness, that's nice. But the historic debate here is quite different. About ten years ago there was one of those memorial debates about the student movement in Germany and I was on the panel with Joschka Fischer and Daniel Cohn-Bendit, right at the beginning of the Balkan wars. And when we had some rouge put on before we went before the cameras, Cohn-Bendit went like this and said: "Hach, I'm gonna mix up this group now. KD, you are moralistic, so you're probably in favor of the invasion, but the others …" Well and then he proposed to put the Bundeswehr on march to the Balkans, and, at that debate, I said, "You are warmongers." And, since that debate, which ran on the regional channels, I have not been invited again to any of those official celebratory debates.

Tom Hayden: I've been called a leader twice and I understand the label, but I don't think of myself as a leader so much as a follower and elder who is trying to find a proper role to play in the struggle over the memory of the past and the emergence of all these new movements. With respect to the establishment issue: a very good question. In my forthcoming book, I will have a chapter called "I Sold Out" (*audience laughter*), and it will be the most sophisticated explanation you've ever read about how people sell out. The most crucial element of it is never knowing that you have sold out. It's like becoming an alcoholic instead of a drinker. Then you need interventions to let you know that you've sold out. And when I was in office, I found that I had some freedom and I was called the conscience of the Senate. But it was like the freedom of a wild animal in large cage. And then I retired, because we have term limits. And nothing about the system was changed by my presence in it. I might have been helpful to movements. I was helpful to my constituents.

So I think, one, the lesson I learned was the system can't be changed from within, but that there are compartments in the system that should be occupied by real progressives, because you can claim resources, you can have press conferences, you can hire staff, you can introduce legislation that nobody else will—a sort of social democratic approach, which, because we don't have much of a third-party tradition in America, is unusual. We're like having a left wing of the Democratic Party within the Democratic Party. But, knowing the left wing, it will be, like, ten percent. It will never be a majority party. So that leaves you realizing that politics has to be in the service of movements, or otherwise it's just in the service of yourself. Because you'll always be a minority in office. But if you align yourself with social movements, you'll bring majority support to some big issues. That's not an appeal for people to enter electoral politics. I'm neutral on that issue.

Bernardine Dohrn: I want to say one thing back to KD and Michael, because you're having a moment of envying us, [and] I'm not sure why. The only advantage we have is that we live, you know, in the middle of the monster at the moment. Dr. King in the last year of his life said, "The greatest purveyor of violence on the earth today is my own country." I think that's still true, speaking as a citizen of the United States. And that puts on us, that's what I was trying to say before, a special obligation. And it creates a special set of contradictions and contexts. I don't want to be defensive about your question, of course we are bourgeois in the sense that we live in the same house [for a long period]. I've raised three children, helped our parents die and, you know, now we're a little bit free again to raise hell more and that's what I'm hoping to do. Both Tom and I are what I call stunt academics, you know, we're not real academics . . .

Tom Hayden: Speak for yourself.

Bernardine Dohrn: . . . So, you know, we're kind of clinging to the wall, you know, of respect. I mean, how could I be teaching at a law school? The irony is not lost on anyone, you know (*audience laughter*). I think it's great. I teach human rights. I take them to South Africa. I take them to Rwanda. We go inside jails. If you're up against the criminal justice system in America, every day in court with your students, you see a lot about power.

KD Wolff: Well, I understand where you are coming from, but I'm not really envious. But I must tell you there is a huge difference. And I just want to tell a story that might illustrate that a bit. As you know, as an exchange student in high school I stayed in Marshall, Michigan, a town of 10,000. It voted eighty percent for Nixon [in 1960]. Main Street Marshall is like the main street of any little town in the Midwest, except for a fountain. And there was a kind of a thermometer put up and people were distributing leaflets for a cancer drive and collecting donations. And I was sixteen years old and, without even thinking, I asked my host parents, "Who allowed them to do that?" And my American host parents, they wouldn't understand the question. Because, of course, you can put up a thermometer in the street at the fountain, and you can collect donations, and distribute leaflets on a cancer drive or something else, and that's part of your democratic heritage. And the way you can fight the monster from within: you're still part of a democratic tradition that is really yours. And we are claiming a little bit of it, too, so.

Tom Hayden: I have two children who are in their thirties and they are political to the bone, but they don't do anything political. They are both artists, and my son is a graffiti artist, who is totally committed to what he calls the Hip-hop generation. Does he vote? Yep. Does he support community organizing? Yes. Is he political? Yes. But for him there is not enough happening to go into the streets except for the once-a-year large march. But if the moment ever came, you know, if the force ever started to be felt in the air, there are a lot of people like him who would be out in the streets. It's not, that he's not in the streets. It's just that he's waiting for something. You may know what it is. You're saying that there is something coming.

Notes

1. The said discussions were:

   i) A public discussion with Rainer Langhans on 19 May 2005, following a screening of the film *Viva Maria!* (F/I 1965, Louis Malle, director). Moderator: Jakob J. Köllhofer (German-American Institute, Heidelberg).

   ii) A public discussion with Bernardine Dohrn, Helen Garvy, Tom Hayden, and Robert Pardun on 20 May 2005, following a screening of the documentary *Rebels with a Cause* (United States 2000, Helen Garvy, director). Moderator: Martin Klimke.

   iii) A roundtable discussion on 21 May 2005 termed "SDS Meets SDS: A Retrospective," featuring Bernardine Dohrn, Tom Hayden, Michael Vester, and KD Wolff. Moderator: Bernd Greiner (Hamburg Institute for Social Research).

   iv) A general discussion on 22 May 2005, concluding the proceedings of the conference "The 'Other' Alliance: Political Protest, Intercultural Relations, and Collective Identities in West Germany and the United States, 1958–1977." Moderator: Wilfried Mausbach.

   v) A public discussion with Bernardine Dohrn on 22 May 2005, following a screening of the documentary *The Weather Underground* (United States 2004, Sam Green and Bill Siegel, directors). Moderator: Carla MacDougall.

   All screenings and discussions took place at the German-American Institute Heidelberg (DAI), except (iv), which—like all other academic proceedings of the conference—was held at the Internationales Wissenschaftsforum Heidelberg (IWH). A warm thank you to both institutions for their wonderful hospitality.

2. Raymond Williams, *Culture and Society, 1780–1950* (London, 1958).
3. Raymond Williams, *The Long Revolution* (London, 1961).
4. E. P. Thompson, ed., *Out of Apathy* (London, 1960).
5. See U.S. Senate Committee on the Judiciary. Subcommittee to Investigate the Administration of the Internal Security Act and Other Internal Security Laws. Hearings, 91st Congress, 1st Session. Testimony of Karl Dietrich Wolff, 14 and 18 March 1969 (Washington, D.C., 1969).
6. John Kenneth Galbraith, *The Affluent Society* (Boston, 1958).
7. Theodor W. Adorno et al., *The Authoritarian Personality* (New York, 1950).
8. Zabriskie Point (United States 1970, Michelangelo Antonioni, director).

Contributors

John Abromeit is assistant professor in the Department of History at SUNY, Buffalo State. He is co-editor with W. Mark Cobb of *Herbert Marcuse: A Critical Reader* (New York, 2004) and (with Richard Wolin) of *Herbert Marcuse: Heideggerian Marxism* (Lincoln, NE, 2005). He is currently finishing an intellectual biography of the young Max Horkheimer.

Karin Bauer is associate professor and chair of the Department of German Studies at McGill University. A wide variety of authors and topics are examined in her publications, which include a book entitled *Adorno's Nietzschean Narratives* (Albany, 1999) and articles on Habermas, Benjamin, and Bachmann. Recently, she published *Everybody Talks About the Weather: The Writings of Ulrike Meinhof* (New York, 2008). She is presently working on issues connected to the formation of alternative cultures and counter-publics.

Detlev Claussen is professor of sociology and theory of culture and science at the University of Hannover. He has researched the phenomena of violence and terror since the 1960s, publishing widely on violence, anti-Semitism, and racism. Monographs include *List der Gewalt* (Frankfurt am Main and New York, 1982); *Grenzen der Aufklärung* (Frankfurt am Main, 1987, 4th edition 2005, English translation Berkeley, forthcoming); *Was heißt Rassismus?* (Darmstadt, 1994); *Aspekte der Alltagsreligion* (Frankfurt am Main, 2000); *Theodor W. Adorno: Ein letztes Genie* (Frankfurt am Main, 2003), translated as *Theodor W. Adorno: One Last Genius* (Cambridge, MA, 2008); also *Béla Guttmann: Weltgeschichte des Fußballs in einer Person* (Berlin, 2007). He is currently writing a contemporary critique of culturalist perceptions in world society.

Belinda Davis, associate professor of history at Rutgers University, is author of *Home Fires Burning: Food, Politics, and Everyday Life in World War I Berlin* (Chapel Hill, 2000) and co-editor with T. Lindenberger and M. Wildt of *Alltag—Erfahrung—Eigensinn: Historisch-anthropologische Erkundungen* (Frankfurt am Main and New York, 2008). She is currently completing a book on "The Internal Life of Politics: The 'New Left' in West Germany, 1962–1983."

Ingrid Gilcher-Holtey, professor of contemporary history at the University of Bielefeld, is an associate member of the Centre de Sociologie Européenne (MSH-Paris) and was visiting professor at St Antony's College Oxford in 2008–09. Her main publications include *"Die Phantasie an die Macht"*: *Mai 68 in Frankreich* (Frankfurt am Main, 2001); *Die 68er Bewegung: Deutschland - Westeuropa, USA* (Munich, 2008); *Eingreifendes Denken: Die Wirkungschancen von Intellektuellen* (Velbbrück, 2007); *1968: Vom Ereignis zum Mythos* (Frankfurt am Main, 2008); and *1968: Eine Zeitreise* (Frankfurt am Main, 2008).

Maria Höhn is associate professor of history at Vassar College. She is author of *GIs and Fräuleins: The German American Encounter in 1950s West Germany* (Chapel Hill, 2002) (published in German as *Amis, Cadillacs, "Negerliebchen": GIs im Nachkriegsdeutschland*), and co-editor with Seungsook Moon of *Over There: Living with the American Military Empire* (Durham, 2010). She has written additionally on German and American debates on interracial marriage, on the collaboration between German students and Black Panther GIs during the Vietnam War, and on how African-American civil rights activists imagined Germany.

Georgy Katsiaficas has been active in social movements including the anti-Vietnam movement since 1969. A target of the FBI's COINTELPRO program, he was classified "Priority 1 ADEX," meaning that, in the event of a national emergency, people like him were to be immediately arrested. For eleven years, he worked in Ocean Beach, California (as described in Andre Gorz's book *Ecology as Politics*) as part of a radical countercultural community. After living in Berlin for a year and a half, he wrote a book on 1968 globally, as well as *The Subversion of Politics: European Autonomous Social Movements and the Decolonization of Everyday Life* (Oakland 2006). For years he was active in the cause of Palestinian rights. A graduate of MIT and UCSD (where he studied with Herbert Marcuse), he is currently based at Chonnam National University in Gwangju, South Korea, where he is finishing a book on Asian uprisings. Together with Kathleen Cleaver, he co-edited *Liberation, Imagination, and the Black Panther Party* (New York, 2001).

Martin Klimke is a research fellow at the German Historical Institute, Washington, DC and the Heidelberg Center for American Studies (HCA) at the University of Heidelberg, Germany. He is the coordinator of the international Marie Curie project "European Protest Movements Since 1945," supported by the European Union, and co-editor of, among others, *1968 in Europe: A History of Protest and Activism, 1956–77* (New York, 2008). His latest publication is *The Other Alliance: Global Protest and Student Unrest in West Germany and the United States, 1962–1972,* (Princeton, 2010).

Carla MacDougall is a PhD candidate in Modern German History at Rutgers University, where she is completing a dissertation on popular protest against urban renewal in West Berlin.

Wilfried Mausbach is the Executive Director of the Heidelberg Center for American Studies (HCA). He is the author of *Zwischen Morgenthau und Marshall: Das wirtschaftspolitische Deutschlandkonzept der USA 1944–1947* (Düsseldorf, 1996), and co-editor with Andreas W. Daum and Lloyd C. Gardner of *America, the Vietnam War, and the World: Comparative and International Perspectives* (New York, 2003).

Susanne Rinner is assistant professor of German studies at the University of North Carolina at Greensboro and research fellow at the university's Center for Critical Inquiry. She received her PhD from Georgetown University and her MA from Washington University; she also studied at the Freie Universität Berlin. Her research focuses on twentieth-century and contemporary German literature, film, and culture, particularly from the 1960s and 1970s. She has published on the representation of the German student movement and is completing a book on "The Sixties in the German Literary Imagination."

Detlef Siegfried, PhD, is associate professor of modern German history and cultural history at the University of Copenhagen. His research areas include European popular cultures, left-wing radicalism, history of social sciences, historiography, and historical culture. Selected publications: *Time Is on My Side: Konsum und Politik in der westdeutschen Jugendkultur der 60er Jahre* (Göttingen, 2008); *Sound der Revolte: Studien zur Kulturrevolution um 1968* (Weinheim, 2008); and, co-edited with Axel Schildt, *Between Marx and Coca-Cola: Youth Cultures in Changing European Societies, 1960–1980* (New York and Oxford, 2006).

Jeremi Suri is E. Gordon Fox professor of history and director of the European Union Center of Excellence at the University of Wisconsin, Madison. He is the author of three books: *Power and Protest: Global Revolution and the Rise of Détente* (Cambridge, MA, 2003); *The Global Revolutions of 1968* (New York, 2007); and *Henry Kissinger and the American Century* (Cambridge, MA, 2007).

Bibliography

Abromeit, John. "The Dialectic of Bourgeois Society: An Intellectual Biography of the Young Max Horkheimer, 1895–1937." PhD diss., University of California, Berkeley, 2004.

Abromeit, John, and W. Mark Cobb, eds. *Herbert Marcuse: A Critical Reader.* London and New York: Routledge, 2004.

Adorno, Theodor W. "How to Look at Television," *Quarterly of Film, Radio, and Television* 8, no. 3 (1954): 214–35.

Adorno, Theodor. *Critical Models: Interventions and Catchwords.* Trans. Henry Pickford. New York, 1998.

———. *Gesammelte Schriften.* 20 vols. Ed. Rolf Tiedemann. Frankfurt am Main, 1970–1980.

———. *Minima Moralia: Reflections from Damaged Life.* Trans. E. F. N. Jephcott. London, 1974.

———. *Negative Dialectics.* Trans. E. B. Ashton. New York, 1973.

———. *Notes to Literature.* vol. 1. Trans. Shierry Weber Nicholsen. New York, 1991.

———. *The Stars Down to Earth, and Other Essays on the Irrational in Culture.* New York, 1994.

Adorno, Theodor W., Else Frenkel-Brunswick, Daniel Levinson, and R. Nevitt Sanford. *The Authoritarian Personality.* New York, 1950.

"Adorno/Marcuse Correspondence on the German Student Movement." Trans. Esther Leslie, *New Left Review,* no. 233 (January/February 1999): 125.

Agosti, Aldo, Luisa Passerini, and Nicola Tranfaglia, eds. *La cultura et i luoghi del '68.* Milan, 1991.

Ahonen, Pertti. *After the Expulsion: West Germany and Eastern Europe, 1945–1990.* Oxford, 2003.

Albrecht, Clemens, Günter C. Behrmann, Michael Bock, Harald Homann, and Friedrich H. Tenbruck, eds. *Die intellektuelle Gründung der Bundesrepublik: Eine Wirkungsgeschichte der Frankfurter Schule.* Frankfurt am Main and New York, 1999.

Alsheimer, Georg W. "Amerikaner in Vietnam." *Das Argument* 8, no. 36 (1966).

Anderson, Benedict. *Imagined Communities: Reflections on the Origins and Spread of Nationalism.* London, 1983.

Angster, Julia. *Konsenskapitalismus und Sozialdemokratie: Die Westernisierung von SPD und DGB.* Munich, 2003.

————. "'Safe By Democracy': American Hegemony and the 'Westernization' of West German Labor." *Amerikastudien/ American Studies* 46, no. 4 (2001): 557–72.

Appiah, Kwame Anthony. "Is the Post- in Postmodernism the Post- in Postcolonial?" *Critical Inquiry* 17, no. 2 (1991): 336–57.

Ash, Timothy Garton. *In Europe's Name: Germany and the Divided Continent.* New York, 1993.

Assmann, Jan. *Das kulturelle Gedächtnis: Schrift, Erinnerung und politische Identität in frühen Hochkulturen,* 2nd ed. Munich, 1997.

Atget, Eugene, and Laure Beaumont-Maillet, eds. *1968 The Magnum Photographs: A Year in the World.* Paris, 1998.

Aust, Stefan. *Der Baader-Meinhof Komplex.* Hamburg, 1986.

Bade, Klaus J., et al., eds. *Deutsche im Ausland, Fremde in Deutschland: Migration in Geschichte und Gegenwart.* Munich, 1992.

Baier, Lothar, et al. *Die Früchte der Revolte: Über die Veränderung der politischen Kultur durch die Studentenbewegung.* Berlin, 1988.

Balfour, Sebastian. *Castro.* London, 1995.

Bandy, Joe, and Jackie Smith, eds. *Coalitions Across Borders: Transnational Protest and the Neoliberal Order.* Lanham, MD, 2005.

Baring, Arnulf. *Machtwechsel: Die Ära Brandt-Scheel.* Stuttgart, 1982.

Baranowski, Shelley. *Strength through Joy: Consumerism and Mass Tourism in the Third Reich.* Cambridge, 2004.

Bauer, Karin, ed. *Everybody Talks About the Weather... We Don't.* New York, 2008.

Bauer, Wilhelm. "Positionen in Vietnam." *Neue Kritik* 6, no. 29 (1965).

Bauerkämper, Arnd, Konrad H. Jarausch, and Marcus M. Payk, eds. *Demokratiewunder: Transatlantische Mittler und die kulturelle Öffnung Westdeutschlands 1945–1970.* Göttingen, 2005.

Bauman, Zygmunt. *Modernity and the Holocaust.* Ithaca, 1992.

Baumann, Michael. *Wie alles anfing.* Munich, 1975.

Bauß, Gerhard. *Die Studentenbewegung der sechziger Jahre.* Cologne, 1977.

Bauschinger, Sigrid, Horst Denkler, and Wilfried Malsch, eds. *Amerika in der deutschen Literatur: Neue Welt, Nordamerika, USA.* Stuttgart, 1975.

Becker, Jillian. *Hitler's Children: The Story of the Baader-Meinhof Terrorist Gang.* London, 1977.

Behrends, Jan C., Árpád von Klimo, and Patrice G. Poutrus, eds. *Anti-Amerikanismus im 20. Jahrhundert: Studien zu Ost- und Westeuropa.* Bonn, 2005.

Bell, Daniel. *The Cultural Contradictions of Capitalism.* New York, 1996.

Bender, Thomas, ed. *Rethinking American History in a Global Age.* Berkeley, 2002.

Benjamin, Walter. *Gesammelte Schriften.* Frankfurt am Main, 1981.

Berding, Helmut, ed. *Nationales Bewusstsein und kollektive Identität.* Frankfurt am Main, 1994.

Berendt, Joachim-Ernst. *Das Leben – ein Klang: Wege zwischen Jazz und Nada Brahma*. Munich, 1996.

Bergem, Wolfgang, ed. *Die NS-Diktatur im deutschen Erinnerungsdiskurs*. Opladen, 2003.

Berghahn, Volker R. *America and the Intellectual Cold Wars in Europe: Shepard Stone Between Philanthropy, Academy, and Diplomacy*. Princeton, 2001.

Bergmann, Uwe, Rudi Dutschke, Wolfgang Lefèvre, and Bernd Rabehl. *Rebellion der Studenten oder Die neue Opposition*. Reinbek, 1968.

Bergner, Christoph. "Zum 90. Jahrestag des Beginns der Armeniervernichtung im Osmanischen Reich," *Evangelische Verantwortung*, no. 4 (2005): 1–5.

Beschloss, Michael, ed. *Taking Charge: The Johnson White House Tapes, 1963–1964*. New York, 1997.

Bessel, Richard ed. *Life in the Third Reich*. Oxford, 1987.

Bill, James A. *The Eagle and the Lion: The Tragedy of American-Iranian Relations*. New Haven, 1988.

Black, Jeremy. *Maps and History: Constructing Images of the Past*. New Haven and London, 1997.

Bloom, Alexander, and Wini Breines, eds. *"Takin' It to the Streets": A Sixties Reader*. New York, 1995.

Bloxham, Donald. *Genocide on Trial: War Crimes Trials and the Formation of Holocaust History and Memory*. New York, 2001.

Böckelmann, Frank, and Herbert Nagel, eds. *Subversive Aktion: Der Sinn der Organisation ist ihr Scheitern*. Frankfurt am Main, 1976.

Bodnar, John. *Remaking America: Public Memory, Commemoration, and Patriotism in the Twentieth Century*. Princeton, 1992.

Bohrer, Karl-Heinz. *Die gefährdete Phantasie, oder Surrealismus und Terror*. Munich, 1970.

Borstelmann, Thomas. *The Cold War and the Color Line: American Race Relations in the Global Arena*. Cambridge, 2003.

Bracher, Karl Dietrich, Wolfgang Jäger, and Werner Link. *Republik im Wandel, 1969–1974: Die Ära Brandt*. Stuttgart, 1986.

Brandes, Volkhard. *Wie der Stein ins Rollen kam: Vom Aufbruch in die Revolte der sechziger Jahre*. Frankfurt am Main, 1988.

Breidenbach, Joana, and Ina Zukrigl. *Tanz der Kulturen: Kulturelle Identität in einer globalisierten Welt*. Reinbek, 2000.

Breitenbach, Dieter. *Das Afrika- und Asienbild bei deutschen Studenten*. Berlin and Bonn, 1964.

Brigl, Kathrin, and Siegfried Schmidt-Joos. *Fritz Rau: Buchhalter der Träume*. Severin, 1985.

Brockmann, Stephen. *Literature and German Reunification*. Cambridge, 1999.

Brückner, Peter. *Ulrike Meinhof und die deutschen Verhältnisse*. Berlin, 2001.

Brünn, Dieter, ed. *Widerstand in der US-Armee: GI-Bewegung in den siebziger Jahren*. Berlin, 1986.

Brunn, Hellmut, and Thomas Kirn, eds. *Rechtsanwälte - Linksanwälte: 1971 bis 1981 - das Rote Jahrzehnt vor Gericht.* Frankfurt, 2004.

Bucur, Maria. *Birth of a Nation: Commemorations of December 1, 1918, and National Identity in Twentieth-Century Romania.* West Lafayette, IN, 2001.

Budde, Gunilla, Sebastian Conrad, and Oliver Janz, eds. *Transnationale Geschichte: Themen, Tendenzen und Theorien.* Göttingen, 2006.

Budick, Sanford, and Wolfgang Isers, eds. *The Translatability of Cultures: Figurations of the Space Between.* Stanford, 1996.

Buhmann, Inge. *Ich habe mir eine Geschichte geschrieben.* Frankfurt, 1988.

Buisseret, David, ed. *Monarchs, Ministers and Maps: The Emergence of Cartography as a Tool of Government in Early Modern Europe.* Chicago, 1992.

Bürger, Peter. *Theory of the Avant-Garde.* Trans. Michael Shaw. Minneapolis, 1984.

Cahnman, Werner J. *Völker und Rassen im Urteil der Jugend: Ergebnisse einer Untersuchung an Münchner Schulen.* Munich, 1965.

Califano, Joseph A., Jr. *The Student Revolution: A Global Confrontation.* New York, 1970.

Caute, David. *The Year of the Barricades: A Journey through 1968.* New York, 1988.

Chaussy, Ulrich. *Die drei Leben des Rudi Dutschke: eine Biographie.* Berlin, 1993.

Cheles, Luciano, Ronnie Ferguson, and Michalina Vaughan, eds. *Neo-Fascism in Europe.* London, 1991.

Chin, Rita. *The Guestworker Question in Postwar Germany.* New York, 2007.

Claussen, Detlev. *Aspekte der Alltagsreligion: Ideologiekritik unter veränderten gesellschaftlichen Verhältnissen.* Frankfurt am Main, 2000.

———. *Theodor Adorno: Ein letztes Genie.* Frankfurt am Main, 2003.

Claussen, Detlev, and Regine Dermitzel, eds. *Universität und Widerstand: Versuch einer Politischen Universität in Frankfurt.* Frankfurt am Main, 1968.

Clemens, Clay. *Reluctant Realists: The Christian Democrats and West German Ostpolitik.* Durham, 1989.

Clutterbuck, Richard. *Terrorism, Drugs and Crime in Europe: After 1992.* London, 1990.

Cohen, Asher, Joav Gelber, Charlotte Wardi, and Raul Hilberg, eds. *Comprehending the Holocaust: Historical and Literary Research.* Frankfurt am Main and New York, 1988.

Cohen, Robert. "The Political Aesthetics of Holocaust Literature: Peter Weiss's *The Investigation* and Its Critics." *History and Memory* 10, no. 2 (1998): 43–67.

Cohn-Bendit, Daniel. *Wir haben sie so geliebt, die Revolution.* Frankfurt am Main, 1987.

Cole, Tim. *Selling the Holocaust: From Auschwitz to Schindler - How History is Bought, Packaged, and Sold.* New York, 1999.

Colley, Linda. *Britons: Forging the Nation, 1707–1837.* New Haven, 1992.

Confino, Alon. *Germany as a Culture of Remembrance: Promises and Limits of Writing History.* Chapel Hill, 2006.

Conrad, Sebastian. "Doppelte Marginalisierung: Plädoyer für eine transnationale Perspektive auf die deutsche Geschichte." *Geschichte und Gesellschaft* 28, no. 2 (2002): 145–69.

Conrad, Sebastian, and Shalina Randeria, eds. *Jenseits des Eurozentrismus: Postkoloniale Perspektiven in den Geschichts- und Kulturwissenschaften.* Frankfurt am Main and New York, 2002.

Conradt, David P. *The West German Party System: An Ecological Analysis of Social Structure and Voting Behavior, 1961–1969.* London, 1972.

Cooper, Alice Holmes. "Public-good Movements and the Dimensions of Political Process: Postwar German Peace Movements." *Comparative Political Studies* 29, no. 3 (1996): 267–89.

Cortright, David. *Soldiers in Revolt: The American Military Today.* New York, 1975.

Cosgrove, Denis, and Stephen Daniels, eds. *The Iconography of Landscape: Essays on the Symbolic Representation, Design and Use of Past Environments.* New York, 1988.

Cull, Nicholas John. *The Cold War and the United States Information Agency: American Propaganda and Public Diplomacy, 1945–1989.* New York, 2008.

Dabrowski, Patrice M. *Commemorations and the Shaping of Modern Poland.* Bloomington, IN, 2004.

Daum, Andreas W., Lloyd C. Gardner, and Wilfried Mausbach, eds. *America, the Vietnam War, and the World: Comparative and International Perspectives.* New York, 2003.

Davis, Angela. *Angela Davis—an Autobiography.* New York, 1988.

Davis, Belinda. *The Internal Life of Politics: The "New Left" in West Germany, 1962–1983.* Forthcoming.

———. "Transnation/Transculture: Gender and Politicization in and out of the BRD, 1950s–1970s," in *Gender in Trans-it: Transkulturelle und Transnationale Perspectiven/ Transcultural and Transnational Perspectives,* ed. Martina Ineichen et al. Zurich, 2009, 51–67.

———. "What's Left? Popular and Democratic Political Participation in Postwar Europe." *American Historical Review* 113, no. 2 (2008): 363–90.

Davis, Belinda, et al., eds. *Alltag—Erfahrung—Eigensinn: Historisch-anthropologische Erkundungen.* Frankfurt, 2008.

DeBenedetti, Charles, with Charles Chatfield. *An American Ordeal: The Antiwar Movement of the Vietnam Era.* Syracuse, 1990.

Debord, Guy. *Die Gesellschaft des Spektakels.* Berlin, 1996.

Debray, Régis. *Éloges.* Paris, 1986.

———. *Kritik der Waffen.* Reinbek, 1975.

———. *Revolution in der Revolution.* Munich, 1967.

DeGroot, Gerard J., ed. *Student Protest: The Sixties and After.* New York, 1998.

della Porta, Donatella, et al., eds. *Social Movements in a Globalizing World.* London, 1999.

della Porta, Donatella, Hanspeter Kriesi, and Dieter Rucht, eds. *Social Movements in a Globalizing World.* New York, 1999.

Demirovic, Alexander. *Der nonkonformistische Intellektuelle.* Frankfurt am Main, 1999.

Doering-Manteuffel, Anselm. *Wie westlich sind die Deutschen? Amerikanisierung und Westernisierung im 20. Jahrhundert.* Göttingen, 1999.

Dreyfus-Armand, Geneviève, et al., eds. *Les années 68: Le temps de la contestation.* Brussels, 2001.

Dubinsky, Karen, et al., ed. *New World Coming: The Sixties and the Shaping of Global Consciousness.* Toronto, 2009.

Duteuil, Jean-Pierre. *Nanterre 1965–66–67–68: Vers le mouvement du 22 mars.* Mauléon, 1988.

Dutschke, Gretchen. *Wir hatten ein barbarisches, schönes Leben: Rudi Dutschke, eine Biographie.* Cologne, 1996.

———, ed. *Rudi Dutschke – Jeder hat sein Leben ganz zu leben: Die Tagebücher, 1963–1979.* Cologne, 2003.

Dutschke, Rudi. *Geschichte ist machbar: Texte über das herrschende Falsche und die Radikalität des Friedens.* Ed. Jürgen Miermeister and Klaus Wagenbach. Berlin, 1980.

———. *Mein langer Marsch: Reden, Schriften und Tagebücher aus zwanzig Jahren.* Hamburg, 1980.

Eco, Umberto. "An Art Oblivionalis? Forget It!" *Publication of the Modern Language Association of America* 103 (1988): 254–61.

Ege, Moritz. *Schwarz Werden: "Afroamerikanophilie" in den 1960er und 1970er Jahren.* Bielefeld, 2007.

Edney, Matthew. *Mapping an Empire: The Geographical Construction of British India, 1765–1843.* Chicago, IL, 1997.

Eßbach, Wolfgang, Joachim Fischer, and Helmut Lethen, eds. *Plessners 'Grenzen der Gemeinschaft': Eine Debatte.* Frankfurt am Main, 2002.

Fahlenbrach, Kathrin, Martin Klimke, and Joachim Scharloth, eds. *The "Establishment" Responds: Power and Protest During and After the Cold War.* Forthcoming.

Fähnders, Walter. *Avantgarde und Moderne 1890–1933.* Stuttgart and Weimar, 1998.

Fehrenbach, Heide. *Race After Hitler: Black Occupation Children in Postwar Germany and America.* Princeton, 2005.

Ferrara, Alessandro. *Reflective Authenticity: Rethinking the Project of Modernity.* London and New York, 1998.

Fichter, Tilman, and Siegward Lönnendonker. *Kleine Geschichte des SDS: Der Sozialistische Deutsche Studentenbund von 1946 bis zur Selbstauflösung.* Berlin, 1977.

Fink, Carole, Philipp Gassert, and Detlef Junker, eds. *1968: The World Transformed.* New York, 1998.

Finkelstein, Norman G. *The Holocaust Industry: Reflections on the Exploitation of Jewish Suffering.* New York, 2000.

Fisher Fishkin, Shelley. "Crossroads of Cultures: The Transnational Turn in American Studies: Presidential Address to the American Studies Association, November 12, 2004." *American Quarterly* 57, no. 1 (2005): 17–57.

Flanzbaum, Hilene, ed. *The Americanization of the Holocaust.* Baltimore and London, 1999.

Foner, Philip S. *The Black Panthers Speak.* 3rd ed. New York, 1995.

Foucault, Michel. *Dispositive der Macht: Über Sexualität, Wissen und Wahrheit.* Berlin, 1978.

———. *Schriften – Dits et Ecrits,* 4 vols. Frankfurt am Main, 2003.

———. *Von der Subversion des Wissens.* Berlin, 1978.

Fousek, John. *To Lead the Free World: American Nationalism and the Cultural Roots of the Cold War.* Chapel Hill and London, 2000.

Fox, Claire F. "Commentary: The Transnational Turn and the Hemispheric Turn." *American Literary History* 18, no. 3 (2006): 638–47.

Frahm, Ole. "Von Holocaust zu Holokaust: Guido Knopps Aneignung der Vernichtung der europäischen Juden." *1999. Zeitschrift für Sozialgeschichte des 20. und 21. Jahrhunderts* 17, no. 2 (2002): 128–38.

François, Etienne, et al., ed. *1968 – ein europäisches Jahr?* Leipzig, 1997.

François, Etienne, and Hagen Schulze, eds. *Deutsche Erinnerungsorte.* 3 vols. Munich, 2001.

Fraser, Ronald, et al. *1968: A Student Generation in Revolt.* New York, 1988.

Frei, Norbert. *1968: Jugendrevolte und globaler Protest.* Munich, 2008.

———. *Vergangenheitspolitik: Die Anfänge der Bundesrepublik und die NS- Vergangenheit.* Munich, 1996.

Fried, Erich. *und Vietnam und.* Berlin, 1996.

Friedberg, Aaron L. *In the Shadow of the Garrison State: America's Anti-Statism and Its Cold War Grand Strategy.* Princeton, 2000.

Friedrich-Ebert-Stiftung, ed. *Urlaub und Tourismus in beiden deutschen Staaten.* Bonn 1985.

Fromm, Erich. *The Working Class in Weimar Germany: A Psychological and Sociological Study.* Trans. B. Weinberger. Warwickshire, 1984.

Furck, Carl-Ludwig. *Das pädagogische Problem der Leistung in der Schule.* Weinheim, 1964.

Gaddis, John Lewis. *Strategies of Containment: A Critical Appraisal of Postwar American National Security Policy.* New York, 1982.

———. *We Now Know: Rethinking Cold War History.* New York, 1997.

Galbraith, John Kenneth. *The Affluent Society.* Boston, 1958.

Galtung, Johan. *Strukturelle Gewalt.* Reinbek, 1975.

Gassert, Philipp. "Amerikanismus, Antiamerikanismus, Amerikanisierung: Neue

Literatur zur Sozial-, Wirtschafts- und Kulturgeschichte des amerikanischen Einflusses in Deutschland und Europa." *Archiv für Sozialgeschichte* 39 (1999): 531–61.

———. *Kurt Georg Kiesinger, 1904–1988.* Munich, 2004.

Gassert, Philipp, and Martin Klimke, eds. *1968: Memories and Legacies of a Global Revolt.* Washington, D.C., 2009.

Gassert, Philipp, and Alan E. Steinweis, eds. *Coping with the Nazi Past: West German Debates on Nazism and Generational Conflict, 1955–1975.* New York, 2006.

Gellner, Ernest. *Nations and Nationalism.* Ithaca, 1983.

Geyer, Michael. "Resistance as Ongoing Project: Visions of Order, Obligations to Strangers, Struggles for Civil Society." *Journal of Modern History* 64 (1992): 217–41.

Gibson, Nigel, and Andrew Rubin, eds. *Adorno: A Critical Reader.* Malden, MA, and Oxford, 2002.

Gienow-Hecht, Jessica C. E. "Shame on US? Academics, Cultural Transfer, and the Cold War: A Critical Review." *Diplomatic History* 24, no. 3 (2000): 465–94.

Giesen, Bernhard. *Intellectuals and the German Nation: Collective Identity in an Axial Age.* Trans. Nicholas Levis and Amos Weisz. New York, 1998.

Giessler, H. J. *APO-Rebellion Mai 1968.* Berlin, 1968.

Gilcher-Holtey, Ingrid. *Die 68er Bewegung: Deutschland – Westeuropa – USA.* Munich, 2001.

———. *Die Phantasie an die Macht: Mai 68 in Frankreich.* Frankfurt am Main, 2003.

———. "Der Transfer zwischen den Studentenbewegungen von 1968 und die Entstehung einer transnationalen Gegenöffentlichkeit." *Berliner Journal für Soziologie* 10, no. 4 (2000): 485–500.

———, ed. *1968 – Vom Ereignis zum Gegenstand der Geschichtswissenschaft.* Göttingen, 1998.

Gillis, John R, ed. *Commemorations: The Politics of National Identity.* Princeton, 1994.

Glaser, Hermann, ed. *Jugend-Stil, Stil der Jugend: Thesen und Aspekte.* Munich, 1971.

Göhring, Martin, ed. *Europa – Erbe und Aufgabe: Internationaler Gelehrtenkongress Mainz 1955.* Wiesbaden, 1956.

Gräser, Marcus. "Weltgeschichte im Nationalstaat: Die transnationale Disposition der amerikanischen Geschichtswissenschaft." *Historische Zeitschrift* 283, no. 2 (2006): 355–82.

Gregory, Derek. *Geographical Imaginations.* Cambridge, MA, 1994.

Gress, David. *From Plato to NATO: The Idea of the West and Its Opponents.* New York, 1998.

Grünbacher, Armin. "Sustaining the Island: Western Aid to 1950s West Berlin." *Cold War History* 3, no. 3 (2003): 1–23.

Habermas, Jürgen. *Toward a Rational Society: Student Protest, Science, and Politics.* Trans. Jeremy J. Shapiro. Boston, 1970.

Halbwachs, Maurice. *The Collective Memory.* Trans. Francis J. Ditter, Jr., and Vida Yazdi Ditter. New York, 1980.

Halliday, Fred. "The Ends Of Cold War." *New Left Review* 180 (March-April 1990): 5–24.

Hanshew, Karrin. "Militant Democracy, Civil Disobedience and Terror: Political Violence and the West German Left during the 'German Autumn' 1977." *AICGS Humanities Volume* 14 (2003): 20–46.

Harley, J. B., and David Woodward, eds. *The History of Cartography.* 4 vols. Chicago, 1987–1998.

Harrison, Hope M. *Driving the Soviets Up the Wall: Soviet–East German Relations, 1953–1961.* Princeton, 2003.

Harvey, Elizabeth. *Women and the Nazi East: Agents and Witnesses of Germanization.* New Haven, 2003.

Hayes, Peter. *Lessons and Legacies: The Meaning of the Holocaust in a Changing World.* Evanston, IL, 1991.

Haus der Geschichte der Bundesrepublik Deutschland, ed. *Endlich Urlaub! Die Deutschen reisen.* Cologne, 1996.

Heitmeyer, Wilhelm, and Hans-Georg Soeffner, eds. *Gewalt: Entwicklung, Strukturen, Analyseprobleme.* Frankfurt am Main, 2004.

Herb, Guntram Henrik. *Under the Map of Germany: Nationalism and Propaganda 1918–1945.* London and New York, 1997.

Herbert, Ulrich, ed. *Wandlungsprozesse in Westdeutschland: Belastung, Integration, Liberalisierung 1945–1980.* Göttingen, 2002.

Herf, Jeffrey. "War, Peace, and the Intellectuals: The West German Peace Movement." *International Security* 10 (spring 1986): 172–74.

Hildebrand, Klaus. *Von Erhard zur Großen Koalition, 1963–1969.* Stuttgart, 1984.

Hilwig, Stuart. *Italy and 1968: Youthful Unrest and Democratic Culture.* London, 2009.

Hirsch, Marianne. *Family Frames: Photography, Narrative, and Postmemory.* Cambridge, 1997.

Hobsbawm, Eric J. *Nations and Nationalism Since 1780: Programme, Myth, Reality.* New York, 1990.

Hobsbawm, Eric J., and Terence Ranger, eds. *The Invention of Tradition.* New York, 1983.

Hochgeschwender, Michael. *Freiheit in der Offensive? Der Kongreß für kulturelle Freiheit und die Deutschen.* Munich, 1998.

Hodenberg, Christina von, and Detlef Siegfried, eds. *Wo '1968' liegt: Reform und Revolte in der Geschichte der Bundesrepublik.* Göttingen, 2006.

Hogan, Michael. *A Cross of Iron: Harry S. Truman and the Origins of the National Security State, 1945–1954.* New York, 1998.

Höhn, Maria. "The Black Panther Solidarity Committees and the *Voice of the Lumpen.*" *German Studies Review* 31, no. 1 (2008): 133–55.

———. *GIs and Fräuleins: The German American Encounter in 1950s West Germany.* Chapel Hill, 2002.

Horkheimer, Max. *Critical Theory.* Trans. M. J. O'Connell. New York, 1992.

———. *Between Philosophy and Social Science: Selected Early Writings.* Trans. G. Frederick Hunter, Matthew S. Torpey, and John Torpey. Cambridge, MA, 1993.

———. *Dawn and Decline: Notes 1926–1931 and 1950–1969.* Trans. Michael Shaw. New York, 1978.

———. *Gesammelte Schriften.* Ed. Alfred Schmidt and Gunzelin Schmid Noerr. 19 vol. Frankfurt am Main, 1996.

———, ed. *Studien über Autorität und Familie: Forschungsberichte aus dem Institut für Sozialforschung.* Paris, 1936.

Horn, Gerd-Rainer, and Padraic Kenney, eds. *Transnational Moments of Change: Europe 1945, 1968, 1989.* Lanham, MD, 2004.

Hosek, Jennifer. "Cuba and the Germans: A Cultural History of an Infatuation." PhD diss., University of California Berkeley, 2004.

Husson, Édouard. "1968: événement transnational ou international? Le cas de la France et de la République Fédérale d'Allemagne." *Revue d'Allemagne et des pays de langue allemande* 35, no. 2 (2003): 179–88.

Iriye, Akira. "AHR Conversation: On Transnational History." *American Historical Review* 111, no. 5 (2006): 1440–64.

———. "The Internationalization of History." *American Historical Review* 94, no. 1 (1989): 1–10.

———. "On the Transnational Turn." *Diplomatic History* 31, no. 3 (2007): 373–76.

Iriye, Akira, and Pierre Saunier, eds. *The Palgrave Dictionary of Transnational History.* London, forthcoming.

Jaeger, Friedrich, and Burkhard Liebsch, eds. *Handbuch der Kulturwissenschaften,* 3 vols. Stuttgart and Weimar, 2004.

Jameson, Fredric, ed. *Aesthetics and Politics.* London and New York, 1977.

Jarausch, Konrad, and Michael Geyer. *Shattered Past: Reconstructing German Histories.* Princeton, 2003.

Jay, Martin. *The Dialectical Imagination: A History of the Frankfurt School and the Institute of Social Research, 1923–1950.* Berkeley, Los Angeles, and London, 1996.

Juchler, Ingo. *Die Studentenbewegungen in den Vereinigten Staaten und der Bundesrepublik Deutschland der sechziger Jahre: Eine Untersuchung hinsichtlich ihrer Beeinflußung durch Befreiungsbewegungen und –theorien aus der Dritten Welt.* Berlin, 1996.

Judt, Tony. *Postwar: A History of Europe since 1945.* New York, 2005.

Junker, Detlef. *Power and Mission: Was Amerika antreibt.* Freiburg, 2003.

————, et al, eds. *The United States and Germany in the Era of the Cold War, 1945–1990: A Handbook*. 2 vols. New York, 2004.

————, et al, eds. Die USA und Deutschland im Zeitalter des Kalten Krieges 1945 - 1990 : ein Handbuch. 2 vols. Stuttgart, 2001.

Junker, Detlef, and Thomas Maulucci, eds. *GIs in Germany: The Social, Economic, Military, and Political History of the American Military Presence*. New York, forthcoming.

Kaelble, Hartmut, Martin Kirsch, and Alexander Schmidt-Gernig, eds. *Transnationale Öffentlichkeiten und Identitäten im 20. Jahrhundert*. Frankfurt am Main and New York, 2002.

Kansteiner, Wulf. "Nazis, Viewers and Statistics: Television History, Television Audience Research and Collective Memory in West Germany." *Journal of Contemporary History* 39, no. 4 (2004): 575–98.

Kastner, Jens and David Mayer, eds. *Weltwende 1968? Ein Jahr aus globalgeschichtlicher Perspektive*. Vienna, 2008.

Katsiaficas, George. *The Imagination of the New Left: A Global Analysis of 1968*. Boston, 1987.

————. "Remembering the Kwangju Uprising." *Socialism and Democracy*, no.1 (2000): 85–107.

————. *The Subversion of Politics: European Social Movements and the Decolonization of Everyday Life*. Oakland, 2006.

Katsiaficas, George, and Kathleen Cleaver, eds. *Liberation, Imagination and The Black Panther Party*. New York, 2001.

Kätzel, Ute. *Die 68erinnen*. Berlin, 2002.

Keitz, Christiane. *Reisen als Leitbild: Die Entstehung des modernen Massentourismus in Deutschland*. Munich, 1997.

Kellner, Douglas, ed. *Herbert Marcuse: Toward a Critical Theory of Society*. New York and London, 2001.

Kenkman, Alfons. *Wilde Jugend: Lebenswelt großstädtischer Jugendlicher zwischen Weltwirtschaftskrise, Nationalsozialismus, und Währungsreform*. Essen, 1996.

Kersting, Franz-Werner. "Helmut Schelskys 'Skeptische Generation' von 1957: Zur Publikations-und Wirkungsgeschichte eines Standardwerks." *Vierteljahrshefte für Zeitgeschichte* 50, no. 3 (2002): 465–95.

Klimke, Martin. *The Other Alliance: Student Protest in West Germany and the United States in the Global Sixties*. Princeton, 2010.

Klimke, Martin, and Joachim Scharloth, eds. *1968 in Europe: A History of Protest and Activism, 1956–77*. New York and London, 2008.

Klimke, Martin, and Joachim Scharloth, eds. *1968 in Europe: A Handbook on National Perspectives and Transnational Dimensions of 1960s/70s Protest Movements*. New York, 2008.

————, eds. *1968: Handbuch zur Kultur- und Mediengeschichte der Studentenbewegung*. Stuttgart, 2007.

Knabe, Hubertus. *Die unterwanderte Republik: Stasi im Westen*. Munich, 2001.

Koenen, Gerd. *Das Rote Jahrzehnt: Unsere kleine deutsche Kulturrevolution 1967–77.* Cologne, 2001.

———. *Vesper, Ensslin, Baader: Urszenen des deutschen Terrorismus.* Cologne, 2003.

Kolb, Ulrike. *Frühstück mit Max.* Stuttgart, 2000.

König, Helmut, Michael Kohlstruck, and Andreas Wöll, eds. *Vergangenheitsbewältigung am Ende des 20. Jahrhunderts.* Opladen and Wiesbaden, 1998.

Korn, Salomon. *Geteilte Erinnerung: Beiträge zur 'deutsch-jüdischen' Gegenwart.* Berlin, 1999.

Kotkin, Stephen. *Armageddon Averted: The Soviet Collapse, 1970–2000.* New York, 2001.

Kraft, Sandra. "Vom Autoritätskonflikt zur Machtprobe: Die Studentenproteste der 60er Jahre als Herausforderung für das Establishment in Deutschland und den USA," Ph.D. diss., University of Heidelberg, 2008.

Krahl, Hans-Jürgen. *Konstitution und Klassenkampf: Zur historischen Dialektik von bürgerlicher Emanzipation und proletarischen Revolution.* Frankfurt am Main, 1971.

Kraus, Chris, and Sylvère Lothringer, eds. *Hatred of Capitalism.* Los Angeles, 2003.

Kraushaar, Wolfgang. *1968 als Mythos, Chiffre und Zäsur.* Hamburg, 2000.

———, ed. *Frankfurter Schule und Studentenbewegung: Von der Flaschenpost zum Molotowcocktail, 1946–1995.* 3 vols. Hamburg, 1998.

———, ed. *Die RAF und der linke Terrorismus.* 2 vols. Hamburg, 2006.

Kraushaar, Wolfgang, Karin Wieland, and Jan Philipp Reemtsma, *Rudi Dutschke Andreas Baader und die RAF.* Hamburg, 2005.

Krebs, Mario. *Ulrike Meinhof: Ein Leben im Widerspruch.* Hamburg, 1989.

Kroegel, Dirk. *Einen Anfang finden! Kurt Georg Kiesinger in der Außen- und Deutschlandpolitik der Großen Koalition.* Munich, 1997.

Kruip, Gudrun. *Das 'Welt'-'Bild' des Axel Springer Verlags: Journalismus zwischen westlichen Werten und deutschen Denktraditionen.* Munich, 1998.

Kundrus, Birthe, ed. *Phantasiereiche: Zur Kulturgeschichte des deutschen Kolonialismus.* Frankfurt am Main and New York, 2003.

Leffler, Melvyn P. *A Preponderance of Power: National Security, The Truman Administration, and the Cold War.* Stanford, 1992.

Leggewie, Claus. "1968: Ein transatlantisches Ereignis und seine Folgen," in *Die USA und Deutschland im Zeitalter des Kalten Krieges 1945–1990: Ein Handbuch,* ed. Detlef Junker (Stuttgart, Munich, 2001), 632–43.

Lethen, Helmut. *Verhaltenslehren der Kälte: Lebensversuche zwischen den Kriegen.* Frankfurt am Main, 1994.

Levy, Daniel, and Natan Sznaider. *Erinnerung im globalen Zeitalter: Der Holocaust.* Frankfurt am Main, 2001.

———. "Memory Unbound: The Holocaust and the Formation of Cosmopolitan Memory." *European Journal of Social Theory* 5, no. 2 (2002): 87–106.

Linton, Derek. *Who Has the Youth, Has the Future: The Campaign to Save Young Workers in Imperial Germany.* Cambridge, 1991.

Logevall, Fredrik. *Choosing War: The Lost Chance for Peace and the Escalation of War in Vietnam.* Berkeley, 1999.

Lönnendonker, Siegward, and Tilman Fichter, eds. *Freie Universität Berlin 1948–1973, Hochschule im Umbruch, Teil IV: 1964–1967.* Berlin, 1975.

Lönnendonker, Siegward, Tilman Fichter, and Jochen Staadt, eds. *Hochschule im Umbruch, Teil V: Gewalt und Gegengewalt (1967–1969).* Berlin, 1983.

Lönnendonker, Siegward, Bernd Rabehl, and Jochen Staadt, eds. *Die antiautoritäre Revolte: Der Sozialistische Deutsche Studentenbund nach der Trennung von der SPD.* Wiesbaden, 1999.

Lotz, Rainer E. *Black People: Entertainers of African Descent in Europe, and Germany.* Bonn, 1997.

Lowen, Rebecca S. *Creating the Cold War University: The Transformation of Stanford.* Berkeley, 1997.

Lowenthal, Leo. *False Prophets: Studies on Authoritarianism.* New Brunswick, NJ, and Oxford, 1987.

Maase, Kaspar, et al., eds. *Amerikanisierung der Alltagskultur? Zur Rezeption US-amerikanischer Populärkulture in der Bundesrepublik und in den Niederlanden.* Hamburg, 1990.

Mailer, Norman. *Advertisements for Myself.* New York, 1959.

Marchart, Oliver, Vrääth Öhner, and Heidemarie Uhl. "Holocaust Revisited: Lesarten eines Medienereignisses zwischen globaler Erinnerungskultur und nationaler Vergangenheitsbewältigung." *Tel Aviver Jahrbuch für deutsche Geschichte* 31 (2003): 307–34.

Marcus, Greil. *Lipstick Traces: A Secret History of the Twentieth Century.* Cambridge, MA, 1989.

Marcuse, Herbert. *The Aesthetic Dimension: Towards a Critique of Marxist Aesthetics.* Boston, 1978.

———. *A Critique of Pure Tolerance.* Boston, 1969.

———. *Eros and Civilization.* Boston, 1955.

———. *An Essay on Liberation.* Harmondsworth, 1972.

———. *Heideggerian Marxism.* Ed. Richard Wolin and John Abromeit. Lincoln, NE, 2005.

———. *The New Left and the 1960s: Collected Papers of Herbert Marcuse,* 3 vols. Ed. Douglas Kellner. New York and London, 2005.

———. *One-Dimensional Man.* Boston, 1964.

———. *Versuch über die Befreiung.* Frankfurt am Main, 1969. (2 edition, Frankfurt am Main, 1972.

Markovits, Andrei. "On Anti-Americanism in West German." *New German Critique,* no. 34 (1985): 3–27.

Markovits, Andrei, and Philip Gorski. *The German Left: Red, Green and Beyond.* New York, 1993.

Marßolek, Inge, and Adelheid von Saldern, eds. *Radiozeiten: Herrschaft, Alltag, Gesellschaft (1924–1960)*. Berlin, 1999.

Martin, Peter, and Christine Alonzo, eds. *Zwischen Charleston und Stechschritt: Schwarze im Nationalsozialismus*. Hamburg and Munich, 2004.

Marwick, Arthur. *The Sixties: Cultural Revolution in Britain, France, Italy, and the United States, c.1958–c.1974*. New York, 1998.

Mausbach, Wilfried. "'Man muss die ganze Wut diesen Herrenrassenbanditen ins Gesicht schreien': Die 68er und die nationalsozialistische Vergangenheit." *Deutschlandarchiv* 38, no. 2 (2005): 273–80.

May, Ernest R. "Writing Contemporary International History." *Diplomatic History* 8, no. 2 (1984): 103–14.

McAdam, Doug, and Dieter Rucht. "The Cross-National Diffusion of Movement Ideas." *Annals of the American Academy of Political and Social Science* 528 (1993): 56–74.

McNamara, Robert S. (with Brian VanDeMark). *In Retrospect: The Tragedy and Lessons of Vietnam*. New York, 1995.

Mintz, Alan. *Popular Culture and the Shaping of Holocaust Memory in America*. Seattle and London, 2001.

Mohr, Reinhard, and Dany Cohn-Bendit. *1968: Die letzte Revolution, die noch nichts vom Ozonloch wusste*. Berlin, 1988.

Montagu, Ivor. *Germany's New Nazis*. London, 1967.

Moreau, Patrick. *Les Héritiers due IIIe Reich: L'extrême Droite Allemands de 1945 à nos Jours*. Paris, 1994.

Moses. A. D. "The Forty-Fivers: A Generation Between Fascism and Democracy." *German Politics and Society* 17, no. 1 (1999): 94–126.

Mueller, Harald, and Thomas Risse-Kappen. "Origins of Estrangement: The Peace Movement and the Changed Image of America in West Germany." *International Security* 12, no. 1 (1987): 52–88.

Müller, Hermann. *Rassen und Völker im Denken der Jugend*. Stuttgart, 1967.

Mumford, Lewis. *The Myth of the Machine, vol. 2: The Pentagon Power*. New York, 1970.

Mushaben, Joyce Marie. "Grassroots and Gewaltfreie Aktionen: A Study of Mass Mobilization Strategies in the West German Peace Movement." *Journal of Peace Research* 23, no.2 (1986): 141–54.

Nagel, Katja. "Die Provinz in Bewegung. Studentenunruhen in Heidelberg 1964 bis 1974," Ph.D. diss., University of Heidelberg, 2008.

Nagle, David. *The National Democratic Party: Right Radicalism in the Federal Republic of Germany*. Berkeley, 1970.

Naumann, Klaus. "Sympathy for the Devil? Die Kontroverse um Hannah Arendts Prozeßbericht 'Eichmann in Jerusalem.'" *Mittelweg 36*, no. 1 (1994): 65–79.

Negt, Oskar. *Achtundsechzig: Politische Intellektuelle und die Macht*. Göttingen, 1995.

Nehring, Holger. "'Westernization': A New Paradigm for Interpreting West European History in a Cold War Context." *Cold War History* 4, no. 2 (2004): 175–91.

Nelson, Daniel. *Defenders or Intruders? The Dilemma of U.S. Forces in Germany.* Boulder, CO, 1987.

Neocleous, Mark. "Off the Map: On Violence and Cartography." *European Journal of Social Theory* 6, no. 4 (2003): 409–25.

Niethammer, Lutz. *Kollektive Identität: Heimliche Quellen einer unheimlichen Konjunktur.* Reinbek, 2000.

Nolan, Mary. "Anti-Americanism and Americanization in Germany." *Politics and Society* 33, no. 1 (2005): 88–122.

Nora, Pierre. "Between Memory and History: Les Lieux de Mémoire." *Representations* 26, no. 1 (1989): 7–24.

———, ed. *Les lieux de mémoire.* 7 vols. Paris, 1984–1992.

Novick, Peter. *The Holocaust in American Life.* Boston and New York, 1999.

Ortoleva, Peppino. *Saggio sui movimenti del 1968 in Europa e in America.* Rome, 1988.

Osterhammel, Jürgen. "Die Wiederkehr des Raumes: Geopolitik, Geohistorie und historische Geographie." *Neue Politische Literatur* 43, no. 3 (1998): 374–97.

Ott, Ulrich, and Friedrich Pfäfflin, eds. *Protest! Literatur um 1968.* Eine Ausstellung des Deutschen Literaturarchivs in Verbindung mit dem Germanistischen Seminar der Universität Heidelberg und des Deutschen Rundfunkarchiv im Schiller-Nationalmuseum Marbach am Neckar. 1998.

Painter, David S. *The Cold War: An International History.* London and New York, 1999.

Pal, Adesh, and Tapas Chakrabarti, eds. *Critiquing Nationalism, Transnationalism, and Indian Diaspora.* New Delhi, 2006.

Pasolini, Pier Paolo. *Freibeuterschriften: Aufsätze und Polemiken über die Zerstörung des Einzelnen durch die Konsumgesellschaft.* Berlin, 1978.

Passerini, Luisa, ed. *International Yearbook of Oral History and Life Stories: Memory and Totalitarianism.* London, 1992.

Patel, Kiran Klaus. "Überlegungen zu einer transnationalen Geschichte." *Zeitschrift für Geschichtswissenschaft* 52, no. 7 (2004): 626–45.

Patterson, James T. *Grand Expectations: The United States, 1945–1974.* New York, 1996.

Pendas, Devin O. *The Frankfurt Auschwitz Trial, 1963–65: Genocide, History and the Limits of the Law.* Cambridge and New York, 2006.

Picht, Georg. *Die deutsche Bildungskatastrophe.* Munich, 1964.

Plessner, Helmuth. *Gesammelte Schriften.* Frankfurt am Main, 1985.

———. *Grenzen der Gemeinschaft: Eine Kritik des sozialen Radikalismus.* 2nd ed. Frankfurt am Main, 2002.

Plogstedt, Sibylle. *Im Netz der Gedichte: Gefangen in Prag nach 1968.* Berlin, 2001.

———, ed. *Vietnam-Kongreß*. Berlin, 1968.

Poiger, Uta. *Jazz, Rock, and Rebels: Cold War Politics and American Culture in a Divided Germany.* Berkeley, 2000.

Pojmann, Wendy, ed. *Migration and Activism in Europe Since 1945.* New York, 2008.

Prakash, Gyan, and Kevin M. Kruse, eds. *The Spaces of the Modern City: Imaginaries, Politics and Everyday Life.* Princeton, 2008.

Portes, Alejandro, and Josh DeWind, eds. *Rethinking Migration: New Theoretical and Empirical Perspectives.* New York, 2007.

Rabehl, Bernd. *Am Ende der Utopie: Die politische Geschichte der Freien Universität Berlin.* Berlin, 1988.

———. *Feindblick: Der SDS im Fadenkreuz des 'Kalten Krieges'.* Berlin, 2000.

———. *Rudi Dutschke: Revolutionär im geteilten Deutschland.* Dresden, 2002.

Rabinowitz, Dorothy. *New Lives: Survivors of the Holocaust Living in America.* New York, 1976.

Rauhut, Michael, and Thomas Kochan, eds. *Bye Bye, Lübben City: Bluesfreaks, Tramps und Hippies in der DDR.* Berlin, 2004.

Reich, Wilhelm. *Was ist Klassenbewußtsein? Ein Beitrag zur Neuformierung der Arbeiterbewegung.* Pirated, n.p, n.d., reprinted from a 1934 publication.

Reichel, Peter. *Erfundene Erinnerung: Weltkrieg und Judenmord in Film und Theater.* Munich, 2004.

———. *Politik mit der Erinnerung: Gedächtnisorte im Streit um die nationalsozialistische Vergangenheit.* Munich, 1995.

———. *Vergangenheitsbewältigung in Deutschland: Die Auseinandersetzung mit der NS-Diktatur von 1945 bis heute.* Munich, 2001.

Resetarits, Willi, and Hans Veigl, eds. *Beatles, Bond, und Blumenkinder: Unser Lebensgefühl in den sechziger Jahren.* Vienna, 2003.

Ribbe, Wolfgang, ed. *Geschichte Berlins, vol. 2: Von der Märzrevolution bis zur Gegenwart.* 3rd rev. and exp. ed. Berlin, 2002.

Richards, Fred. *Die NPD: Alternative oder Wiederkehr?* Munich, 1967.

Richie, Alexandra. *Faust's Metropolis: A History of Berlin.* New York, 1998.

Roseman, Mark, ed. *Generations in Conflict: Youth Revolt and Generation Formation in Germany 1770–1968.* Cambridge, 1995.

Rosenberg, Rainer, Inge Münz-Koenen, and Petra Boden, eds. *Der Geist der Unruhe: 1968 im Vergleich. Wissenschaft – Literatur – Medien.* Berlin, 2000.

Rosenfeld, Alvin H. *Thinking About the Holocaust: After Half a Century.* Bloomington, IN and Indianapolis, 1997.

Roth, Günther, and Claus Wittich, eds. *Economy and Society: An Outline of Interpretive Sociology.* New York, 1968.

Rucht, Dieter. "Mesomobilization: Organizing and Framing in Two Protest Campaigns in West Germany." *The American Journal of Sociology* 98, no. 3 (1992): 555–96.

Rupieper, Hermann-Josef. *Die Wurzeln der westdeutschen Nachkriegsdemokratie: Der amerikanische Beitrag 1945–1952.* Opladen, 1993.

Rüsen, Jörn, ed. *Westliches Geschichtsdenken: Eine interkulturelle Debatte*. Göttingen, 1999.

Salzinger, Helmut. *Rock Power oder Wie musikalisch ist die Revolution? Ein Essay über Pop-Musik und Gegenkultur*. Frankfurt am Main, 1972.

Sartre, Jean-Paul. *Plädoyer für die Intellektuellen: Interviews, Artikel, Reden, 1950–1973*. Reinbek, 1995.

Sauer, Thomas. *Westorientierung im deutschen Protestantismus? Vorstellungen und Tätigkeit des Kronberger Kreises*. Munich, 1998.

Schelsky, Helmut. *Die skeptische Generation: Eine Soziologie der deutschen Jugend*. Düsseldorf and Cologne, 1957.

Schenk, Frithjof Benjamin. "Mental Maps: Die Konstruktion von geographischen Räumen in Europa seit der Aufklärung." *Geschichte und Gesellschaft* 28, no. 3 (2002): 493–514.

Schildt, Axel. *Ankunft im Westen: Ein Essay zur Erfolgsgeschichte der Bundesrepublik*. Frankfurt, 1999.

———. *Moderne Zeiten: Freizeit, Massenmedien und „Zeitgeist" in der Bundesrepublik der 50er Jahre*. Hamburg, 1995.

Schildt, Axel, and Detlef Siegfried, eds. *Between Marx and Coca-Cola: Youth Cultures in Changing European Societies 1960–1980*. New York and Oxford, 2006.

Schildt, Axel, Detlef Siegfried, and Karl Christian Lammers, eds. *Dynamische Zeiten: Die 60er Jahre in den beiden deutschen Gesellschaften*. Hamburg, 2000.

Schiller, Nina Glick, Linda Basch, and Cristina Blanc-Szanton, eds. *Towards a Transnational Perspective on Migration: Race, Class, Ethnicity, and Nationalism Reconsidered*. New York, 1992.

Schissler, Hanna, ed. *The Miracle Years: A Cultural History of West Germany, 1949–1968*. Princeton, 2001.

Schlauch, Wolfgang. "Reliable Partnership? Perspectives on Recent German-American Relations." German Studies Review 8, no. 1 (1985): 107–25.

Schlink, Bernhard. *Der Vorleser*. Zurich, 1995.

Schlögel, Karl. *Im Raume lesen wir die Zeit: Über Zivilisationsgeschichte und Geopolitik*. Munich, 2003.

Schmidt, Alfred. *Emanzipatorische Sinnlichkeit: Ludwig Feuerbachs Anthropologischer Materialismus*. Munich, 1988.

Schmidtke, Michael. *Der Aufbruch der jungen Intelligenz: Die 68er Jahre in der Bundesrepublik und den USA*. Frankfurt am Main and New York, 2003.

Schneider, Christina, Cordelia Stillke, and Bernd Leineweber. *Das Erbe der Napola: Versuch einer Generationengeschichte*. Hamburg, 1996.

Schneider, Peter. *Eduards Heimkehr*. Berlin, 1999.

Schoenbaum, David. *The Spiegel Affair*. New York, 1968.

Schönwälder, Karin, et al. *Siedlungsstrukturen von Migrantengruppen in Deutschland*. Berlin, 2007.

Schrecker, Ellen. *No Ivory Tower: McCarthyism and the Universities*. New York and Oxford, 1986.

Schubert, Michael. *Der schwarze Fremde: Das Bild des Schwarzafrikaners in der parlamentarischen und publizistischen Kolonialdiskussion in Deutschland von den 1870er bis in die 1930er Jahre.* Stuttgart, 2003.

Schulenburg, Lutz. ed., *Das Leben ändern, die Welt verändern! 1968 – Dokumente und Berichte.* Hamburg, 1998.

Schultz, Hans-Dietrich. "Raumkonstrukte in der klassischen deutschsprachigen Geographie des 19./20. Jahrhunderts im Kontext ihrer Zeit: Ein Überblick," *Geschichte und Gesellschaft* 28, no. 3 (2002): 343–77.

Schulzinger, Robert D. *A Time for War: The United States and Vietnam, 1941–1975.* New York, 1997.

Schuster, Jacques. *Heinrich Albertz – der Mann, der mehrere Leben lebte: eine Biographie.* Berlin, 1997.

Schwendter, Rolf. *Theorie der Subkultur.* 2nd ed. Hamburg, 1993.

Schwind, Hans-Dieter, and Jürgen Baumann, eds. *Ursachen, Prävention und Kontrolle von Gewalt: Analysen und Vorschläge der Unabhängigen Regierungskommission zur Verhinderung und Bekämpfung von Gewalt,* vol. 2. Berlin, 1990.

Seton-Watson, Hugh. *Nations and States: An Enquiry into the Origins of Nations and the Politics of Nationalism.* London, 1977.

Seuss, Jürgen, Gerold Dommermuth, and Hans Maier. *Beat in Liverpool.* Frankfurt am Main, 1965.

Shandler, Jeffrey. *While America Watches: Televising the Holocaust.* New York, 1999.

Siegfried, Detlef. *Time Is On My Side: Konsum und Politik in der westdeutschen Jugendkultur der 60er Jahre.* Göttingen, 2006.

Siepmann, Eckhard, et al., eds. *CheShahShit. Die sechziger Jahre zwischen Cocktail und Molotow.* Berlin, 1984.

Simmel, Georg. *Philosophische Kultur: Über das Abenteuer, die Geschlechter und die Krise der Moderne.* Berlin, 1983.

Slobodian, Quinn. "Radical Empathy: The Third World and the New Left in 1960s West Germany." PhD Diss., New York University, 2008.

Smith, Jennifer B. *An International History of the Black Panther Party.* New York and London, 1999.

Sorensen, Thomas. *The Word War: The Story of American Propaganda.* New York, 1968.

Spode, Hasso, ed. *Goldstrand und Teutongrill.* Berlin, 1996.

Stauth, Georg. *Authentizität und kulturelle Globalisierung: Paradoxien kulturübergreifender Gesellschaft.* Bielefeld, 1999.

Steege, Paul. *Black Market, Cold War: Everyday Life in Berlin, 1946–1949.* Cambridge, 2007.

Steinbacher, Sybille. *Auschwitz: Geschichte und Nachgeschichte.* Munich, 2004.

Suri, Jeremi. "Explaining the End of the Cold War: A New Historical Consensus?" *Journal of Cold War Studies* 4 (2002): 60–92.

————. *Henry Kissinger and the American Century.* Cambridge, MA, 2007.

————. *Power and Protest: Global Revolution and the Rise of Détente.* Cambridge, MA, 2003.

————, ed. *The Global Revolutions of 1968.* New York, 2007.

Tanner, Jakob, and Sigrid Weigel, eds. *Gedächtnis, Geld und Gesetz: Vom Umgang mit der Vergangenheit des Zweiten Weltkriegs.* Zürich, 2002.

Tasman, Coen. *Louter Kabouter: Kroniek van een Beweging 1969–1974.* Amsterdam, 1996.

Taubman, William. *Khrushchev: The Man and His Era.* New York, 2003.

Taylor, Charles. *The Ethics of Authenticity.* Cambridge and London, 1991.

Tent, James F. *The Free University of Berlin: A Political History.* Bloomington, IN, 1988.

Teodori, Massimo, ed. *The New Left: A Documentary History.* Indianapolis and New York, 1969.

Thelen, David. "The Nation and Beyond: Transnational Perspectives on United States History." *Journal of American History* 86, no. 3 (1999): 965–75.

————. "Of Audiences, Borderlands, and Comparisons: Toward the Internationalization of American History." *Journal of American History* 79, no. 2 (1992): 432–62.

Thompson, E. P., ed. *Out of Apathy.* London, 1960.

Tiedemann, Rolf, ed. "Fernsehen als Ideologie" in *Eingriffe,* vol. 10.2 of *Gesammelte Werke,* Frankfurt am Main, 1977, 518–32.

Trilling, Lionel. *Das Ende der Aufrichtigkeit.* Frankfurt am Main, 1989.

Trommler, Frank, ed. *Berlin: The New Capital in the East. A Transatlantic Appraisal.* New York, 2000.

Trommler, Frank, and Elliot Shores, eds. *The German-American Encounter: Conflict and Cooperation between Two Cultures, 1800–2000.* New York and Oxford, 2001.

Trotha, Trutz von, ed. *Soziologie der Gewalt.* Opladen, 1997.

Tuathail, Gearóid Ó. *Critical Geopolitics: The Politics of Writing Global Space.* Minneapolis, 1996.

Tuch, Hans N. *Communicating with the World: U.S. Public Diplomacy Overseas.* New York, 1990.

Tyrrell, Ian. "American Exceptionalism in an Age of International History." *American Historical Review* 96, no. 4 (1991): 1031–55.

Uesseler, Rolf. *Die 68er: APO, Marx und freie Liebe.* Munich, 1998.

Vague, Tom. *The Red Army Fraction Story, 1963–1993.* Edinburgh, 1994.

Van Deburg, William L. *New Day in Babylon: The Black Power Movement and American Culture, 1965–1975.* Chicago and London, 1992.

Varon, Jeremy. *Bringing the War Home: The Weather Underground, the Red Army Faction, and Revolutionary Violence in the Sixties and Seventies.* Berkeley, 2004.

Vester, Michael, et al. *Soziale Milieus im gesellschaftlichen Strukturwandel.* Frankfurt am Main, 1991.

Watts, Max. *US-Army – Europe: Von der Desertion zum Widerstand in der Kaserne oder wie die U-Bahn zur RITA fuhr.* Berlin, 1989.

Weigel, Sigrid. "'Generation' as a Symbolic Form: On the Genealogical Discourse of Memory since 1945." *Germanic Review* 77, no. 4 (2002): 264–77.

Weinhauer, Klaus. *Schutzpolizei in der Bundesrepublik: Zwischen Bürgerkrieg und Innerer Sicherheit.* Paderborn, 2003.

Wells, Tom. *The War Within: America's Battle over Vietnam.* Berkeley, 1994.

Welzer, Harald. *Das soziale Gedächtnis: Geschichte, Erinnerung, Tradierung.* Hamburg, 2001.

Wetzel, David, ed. *From the Berlin Museum to the Berlin Wall: Essays on the Cultural and Political History of Modern Germany.* Westport, CT, and London, 1996.

Wheatland, Thomas. *The Frankfurt School in Exile.* Minneapolis, MN, 2009.

Wiggershaus, Rolf. *The Frankfurt School: Its History, Theories, and Political Significance.* Trans. Michael Robertson. Cambridge, MA, 1994.

Williams, Raymond. *Culture and Society, 1780–1950.* London, 1958.

———. *The Long Revolution.* London, 1961.

Wittmann, Rebecca. *Beyond Justice: The Auschwitz Trial.* Cambridge, MA, 2005.

Wolff, Kurt H., and Barrington Moore, Jr., eds. *The Critical Spirit: Essays in Honor of Herbert Marcuse.* Boston, 1968.

Wolfrum, Edgar. *Geschichtspolitik in der Bundesrepublik Deutschland: Der Weg zur bundesrepublikanischen Erinnerung 1948–1990.* Darmstadt, 1999.

Wood, Denis, *The Power of Maps.* New York, 1992.

Young, James E. *At Memory's Edge: After-Images of the Holocaust in Contemporary Art and Architecture.* New Haven and London, 2000.

Young, Robert J. C. *Colonial Desire: Hybridity in Theory, Culture and Race.* London, 1995.

Young-Bruehl, Elizabeth. *Hannah Arendt: For Love of the World.* New Haven and London, 1982.

Index